West German Industry and the Challenge of the Nazi Past,

1945–1955

West German Industry and the Challenge of the Nazi Past, 1945–1955

by S. Jonathan Wiesen

The University of North Carolina Press · *Chapel Hill and London*

Set in Cycles and Arepo types
by Tseng Information Systems
Manufactured in the United States of America

The paper in this book meets the guidelines
for permanence and durability of the Committee
on Production Guidelines for Book Longevity
of the Council on Library Resources.

Library of Congress Cataloging-in-Publication Data
Wiesen, S. Jonathan.
West German industry and the challenge of the Nazi past,
1945-1955 / by S. Jonathan Wiesen.
p. cm.
Includes bibliographical references and index.
ISBN 0-8078-2634-0 (cloth : alk. paper)
1. Industries—Germany—History—20th century.
2. Reconstruction (1939-1951)—Germany.   3. National
socialism—Germany.   4. Corporations—Public relations
—Germany—Case studies.   5. Industrial mobilization—
Germany—History—20th century.   6. Defense industries
—Germany—History—20th century.   7. Forced labor—
Germany—History—20th century.   8. World War,
1939-1945—Prisoners and prisons, German.   9. Fried.
Krupp AG—History.   10. Siemens Aktiengesellschaft—
History.   I. Title.
HC286.5 .W524   2001
338.0943'09045—dc21   2001023566

Portions of this book have appeared previously, in
somewhat different form, as "Overcoming Nazism:
Big Business, Public Relations, and the Politics of
Memory, 1945-50," *Central European History* 29, no. 2
(1996): 201-26, and "Mass Society, America, and the
Decline of the West," in *Technologie und Kultur: Europas
Blick auf Amerika vom 18. bis zum 20. Jahrhundert,*
ed. Ursula Lehmkuhl and Michael Wala, 203-24
(Cologne: Böhlau, 2000), and are reprinted
here with permission.

05 04 03 02 01   5 4 3 2 1

For my mother and in loving memory of my father

Contents

Illustrations

Acknowledgments

It is with tremendous gratitude that I acknowledge the individuals and organizations who supported this project from its inception. Without them this book would never have been possible.

During my early years in graduate school, when I was searching for a dissertation topic, I benefited greatly from the support of the German Historical Institute in Washington, D.C., which organized a summer tour of German archives. On the trip, I met many kind scholars and fellow graduate students who encouraged me to pursue this theme, despite my initial concern that industrialists might not have anything to say about National Socialism.

I am grateful to Brown University and the Department of History, which supported my graduate work with fellowships, teaching assistantships, and proctorships. Fellowships from the German Academic Exchange and the Berlin Program for Advanced German and European Studies at the Free University of Berlin (sponsored in part by the Social Science Research Council) enabled me to undertake an exhausting but rewarding nineteen months of research in Germany. Many thanks also to Berlin program coordinator Ingeborg Mehser for her support and expert German proofing skills. I am also beholden to my friends in Cologne (in particular Tanja Klinkert, who provided me with a guest room during every research visit).

While in Germany I became indebted to many archivists and historians who generously supplied me with primary materials and consistent encouragement. Archivists at Bayer, Degussa, Krupp, Mannesmann, Siemens, Thyssen, and the Augsburg Chamber of Industry and Commerce all made their collections available to me with few limitations and much support. Dr. Jürgen Weise at the Rheinisch-Westfälisches Wirtschaftsarchiv graciously tolerated my extended research in the Gutehoffnungshütte collection and my hundreds of requests for photocopies. The librarians at the Institut der Deutschen

Wirtschaft were also most helpful in providing me with material throughout my many months in Cologne. Werner Bührer at the Technische Universität, Munich, provided me with his personal collection of documents, and Paul Erker at the Free University of Berlin kindly opened his office to me and arranged for me to present my findings at Wolfram Fischer's university colloquium. Also, I would like to thank the ASU's director Gerd Habermann for making the organization's library available to me. Likewise, I am grateful to Johannes Stemmler, former BKU managing director, and his successor Willibert Kurth for generously granting me their time and access to the BKU's publications. I would also like to express my deep gratitude to the archivists at the numerous public and private archives in the United States and Germany.

In Germany and America I also had the good fortune of speaking and corresponding with a number of individuals with firsthand knowledge of the period and subject under examination. Special thanks go to Berthold Beitz, F. C. Delius, Benjamin Ferencz, John Kenneth Galbraith, Jürgen Heinrichsbauer, Fritz Hellwig, Otto Kranzbühler, Bernhard Plettner, and Paul Jürgen Reusch.

My work has benefited greatly from the knowledge and enthusiasm of my colleagues in the fields of European and American history. Our discussions in classrooms, conferences, and e-mail correspondences and over German beers have helped me incalculably over the last few years. I thank Keith Allen, Frank Biess, Dirk Bönker, Susanne Brown-Fleming, Deborah Cohen, Michele Elvy, Christopher Ely, Gabrielle Friedman, Neil Gregor, Michael Gross, Renate Köhne-Lindenlaub, Robert Moeller, James Patterson, Mark Ruff, Pamela Swett, Henry Turner, and Jonathan Zatlin for providing me with documents and for engaging with my ideas so carefully and sophisticatedly. I am also grateful to my colleagues at Colgate University and Southern Illinois University Carbondale for their insights and their support as I tried to balance writing and full-time teaching. Thanks also to Saskia Coenen for her tireless assistance as I prepared my manuscript. My gratitude also goes to Lewis Bateman for supporting this book from the outset as well as to the editors and the two outside readers for the University of North Carolina Press for their painstaking reading of my manuscript and their detailed, penetrating, and invaluable comments on my work.

A few individuals deserve special mention. I could not have written this book without the help of Peter Hayes, who has offered his encouragement and his expert knowledge of German industry from this project's inception. Likewise, Mary Gluck and Abbott Gleason at Brown University have provided invaluable support over the years and have taught me how to understand my work within the broader intellectual developments of twentieth-century Europe and America. I would also like to express my deep gratitude to Gerald Feldman at the University of California, Berkeley, who has been a generous advocate of my work for many years now. His knowledge and good counsel have had a wonderfully positive effect on my graduate studies and my first years teaching, even as I have been several thousand miles from my alma mater. My final and deepest gratitude goes to Volker R. Berghahn. A more dedicated, available, and unselfish adviser is impossible to imagine. His tireless support of his students both professionally and personally, in his office and at his home, is legendary. Although busy with teaching and research, he always made time for his students—to read their work, to write another letter of recommendation, to prop them up. His knowledge of German history and his ability to tease out the historian in me have been masterful. I am profoundly indebted to him.

I would like, finally, to thank my family and especially my mother for many years of unquestioning devotion and support. This book is for them and for Natasha, whose careful readings, endless encouragement, and sweetness have sustained me through the process of writing this book.

Glossary and Abbreviations

ASM	Aktionsgemeinschaft Soziale Marktwirtschaft (Action Group for the Realization of the Social Market Economy)
ASU	Arbeitsgemeinschaft selbständiger Unternehmer (Working Association of Independent Businessmen)
BdA	Bundesvereinigung deutscher Arbeitgeberverbände (Federation of German Employers' Association)
BDI	Bundesverband der Deutschen Industrie (Federation of German Industry)
BKU	Bund katholischer Unternehmer (Federation of Catholic Industrialists)
CDU	Christlich-Demokratische Union (Christian Democratic Union)
Claims Conference	Conference on Jewish Material Claims against Germany
DAF	Deutsche Arbeitsfront (German Labor Front)
DGB	Deutscher Gewerkschaftsbund (German Trade Union Federation)
DI	Deutsches Industrieinstitut (German Industry Institute)
DIG	Deutsche Industriegemeinschaft (precursor organization to the DI)
DIHT	Deutscher Industrie- und Handelstag (German Association of Industry and Commerce)
ECSC	European Coal and Steel Community
ERP	European Recovery Plan (Marshall Plan)

FRG	Federal Republic of Germany (West Germany)
GDR	German Democratic Republic (East Germany)
GHH	Gutehoffnungshütte (a heavy industry firm in Oberhausen)
HICOG	Office of the U.S. High Commissioner for Germany
IHK	Industrie- und Handelskammer (Chamber of Industry and Commerce)
JCS 1067	U.S. Joint Chiefs of Staff policy directive 1067
KPD	Kommunistische Partei Deutschlands (Communist Party of Germany)
NSDAP	Nationalsozialistische Deutsche Arbeiterpartei (National Socialist German Workers Party—Nazi Party)
NWDR	Nordwestdeutsche Rundfunk (Northwest German Radio)
RDI	Reichsverband der Deutschen Industrie (Reich Federation of German Industry)
S&H	Siemens & Halske
SED	Sozialistische Einheitspartei Deutschlands (Socialist Unity Party of Germany)
SPD	Sozialdemokratische Partei Deutschlands (Social Democratic Party of Germany)
SS	Schutzstaffel (Nazi security echelon)
SSW	Siemens-Schuckertwerke
Treuhand	Stahltreuhändervereinigung (Steel Trustees Administration)
Vorstand	company board of directors/management board
VSt	Vereinigte Stahlwerke (United Steel Works)
WES	Wirtschaftsvereinigung Eisen- und Stahl (Iron and Steel Trade Association)
WWI	Wirtschaftswissenschaftliches Institut der Gewerkschaften (economics and social science research and policy institute established and supported by the DGB)

West German Industry and the Challenge of the Nazi Past,
1945–1955

Introduction

On 16 February 1999 German chancellor Gerhard Schröder held a press conference to address the theme of German corporate behavior under National Socialism. Flanked by some of the country's leading industrial and banking executives, Chancellor Schröder announced that twelve German firms would establish a $1.7 billion fund known as the German Companies Foundation Initiative: Remembrance, Responsibility, and Future (Stiftungsinitiative deutscher Unternehmen: Erinnerung, Verantwortung und Zukunft).[1] The fund was a long-awaited acknowledgment that Germany's companies and its government bore a responsibility to address the role of industry in the crimes of National Socialism. More specifically, the fund was to provide financial compensation to aging forced and slave laborers who had been compelled to work in German factories, in concentration and death camps, and on German farms during World War II.[2] Despite the sponsors' declarations of moral responsibility toward Germany's victims, Schröder made it clear that the new foundation was less an expression of contrition than a pragmatic response to survivors' legal actions against Germany's major firms. Indeed, in the words of the chancellor, the fund would "counter lawsuits, particularly class action suits, and remove the basis of the campaign being led against German industry and our country."[3]

Schröder's contention that German corporations—and indeed Germany—were targets of an unjustified "campaign" tarnished this first coordinated public admission of industrial complicity in the crimes of National Socialism. What was meant to be a courageous display of corporate responsibility instead provoked the anger of Holocaust survivors and their families. "This is an inadequate and embarrassing statement," commented a Munich lawyer who represented thousands of the plaintiffs. "It is not a question of campaigns by anybody. It is a question of Holocaust victims' rights that have been denied by these corporations for decades."[4]

Schröder's sentiments were not unprecedented. Rather, they were the culmination of a sometimes vigilant, sometimes self-pitying, fifty-year effort by West Germany to contain the legacy of corporate complicity in Nazi crimes — from the use of forced and slave labor, to the "Aryanization" of Jewish property, to war profiteering. German industry's decision in 1999 to compensate Holocaust survivors was, to be sure, a welcome development at the end of the twentieth century. What has grown to become a fund of 10 billion deutsche marks affecting 1.5 million survivors represented a genuine watershed in corporate and national attitudes toward National Socialism:[5] in 1999 Germany openly acknowledged the role of its companies in the Holocaust. But the flashes of industrial defiance, the language of self-victimization, and the overriding desire for damage control that accompanied negotiations between industry, the U.S. and German governments, and survivors' lawyers harkened back to the years immediately following World War II, when German industrialists—indeed all Germans—struggled to ward off indicting reminders of the recent past.

This book focuses on the first decade of postwar West Germany, when defeat, military occupation, and the Cold War forced Germans to confront National Socialist crimes and reorient themselves to a new political, economic, and ideological setting. Among the most vocal participants in this collective rethinking were the country's business leaders. Caught between the legacy of Nazism and their new responsibilities as economic leaders, industrialists began working through the implications of the recent past. How did business leaders come to terms with National Socialism and their own accommodations to Hitler? Did industrialists reconcile themselves to political democracy after twelve years of dictatorship? Was industry able to remake its public image at a time when the past and present behavior of "capitalism" assumed such political importance?

This book will answer these questions by considering West German industrial mentalities as case studies in collective memory, public relations, and self-presentation—as the locus for a dialogue among industrialists about the role of the economy in the Third Reich and the social and political responsibilities of big business in a post-Hitler, Cold War society. From 1945 to 1955, industrialists, with the help of business leaders and publicists across the Atlantic, actively confronted and manipulated the past. In doing so, they simultaneously countered their present-day philosophical and political enemies and constructed new frameworks within which to understand themselves in a democratic and increasingly prosperous Germany.

This study proceeds from the assumption that in the aftermath of World War II, German industry underwent a major legitimation crisis.[6] It was not, as such, a structural crisis of capitalism, but one of image and perception, and it arose from German industrial complicity in the crimes of National Socialism. After 1945 West German industry found itself on the defensive, forced to explain its compromised past and create a sanitized collective identity that would protect companies and their leaders from Allied retribution and keep Germans from rejecting free enterprise as an economic system. Importantly, the subjective crisis of "German capitalism" did not originate with accusations of criminality under Hitler. From the economic privations and governmental fiats of World War I, to the chaotic inflation of the early Weimar years, to the World Economic Crisis of the 1930s, German industry was already accustomed to fending off critics. Indeed one can go back further, to the nineteenth and early twentieth centuries, when companies in the United States and Europe felt the need to justify business practices that segments of the public deemed to be self-serving, exploitative, or immoral.[7]

But industry's long-standing image problem was greatly exacerbated in Germany by the record of business cooperation with Hitler and the persistence of this legacy into the postwar years. West German companies emerged from World War II with their national and international reputations in tatters, and they immediately faced the challenge of infusing a new morality into capitalism — of relegitimating free enterprise at a time when its leaders were being linked to the most heinous of crimes. In the first decade after 1945, German industrialists saw themselves as surrounded by hostile forces designed to dishonor them and their companies. They bemoaned the fact that journalists, politicians, and union leaders in both Eastern Europe and the West were propagating and politicizing the collective misdeeds of "capitalism" in the form of speeches, slogans, books, and articles.

Contrary to a popular assumption today, West German industry did not wait until recent years to take these narratives of corporate guilt very seriously. In the late 1940s and early 1950s, business leaders recognized that their cooperation with Nazism had damaged individual and company reputations and, indeed, resulted in the criminal prosecution and imprisonment of prominent businessmen. Industrialists coordinated defensive, and often crude, responses to these indictments, whether through the medium of self-exculpatory publications or in courtroom defenses in Nuremberg. This book will pay substantial attention to these strategies of self-exoneration. Yet industry also tried to overcome its legitimation crisis by celebrating and taking responsibility for West Germany's economic rebirth that began to take hold in the late 1940s and early 1950s. Alongside their negative confrontations with the legacy of Nazism, industrialists were also employing more *positive* methods of overcoming their publicity crisis. During the years of the "Economic Miracle," they created and marketed a new industrialist persona devoted to corporate responsibility and social harmony, attributes that stood in stark contrast to the crimes being imputed to German industry. Ultimately, industry's dual process of looking backward with trepidation and looking forward with confidence revealed the fraught and tentative self-understanding not just of business elites but of West Germans more generally in the early years of the Federal Republic of Germany (FRG).

Public Relations and Collective Memory

This book diverges from existing literature by choosing as its subject not the West German economy per se, but the mental world and self-presentation of its representatives. Fifteen years ago Volker Berghahn already bemoaned the fact that we know very little about postwar industrialists as a distinct group with shared social backgrounds and ideological assumptions. Berghahn cited Ralf Dahrendorf's 1962 observation that "the least known elite group of the society of the Federal Republic is at the same time the one which is giving it its shape . . . as creator and beneficiary of the Economic Miracle."[8] The same assertion still applies forty years later.[9]

In most literature about the West German economy, the industrialist usually appears in his capacity as the head of a firm, the defender of the bottom line, or a power jockey in West Germany's capital, Bonn. We know much about material reconstruction, industrial relations, and business leaders' political and economic strategies and philosophies.[10] But we know remarkably little about the industrialist's understanding of National Socialism and the extent to which the twelve years under Hitler informed postwar business attitudes and behaviors. Beneath the pragmatic exterior of the German industrialist, I hope to demonstrate, lay a wealth of untapped cultural attitudes and anxieties that were intimately tied to the past and to the rapid changes of the present. Like all Germans, industrialists struggled with the defeat of Germany and reconstruction of the economy, the fate of the country's youth, the threat of communism, and the fear of social leveling and moral decay.

In approaching these various themes, this book uses the relationship between collective memory and public relations as its organizing construct. Since the late 1980s the loose and malleable concept of "memory" has found its way into every academic discipline. Scholars have explored all aspects of the theme of memory—its cognitive, psychological, neurobiological, social, and cultural dimensions—thus producing a voluminous body of literature.[11] For historians of modern Germany, the interest in memory is not new. For over fifty years historical memory has been the centerpiece of heated discussions about how—or if—East and West Germany have "come to terms" with Nazism and the Holocaust.[12]

For a long time there existed a widely accepted, but now increasingly challenged, interpretation of memory in West Germany's early postwar years. It held that in the immediate aftermath of Nazism and throughout the Konrad Adenauer years (1949–63), West Germans ran away from their collective experience of National Socialism. They neither acknowledged nor struggled with their country's tainted past, nor did they mourn the loss of a political system and a dictator in whom they had once invested so much faith. This theory of repression (*Verdrängung*) is most closely associated with Margarete and Alexander Mitscherlich, whose classic work *The Inability to Mourn* defined the discussion about memory in early West Germany for decades.[13] During the late 1950s and 1960s, they argued, West Germans retreated into their newly gained material comforts, pushing aside the horrifying events of their recent past and their own enthusiastic embrace of a criminal system. In a state of collective denial, Germans refused to mourn the "father" Hitler, their lost object of affection, and instead escaped from their melancholia into an orgy of wealth and consumption.[14]

While the above theory offers a compelling account of postwar Germany's seeming flight from its past into material success, this book will move beyond the Mitscherlich thesis and its psychological understanding of memory. By studying West German industry's defensive and aggressive relationship to the recent past, I will offer an alternative view of postwar memory as present and active. Industrialists and other Germans in fact spent much time grappling with the legacy of National Socialism. They did not engage in wrenching confessions of guilt about the Holocaust and the relationship of their companies to mass crimes. But they certainly did not and could not forget the past, and this forced memory took many forms. For industrialists, memory entailed a dual process of denying the sins imputed to German business and reinventing the "new industrialist," who would lead the German economy to prosperity and remodel embattled businessmen into corporate citizens.

In shifting away from the concept of repressed memory, I am drawing on the work of French sociologist and Émile Durkheim protégé Maurice Halbwachs, who is now regarded as the father of collective memory studies.[15] Halbwachs's theory of memory differed from the psychoanalytic model employed by the Mitscherlichs. The Mitscherlichs saw memory as something passive and hidden, lying deep within the subconscious, to be retrieved with the help of analysis, trauma, or visible and aural reminders.[16] In contrast to this Freudian model, Halbwachs articulated memory as a conscious, collective, and purposeful process. Neither passive nor personal, memory takes place in a complex web of social and performative practices. The snapshots that constitute individual memory, according to Halbwachs, are ephemeral and have no lasting life outside the context of a group. Memory is embedded in a network of power relations, customs, discourses, and symbols. A group sustains itself by manipulating images of the past for present purposes, and individuals within a group experience their own personal memories through the lens of broader group narratives. According to Halbwachs, therefore, memory is more appropriately seen as "commemoration," an active process dependent on collective agency and rational choice.

It is fruitful to consider West German industry's confrontation with Nazism as an example of collective memory. But the question remains of where to locate industrial memory. While scholars of national identity have looked to monuments, statues, and public ceremonies, I have looked to public relations as the locus of memory.[17] By definition publicity entails a process of remembering and forgetting. It is about the conscious selection and purposeful presentation of images from the past. It is about self-invention and self-promotion. If public relations is an obvious site of memory in any free-market economy, in the context of postwar Germany, when economic reconstruction and reindustrialization dominated newspaper headlines, industrial publicity became one of the most conspicuous and important repositories of institutional and group memory. The experience of Nazism and the priorities vested in economic rebirth after 1945 added a sense of urgency to preexisting practices of industrial publicity. In post-Nazi Germany, business public relations was not only about a firm's desire to sell itself and project goodwill in order to generate profits and retain customers. Alongside this universal quest to promote their firms and products, West German industrialists had the added burden of clarifying their own and their companies' behavior under a dictatorship. This need for business both to conform to the established norms of corporate publicity and to confront and explain more serious accusations of criminality was unique among all German institutions and professions. This "double burden"—conventional corporate self-promotion and the need to both confront and justify a putatively sinister past—provided West German industry with a challenge of tremendous proportions.

Importantly, however, during the early postwar years industrial publicity was not only about confronting the legacy of Nazism. In the late 1940s and early 1950s, industrialists unveiled their new public image at cultural gatherings, in films, at trade fairs, and in popular literature. While memories of National Socialism were always present at these events and in these media, industry's active role in the country's public life reveals that more was at stake than simply fending off accusations of complicity. Industrialists' participation in the political, social, and cultural discourses of the day sheds light on broader preoccupations in early West Germany, from understanding economic and political democracy, to debating the meaning of mass culture, to diagnosing the state of "the West." Thus while memory stands at the center of my analysis, this book's focus also moves beyond the explicit attempts to come to terms with the past.

The Industrial Milieu

In presenting industry as a collective group, one inevitably encounters the problem of definitions: How does one differentiate between the generalizing categories of "industry," "business," and "big business"? Like many studies about the economy, this book uses these terms interchangeably. Industry, I contend, encompasses a broad community of owners, firm directors, businessmen, company spokesmen, economic publicists, and managers, brought together by a shared commitment to profit, private property, and productivity.[18] While West German industry was, of course, quite diverse with respect to product lines, company size, and marketing strategies, the very urgency of public relations after Hitler demanded that its representatives de-emphasize their differences in favor of a unified front.[19] My reductive use of "industry," "big business," and "business," therefore, mirrors industrialists' *own* attempts to create a fortified linguistic and political community in the face of past memories and present political enemies.

The broad use of the term "industry" also reflects specific concepts in the German language that, while defying easy translation, reveal the malleable nature of business leaders' self-understanding and the hopes embodied in vague and imprecise terminology. The first term is *die Wirtschaft*. Germans employ this expression not only in its literal sense of "the economy" but also to connote "business and finance," or simply "industry." While this linguistic conflation between the economy and business is the result of the obvious correlation between the two terms, it was quite an advantageous one for German industrialists after the war. By identifying the economy with industry (to the obvious exclusion of trade unions), business leaders were able to portray the material successes of postwar Germany as their creation. The term *die Wirtschaft* facilitated industrialists' attempts to depict themselves as the nation's providers and protectors—as the economy incarnate. Who was responsible for Germany's material and spiritual recovery after 1945? *Die Wirtschaft*.

A second term, and a much more prominent one in this book, is *Unternehmer*. The primary meaning of *Unternehmer* is "entrepreneur." Yet it also doubles in German as "industrialist," by no means a synonymous concept. If an entrepreneur risks his personal capital to build a company, an industrialist, while possibly *also* an entrepreneur, is primarily a manufacturer, owner, or director of a middle-sized or large firm.[20] This merging of large and small business into one German word is of fundamental importance in postwar public relations. At a time when the behavior of big business, capitalism, or *Grossindustrie* (big industry) was largely discredited, it behooved leaders of large companies to identify with a less compromised and still romanticized symbol of the business world: the small-time entrepreneurs who were at one with their capital, their employees, and the workings of their firms. I hope to demonstrate that industrialists took refuge in the powerful looseness of the term *Unternehmer*, which they transformed into a metaphor for all of *homo economicus* and employed for their own purposes. They created a "new industrial image" (*Das neue Unternehmerbild*) that combined symbols of an older, untroubled past with images of West Germany as a rapidly expanding economic powerhouse. With the conscious effort of industrialists, the *Unternehmer* and *Unternehmertum* ("business" or "the qualities of the *Unternehmer*") became normative concepts, bearing emotive connotations that the English words "industrialist" and "business" simply do not have.

This industrial language did not exist in a vacuum; it constituted and reflected common values held by individuals tied to industry. These values, which, importantly, underwent a transformation during the 1950s,[21] included a shared suspicion of or even hostility to organized labor, a paternalist relationship to the worker, a deep-seated conservatism and cultural pessimism, and a devotion (in word, if not necessarily in deed) to the concepts of individual and economic freedom. If we accept the premise that industry is not so diverse as to defy any generalization, then business can best be seen as a separate milieu. This "business world" of the late 1940s and early 1950s showed a remarkable continuity with the Weimar and Nazi years; the same figures dined together, spent leisure time with one another, attended each other's family events, and talked about politics and business into the early morning hours. There was, in short, a common German business ethos and community that was part linguistic, part social, and partly defined by shared experiences and memories. It revolved around upper middle-class values, cultural elitism, and memories of "better days," when the industrialist was king of his company, unmolested by politicized workers and an interventionist state.

After 1945 the most significant feature of this milieu was the shared experience of National Socialism. While industrialists always traveled in close circles, spoke the same language, and felt embattled by the government and labor, after the war the legacy of Nazism and the accusations of guilt brought businessmen even closer together. The industrial milieu was now defined not only by older cultural notions of an economic bourgeoisie (*Wirtschaftsbürgertum*) but by memories of Nazism and experiences of the armaments boom, war boards, Aryanization, direct government controls, and compulsory labor.

The collective dimensions of West German industry were not only psychological. They were also political. In most market economies, industry must project a certain unity, not only for personal or public image reasons but also to exact tangible political gains that will benefit individual companies and the economy more generally. This book relies on the assumption that industrialists must and do organize their interests and resources for the broader benefit of the economy and in response to developments within the society and politics. They build working groups, lobbying agencies, and publicity commissions in order to press their political and economic interests in a democratic setting.[22] By bringing in these social and political dimensions, I hope to show the convergence of public relations, language, politics, and ideology.

The Scope of This Study

This study is organized both thematically and chronologically. This structure reveals the extent to which looking back and looking forward were parallel and overlapping processes in postwar West Germany—how the legacy of Nazism always informed industrial discourses in the 1940s and 1950s, whether about labor and democracy or culture and mass society. The book is framed less by specific domestic and international political developments than by the multiple strains of industrial self-understanding and self-presentation, which cannot be encapsulated in a discrete chronological narrative.

Chapter 1 looks specifically at one firm—the electrical giant Siemens—as a case study in company memory. By focusing chiefly on the summer of 1945 and the desperate writing of a Siemens apologia in a destroyed Berlin, I present memory as a calculated process of creation and re-creation. I look at managerial meetings and the attempts to create a company narrative, particularly about the Nazi period, that would salvage the reputation of the firm when it was being accused of the most heinous crimes. While the narrative strategies and political events highlighted were uniquely dramatic in Berlin, Siemens's response to the politics of the past was common throughout a defeated Germany, from company to company and businessman to businessman.

Chapter 2 moves from one company to industry as a larger collectivity. It begins with a discussion of the political events surrounding industry's occupation, deconcentration, dismantling, denazification, and prosecution in Nuremberg. Rather than emphasizing the details of Allied policies, however, I use these official developments as the context in which to examine industrial public relations and the strategies for creating a unified interpretation of National Socialism during the Nuremberg trials of industrialists. The chapter concludes with a discussion of how the Nazi past was instrumentalized and manipulated not just for publicity purposes, but as part of a lingering political contest between industry and organized labor.

Chapter 3 is about the introduction of the concept of public relations in West Germany after the war. By focusing on the activities of a national industrial public relations agency, the Deutsches Industrieinstitut (DI) (German Industry Institute) and other organizations, I look at how industrialists coordinated the presentation of a new *"Unternehmer* type" based on political engagement and social goodwill. While the U.S. economist Milton Friedman once said that a company's greatest social responsibility is increasing profit, West German industrialists discovered that such a view was unacceptable after National Socialism.[23] In a highly charged political context defined by finger-pointing and contested memories, industry cultivated a much more humane rationale for business activity. The DI helped instill the new industrial ethos in young businessmen and the broader public.

Chapter 4 examines how this new industrialist image was marketed. I focus on various media—books, pamphlets, films, trade fairs, and a company's products—that were used to promote market economics and the reworked image of its leaders. I demonstrate how the desire to sell free enterprise and promote its representatives converged with the persistent need to account for past behavior under National Socialism.

Chapter 5 explores the broader intellectual backdrop to the re-creation of industry. I focus on the concept of cultural decline as a critical dimension of postwar industrial ideology. More specifically, I demonstrate how industrialists engaged in contemporary discussions about mass society, democracy, totalitarianism, and the state of "the West," while, at the same time, using artistic patronage as a means of remaking themselves as social and cultural elites.

Chapter 6 moves from public relations to human relations. I shift focus from the self-invention of German industry to attempts to reshape the worker in the businessman's own image. I argue that while industrialists postured aggressively against the unions in the late 1940s and early 1950s, they soon discovered a more effective strategy for attaining their political and publicity aims: wooing the worker through less confrontational means. By exposing the dangers of collectivism and the virtues of capitalism, industrialists hoped to educate workers in pro-market, middle-class values and to convert them into their own *Unternehmer.*

Chapter 7 returns to the themes of textual production and memory by exploring the genesis of two apologias written on behalf of German big business in the early 1950s. The books, Baron Tilo Freiherr von Wilmowsky's *Warum wurde Krupp verurteilt?* and Louis Lochner's *Tycoons and Tryant,* reflect the collaborative efforts by U.S. and West German businessmen, conservatives, and "Cold War Liberals" to bury memories of Nazism and secure the FRG as a bulwark against communism. Finally, in my conclusion I return to the question of memory and business guilt today and consider the implications of industrialists' behavior for broader debates about West German culture and society.

German Industry and National Socialism: A Brief Overview

Before moving into a discussion of German industry and memory after 1945, it is necessary to offer an overview of the relationship between business and National Socialism. While this book, by virtue of its focus on memory, moves back and forth between the Nazi years and postwar developments and mentalities, it is important that I provide some sense of the key events and themes that would come to haunt German industry after the collapse of the Third Reich.

We must begin our examination of corporate complicity in the final years of the Weimar Republic, for it is on this period, before the Nazis came to power in 1933, that most of industry's postwar critics focused their attention.[24] Until recently, most debates revolved around the claim that German big business was responsible for the rise of Hitler. This argument has had multiple incarnations, but its basic assumption is that Hitler could not have come to power without the financial and ideological support of German businessmen.[25] Fascism, according to the Marxist version of this argument, was a natural outgrowth of "monopoly" or "finance" capitalism, and during the Great Depression Weimar businessmen discovered a natural kinship with Adolf Hitler, who promised to crush the labor movement and protect capitalist interests.[26] German industry was responsible for financing the Nazi Party[27] and ultimately, to use the common parlance of postwar debates, helped "lift Hitler into the saddle" (*in den Sattel heben*).

During the Cold War the pre-1933 relationship between industrialists and the Nazi Party became the cornerstone not just of propaganda for or against capitalism, but also of more dispassionate discussions about the relationship between business and fascism. But the polemical literature against capitalism, often stemming from East Germany (German Democratic Republic, or GDR) and the Soviet Bloc, usually provoked the most acrimonious debate. The official ideology of the communist GDR was rooted in the idea that the capitalist West German state was simply a continuation of the fascist regime. To make this case, GDR publicists and propagandists drew attention to the fact that many businessmen prominent in the Nazi economy maintained their wealth and status after 1945 in West Germany. While it is indeed the case that most industrialists escaped a purging under Chancellor Konrad Adenauer, the GDR portrayed this rather crudely as evidence of the ideological affinity between fascism and capitalism. Communist publications focused primarily on the years of Hitler's rise to power in order to establish the putative links between capitalism and the triumph of fascism. In turn, businessmen spent much energy during the Cold War fending off the accusation that they had brought Hitler to power through their financial intervention.

After many decades of debate, scholars now have ample evidence that

Weimar businessmen neither sympathized with nor funded the Nazi Party to any great measure. As Henry Turner and others have demonstrated, industrialists did not flock to Hitler en masse. To be sure, some individual industrialists—most notably the Ruhr magnates Fritz Thyssen and Emil Kirdorf—did offer financial and moral support for the Nazis before 1933. But the party was largely self-supporting and depended on its own members for contributions, as well as on a diverse group of supporters representing all middle-class professions and small business.

This is not to say that industrialists were politically aloof during Weimar, as they would claim after the war.[28] They certainly paid close attention to Hitler's views on the economy, and in a notorious gesture that would haunt them after the war, Ruhr leaders invited the future chancellor to air his views at the Düsseldorf Industry Club in January 1932. The questionable assumption that industrialists resoundingly applauded Hitler after his speech constituted part of the "evidence" of business complicity in Hitler's rise.[29] Despite their overall distaste for the rabble-rousing Hitler, however, Weimar industrialists made no secret of their antirepublicanism, their anticommunism, and their support of authoritarian solutions to the economic and political crisis of the early 1930s.[30] In the midst of the Depression in 1932, some businessmen indeed countenanced the participation of the Nazis in a business-friendly government. But one cannot say that they conspired to bring Hitler to power in January 1933.

What is remarkable about these discussions of pre-1933 industrial complicity is that they turned on events that were ultimately the least provable and the least damning when it comes to the relationship between big business and Nazism. It is not difficult, however, to account for this preoccupation with the last years of Weimar. During the Cold War the question of fascism's organic relationship to capitalism served more immediate ideological and political goals (on both sides) than did the specifics of the Nazi Holocaust and industry's relationship to heinous acts of persecution and murder. While issues of slave labor, or Aryanization, could be—and indeed were—cited as examples of industrial exploitation, they did not fit as readily into discussions of the *structures* of capitalism, which grounded any legitimate Marxist analysis.

At the same time, this book argues that, like industrialists themselves, West and East German scholars, politicians, and pundits never actually ignored the behavior of German industry after Hitler's rise to power. In fact, in the first few years after 1945, before the Cold War became a fait accompli, industry's relationship to war crimes and crimes against humanity played a prominent role in discussions of corporate complicity. However, as Cold War tensions escalated and the West German economy grew increasingly healthy, the more odious aspects of business behavior after 1933 were relegated to the background. Yet it is in the twelve years of the Third Reich that true industrial culpability lies. For after 1933, industry benefited greatly from Nazi policies. The Nazi Party was, to be sure, founded, in part, on an anti–big capital, pro-shopkeeper platform, and Hitler selectively exploited a petit bourgeois *ressentiment* of big business throughout the 1920s and early 1930s. Once in power, however, the Nazis implemented policies that favored large business rather than small and medium-sized firms. In the 1920s firms had begun to combine their capital as a means of limiting competition and costs and maximizing profits, as evidenced by the founding of the IG Farben chemical combine in 1925 and the United Steel Works (Vereinigte Stahlwerke, or VSt) in 1926. After 1933 the Nazis did nothing to disturb the top-heavy, cartelized economy; indeed they promoted it, as Hitler's rearmament of Germany depended on large steel, electrical, chemical, automotive, and aircraft companies that could efficiently produce capital goods and war matériel.[31]

Importantly, despite his desire for some measure of state oversight of the economy—and its leaders—Hitler essentially left undisturbed the structural foundations of the market economy. There was no expropriation or nationalization of industry, and the private sector was protected—and indeed flourished—during the economic recovery of the prewar years.[32] The 1930s witnessed increased investments and output and a generally expanding economy, and industrialists demonstrated their gratitude, at least nominally, through organizations such as Heinrich Himmler's Freundeskreis (Circle of Friends), a part honorary/part advisory group under the auspices of the SS, which brought together leading men of business and agriculture to confer with the regime on economic and cultural matters and to raise industry funds for the party.[33] Aside from their participation in the Himmler circle, prominent industrialists also served as members of the German Economic Ministry's Economic Groups, which represented the Nazi regime's attempts to maintain consistency in economic policy and some centralized overseeing of steel production, mining, trade, agriculture, and food processing. By 1939 there were forty-six Economic Groups.[34]

Finally, industrialists served as so-called *Wehrwirtschaftsführer* (military procurement officers), who were first appointed in 1935 by the Wehrmacht as counterweights to the Nazi Party military organizations. Firm directors who bore this title helped spread official army, as opposed to Nazi, propaganda in companies. During the war the appointment developed into an instrument of the Nazi Party, with *Wehrwifus* advising armaments minister Fritz Todt and his successor Albert Speer on technical and economic matters.[35]

While National Socialism unquestionably benefited industry, one must be cautious in generalizing about industrialists' responses to Nazi policies.[36] Some leaders of small and large businesses became devoted adherents to the regime, while others remained skeptical and detached, to the extent possible, from political activities. But most business leaders made, at the very least, a cautious peace with the new government that had revived the economy and crushed organized labor.

When it came to the racist policies of the government before 1938, industrialists maintained considerable room to maneuver, and their behavior ranged from outright support to, on a rare occasion, defiance. Beginning in 1933 most firms dutifully (and often eagerly) began eliminating Jewish employees and managers, and many company directors joined the NSDAP (Nationalsozialistische Deutsche Arbeiterpartei) and the SA (Sturmabteilung), the Nazis' brownshirted stormtroopers. In larger firms such as IG Farben or the Deutsche and Dresdner Banks, executives often had even more latitude to maneuver, and they sometimes decided on a case-by-case basis to retain a Jewish board member or even to retrieve him from prison.[37] Eventually, however, most company executives carried through with the "dejudaization" of their management.[38] Acts of heroism were rare, and there was always an element of self-preservation in an attempt to "protect" a Jewish board member. The seemingly nonconformist behavior of some company leaders during this early period represents a thorny moral and historical problem. For example, when a non-Jewish company executive helped a Jew to emigrate, sometimes rendering both financial and moral support, this could be interpreted as a selfless act on behalf of a persecuted friend. Indeed it was not uncommon, after the war, for émigré businessmen to reestablish contact with former colleagues or testify in denazification cases on behalf of those business partners who had helped them flee Nazi Germany. On the other hand, by helping or encouraging a Jew to leave a firm or flee the country, company executives were doing exactly what the Nazi regime had ordained. Industrialists' self-proclaimed altruism toward Jews helped implement the very racist measures that, after they war, they claimed to have despised.

After 1936 the comfortable relationship between industry and Nazism grew rockier. Most industrialists were embittered by the Nazis' introduction of state intervention, in the form of Hitler's Four Year Plan to make Germany economically self-sufficient and to ready Germany for war by 1940.[39] In August 1939, in preparation for war, the plenipotentiary for the Four Year Plan placed the various organizations relating to the economy (for example, the Ministries of Economics, Food and Agriculture, and Labor and the Reich Price Control Commission) directly under its control. Private industry also felt challenged by the regime's state-run Hermann Göring Works (Hermann Göringwerke), an extensive construction and mining undertaking that competed directly with the heavy industry firms of the Ruhr.[40] During World War II, private industry cooperated with but also felt pressured by the state, which demanded manufacturing quotas and controlled manpower, prices, and the rationing of raw materials.[41] Industrialists also watched with frustration as SS leader Heinrich Himmler created a network of construction, agricultural, and consumer product companies run by the SS, and thus owned by the state.[42]

The Nazi regime's challenges to private industry must be placed in their correct context. Despite consistent complaints about state intervention in the economy, most industrialists, in fact, maintained considerable power to make their own business decisions without governmental interference, even during the war.[43] Large and many medium-sized and small firms were still, for the most part, in charge of their production priorities, long-term planning, and daily operations. And despite any tensions between industry and the Nazi regime, the business world did not register an overall dissatisfaction with Hitler's rule or his ideological aims. Quite the contrary, industrialists benefited directly and indirectly from German rearmament and Nazi racism, and many brought Hitler's *Führerprinzip* (leadership principle) of strict obedience and hierarchy, as well as his vision of a thousand-year, racially pure Reich, directly to their factories. Industrialists also took some measure of satisfaction in Hitler's crushing of the labor unions in 1933. Moreover, the outright appropriation of Jewish firms, or the fire-sale prices paid to Jews as they sought to sell their businesses and leave Germany quickly (Aryanization) is a disturbing example of industry's exploitation of Hitler's ideological aims.[44] The outbreak of World War II in 1939 only increased the opportunity to secure lucrative military contracts or to Aryanize Jewish businesses.

If we look at the summer of 1940, when Germans savored the Wehrmacht's rapid military victories across Europe, companies (whether small firms or large corporations) enthusiastically followed the army into every occupied country, taking over firms from France and the Netherlands to Czechoslovakia and Poland. When the German army was firmly established in these territories, industry exploited raw materials, seized private and public companies, and forced local citizens into hard labor.[45]

This penetration of industry into occupied Europe led to the most incriminating aspect of business behavior during the Third Reich: the exploitation of POW, forced civilian, and concentration camp labor.[46] Large companies fanned out into occupied Europe, seizing the assets and installations of foreign firms or setting up satellite factories near ghettos and death camps. The most notorious case is that of IG Farben, which built a synthetic rubber plant a few miles from the Auschwitz/Birkenau death camp.[47] The treatment of the prisoners in the multitude of labor camps and factories varied greatly, depending on race, national origin, time period, type of camp, or individual firm.[48] In accordance with the Reich's strict hierarchies regarding foreign labor, Jews in occupied Eastern Europe were considered most expendable. If they did not die from sheer exhaustion or sickness in a work camp, they were gassed at the nearest killing centers in Poland.[49]

In most cases companies provided meager, if any, wages to the workers, instead paying a "fee" to the SS, which had "sold" this labor to the private companies. During the course of the war, as their firms lost manpower to the Wehrmacht, industrialists began bringing forced foreign labor (particularly Poles, Russians, and Ukrainians) and concentration camp inmates back to their plants within Germany's borders. From larger companies, like Volkswagen, Daimler-Benz, Krupp, and Siemens, to small and medium-sized firms, thousands of businesses took advantage of the Nazis' forced and slave labor programs. The millions of foreign workers who labored for Hitler's war effort on German soil often toiled in abysmal conditions, subject to death by disease, exhaustion, or the caprice of an SS or company watchman.[50]

Accounting for industrial participation in the labor program is complicated, given the different circumstances throughout Germany and occupied Europe. Certainly before the war, industrialists never perceived a massive influx of foreign workers as beneficial to their companies; indeed, often it was not. During the war years, the armaments ministry made production demands on German companies, and Nazi Plenipotentiary for Labor Fritz Sauckel, in conjunction with the SS, made available to industry a steady supply of forced and slave laborers. As we will see, after the war, industry portrayed these governmental mandates and the use of captured labor as unwelcomed fiats, which companies had no choice but to obey under war conditions. Undoubtedly, companies were pressured to produce for the Wehrmacht and the "Fatherland." But they also used forced and slave labor to profit from the war and, more pragmatically, to survive the war after losing manpower to the armed forces.[51] Regardless of the complexities, the reality remains that companies themselves actively participated at all levels of the compulsory labor program, with apparently little mind to the moral implications of their brutal actions. Industrialists actively sought out Eastern European civilians and concentration camp laborers whom they knew they could treat as expendable. The broad picture is one of opportunism, in which companies took advantage of the vagaries of war to keep factories running and profits flowing.[52] But only a combination of factors—outright greed, intimidation, the urge to keep businesses afloat, anti-Semitism, and anti-Slavic sentiments—can truly account for the overwhelming complicity of German firms in the Nazi economy and the Holocaust.

By the time the war was over in 1945, companies of all sizes had been tied inextricably to the crimes of the Third Reich. Germany's companies had produced and delivered the Zyklon B for the gas chambers; they had constructed tanks and cannons; they had benefited from stolen Jewish property; and they had plundered companies. It was now up to the Allies and Germans themselves to account for the country's descent into war and industrialized mass murder.

CHAPTER ONE

A Company Encounters the Past:
The Case of Siemens

German industry in the aftermath of the Nazi defeat is a study in contradictions. On one hand, we are confronted with images of utter destruction and chaos: factories bombed into oblivion, company managers arrested or on the run, employees wandering the streets looking for food and water.[1] On the other hand, recent literature has offered us a more nuanced picture, one of widespread but often superficial damage, respectful if cool relations with the occupying powers, and well-coordinated and swift infrastructural rebuilding.[2] Bomb damage was not as great as originally believed, and industrial capacity, while badly shaken, remained relatively high. For the first two years after the war, West German industry was undoubtedly in dire straits with respect to production. But it still held immense economic potential.

While over the last few years historians have tempered earlier portrayals of sweeping physical devastation, they cannot diminish the subjective experience of horror that accompanied defeat and destruction. If actual physical damage varied from factory to factory and region to region, all industrialists seemed to share in the experience of national and spiritual collapse. This sense of trauma was apparent when the German electrical firm Siemens & Halske (S&H) observed its 100th anniversary in 1947. For a century Siemens had prided itself on its national and international reputation. It was known worldwide for its entrepreneurial and technological ingenuity and respected for its progressive approach to labor relations, organizational power structures, and international trade.[3] Yet two years after the end of World War II, the company directors chose to forgo all centennial festivities. There were no parties or fireworks but, rather, a simple and sober announcement posted throughout the Siemens factories. It read as follows:

Fate does not allow us to celebrate this day as we surely would have done under other circumstances—with the lively participation of the whole world. All of us know how much our company has been affected by the catastrophe of our Fatherland. Many of our employees have lost their lives. A great part of our factories have been destroyed. We have lost our Siemensstadt works and all of our foreign patents. In Berlin and in the eastern zone our stocks and bank accounts have been confiscated and . . . our factories appropriated. Despite all these misfortunes, we have decided . . . to rebuild. This task has demanded from us inordinate diligence, and hard work still faces us. We must find strength . . . in the memory of our proud history. Let us celebrate this significant day in quiet reflection. Let us look into the past with pride and into the future with hope. In the spirit of our company's founder, let us rebuild with strong hearts and unbending confidence, through peaceful competition among all nations, and with the blessing of our people and of humanity.[4]

This declaration, with its tones of self-pity and mournful optimism, represented the culmination of two of the most tumultuous years in the firm's history. Since the end of World War II, Siemens, Germany's largest producer of electrical products, had struggled to rebuild not only its factories but also its reputation. Like many other large German companies, Siemens had compromised itself in multiple ways during the Third Reich, from producing armaments to employing concentration camp labor. Siemens may have once enjoyed a proud past, yet put to the greatest moral test during the Third Reich, it was both unable and unwilling to resist the allures and demands of the Nazi economy. In 1945, immediately after the war, this record of complicity would begin to haunt the firm. Two years later and a century after its founding, Siemens was in no mood to celebrate.

This chapter illustrates how a company like Siemens, amidst accusations of war crimes and crimes against humanity, created a self-image of the sad but noble victim of Nazi and Allied policies. Through the example of one firm, I hope to demonstrate how, in the early postwar years, companies tried not only to rebuild themselves physically but also to salvage their reputations. Already in the summer of 1945 they began to recall glorious moments in their past, while portraying themselves as persecuted resisters against National Socialism. This self-characterization did not come easily. It had to be created by company directors, who carefully crafted a narrative that defended a firm's involvement in the Nazi economy and asserted a company's moral purity. But in the immediate aftermath of World War II, a hostile public and wary Allied occupation officials were not yet ready to accept these industrial self-inventions.

Destruction at Siemens-Berlin as a result of Allied bombing, 1944 (courtesy of Siemens AG, Siemens Forum, Munich)

Siemens at the End of World War II

Siemens AG, headquartered in Munich and Erlangen, is the largest electro-technical firm in Europe and the second largest in the world.[5] Although this multinational firm originally built its name on radios and telephones, Siemens is now a world leader in electronics, digital communications, and elec-tromechanical manufacturing. While today Siemens is adapting comfortably to the information age, with an extensive public relations network spanning the globe, fifty years ago the company was in a catastrophically different situa-tion. In 1945 Siemens's factories lay in ruins, destroyed by Allied bombs and postdefeat dismantling.

Numerous eyewitness testimonies deposited today in the Siemens archive offer a fascinating and unrelenting barrage of violent images from the spring and summer of 1945—scenes of bloodshed and street fighting, plundering troops, and scared Berliners hunkered down in the company library or in air-raid shelters as they await the Soviet troops' arrival.[6] From these many chronicles one can grasp the sense of resignation and the deep-seated fear of the "communist invaders" that hung over the House of Siemens in the days immediately before Germany's surrender. Firsthand narratives usually begin when the Russians pushed into the Siemensstadt (literally, Siemens

City) neighborhood of Berlin on 26 April, six days after production operations had been shut down for good.[7] As the troops approached the company building, there was little for the directors and employees to do but worry and wait and, in the words of one witness, to go through all the floors to make sure "everything was in order."[8] As the troops surrounded the corporate headquarters, frantic employees tore from the walls the company's portraits of Adolf Hitler and set them aflame. This last-minute attempt to remove all vestiges of National Socialism, however, did little to calm the wrath of the Soviet army, which, upon arrival, quickly transformed the company into a site of murder, arrests, rape, and pillage.[9]

A few days after Germany's unconditional surrender on 8 May, more employees began to trickle back to Siemensstadt. It was immediately evident that many workers and managers had not survived the street fighting and bombing raids. Suicide had been a common end for many.[10] On 4 May a report reached the company that sixty-five employees had taken their own lives, among them the chairman of the Berlin Works Council, who had committed suicide with his wife and children after burning their house to the ground.[11] In the following days and weeks the instances of death and suicide found their way up the corporate ladder. Five members of the managing boards of Siemens-Schuckertwerke (SSW) and S&H were confirmed dead or would soon meet their ends.[12] The chairmen of the two managing boards, Dr. Heinrich von Buol and Dr. Rudolf Bingel, as well as the directors of the Berlin research and radio production labs, had been arrested and were en route to Moscow.[13] The Russians had received orders to capture the most technologically knowledgeable directors and specialists, who were to be brought to the Soviet capital for interrogation and eventual forced employment in electrotechnics, rocket sciences, and optics.[14] The Soviets' plans did not, however, meet with success. Bingel died on the way to the Soviet Union in an internment camp in Landsberg an der Warthe, while Buol swallowed poison shortly after arriving at Lubjanka prison in Moscow.[15]

The deaths of a number of employees and chief officers were not the only problems facing Siemens. The Soviets immediately began dismantling the factory piece by piece and carting it off to be reassembled in the eastern zone of occupation and in the USSR. According to the simple but revealing rationale of one Russian colonel who directed the dismantling efforts, "Hitler Kaputt, Berlin Kaputt, Siemens Kaputt."[16] The Siemens employees responded to the Soviets' demands with a mixture of obsequiousness and defiance. Some spoke of sabotaging the dismantled equipment, while the majority saw full cooperation as the only means of securing their own survival and that of the firm. In a stark reminder of the sense of denial that pervaded a defeated Germany, one employee found it unfathomable that the Soviets should have the gall to claim Siemens's machinery as their "war trophies."[17] The Soviets spent the next many months carting off tons of machinery, communications and laboratory equipment, test reports, technical documents, patents, and company bank accounts.[18]

By the end of June, Siemens was in a state of complete turmoil. Factory floors looked liked scarred battlefields, and hundreds of employees and middle-level managers had fled west without company approval, following in the footsteps of those who in February had been authorized to leave for Bavaria to establish three new administrative centers for the company.[19] During the spring and summer, the continued flight of the Siemens middle management got so bad that the remaining company directors issued a warning forbidding all departmental and factory leaders from traveling "beyond the Elbe" without prior permission.[20]

With the disappearances and deaths of most of the high- and middle-level managers, Siemens remained officially leaderless—without guidance and without a counterweight to the Soviets' seemingly arbitrary actions. Communications had yet to be reestablished with the directors in Nuremberg and those en route to Munich. Had the phone lines been in service, the Berlin Central would have heard tales of a different form of chaos, with company directors meeting their deaths during their flight west or interned behind barbed wire after being stopped by the Americans. The Berlin managers would also soon learn of the arrest and detention of the supervisory board director and "Head of House," Hermann von Siemens, who would remain in U.S. internment until January 1948.[21]

In mid-July the Russian troops left Siemensstadt after handing over jurisdiction to the British occupation, in accordance with Allied plans drawn up at the end of 1944. The remaining managers in Berlin began pulling pieces together. The most immediate task was to assemble a new board of directors. Wolf-Dietrich von Witzleben, who had been the personnel director for both firms during the war, was unanimously chosen as chairman.[22] Other members of the new managerial board included Fritz Jessen, who had led both companies' financial divisions, as well as Bruno Pohlmann and Theodor Frenzel from S&H and Hanns Benkert and Georg Leipersberger from SSW.

With the new board in place, the first order of business was to assess the damage to the firm. Of the 23,100 machines in the Berlin works, the Soviets had confiscated 22,700. Buildings covering 40 percent of the entire factory area were destroyed. Gone was everything from machine tools, furnaces, welding equipment, and pumps to the last office telephones, typewriters, slide rules, and pencils. When the damage was totaled, S&H had lost 98 percent of its prewar capacity in Berlin due to Soviet dismantling, and SSW had lost 85 percent.[23] The company had incurred a loss of 2,100 million reichsmarks, or three-fourths of its prewar value.[24] For the House of Siemens, however, the destruction was not yet over.

A Company Encounters the Past   21

A Legacy of Complicity

On 16 July 1945 Siemens's newly chosen directors met at the office of Hanns-Henning von Pentz, a fourteen-year veteran of the managerial board, to discuss a subject that was, in director Witzleben's estimation, "of extreme urgency."[25] The matter concerned the collection of materials that would "diffuse all claims the Allied side could raise against us with respect to the Jewish Question."[26] Amidst the rubble of Berlin, the directors would take the first steps in confronting a theme that would haunt Siemens long after it had risen from the ruins of a defeated Berlin. They called for an investigation into the "employment of Jews during the war—the time period, the number, the use, the responsible agencies, the withdrawal of the Jews, and the measure enacted, etc." In short, the company, in the words of Witzleben's assistant, aimed to understand its "Jewish problem."[27]

In organizing a brainstorming session on this theme, Witzleben initiated what would become a long-term effort to deflate the shameful legacy of German industry's forced and slave labor program. The wartime employment of Jewish and non-Jewish laborers in Siemens's factories has remained until today the most nagging issue to have emerged from the Nazi years, one that has manifested itself in lawsuits, public relations campaigns, internal investigations, and a slew of published exposés about the war crimes of Europe's largest electrical firm.[28] While Siemens is by no means unique in its use of forced and slave laborers in its factories and in occupied Eastern Europe, this company's program, nonetheless, was possibly the most extensive, spanning a wide range of factory installations and concentration camps, from Auschwitz to Buchenwald to Sachsenhausen. It affected Jews and non-Jews alike who were to work long hours often in the most abysmal conditions.

There are, in effect, two issues at stake in a discussion of the relationship of Siemens to forced and slave labor. The first concerns Jews and non-Jews who worked in Siemens's Berlin factories against their will. Shortly after the German invasion of Poland in 1939, the Nazis began to transport Polish civilians to Berlin to fill a labor shortage and to work at Siemens alongside Germans and other foreign employees who had voluntarily come earlier. At the same time, the Berlin labor office also allocated to the company its first group of Jewish women. There immediately followed larger influxes of workers from Berlin's Jewish community, whom the government had assigned to work at Siemens for regular wages but without the opportunity for any company benefits or overtime pay.

By the end of 1940 approximately 2,000 Jewish workers had been drafted to work in SSW and S&H, many of them still residing in their apartments in Siemensstadt or greater Berlin.[29] Their stay at Siemens was, for all intents and purposes, a short detour on the way to "resettlement" in the east.

Prisoners at forced labor, building airplane parts at the Siemens factory at Bobrek, a subcamp of Auschwitz (Charles Stein, courtesy of the U.S. Holocaust Memorial Museum Photo Archives, Washington, D.C.)

Exactly a year later, in December 1941, Nazi authorities informed the company that Berlin's remaining Jews were to be evacuated from the city by the end of 1942.[30] Recognizing an opportunity to achieve their state-dictated production goals with cheap labor, Siemens and other Berlin companies offered to take in the last Jewish workers at company expense. The company was motivated in part by humanitarian feelings (according to Wilfried Feldenkirchen)[31] and in part by a belief that assimilated German Jews could work more productively—more like "Aryans"—than other nationalities, namely Slavs, whose racial inferiority and cultural differences supposedly impeded their integration into an efficient and harmonious system of production.[32] For these Berlin Jews, the stint at Siemens was borrowed time. By the beginning of 1943, all of these approximately 2,000 Jews had been transported from the Siemens factories to Auschwitz, where most of them were gassed upon arrival.[33] In most instances Siemens replaced these Jews with larger influxes of POWs and non-Jewish forced workers (*Ostarbeiter*) from Poland, the Baltic countries, Ukraine, and Russia.[34]

The second example of forced and slave labor was Siemens's use of Jewish and non-Jewish concentration camp inmates during the later stages of the war. Many of these inmates had come from the German-occupied areas of

Workers from the Soviet Union at forced labor in a Siemens factory in Berlin. The women wear badges with the OST insignia, identifying them as *Ostarbeiter,* workers from the Eastern European occupied territories. (Dokumentationsarchiv des Österreichischen Widerstandes, courtesy of the U.S. Holocaust Memorial Museum Photo Archives, Washington, D.C.)

Eastern Europe. According to Auschwitz commandant Rudolf Höss, who was tried and executed in 1946, Siemens had obtained 1,200 women from his camp in 1943 and about 1,500 in 1944, all of whom were employed eight miles down the road from Auschwitz in the subcamp of Bobrek, manufacturing electrical switches for aircraft.[35] During the war 550 Jewish women were also forced to work in the Siemens Nuremberg factory after first passing through the concentration camp Flossenbürg. Twelve hundred female prisoners in Sachsenhausen were put to work in Siemens's Werner Works in Berlin. The company also made use of the prisoners in the camps of Buchenwald and Groß-Rosen, and they set up their largest forced labor enterprise in the women's concentration camp Ravensbrück, where 2,300 prisoners worked in harsh conditions for Siemens in the assembly-line production of microphones, telephones, and other telecommunications products.[36] In the latter stages of the war, concentration camp inmates were also brought into Berlin, where they were housed in a work camp in the Berlin suburb of Haselhorst. According to the concluding assessment of a later report by the Conference on Jewish Material Claims against Germany (Claims Conference), "The Siemens concern reaped the full benefit from this slave work without any pecuniary compensation for the victims or the least care for their welfare."[37]

During the summer of 1945, Berlin politics began heating up along ideological lines, as communists, socialists, and Christian parties vied for the allegiance of the divided capital's demoralized populace. As Berlin's political parties reestablished themselves at the grass roots, Siemens's participation in the Nazi economy and the Holocaust took on great symbolic importance in both the Soviet and the Western sectors of the city. Almost overnight the rhetoric of class conflict had returned to the factory floors in the destroyed capital. While twelve years of an imposed *Betriebsgemeinschaft* (factory community) had attempted to keep German workers from opposing their bosses (although not always successfully), the Nazis' utopian workplace rhetoric was exposed as an illusion after 1945.[38] In May of 1945, with the encouragement of Berlin's newly revived SPD (Sozialdemokratische Partei Deutschlands) (Social Democratic Party of Germany), and especially the communist leadership (which quickly reestablished the moribund KPD [Kommunistische Partei Deutschlands] [Communist Party of Germany]), workers began organizing themselves. They called for a nationalization of industry and a removal of the "monopoly capitalists" whom they saw as having conspired with Hitler to destroy organized labor and conquer Europe. Since German business leaders had been so quick to subordinate humanity to profit, argued the parties on the Left, the only solution would be to turn their industries into wards of the state, which would protect its citizens from the inhumane effects of capitalism.

It is important to emphasize that the equation of free enterprise and the recent catastrophes of the Great Depression and the Third Reich was a tool wielded not just by the communist leadership in the Soviet zone of occupation but by the major political parties forming throughout divided Germany. In the early postwar years, Germans across the political spectrum harbored doubts about the ability of capitalism to withstand the temptations of state-sponsored aggression. They drew on previous critiques of capitalism that had come to a climax during the Great Depression, when capitalism had proven itself incapable of preventing unimaginable misery.

The SPD, whose leadership consisted of a number of socialists who had been persecuted by the Nazis, made no mistake about who bore the lion's share of the blame for Hitler. According to the party's May 1946 guidelines, it was the "forces of high capitalism and reaction," which had tried in the 1920s "to escape the socialist consequences of democracy," thus paving the way for Hitler's destruction of "democratic opinion formation" and the working class.[39] Business behavior under Nazism became instrumental in the SPD's early efforts in West Germany to nationalize major industries and democratize the workplace—political projects that had been left over from the Weimar years. Until the mid-1950s, when they abandoned the desire for a radical reordering of the West German economy, the labor unions also held similar views about the relationship between industrial crimes and the need for economic restructuring.[40]

Likewise the new Christian Democratic Union (Christlich-Demokratische Union, or CDU), a diverse grouping of conservative, Catholic, and neoliberal traditions, displayed in its early years a deep suspicion of capitalism. The CDU platform of 1947, the so-called Ahlen Program, represented the high point of the party's Christian socialist, antimarket orientation: "The capitalist economic system has failed to do justice to the vital political and social interests of the German people. Following the terrible economic, political, and social collapse as a consequence of criminal power politics, only a fundamental renewal is conceivable."[41] Drawing on the tradition of political Catholicism, which saw the welfare state as an expression of Christian brotherly love and solidarity, the CDU's left wing argued that some measure of governmental intervention would thenceforth be necessary to protect the public and the weaker parts of society from the effects of unfettered capitalism. Many Catholics had since the 1920s condemned the increasing materialism penetrating Europe, which they associated with capitalism and the influence of the United States. The early CDU, as a "big tent" party, embraced both anti-Marxist and anticapitalist sentiments. While the CDU, under Konrad Adenauer's leadership as West Germany's first chancellor, eventually abandoned the aim of a more fundamental reordering of the economy, its initial impetus toward Christian socialism would continue to resonate in respected publications like the *Frankfurter Hefte*, whose antifascist editors, Walter Dirks and Eugen Kogon, combined their promotion of democratic-socialist "new ordering" with a broader vision of European unity.[42]

Despite the shared suspicion of capitalism in these early political platforms, the KPD, much more than the SPD and the left-wing Christian Democrats, spearheaded the campaign against Siemens in the summer of 1945. Communist politicians, journalists, and Siemens workers began locating vestiges of Nazism on the Siemens managerial boards, which despite the deaths of their chairmen, reconstituted themselves with many of the same members who had led the firm during the years of rearmament and war. Suspicions immediately fell on director Benkert, who, along with Pohlmann, had been an active member of the NSDAP and who had earnestly incorporated Nazi labor terminology into his speeches at company gatherings.[43] The former director of SSW *Kleinbauwerk,* Benkert became during the next couple of years the favorite target of the KPD organ *Neues Deutschland,* which repeatedly published articles attacking the former "connection man to the SS" and his firm.[44] Benkert, *Neues Deutschland* pointed out, was under suspicion for his activities as chairman of the Organization of German Engineers, as a "coworker of Speer and friend of Todt," and as special emissary of the Reich minister for economics and production.[45] Benkert had also compromised himself through his participation in the firm's forced labor program. Benkert had in the early 1940s written a memorandum titled "On the Use of Foreign Labor," in which he had explicitly promoted the physical punishment of prisoners when more gentle measures for keeping them productive no longer sufficed.[46]

Witzleben, on the other hand, had never been a member of the party. If he felt, however, that this fact placed him beyond political reproach, the chairman was sadly mistaken. Witzleben presents the classic case of the non-party-affiliated businessman who, nonetheless, in numerous ways helped realize the Nazis' ideological aims. In the early 1940s the Nazis bestowed on Witzleben the honorary title of *Wehrwirtschaftsführer.*[47] While Witzleben insisted that this was an empty appellation (a denazification tribunal later would conclude as much), he could not claim to have stood on the sidelines while his firm sullied its good name with Hitler's anti-Jewish measures. In a 1938 note to the head of the Berlin police, Witzleben boasted of his company's exemplary anti-Jewish stance and its efforts to force its Jewish employees to emigrate.[48] As personnel director of both S&H and SSW, Witzleben had also taken an active part in the procurement of forced laborers and the establishment of factory security forces that would ensure the "orderly behavior of the foreign workers" and prevent breaches of conduct in concentration camps.[49]

In early July 1945, as they were beginning to hear the accusations raised against them, Siemens's directors received a tangible reminder that their pasts would not easily be forgotten. British radio services reported that 100 industrialists had been arrested in Bavaria, among them Karl Knott, the head of Siemens's Nuremberg works.[50] Immediately, the nervous board members in Berlin began designating their successors, in preparation for their own potential arrest by the British police.[51] Throughout Germany, top company directors were being detained for having contributed in some way to National Socialist rule. Some would spend only a couple of days in custody; others would spend several years. The Americans captured aircraft entrepreneur Willy Messerschmitt in May. Steel magnate Alfried Krupp von Bohlen und Halbach was captured in Essen on 11 April and would not be released until the beginning of 1951, after conviction and a prison term.[52] Wilhelm Zangen of Mannesmann Steel was arrested in July but was released four months later.[53] And Fritz Thyssen, formerly Hitler's most enthusiastic supporter (and later opponent) in the Ruhr, was picked up by the British in April and held until his denazification in 1948. Yet while Germany's most illustrious businessmen and company namesakes were being rounded up in the spring and summer of 1945, less prominent board members remained confident that they would be spared the wrath of the victors. These hopes would be dashed, as we will see, during the fall and winter, when the Allies launched a massive wave of arrests designed to root out possible war criminals from the ranks of German industry.[54]

More troubling for businessmen than the rounding up of individual directors was the dark shadow these arrests cast on their companies. Germany's industrialists were being pursued not simply as individuals but as representatives of their businesses. The pursuit of individual company directors was accompanied not only by published details of the Nazis' forced and slave labor program, but by a host of other claims, including willfully embracing Hitler's rearmament aims, cooperating with the DAF (Deutsche Arbeitsfront) (German Labor Front), promoting the Nazi ideology in company newsletters, and financing the NSDAP before and after 1933. Thus when it met in mid-July to discuss the company's "Jewish Question," the Siemens board was actually taking the first steps toward a much broader plan of attack, one that entailed the direct rebuttal of these numerous accusations, of which anti-Semitism was only one, albeit the most potentially damaging.

Memory in Action: Rewriting the Company Past

A week before the meeting, board member Fritz Jessen made the first attempt to coordinate a response to these mounting claims when he distributed to his colleagues a memorandum titled "On the Question of the War Criminality of Siemens."[55] In this short directive we can discover some of the interpretive strategies that the firm would consistently embrace as it tried to fend off criminal charges. Jessen listed point by point the tactics he felt Siemens should adopt when confronted by accusations of wrongdoing under the Nazis. He began with the theme of war production. Like all major firms, Siemens was being accused of having benefited from Germany's rearmament in the 1930s and from the increasingly lucrative contracts to produce war matériel. Although it had never manufactured tanks and guns, Siemens had indeed contributed greatly to Germany's war effort by producing everything from telephones, telegraphs, and radios to military floodlights and the electrical components of U-boat and airplane engines. By mid-1943 Siemens's Werner Works was selling 80 percent of its products to the Wehrmacht, half of which went to the Luftwaffe.[56] According to a 1960 Claims Conference report, Siemens, alongside its aircraft production, had participated in the construction of V1 and V2 rockets, and the company's building subsidiary, the Siemens *Bauunion*, had obtained some of the largest war-related construction contracts throughout occupied Europe.[57]

However desperate to distance itself from the belligerent policies of the Nazis, Siemens could not very well deny having manufactured for purposes of war. Rather, it chose to portray this production as the unsavory but unavoidable result of governmental pressure and corporate self-preservation. In his memo Jessen expressed this interpretation in clear terms: Siemens had never *chosen* to soil its hands with such military contracts. War production, Jessen wrote, was anathema to the company's philosophy. Siemens, he argued, had always concentrated on electrotechnics and had avoided "foreign production"—no war materials, no tanks, no munitions. If Siemens had deviated from this declared company policy during the Third Reich, Jessen wrote, it had done so only under pressure from the Nazis and only in very "exceptional" circumstances. Ultimately, the company's refusal to get more involved in war production, Jessen wrote, had been "a source of personal danger" to the firm directors. Finally, in the July directive, Jessen also denied that his firm had supported the Nazis financially, and he insisted that "as long as it was in any way possible . . . [Siemens had] always resisted the Nazis' persecution of non-Aryans and Free Masons, etc."[58]

In all of these claims, the director was revealing his carefully selective memory. Like all other companies, Siemens had indeed felt pressure to accede to the state's demands. For example, the firm was pressed to make mandatory contributions to the Nazi "charity" organizations such as the Winterhilfe and the Adolf Hitler Spende.[59] While it did attempt to keep these donations to a minimum, Siemens certainly never avoided paying them. Jessen also failed to mention that Rudolf Bingel had been an active member of Heinrich Himmler's Circle of Friends. Bingel had, in fact, donated substantial amounts of money to the Freundeskreis in the name of Siemens.[60] And as we will see below, the company would also have trouble substantiating the claim that it helped persons persecuted by the Nazis.

Jessen's memorandum was a combination of truths, half-truths, and inaccuracies. Yet the document was intended not as a detailed study but, rather, as a strategy proposal to the fellow board members. In distributing these publicity guidelines to his colleagues, Jessen was, of course, preaching to the converted, who had experienced with him the twelve years of National Socialist rule. But the director saw as imperative the creation of a unified strategy that the company could readily call on in the face of allegations of war criminality. The challenge for Siemens was now to transform Jessen's suggestions into a more nuanced and convincing portrayal of its own behavior.

At its mid-July meeting the board decided that "for the benefit of the Allies"[61] it would prepare as quickly as possible a multipaged document disavowing any link to the "Hitler regime" and highlighting the contributions Siemens had made to Germany throughout its almost 100-year history. It would then attach to this glowing company profile two enclosures addressing the most incriminating issues relating to the Third Reich. The first item was to deal with the company's Aryanization of a Belgian firm called Automatique Electrique S.A., which Siemens had controlled in absentia from March 1942 until September 1944 after the Wehrmacht had driven the company's U.S. owner from his directorial post. The second addendum was to deal with the most sensitive issue that had been the ostensible purpose of the July meeting: the "Jewish Question" and the company's general position on forced and slave labor.

Following the meeting on 16 July, Director Pentz took charge of this exculpatory effort. For the last two weeks of the month, as accusations against the firm began to accumulate, he presided over the feverish preparation of three working drafts—the main defense and the two additional reports. On 31 July the director's exhausted assistants handed him a draft of the basic manuscript, with the title "The Behavior of the House of Siemens during the Hitler Regime," and working drafts of the addenda.[62]

It is not surprising that the drafts adhered closely to Fritz Jessen's strategy of emphasizing the peaceful nature of the firm. Yet they also made a meticulous effort not simply to rebut specific claims of complicity but also to reconceptualize the entire relationship between Siemens and National Socialism. The document is, therefore, worth focusing on in some detail, as it reveals the early strategies of self-defense that industry would employ, in an even more coordinated fashion, throughout the late 1940s and 1950s.

Siemens's strategy was simple and commonsensical: defy the allegations against the firm by depicting the company and its managers in an unequivocally positive light. If the company was currently being treated as expendable by the Soviet occupation, show why Siemens was in fact indispensable to the postwar economic recovery; if Siemens was being labeled a war criminal firm (*Kriegsverbrecherfirma*), then emphasize the peaceful and humanitarian aims of the company; if the company was being accused of having exploited workers, then demonstrate Siemens's progressive track record vis-à-vis its employees; most importantly, if the firm was being accused of having embraced National Socialism and having worked toward the realization of its aims, then argue that the opposite had been true—that the company had in fact opposed the Nazis from start to finish, in word and deed. In this approach there was little room for nuance and subtlety. The reputation of the company was on the line, and Siemens had to set the tone early for its campaign to save its name. The manuscript began on a confident and defiant note:

> In the months before the end of the European war and during the following period, questions about the German "war industry" have come to the fore. According to the Allies' explanation, the elimination of the German "war industry" is necessary in order to, on one hand, make impossible a rearmament of Germany and, on the other hand, because this "war industry" supported Hitler and helped him into the saddle, presumably because they were both of the same mind. In addition, German industry is being attacked for its use and treatment of foreign workers, Jews, prisoners of war, and concentration camp inmates. In Germany these claims are being repeated in part, with the additional one that the Siemens firm is a war-profiteer of the worst kind. We cannot let these claims remain unanswered. We owe it to the almost 100-year history of our house, to our employees, and to ourselves to fully clarify these accusations, both for the [public] abroad and for Germany.[63]

With this direct appeal in the name of company loyalty, the manuscript appeared eager to launch straight into a discussion of industry and National Socialism. But instead it quickly shifted from the Nazi theme in favor of a discussion of the company's indispensability to Germany's reconstruction process. Titled "The Significance of the House of Siemens for the Rebuilding of Germany," this first section played effectively on the Allied concern over Germany's current economic devastation. Before the war Siemens, the manuscript pointed out, had been responsible for 40 percent of Germany's electrical industrial production. Now a ruined Germany had little means of obtaining its basic needs, to which reelectrification was central. Without electricity, the essay admonished, there would be no lighting, no electric transportation, and no news service. And without these basic necessities, "Germany will remain for an unforeseen period of time an open and bleeding wound on the economic body of Europe and the entire world."[64] Undoubtedly, from the wiring of refrigerators and radios to electrical cables for streetcars, electricity was indispensable to the country's infrastructural recovery. Siemens took full advantage of this reality when beseeching the Allies to spare their firm further devastation.

Yet more valuable to postwar reconstruction than the company's electro-technical contributions were what the manuscript called the "spirit and aims of the House of Siemens." By accentuating the words and ideals of the company's founding fathers — by articulating Siemens's "corporate identity" — the manuscript hoped to impress upon its readers the extent to which Siemens was philosophically removed from the reckless and evil behavior being attributed to it. Accordingly, the essay had as its centerpiece the company's long-standing devotion to peaceful scientific progress and international cooperation. It celebrated company founder Werner von Siemens's contributions to humankind as inventor, entrepreneur, scholar, and technician and referred readers to his published memoirs.[65] The essay pursued this theme of selfless and moral industrial production with an almost poetic flourish, at one point presenting the amusingly incongruous scene of the founder's son and successor Carl Friedrich von Siemens delivering a speech about brotherly love to an audience of New York meatpacking executives in 1931. Finally, this first section attempted to curry favor with its Allied readers by emphasizing the extent to which Siemens, until the war, had been embraced by both the Soviet Union and Great Britain not only for its products but for its devotion to progressive social welfare — from the eight-hour day to company pension plans.[66]

It is important to mention that this emphasis on the company spirit does not, in and of itself, betray a unique deceptiveness on the part of the firm. This type of ardent self-promotion has been a well-tested publicity strategy for a long time. In order to avoid the impression that it functions only from a selfish desire to maximize profit, a company injects a sense of purpose — a higher calling — into its seemingly amoral, economic behavior. Certainly Siemens did have reason to be proud of its history of sociopolitical engagement, as well as its generous policies in the areas of wages, insurance, child care, and company housing. In light of the company's complicity with Hitler, however, the manuscript's emphasis on the firm's commitment to social progress appears as a cynical attempt to mollify a hostile readership at any cost.

This preemptive move should not be surprising. Before attempting to deal with the charge of complicity, Siemens first had to remind its readers of its honorable history of smiling employees, garden villages, and ample vacation time that preceded the Nazi regime. Only then would the essay be poised to argue that any complicity under the Third Reich was, at best, an aberration. The firm was being accused of the most immoral behavior, and its greatest challenge was to reinstill in its buying public and in Western governments the confidence that they were dealing with a reputable and ethically conscientious company.

After portraying the company as an economically and morally vital force for the new Germany, the memorandum then turned to the unavoidable theme of Nazism. Rebutting all accusations on this point was hardly easy, given that the company had indeed committed many of the acts for which it was being called to task. Rather than deny that the company had been an essential force in the Nazi economy, the essay cast the behavior in question in a tragically heroic light by portraying Siemens's accommodation to the Nazi regime not as criminal behavior but as a mixture of defiance and resignation in the face of Nazi terror. In order to make this case, the essay expanded on the interpretation that Jessen had offered earlier in the month: Hitler had placed the firm under constant pressure to increase production and to go against the company spirit by manufacturing products not directly related to electro-technics. But Siemens had resisted the Nazi demands to the best of its ability. When it refused to make installations for warplanes, air force general field marshal Erhard Milch threatened to arrest the company's directors. When it refused to build a Graphite Electrode factory (*Graphitelektrodenfabrik*), the firm leaders were threatened with imprisonment in concentration camps or a bullet in the head. When Robert Ley of the DAF visited the company in 1942, Hermann von Siemens and his employees refused to greet him with "Heil Hitler."

But in the face of these constant psychological and physical threats, the argument continued, Siemens could not resist the demands of the state for long, and it had begun acceding to its request for armaments. Yet, argued the essay, the company never became a "defense firm," for it fulfilled these military orders only through makeshift subsidiaries, which could be easily dissolved or transferred to peaceful production when the Nazis were gone.[67] Even as munitions orders increased, the essay argued, Siemens remained opposed on principle to the state's demands, and this reluctance even helped contain, indirectly, the Nazis' destructive war capabilities. "One could perhaps say that the leadership of the firm should have resisted absolutely every form of cooperation in the armaments sector. There is no doubt, however, that the prior directors would have been treated as saboteurs." Moreover, "through their tactics of restraint, they held production in this area to a minimum and prevented much more."[68]

The essay expanded on this theme of resistance by disavowing any link between the company and national politics. The defining philosophy of the company was that "politics has no place in our house!" and "political propaganda stops at the door of the firm."[69] Carl Friedrich von Siemens, the head of Siemens from 1919 to 1940, had himself been quite active in politics and had served as a Reichstag deputy in the early 1920s, representing not a conservative party, as was typical for Weimar industrialists involved in politics, but the liberal German Democratic Party.[70] This particular example of public engagement, the essay suggested, was hardly "politics as usual" but, rather, a manifestation of the company's fundamental service ethic. When a Siemens director did choose to serve "the Fatherland" by entering national politics, he did so only as a candidate of the "democratic party," which had defended the Weimar Republic until its collapse.

The purpose of this insistent disavowal of politics is clear: if National Socialism was an inherently "political" movement, then refusing to allow political activities on the factory floor removed from Siemens the stain of criminal complicity. By demonstrating founder Werner von Siemens's and his sons' determination to keep all politics out of the firm, the essay hoped to maintain the image of an enterprise devoted purely to technological research. Governments may come and go, but Siemens was always there, producing electricity in the service of science and humanity. Industrialists—whether steel barons, managers, or chemical engineers—consistently disavowed any relationship to "politics" as they struggled to distance themselves from National Socialism.

If Siemens had always been democratically inclined and had rejected authoritarian political solutions before 1933, how, then, was the essay to deal with the firm's relationship to politics *after* Hitler's *Machtergreifung* (seizure of power)? During this period, the essay argued, the firm had never supported the Nazis "of its own free will."[71] In fact it had resisted the Nazis from the outset. Already in early 1933 C. F. Siemens had boldly declared his opposition to Hitler, predicting, "like a seer," that National Socialism would lead to a "horrible and bloody" end.[72] Immediately after Hitler's accession to power, the essay continued, C. F. Siemens resigned all of his public posts, and when he died in 1941, the Nazis refused to attend his funeral or to allow the publication of the funeral oration. By undercontributing to the Nazis' charitable funds, the company made itself the target of angry letters and visits from government officials, who reminded the firm that other companies were giving much more money than Siemens. Siemens, the essay continued, had never knowingly sold stock to Nazis, nor did it benefit from seized Jewish and foreign property, except for one exception in France[73] and the Belgian case discussed in the appendix. Siemens, the document concluded, had never been out to profit from a relationship with National Socialism. Admittedly, "without sufficient profit, there is no way of progressing and evolving." But "the desire for profit must not be the driving motive behind work, but rather the will toward the improvement of technology . . . and the service of progress."[74] In other words, the essay concluded, the House of Siemens had remained technologically and ideologically aloof from National Socialism and the allure of profit. Siemens, in short, had survived the Third Reich morally pure.

At this point we must consider what was at stake for Siemens in presenting this sanitized portrayal of its behavior, which in reality was marked by many instances of greed and opportunism. Importantly, some of the facts highlighted in the manuscript were not inventions as such. The company's long-standing resistance to *Fremdfabrikation* ("foreign" production, i.e., outside the area of electrotechnology) is well documented.[75] Similarly, the portrayal of Siemens as cautious and hesitant vis-à-vis the Nazis can be seen as an accurate reflection of some of the misgivings that did pervade the business community from 1933 to 1945. But the actions of firms like Siemens speak louder than their words. If Germany's industrialists had doubts about whether National Socialism was good for business, they nonetheless were able to overcome them and cooperate with a regime that demanded their services. Were, then, the Siemens directors in the summer of 1945 entirely disingenuous when they depicted themselves as opponents of the National Socialist government? Or did they sincerely believe that despite the more than nominal cooperation of some of its directors, Siemens *as an organization* had all along been an enemy of the Nazi regime? The answers to these question lie, in part, in the realm of individual and group psychology. With the destruction of National Socialism, most individuals and organizations that had supported the regime were wont to interpret their behavior as the result of external pressure or as a mask they wore to hide their true "internal emigration" from Nazi ideals. The struggle to survive the postwar purge of Germany's Nazi elements often led to embellished accounts—indeed whitewashes—of personal behavior, and business-men were not immune to this temptation. This fact, of course, should not detract from the acts of courage by Germans that did take place from 1933 to 1945. While it would be inappropriate to bestow oppositional status on those company directors who worked with the Nazis without any apparent misgivings, one can use the case of German industry and Nazism to raise more universal questions about the nature of corporate guilt. Do companies transcend the individuals who work for them? More directly, can a company remain untainted by the moral transgressions committed in its name?

These legal and philosophical questions are not without merit. But despite industrialists' protestations to the contrary, corporations *are* often judged according to the standards of individual morality, and Germany's businessmen have always known as much. One must, therefore, see German industrialists' defensiveness less as a genuine ethical position than as a pragmatic response to very real fears and anxieties. In the scramble to avoid punishment for individual acts committed in the name of their firms, German industrialists devised narratives of the past that would be useful not only in exculpating themselves legally, but in refurbishing a corporate self-identity (and identities) that would resonate with the Allies, employees, managers, and the public. The firms could then proceed with the business of reconstruction, unencumbered by the fear of arrest and the memories of the past.

As we have seen, the "resister" was one framework of identity industrialists created after the war. Yet it alone was not sufficient to explain the relationship of big business to National Socialism. In the postwar years, industrialists' oppositional self-image merged with other self-proclaimed identities—the apolitical entrepreneur, the scientist, and most notably, the victim. Already in 1945 industrialists were portraying their "opposition" to National Socialism not only as the product of a sense of outrage at the regime's polices but as a result of actual persecution. Industry argued consistently after the war that big business not only questioned Hitler's policies; it was also the object of his terror. Through threats of punishment, through the forced penetration of ideology into the factory, and through the government's dictation of economic goals, businessmen became victims as well as critics of the Nazis' authoritarian policies.

In exposing this self-image of victimization as an interpretive strategy, one must be careful not to underestimate the elements of terror that certainly contributed to the horrifying success of the Hitler dictatorship. But after the war, apologies for big business went far beyond a sober analysis of political control and intimidation. Rather, they displayed a crass and calculated identification with those who had suffered the most under National Socialism. This was most evident with respect to the "Jewish Question." It was not enough for a company to declare after the war that it had opposed the persecution of Germany's Jews. Businessmen also had to demonstrate that they had actively helped to save Jews *at their own personal risk*. This direct identification with the victim revealed itself clearly in the Siemens manuscript. "Not once did the firm proceed against a Jew or Free Mason on its own initiative," it argued. "On the contrary, it stood up for them to the point of self-sacrifice by helping these employees find positions abroad and by paying them greater transitional payments (*Übergangsbeihilfe*)."[76] By appropriating the status of the Jew and by actually boasting of its credentials as a "pig-sty, democratic-Jewish factory" (Robert Ley reportedly hurled this insult at the company when Hermann von Siemens refused to greet the labor leader with "Heil Hitler"), Siemens could claim that it, too, had been marginalized by the Nazis. On this point the manuscript is unambiguous: Siemens, the Jews, and all of the Nazis' victims shared a common enemy—Adolf Hitler.

It remained to be seen how this appropriation of victimhood would play out in the company's assessment of its own use of Jewish labor, however. When faced with evidence of having employed slave labor, could Siemens still profess to have shared in the plight of Germany's persecuted minorities? As we recall, this issue of forced labor was to be taken up in the so-called Enclosure No. 2. When it was finally finished in October 1945, this addendum had been expanded from a short piece into a forty-three-page essay bearing the title "The Use of Foreign Civilian Workers, Prisoners of War, Jews, and Concentration Camp Inmates in the House of Siemens."[77] Not surprisingly, the essay continued along the same interpretive line set down in the "Behavior of the House of Siemens." The company had been "forced" by the Nazi authorities to use slave labor, but only after holding out as long as possible. When this step became inevitable, the firm did everything in its power to provide clean and comfortable living conditions for the workers. This benevolent treatment of foreign labor can be attested to, argued the report, by the "large number of thank-you letters and requests for employment" that the company had reportedly received from its former forced laborers upon their return home.[78] Ultimately, the essay concluded, Siemens saved the lives of these workers, who under other circumstances might have perished.[79]

Historian Carola Sachse has focused at some length on this report and its reliance on exaggerations and untruths. As she has pointed out, contrary to the report's claims, no company during World War II was ever forced to employ Jews and concentration camp prisoners. Nor, as we have seen, is it the case that Siemens waited as long as possible before employing Jews.[80] While it is surely true that individual prisoners suffered to varying degrees depending on their gender and ethnicity, the nature of their work, and the particular camp and labor conditions, it is inaccurate to claim that prisoners were treated just like Germans or that sanitation and comfort were always of supreme importance. In the oral histories of Ravensbrück survivors, we encounter many reports of backbreaking and humiliating labor conditions, compounded by the reality that these women were terrified and far from home and family.

While the line of defense adopted by the Siemens report is, in Sachse's words, "unsensational" in its by now familiar manipulation of historical reality, it is nonetheless a telling reflection of its immediate historical context, when industry was searching for an interpretive framework for the events of the preceding twelve years.[81] Again, the emphasis on the corporate *Geist* is of fundamental importance. Even when dealing with the most severe example of industrial brutality—forced labor—companies still chose to defend themselves by emphasizing their worker-friendly ethos. Not only in this report on slave labor but also for many years afterward, Siemens repeatedly suggested that its foreign workers had benefited from the progressive stance on which the company so prided itself. While certainly not denying that the workers had been brought against their will to work for Siemens, the company report, and reports of other companies later, insisted that these workers had always been well fed and given much opportunity for relaxation and cultural diversion. Instead of images of grueling labor, these reports offered statistics on leisure and sports, the frequency of group visits to museums and theaters, and the availability of foreign-language books in the company libraries.[82]

Food, housing, and sanitary conditions did, of course, vary from camp to camp and from installation to installation, and the Siemens tract presented (selective) evidence to this effect with dispassionate prose and sober statistics. But it overlooked the often atrocious conditions at its camps, and it avoided any discussion of the moral implications of having using forced labor. Instead there is an exaggerated preoccupation with sanitation and nutrition. If Siemens could produce statistical evidence that the prisoners had been well clothed and well fed (and at additional cost to the firm), then perhaps the deeper moral dilemmas could somehow be bypassed altogether.[83] Today one can still discover in the Siemens archives a rather selective array of testimonies, many gathered by the company's internal Investigative Committee in 1947, all of which coincidentally seem to mitigate the harsh realities of slave labor. Quite conveniently, after the Soviets had confiscated the company papers, Siemens claimed to have lost all written complaints against the firm with respect to labor conditions.[84] One therefore rarely comes across any negative portrayals of Siemens. More common are documents like the letter from a Jewish veterinarian in Berlin who had been forced to work for Siemens. The doctor and his son spent a year and a half working for the Werner Works in Berlin. "While the forced labor at the time depressed us morally," he wrote to Witzleben in the fall of 1945, "I do have to admit that the actual work given to us was enjoyable. We were treated well and respectfully by the overseers and instructors, and one always had the feeling that they tried to meet our wishes as much as it was possible."[85] It would, in the end, be unrealistic to expect an exculpatory effort to concede ethical shortcomings or to wax philosophical about the relationship between profit making and human suffering. Nonetheless, in these texts any sense of moral awareness is lost in a flood of statistics on cabbage, carrots and beets.

The selective use of evidence and the less than subtle adoption of a victim-resister framework in both the "Behavior of the House of Siemens" and the report on forced labor ultimately reveal a superficial understanding of the more complex relationship between the Nazi government and big business, with all of its elements of pressure, opportunism, defiance and moral cowardice. In reality, industry—if looked at collectively—chose to adhere to the demands of the state. But after the war it would certainly not admit as much. In industrialists' attempts to defend past behavior through company profiles, what began in a spirit of confident defiance often degenerated into melodrama and falsehoods.

Rhetorical Fine-Tuning

On 1 August the Siemens board of management had partial and completed manuscript drafts in its possession. The basic themes had been spelled out clearly. Under the Nazis Siemens had remained scientific, apolitical, peaceful, oppositional, and worker friendly. The next step for the directors was to fine tune these arguments. This postcomposition process of exchanging and proofreading drafts offers the powerful image of industrialists sitting in conference rooms, carefully negotiating publicity strategies as their companies lay in ruins around them. Pentz and Witzleben's comments and penciled corrections on these early drafts reveal an effort to fashion a coherent narrative by eliminating potentially ambiguous or damaging turns of phrase. Both directors insisted that the manuscripts maintain a tone as restrained and "strictly objective" as possible, lest they be dismissed as sensationalist or overly biased.[86] Witzleben, for example, suggested that all references containing the word "Nazi" in the original draft be replaced with the more official "National Socialist," so as to avoid the seemingly frivolous, less imposing language of Hitler's opponents. At various other points they questioned candidly whether enough evidence actually existed to support the essays' claims.[87]

Beyond the proofreader's expected lexical and evidentiary queries, Pentz and Witzleben took great pains to consolidate the company's broader view of National Socialism as a force that gave little room for businessmen to map their own fates. They replaced "*Nazi Herrschaft*" (Nazi rule) with "*Hitler-Regime*," in keeping with the company's understanding of state terror as emanating from a small clique of perpetrators surrounding the Führer.[88] They questioned the draft's voluntary references to the albeit "limited" number of Siemens board members who had belonged to the NSDAP. Despite this intention to temper the image of a thoroughly Nazified company directorship, any allusion to Nazis on the managing board, wrote Witzleben, "hardly made a good impression, especially when we have previously always insisted that the company leadership never exercised pressure to join the party."[89]

To the contemporary reader, this verbal hairsplitting may appear a naive attempt to put out a fire with teacups full of water. But it also indicates the inability of the Siemens board members to grasp the extent of the moral disaster that lay behind them in Germany. This meticulous crafting bespeaks the single-mindedness with which Germans in the summer of 1945 embraced any rhetorical device that could mitigate the severity of the claims against them and their country. If shortening a chapter title or padding the biography of "Sir William Siemens" (Wilhelm von Siemens) with a few more honors and marks of British nobility could persuade the Allies to spare Siemens harsh punishment, then the company would have no qualms about undertaking such changes. By portraying themselves as the pawns of a terrifying dictatorship embodied in a single man and his entourage, Germans would relieve themselves of the responsibility of having contributed to the crimes of Nazism. This attempt to personify all criminal activity in Adolf Hitler would become an essential strategy not just of industrialists but of a variety of social and professional groups in postwar Germany. It was not enough simply to depict oneself as a detached and fearful observer of the regime. One also had to offer an explanation for the inability to resist the Nazis even more vigorously than one claimed one had. If the demonic efficiency of the Nazis could be attributed, in the end, to one man, Hitler, then Germans would have lifted from themselves some of the burden of complicity.[90]

In the first half of September the Siemens directors put the finishing touches on the main draft, the slave labor report, and the Aryanization piece.[91] These were then sent to various Allied agencies, as had been originally intended. In 1946 the company sent a copy of the forced labor report to the Berlin office of the U.S. chief of counsel, along with a selection of Siemens-friendly questionnaires filled out by former foreign employees who, of course, testified only to the comfortable work conditions in the firm's wartime installations.[92] Despite the undisguised attempt to lobby the Allies with these company profiles, Siemens was later to claim that these reports had been written only for "internal purposes" and were never intended to be "published."[93] This claim is not accurate. While it may, indeed, be true that the company never conceived of these reports as future best-sellers, the arguments contained in them were, without a doubt, directed not simply at Siemens employees but, by their own private admissions, at the Allied occupation and the world public, which alone held the key to the survival of Germany's firms.

With the composition of the "Behavior of the House of Siemens" and its addenda, Siemens had completed the first of what was to be a series of documents designed to distance the company from its past. A later document, titled "Horror Stories about the Siemens Concern," invoked the familiar narrative, but more forthrightly (and tendentiously) than before: Siemens had never built a gas chamber at Auschwitz; the firm had been forced to accept POWs, Jews, concentration camp inmates, and foreigners; Jews and foreign workers had been paid the same as Germans; Siemens had conducted "passive resistance" against the Nazis.

Fearing that the firm's negative publicity might adversely affect overseas business, Director Pentz sent a copy of this piece to a respected businessman and Siemens friend, Benjamin O'Shea, president and CEO of Union Carbon and Carbine. Pentz asked O'Shea to pass the text around to as many businessmen in the United States as possible. He entreated his American colleague to remember Siemens's corporate integrity. "It would be a tragic thought for me if, as a result of these false reports, you were to have any doubts about the moral behavior of the House of Siemens. . . . We hope that none of our friends abroad are fooled by the malicious slandering of the Siemens Concern and remain convinced that the moral foundations of the House of Siemens have remained unshaken for 100 years."[94]

It should not be surprising that Siemens worried about potential international damage to its reputation. Since the nineteenth century, Siemens had prided itself as a global firm, with large foreign sales and numerous subsidiaries, stretching from Latin America to Africa to Japan. Siemens had entered cooperative agreements with U.S. companies such as Westinghouse in the 1920s and wanted to maintain favorable postwar relations with markets in the United States and elsewhere. Finally, Siemens remembered that during World War I, Britain had confiscated its subsidiaries, and the company was sensitive to any such losses it could suffer again on the international front.

In an interesting response to Pentz's appeal abroad, however, O'Shea wrote back claiming he had never heard any claims against Siemens but promising, nonetheless, that he would "not fail to give your [Siemens's] side of the story to any who are at all interested."[95] Clearly, many foreign businessmen were not yet paying much attention to (or were not hearing about) the accusations leveled against some German companies. But, importantly, reminders of the past engendered the *fear* within Siemens that the company would be damaged internationally. With this attempt to reassure the U.S. business world that Siemens was morally pure, Pentz anticipated German industry's later attempts to reach a foreign audience as it slowly regained its former place in the world market.

These documents ultimately reflect the desperate mood of the early postwar years and the desire by severely damaged companies like Siemens to counter claims that "would damage the reputation and calling of our firm and have a very bad effect on our employees' work."[96] Without the ability to mass produce and distribute these apologias, however, Siemens could hardly expect to dispel the accusations against it. Until 1947 Siemens therefore remained embroiled in controversy about its war criminality, with Benkert and Witzleben going through lengthy denazification proceedings and with the companies' own workers turning on their directors.

Allied Policies toward German Industry

Before we return to tumultuous events in Berlin-Siemensstadt, we must consider the broader circumstances, specifically with regard to Allied industrial policy, that accompanied the writing of early industrial apologies. For companies like Siemens were responding not only to accusations of corporate guilt coming from the political press, but to the actions of the victorious powers, who alone held the key to the survival of a company.

At the end of World War II, the Allies divided Germany (and the capital, Berlin) into four zones administered respectively by the commanders-in-chief of each of the Allied armies. They established an Allied Control Council in Berlin to devise policy affecting Germany as a whole, and in the spring and summer of 1945 the four powers agreed on a number of points, such as the basic need for the denazification of industry (and all German society) and the desire to keep industry from expanding to threatening levels. In July 1945 the Big Three—Joseph Stalin, Harry Truman, and Winston Churchill—met outside Berlin in Potsdam to inscribe these views in writing. What came to be known as the Potsdam Protocol called for the denazification of German industry and the removal of "excessive concentration of economic power" from the defeated country. The Allies agreed to exact reparations through, among other means, the dismantling and appropriation of industrial facilities deemed superfluous or capable of producing war matériel.[97] Potsdam also mandated the issuing of future policy directives regarding German industrial capacity, and it reiterated the Allies' commitment to an international tribunal to try major Nazi criminals.

Despite the spirit of agreement in the summer of 1945, the Allies soon recognized how much they actually differed over the treatment of German industry and its leaders. The British, despite confusion and conflicting policies at local and regional levels, promoted an essentially reconstructive approach to German industry from the outset. They hoped to rebuild Germany according to the ideals of the ruling Labour Party, strengthening the hand of West Germany's unions, nationalizing its basic industries, and introducing economic democracy in the workplace.[98] (The British would later abandon their more radical goal of nationalization.) Similarly, the French were determined to contain German industry without destroying it; their chief interest was less punitive than it was self-promoting—to (re)establish their hegemony within a peacefully reconstructed Europe. While perhaps the most vocal in its desire to check the rebirth of German national might, France was less interested in revamping capitalism than in internationalizing heavy industry in the Ruhr and keeping German business peaceful. This policy culminated in the European Coal and Steel Community (ECSC) of 1950 and French patronage of an industrially vigorous, if carefully monitored, Germany.[99]

The Soviet Union, in turn, made it clear through its actions upon arrival in Germany that the expropriation, nationalization, and dismantling of factories would be its solution to the problems of industrial reconstruction. The Soviets and the formerly exiled communist leadership in Germany saw in the defeat of fascism the final repudiation of capitalism and the opportunity to push through reforms that they had already enacted in the USSR. The Soviets, and later the Socialist Unity Party of Germany (Sozialistische Einheitspartei Deutschlands, or SED) (communist) leadership in East Germany, were, therefore, less intent than the other Allies on purging the economy of Nazi industrialists. According to Soviet doctrine, the overhaul of the entire capitalist system would naturally obviate the need to somehow weed out "bad" industrialists from what was already a corrupt and anachronistic market-oriented system.[100]

The Americans were by far the most divided—and in some ways the harshest—in their treatment of German industry, and their policies deserve close examination. Since the Depression, U.S. politics had been defined by competing conceptions of government and labor and their ability to function as checks on the power of big business.[101] In the 1930s and 1940s a rift between neoliberals and the advocates of a more regulated economy colored the Franklin D. Roosevelt administration's view of fascism and postwar plans for German industry. While the desire after the war to limit severely Germany's economic potential quickly lost the upper hand to more business-friendly schemes, throughout the late 1940s U.S. policy was still, in part, influenced by a lingering fear of the powers and dangers of big business.[102] The Americans were determined to hold German industry accountable for its cooperation with Hitler. Yet they never formulated this desire in anticapitalist terms but, rather, in terms of individual responsibility. The punishment of German business, even from the perspective of the many Americans who attributed Hitler's rise to big business, was conceived of as *promoting* the market system—albeit a more genuinely "free" and humane one—rather than destroying it. If the Soviets and members of the German Left saw capitalism—whether monopoly, finance, or laissez-faire—as intrinsically unstable, the Americans launched a more precise attack on one version of capitalism. To the Americans who campaigned against a strong industrial rebirth, the German economy, made up of a tangle of cartels, price-fixing agreements, and monopolistic combinations, had been the greatest violation of the free market. In other words, while the communists saw capitalism as having spawned fascism, the Americans believed that industrial greed and moral callousness had paved the path to Auschwitz. The Nazis' limiting of economic freedom had been part of their brutal effort to curtail political and personal freedom altogether. According to the Americans, only by smashing the large conglomerations of economic power and controlling trusts and monopolies would Germany become ripe for a more decentralized and peaceful economy, recast according to the U.S. model.[103]

This trust-busting approach to West Germany was embodied in a U.S. Joint Chiefs of Staff policy directive (JCS 1067) of May 1945, which replaced U.S. Treasury Secretary Henry Morgenthau's September 1944 proposal to dismantle the heavy industries of the Ruhr. Morgenthau had not intended, as many scholars and Germans still believe, to "pastoralize" Germany completely (that is, turn the country into farmland). Rather, he wanted to limit Germany's war-making potential and allow for the growth of industry in other parts of Europe.[104] But his proposal was harsh, and it included plans for a major deindustrialization of the Ruhr through, among other means, the flooding of coal mines. From 1945 to this day, Germans have exaggerated the importance of the short-lived Morgenthau Plan as an indication of how brutal occupation policy was. JCS 1067 removed an extensive disabling of German industry from U.S. policy. But it still committed the United States to a punitive industrial policy based on preventing the "rehabilitating of the economy." [105]

JCS 1067 also explicitly outlawed cartels and called for the breakup of large business empires, such as would eventually occur with IG Farben.[106] In the minds of its planners, this new policy directive was to serve as a warning not only to Germany but also to the big trusts in the United States (Du Pont, Standard Oil, General Electric) that harbored monopolistic sentiments. The decartelization of German companies would remind Americans that unchecked economic power could breed political terror in any political context.[107]

During the first three years after World War II, the German economy was under the total control of the Allies, who dictated all policy with respect to production, the import and export of raw materials and heavy industrial goods, agriculture, prices, and wages. Some aspects of JCS 1067 and Potsdam continued to guide U.S. and, to a lesser extent, the other Western Allies' policies through 1949. This was most notable in the controversial, if ultimately limited, dismantling of factories through 1949 and the promulgation of constantly changing Levels of Industry plans, one of which, for example, called for German industrial output to be reduced to 55 percent of the production levels of 1938.[108]

The force of these policies was greatly diminished, however, once the Cold War between the West and the Soviets became a reality. In January 1947 the British and Americans united their zones of occupation in order to coordinate policy, and in July the United States formally abandoned JCS 1067. By 1948, with the growing hostilities between the West and the Soviet Bloc, the Grand Alliance of World War II was dead, and Potsdam was effectively obsolete. Western Allied policy became more uniformly reconstructionist, as embodied in the Marshall Plan and the introduction of the deutsche mark. With the Cold War and the failure of harsh post–World War I policies in mind, the Western Allies aimed instead at integrating a productive industrial Germany into a Western economy and Atlantic community.

Berlin Politics, Workers, and Siemens Guilt

While Western Allied policy would eventually favor the reconstruction of German industry, business leaders could not be sure of this in the initial chaotic years after the war. Indeed, as they crafted their exculpatory company narratives in July 1945, Hanns-Henning von Pentz and his Siemens codirectors were well aware that the Allies were formulating industrial policy across town in Potsdam. The day after Pentz distributed drafts to the other board members, the Big Three signed the Potsdam agreement. The board of directors was aware that it would have to move quickly on its publicity projects if it wanted to have any influence on Allied policies toward its firm.

The problem was that the British, who controlled the sector of Berlin that included Siemensstadt, were not yet sure of how to proceed against Siemens, and their frequent shifts in policy reflect the confusion that accompanied the division of the destroyed capital. In Berlin, a city from which a great many skilled technicians, scientists, and trained managers had fled, the British were also keenly sensitive to the paradox they were creating for themselves as they pursued economic rebuilding and denazification simultaneously. On one hand, they wanted to punish persons they deemed in any way complicit in the crimes of National Socialism. On the other hand, the practicalities of reconstruction demanded a convenient blindness to some past transgressions.[109] Moreover, the political situation in Berlin was extremely tense, as the SPD, the KPD, the CDU, and the Free Democratic Party all sought to establish influence at the grass roots.[110] In the Soviet sector of "Red Berlin," the socialists and communists vied for dominance until 1946, when the communists forcibly absorbed the SPD to form the SED. The now, in effect, dictatorial SED leadership, along with its KPD affiliates in the non-Soviet zones of Germany, would spearhead the efforts after 1946 to remind the world of Siemens's complicity.[111]

In the summer of 1945 the British witnessed the confusing mix of Berlin politics and the legacy of business guilt when Siemens's newly forged factory councils and the communist press in Berlin stepped up their assault on the company directors. On 5 August, while company directors were hard at work on their Siemens documents, the communist *Deutsche Volkszeitung* published an article asserting that Siemens had built and installed the crematoriums and gas chambers in Auschwitz (a claim that has never been proven).[112] This latest assertion had potentially dire consequences for Siemens. With all the turmoil surrounding the company, the last thing Siemens wanted was to be more closely associated with the Final Solution. The board of directors responded instantly to this new development. On 6 August they scrambled to find a lawyer, presumably for a possible lawsuit against the newspapers that were fomenting the campaign against the firm.[113] The next day the Siemens directors wrote to the *Deutsche Volkszeitung* to deny the Auschwitz story. They demanded that the paper retract the claim, which, they argued, "would damage the reputation and calling of our firm and have a very bad effect on our employees' work."[114] When the *Deutsche Volkszeitung* defiantly repeated the Auschwitz claim on 24 August, Siemens decided to take more direct action. Witzleben immediately drafted a letter to General L. O. Lyne of the British military command of Berlin, calling for an investigation into the *Deutsche Volkszeitung* and a cessation of these accusations against the company. "In the interest of the reputation of both firms," wrote an angry Witzleben, "I cannot let these wholly untrue assertions remain unanswered." To aid in dispelling this damaging rumor, Witzleben enclosed a copy of the latest version of "The Behavior of the House of Siemens during the Hitler Regime," with the comment that the memorandum had been "prepared by us, objectively written, and in every respect true." [115] The assertion about the crematoriums stunned the Siemens directors already at work on their careful publicity campaign. This new rumor motivated Witzleben to issue a protest to the British command, although not only out of concern for his firm. Rather, it was the immediate personal consequences it had on Witzleben, whose name had also been "dragged through the mud" by the *Volkszeitung* article. The British, who had administrative control over Berlin-Siemensstadt, apparently took the Auschwitz claims very seriously. On 22 August, the day the second *Deutsche Volkszeitung* article appeared, Witzleben was arrested and brought to a British military command post. He was, according to his own description, immediately forced down into the cellar, where he was stripped of his shoes and suspenders and locked into a wooden cubicle. After two hours of waiting, a whip-wielding soldier eventually prodded him to his interrogation. After he was cross-examined and released, Witzleben made his way back to Siemensstadt on foot. Two days later he was again arrested, this time under suspicion of having delivered secret reports to the Gestapo. He was held for eighteen hours before being interrogated and released. Nothing became of this accusation against him. [116]

Witzleben surely spoke for all of his colleagues when he revealed, in his letter to Commander Lyne, his sense of outrage and wounded pride at being treated like a common criminal. [117] Regardless of the accusations against his firm, including constructing crematoriums and directing the acquisition of slave labor, such treatment did not befit one of the nation's most important industrial leaders. Witzleben felt that such barbarous treatment had not only violated his basic civil rights but threatened the well-being of the economy. In his protest he cleverly took advantage of the desire of the British occupation to see industrial reconstruction proceed apace. "I represent my firm to the British," he argued, "and the way I am being treated has physical and psychological effects that will endanger the reconstruction process." [118]

Galvanized by both the Allies' and almost every political party's concern with the complicity of big business, the Siemens employees themselves continued to expose the Nazi pasts of their board of directors. In September 1945 the employees of the Siemens Werner Works issued a protest against director Benkert, and in December a membership gathering of Siemens employees voted 2,000 to 4 to remove Witzleben, Benkert, and Pohlmann from the Siemens managerial board. [119] Clearly, the firm's employees had turned against the upper management. This vote indicates the extent to which Siemens's own workers were aware of the relationship between industry and National Socialism and how they would not tolerate the continued leadership of individuals who had carried through Hitler's policies. Throughout 1946, in their campaign to socialize the economy, Communist Party politicians and the Siemens factory councils jointly presented new evidence tying the firm and its directors to National Socialist crimes.[120] The firm's supervisory board, however, had no obligation to respond to this information, and the three directors remained in their positions. Benkert, however, was stripped of actual managerial duties in accordance with Allied decrees regarding former members of the NSDAP.[121]

When, at the end of 1946, a denazification board failed to acquit Witzleben and Benkert, the British military government began to take some heat for not acting against the two directors. In January 1947, with the imminent visit to Berlin of the World Federation of Trade Unions, the British began to discuss more drastic measures. A split emerged between the political wing of the British Control Commission, which was responsible for all questions of denazification, and the more pragmatic members of the Economic Section, who were reluctant to dispense with the two directors' services at this crucial time of industrial reconstruction. In January 1947 the Political Branch recommended that the two men "be suspended forthwith," despite the misgivings of the economists. "Unless we can show," wrote Director D. S. Laskey, "that we are not prepared to protect these two men indefinitely, I am afraid that we shall leave ourselves open to strong and justified criticism."[122] The Berlin branch of the Economic and Social Council of the Control Commission agreed, arguing that while "we have to take into consideration the great demand for capable, skilled specialists . . . in the basic industries[,] . . . we cannot allow this situation to continue any longer."[123] The Economics Branch of the military government finally acceded to the pressure and suspended both men from an executive role with Siemens until their appeals went through.[124]

On 1 February 1947 Allied Law No. 52 took effect.[125] According to its terms, the bank accounts of Germany's major companies were to be seized and placed in trust with the Allied Property Control Branches. The British quickly appointed Fritz Jessen to act as financial custodian for Siemens, a move that did little to assuage the wrath of the company's workers, who saw Jessen as a fascist holdover.[126] Both the company and the British government were quick to reassure the workers and the public that Jessen had neither a shady past nor a conflict of interest in representing both the British authorities and the Siemens management. They also tried to assure foreign stockholders that Law No. 52 was not an admission of company complicity in Nazism but merely a financial safeguard while Siemens's fate was decided.

Despite continued attacks from the press, including repeated claims that Siemens had helped build the Auschwitz crematoriums, things began looking up for the company when, at the end of the month, a British appeals court fully exonerated Witzleben.[127] Immediately the company held a referendum on whether he should be reinstated as chairman of the board. Twenty-two thousand members cast ballots and by a narrow 50.8 percent decided in the director's favor.[128] But after so close a vote, the supervisory board still considered not allowing Witzleben to continue in his duties. After brief deliberations the board ultimately reappointed Witzleben as chairman of S&H and SSW. The relieved director immediately posted a circular around the company offices and factories, thanking employees who had stuck by him and offering an olive branch to workers who had called for his removal.

> I am convinced that those employees who, out of ignorance, judged me falsely, will now alter their opinion of me when the true facts about my behavior and that of the company are clarified. German industry—and with it Siemens—now finds itself in the midst of a serious economic crisis. We can overcome it only if we stand together and marshal all of our energies together. In order to be true to the old founding principle of our House that we are a technical-economic enterprise . . . , I call upon all employees of goodwill, regardless of their personal political views, . . . to lend a hand and support me in this endeavor.[129]

With the reinstatement of Witzleben, Siemens began to tone down its frantic publicity activities. By 1947 Siemens could take heart at Cold War developments that led the Western Allies to take less interest in Siemens's crimes. While the Berlin SED pushed through a law to nationalize all industry, its implementation was delayed until the joint administration of Berlin was dissolved altogether, leaving the firm squarely in the Western zones of occupation.[130] With the dissolution of the joint Allied control of Berlin and the reestablishment of the company headquarters in Munich and Erlangen, Siemens felt less vulnerable to the East German rhetoric against finance capitalism. Now, however, Siemens and the rest of German industry would have to focus their attention on the Western Allies' own critique of German capitalism.

I have used the construction of an apologetic company narrative to illustrate the urgency with which German industry tackled the memory of National Socialism in the immediate aftermath of defeat. It is difficult to determine, however, whether these Siemens apologies actually helped temper the bad publicity from which the company suffered or, indeed, restored a positive public image for Siemens. Admittedly, their distribution was always limited, most likely because, as Fritz Jessen suggested and as Benjamin O'Shea's puzzled response indicated, the last thing the company managers wanted to do was inadvertently introduce the images of complicity to individuals who had not already taken an interest in these claims. Of course to anybody who read German newspapers in the early postwar years, the accusations against Siemens were entirely familiar. But in composing the manuscripts for the Allies and the foreign public, Siemens clearly recognized that its future lay as much with a renewed foreign trade as with a domestic market. While the attacks coming from socialists, union leaders, and primarily the Soviet-sponsored communist newspapers could always be met in the political arena, the negative effect that the link to Nazism would have on British and U.S. public opinion was a danger that the company could not ignore. But until German companies could establish official public relations branches, their top managers would have to rely on less systematic publicity activities. While this strategizing amidst the Berlin wreckage could hardly compare to later, industrywide efforts to fend off attacks on capitalism, it is nonetheless clear that firms and individual industrialists were already anticipating the battles to come.

With hindsight it might appear that Siemens was overreacting to the claims against it. The company would never be broken up like IG Farben nor submitted to a highly public prosecution in Nuremberg. From 1945–47, however, the United States seriously considered prosecuting Siemens executives in Nuremberg. The State Department gathered extensive material on the firm but never carried through with this intention.[131] Siemens executives, therefore, *feared* that the company would be divided up, and the firm, along with the rest of German industry, maintained a siege mentality through the late 1940s and early 1950s, even when the possibility of prosecution was behind it and when business was picking up. For more was at stake than the relationship between company reputation and sales figures. To industrialists, accusations of criminal behavior threatened their entire self-perception. While industrialists had grown accustomed to being labeled immoral profiteers, accusations of complicity with the Nazis clearly struck a deeper nerve, one that went beyond a concern for maximizing profit. The thesis of big-business guilt besmirched the entire calling of Germany's industrialists. In accordance with official communist doctrine, but also in the minds of East and West Germans, capitalism became, in the aftermath of World War II, synonymous with National Socialist crimes against humanity, and industrialists took this analogy—or, rather, its damaging application—very seriously.

Siemens was not the only company or individual preparing exculpatory manuscripts during this period. Klaus-Dietmar Henke has focused in great detail on the apologetic testimonial written and distributed by steel director Ernst Poensgen and his colleagues with the VSt in the summer of 1945.[132] In this piece the former VSt director carefully emphasized his own personal honor and his utter lack of knowledge of the Final Solution until after May 1945. After the war, Daimler-Benz directors also drew together an internal report on the company's use of foreign labor, in which they, like Siemens, subordinated any moral grappling to a presentation of the raw "employment figures."[133] However, the Siemens self-profile on which I have focused reveals most plainly the rhetorical tools with which all industry would soon carve out a postwar identity. By drawing on a tradition of service, humanity, and technological progress, and by maintaining their apolitical self-definition, industrialists were able not only to defend their firms but also to rationalize to themselves their accommodation to a criminal regime. By composing such self-defenses, industrialists were constructing a counternarrative of the past, intended as much for themselves as for a limited public. In the summer of 1945 Siemens began to create a new company memory. It drew on an older narrative of entrepreneurial ingenuity and selfless production and reworked it to reflect the challenges that National Socialism had posed. If the Siemens *Geist* was still intact, it was now more multifaceted, embodying claims of civil courage and defiance in the face of a dictator.

These early self-justifications must be ultimately considered in the context of the war and its immediate aftermath. In the summer of 1945 Germans were still reeling from two years of constant bombing and serious economic and social devastation. It had already been clear to many industrial leaders by 1943 that industry would have to plan for a postwar world that followed not victory but defeat.[134] When the end finally came, not just industrialists but all Germans immediately reached for explanations of this catastrophe. Their own experiences during and after the war easily facilitated a view of National Socialism as an evil force that they had never supported. Surrounded by rubble and broken families, it was easy to impose retroactively their current disdain for Nazism onto the 1930s and early 1940s, when so many Germans did support the regime. National Socialism, people could convince themselves, was something they never wanted—at least not in the form that it took: physical destruction, personal privation, and national humiliation. The narratives of opposition to and victimization by Nazism transcended specific professions and social groups; industrialists joined war veterans and politicians in their identification with the heroic and the oppressed.[135] They all shared the view that National Socialism had both betrayed their inner convictions and violated them personally through the hardships it created. But their language often betrayed the extent to which they had accommodated themselves to the Nazi *Volksgemeinschaft*. For example, Siemens's use of the terms "Jewish Question" and "Jewish Problem" to refer to the company's public image difficulties is quite telling. In adopting the anti-Semitic verbiage of the prior decades, Siemens executives were not necessarily expressing the same hate-filled ideas. This choice of words, nonetheless, reveals the extent to which Germans had assimilated the rhetoric of anti-Semitism, even as they attempted to disavow any such sentiments.

After the immediate postwar years, as West German economic reconstruction began in earnest, industrial self-portrayals took on less spontaneous, more coordinated dimensions. Publicity moved beyond the walls of the individual firm and became the joint enterprise of all industrialists. Community memory formed as industrialists began focusing not only on their own stories or those of their firms but on "German industry" as a seemingly unified group. Postwar professional and national identities revealed themselves to be multi-layered. Business leaders understood themselves not simply as members of the House of Siemens but as industrialists and, finally, as Germans.

CHAPTER TWO

The Beginnings of a Collective Identity

For West Germany's largest firms, the defeat of Nazism brought both the hope for a new beginning and the sober realities of Allied policies and damaged reputations. A company like Siemens, which before the war had enjoyed respect at home and abroad, was called to account for its accommodation with the Nazis. To defend itself, it created the story of an uncompromised company past. National Socialism was portrayed as one more challenge, albeit the greatest in the company's history, that Siemens had overcome as it proceeded with the business of peaceful electrotechnological production. In defending itself against charges of complicity, Siemens provided itself with an official company memory that would help its employees and managers face the vicissitudes of economic and political reconstruction.

While the focus of the last chapter was limited to a relatively progressive company and the events in the city of Berlin, I will now expand my discussion to other regions of Germany and other branches of industry. A defiant reinterpretation of National Socialism was not the exclusive privilege of a firm like Siemens, which had once enjoyed a positive national and international reputation. Heavy industry, which had always been considered more reactionary with respect to foreign trade and worker relations, employed similar interpretive methods in the face of accusations of complicity. During the early years of the Cold War, both the Western Allies and German political parties on the Left stepped up their critique of big business, and in response industrialists expanded their publicity efforts beyond the personal self-defense and the company history. In their fight against the Allies' policies of deconcentration, dismantling, and denazification, business leaders in all branches of industry began manipulating memories of the recent past more confidently and more deftly than in 1945. Industrialists positioned themselves not only as representatives of their own companies, but as key players in a domestic and international network of businessmen opposed to a punitive handling of the German economy. Industrialists responded to the prosecutions in Nuremberg, the Allied debates over the future of their firms, and the rebirth of organized labor with a collective sense of outrage and an increasing hope that the public—both at home and abroad—would be receptive to a spirited defense of German big business.

Mass Arrests and the Rebuilding of Industrial Organizations

In the fall of 1945, Allied occupation authorities embarked on a massive effort to capture possible war criminals active in heavy industry. During two raids in October and November, British field security police swept through homes and businesses in the Upper Rhine and Ruhr regions, arresting eighty-three of Germany's most prominent steel and coal magnates. With bank accounts frozen and firms placed in the hands of a control commission, Germany's leading industrialists—from company owners to members of the supervisory boards to high-level managers—were brought to the Düsseldorf central jail and then transferred to various internment camps throughout British-occupied Germany.[1] Most of the detained were interrogated, released, and successfully denazified in a few months. But others would spend almost three years behind barbed wire.[2] Still others were brought to Nuremberg for cross-examination and prosecution for war crimes and crimes against humanity.[3]

The somewhat belated arrest of company managers provoked a tremendous shock among Germany's economic elites. Industrialists found it unfathomable that the Western Allies "could now treat [them] without exception as criminals."[4] This incredulity was revealed during the arrest of Werner Carp, a financier active on several supervisory boards in the Ruhr. When the British arrived in the middle of the night to seize Carp at his luxurious home, the agitated director immediately began insisting that he had been an enemy of Hitler all along and was never a "real Nazi." The British were forced to carry away the pajama-clad executive under a barrage of pleas that he be allowed to contact important friends who would put a stop to the arrest.[5] Carp was probably unaware that these influential colleagues were also on their way to Düsseldorf prison and later to Bad Nenndorf, a sprawling British internment camp near Hanover.[6]

Despite prior rumors that arrests were forthcoming, industrialists were dumbfounded by this turn of events. During the summer of 1945 many business leaders had been given a false sense of security, as U.S. and British military governors conferred closely and amiably with them on a myriad of economic matters.[7] While the Potsdam conference in early August had already dashed hopes that German industry would be left in peace to rebuild itself, few executives who had survived the initial wave of arrests in the early summer could have expected their own capture.

The great majority of business leaders arrested in the fall of 1945 represented the iron and steel industries of the Upper Rhine and Ruhr Valley. Taking advantage of some of the world's largest deposits of coal, the entrepreneurs of the Ruhr had in the nineteenth century presided over the rapid transformation of Germany from a rural country into one of the world's most industrialized nations. If steel for construction and coal for heating had originated in this narrow stretch of land in northwest Germany, so had the tanks and guns of two world wars. According to the Western Allies, heavy industry bore the lion's share of guilt because of its war production. If the Allies could break up the tight network of factories and industries that comprised the Ruhr, then Germany, it was argued, would be prevented from unleashing another war of aggression. Not surprisingly, in response to this view, Ruhr leaders adopted a defiant perspective on this perpetual equation of guilt and heavy industry. "Steel," observed Klöckner's Günter Henle sarcastically, "seemed to contain some hidden poison that turned everyone who came in contact with it into a heinous criminal, beside whom Hitler was a mere fellow traveler."[8]

The arrest and multiyear sidelining of the Ruhr's economic leaders did little to keep business morale and productivity high in West German industry. But it did represent an opportunity for industrialists to reestablish old ties and forge new ones in the Allied internment camps.[9] Until 1948 industrialists circulated through the Allied camp system, often encountering one another on work duty or in the mess hall. For younger industrialists and managers who were lucky or innocent enough to have been spared arrest, the incarceration of their colleagues opened tremendous possibilities for career advancement. A characteristic case was that of Ulrich Haberland, a talented upstart with Bayer and IG Farben who had been groomed during the war for future leadership. After 1945 Haberland avoided arrest at the last minute and remained behind to play a leading role in the revival of the chemical industry while his colleagues sat in prison.[10] Another figure who would play a prominent role in economic reconstruction was Hermann Reusch, the son of Paul Reusch, an outspoken critic of Nazism and until 1942 the head of Gutehoffnungshütte (GHH), the giant steel and coal conglomerate in Oberhausen. On 1 December 1945 the younger Reusch arrived at the company headquarters to find the British police in the process of apprehending the GHH's stunned chairman Hermann Kellermann.[11] Reusch assumed immediate control of the company, and with his boss in prison and his father retired, he quickly established himself as one of the most impassioned and controversial defenders of German industry.

With the wave of arrests in 1945 and 1946, German industry realized that the Allies were determined, at least for the time being, to adhere to the principles embodied in the Potsdam agreement and JCS 1067. Yet it would be a mistake to assume that industrialists were helpless or without a voice during this period. Chambers of Industry and Commerce (IHKs) had, for example, survived the war relatively intact, and with Allied support they instantly assumed a leading position in the infrastructural reconstruction and the protection of local business interests. By the middle of 1946 the IHKs had resumed their publication of newsletters and had reestablished their press organs, whose articles were often reprinted in larger newspapers throughout Germany.[12] While the formation of national industrial organizations would be prohibited until 1949, both regionally and within specific branches of industry we can discover the almost immediate renewal after April 1945 of special interest and business-friendly publicity and lobbying.[13] For example, the Düsseldorf-based Iron and Steel Trade Association (Wirtschaftsvereinigung Eisen- und Stahl, or WES), under the leadership of Klöckner's Günter Henle, reconstituted itself rather effortlessly as the voice of the Ruhr business establishment vis-à-vis the British and later bizonal authorities.[14] In August 1946 Hermann Reusch, who had taken over the helm of the association upon Henle's arrest,[15] helped organize over twenty special interest industrial trade associations into the umbrella association Vereinigung der industriellen Wirtschaftsverbände, which would later become the Bundesverband der Deutschen Industrie (BDI) (Federation of German Industry).[16] As a way of starting up industrial production, the British authorities granted businessmen an advisory voice on an economic council in Minden and, eventually, in a bizonal council in Frankfurt.[17] A financially strapped Britain was hardly in the position in 1946 to pour large resources into occupied Germany; instead it set mechanisms in gear that would help Germans to feed and produce coal for themselves. In light of the practical demands of reconstruction, the Allies were forced to acknowledge German businessmen as junior partners, even as they were purging their ranks. "There can be little doubt," Volker Berghahn has concluded, "that [industrialists'] formal and informal power remained very considerable after the defeat of 1945."[18]

Despite these vehicles for special interest politics, under a military-regulated economy there existed no arena in which industry could exercise truly independent power. Even with the toleration of these local organizations, businessmen were, until the establishment of the British and U.S. bizone at the beginning of 1947, forbidden to travel from one zone of occupation to another, thus shutting off the possibility of any supraregional or international publicity coordination.[19] When business leaders did attempt to vocalize their interests—which were inevitably critical of Allied reparations and denazification policies—they risked angering the authorities and jeopardizing their already precarious positions. In light of these formal obstacles, businessmen relied on more clandestine publicity activities, often calling on foreign colleagues from the Weimar and Nazi years to lobby on their behalf in their respective home countries. But in these attempts to engage foreign citizens in their defense, industrialists time and again tested the resolve of the Allies, who they knew depended on their economic and technical expertise. The promotion of German economic interests demanded a cautious mixture of deference and assertiveness on the part of industry and a carrot and stick approach by the Allies. In their attempts to counter policies they deemed counterproductive, industrialists also tested their own limits and discovered, in the process, a new postwar professional identity.

Hermann Reusch and the Deconcentration of Industry

Among the first challenges that industry faced was the Allied ban on horizontal cooperation as manifested in the policy of deconcentration, whereby the largest firms, particularly the combines of the Ruhr, were to be broken into smaller units in order to harness and redistribute Germany's economic power.[20] Coal was to be separated from steel, the VSt was to be dissolved, and IG Farben was to be broken into its constituent companies.[21] That tempers should flare during the implementation of deconcentration is not surprising. While some more progressive industrialists were glad to see an end to the vertical and horizontal concentration of the Ruhr economy, the intensity with which most industrialists defended their companies attests to the deep despair that pervaded the West German business community.

Industrialists were ill equipped to launch a massive public relations campaign against deconcentration, but they made their disapproval clear through the actions of their spokesmen. Hermann Reusch is worth focusing on in this regard, as he came to embody the Ruhr's stubborn resistance to most aspects of Allied industrial policy. When the British agencies administering the property and holdings of the Ruhr firms—the Steel Trustees Administration (Stahltreuhändervereinigung, or Treuhand) and the North German Iron and Steel Control Commission—attempted to implement the company breakups, Reusch, as acting chair of the WES, took it upon himself to defend heavy industry against this perceived Allied onslaught. He used his own company as a testing ground for a larger battle, in the process jeopardizing his own relationship with the Allies and, more significantly, with his workers. In his negotiations over the practicalities of separating the Hüttenwerk Oberhausen, the GHH's chief mining operation, from its parent firm, Reusch became embroiled in a controversy that revealed the tenuous nature of the power of West German industry.[22]

The controversy began during discussions over the future ownership of the Hüttenwerk's company library, when Reusch suffered an unidentifiable slight at the hands of his negotiating partners representing the recently severed coal interests. During a March 1947 meeting Reusch exacted revenge by insulting the offending party, the Hüttenwerk's factory director. "Tact and politeness are things that one is taught in the cradle," he admonished the board member. "We should not really be surprised, Herr Strohmenger, that we have not discovered these things in you." [23] Upon hearing these words, the Hüttenwerk representative called an immediate halt to the meeting and refused to engage in further discussions with the GHH until Reusch apologized for having offended both him and "his old and honorable parents." [24] Heinrich Dinkelbach, the Treuhand's newly appointed commissioner, was forced to preside over the healing of bruised egos and family honors. In his attempts to bring the injured parties together for a mutual peace offering, Dinkelbach himself became the object of Reusch's wrath. To Reusch the commissioner embodied the sinister policy of deconcentration and the duplicity of those Ruhr industrialists who were now working with the Allies to fulfill their aims. Dinkelbach had been a key industry insider on the VSt managerial board until the end of 1946, but now he was being regarded by some of his colleagues as a collaborator.[25]

For the next three months, Dinkelbach conferred regularly with labor leader Hans Böckler and W. Harris-Burland, the British head of the North German Iron and Steel Commission, over the best means of handling Reusch, who was now launching personal and often crude attacks at Dinkelbach. At one point Reusch tried to discredit Dinkelbach by asserting that employees of the Treuhand participated in orgies at their office headquarters.[26] Dinkelbach wrote to Reusch demanding to know why he deemed it necessary to stoop to such a prurient level. Reusch never answered directly, having been emboldened by the controversy he was causing. He refused to tour the new Hüttenwerk with a British representative, and he ruled out accepting a seat on the newly independent firm's supervisory board.[27]

What was Reusch so angry about? To him and his fellow critics, the Allies had challenged the hallowed concept of private property by breaking apart companies. Reusch actually likened the Allies' industrial policies to the forced Aryanization of Jewish property under Hitler.[28] Industrialists reiterated this stunning comparison between German deconcentration and the confiscation or cheap sale of Jewish businesses under Hitler on other occasions in the following years. This crude analogy not only indicates the extent to which individual industrialists could be insensitive to the tragic plight of Germany's Jews in the 1930s. It also reveals how easily they could distance themselves from the shameful examples of corporate behavior under Nazism, to the point that they would not hesitate to use them as rhetorical weapons against the Allies.

Hermann Reusch, in making his analogy to Aryanization, was, of course, little concerned with what happened to Jewish property under Hitler. Rather, he saw as the ultimate affront the Allies' attempts to strip companies' rightful owners of their property and the fruit of their labors. In his attempt to prevent the breakup of his company, an angry Reusch expressed a sentimental loyalty to the GHH: "I was born here, spent my youth around these works. I made my first trip to the mines in the local collieries of Königsberg, and I grew up entirely with this factory. You could understand for personal and technical reasons why I cannot agree with Mr. Dinkelbach in this matter." [29] Ultimately, Reusch apologized for his insulting attacks. The controversy ground to a halt on 20 June 1947, when he resigned as acting chairman of the WES, admitting that his comments about deconcentration had led to his "overexposure" and had thus constituted a threat to the Ruhr's most influential industrial organization.[30]

Although this anecdote appears a minor and bizarre aside to the serious business of deconcentration, it was to take on a greater symbolic importance in light of later, not-so-frivolous Reusch controversies, which would test the ability of heavy industry to project a more enlightened image to its workers and the world. As the delegated spokesman for heavy industry, Reusch had challenged, albeit with atypically nasty overtones, the Allied aims to reform heavy industry. While it is certainly not the case that all heavy industrialists resisted the Allies, the Ruhr elite nevertheless did place their faith in someone who everyone agreed was "the most bitter and irreconcilable opponent of deconcentration." [31] During this period, steel industries were negotiating with the British and with labor over the introduction of workplace democracy (codetermination) in the Ruhr.[32] Organized labor, with Harris-Burland's help, eventually exacted concessions from management in the form of equal representation on the supervisory board and one representative on the managing board, a solution Reusch, as "master of the house," would forever find unpalatable.[33] Despite their partial victory in 1947 on this issue, the workers of the Ruhr would not easily forget Reusch's attempt to fight what they saw as the reformation and democratization of the German economy. Nor, as we will see, did Reusch forget.

Importantly, Reusch, despite his pugnacious stance vis-à-vis workers' demands, actually echoed a broader distrust of the Allies that transcended class lines and political divisions. Union members and socialists may not have liked Reusch, but they also did not like much of postwar Allied occupation policy, which they saw as punitive, confused, and deconstructive. While workers could countenance the arrest of "Nazi industrialists," they saw the breakup of firms as potentially threatening their own jobs and the economy more generally. The loud public outcries against the Allies' policies also emanated from beyond labor and industrial circles. Many West Germans harbored deep re-

Hermann Reusch in
1952 (Abt. 130, Nr.
45000/67 Gutehoff-
nungshütte Ober-
hausen, courtesy
of the Rheinisch-
Westfälisches
Wirtschaftsarchiv,
Cologne)

sentments toward denazification, which demanded that millions of individuals disprove that they had abetted the Nazi cause. Many Germans refused to
believe that their present hardships were the result of their own support of
Hitler. As the economy remained hampered into the late 1940s, most West
Germans chose their occupiers as the easy targets.[34]

In the end, despite widespread bitterness toward the Allies, Reusch's colleagues within industry thought it wise to refrain from an all-out campaign
against deconcentration. They lacked both a structured public relations apparatus and the sympathy of the world business community, which could weigh
in on behalf of the Ruhr. Indeed, after 1948 some industrialists saw no real
gain in derailing the process of deconcentration. The breakup of coal and
steel actually brought with it advantages by opening up managerial positions
within the newly severed companies. Industrialists were ultimately divided
on the issue of deconcentration, which some smaller firms saw as the de-
served treatment of overly powerful and monopolistic companies. But there
were also more serious issues around which they would all soon rally: dismantling and Nuremberg.

The Campaign against Dismantling

On 5 June 1947 U.S. Secretary of State George C. Marshall announced the European Recovery Plan (ERP) to a commencement audience at Harvard University. The United States, according to the plan, would pump billions of dollars into the European economy. Industries would be rebuilt, foreign commerce would increase, and Europe would be transformed into a community of prosperous Atlantic nations, committed to free trade and anticommunism. The ultimate objective, declared Marshall in his June speech, "was restoring the confidence of the European people in the economic future of their own countries and of Europe as a whole."[35]

The Marshall Plan and the currency reform (see below) instilled hope among West German industry that the Allies had finally moved beyond Potsdam and JCS 1067 and were committed to a consistently benign policy of reconstruction. Industrialists looked to the Marshall Plan as their salvation. But their euphoria was short lived. Big business was sobered by the realization that the Allies remained fully committed to their industrial dismantling policy, which was geared toward reducing the capacity of "war industries" to their level before Hitler had built them up. But while West German industry had felt helpless in the face of Allied deconcentration, the same cannot be said for dismantling.

Dismantling, or in the parlance of the Allies, reparations, offers an example of how German outrage over a particular policy far surpassed the Allies' seriousness toward that policy. To be sure, dismantling was not a frivolous slap at German industry. The Western Allies hoped to rebuild the German economy while also containing its destructive power and the potential to start another war. Hundreds of businesses, small and large, were designated to be partially or entirely torn down, and industry reacted with a collective expression of anger.

In their August 1947 "Level of Industry Plan" the British and the Americans drew up individual lists of over a thousand war industries designated for dismantling. The list was eventually whittled down to 682 companies in October 1947, and until the dismantling of industries came to a halt in 1949, the British and the Americans actually did not place dismantling high on their agenda of economic policies in the Western zones.[36] They were divided about whether it was in the best interests of economic and political recovery literally to tear down factories and, in some cases, deliver their remnants to the Soviet Union (as stipulated under Allied agreements). Regardless of the ambivalence on the Allied side, Germans from all walks of life and political persuasions reacted angrily and vociferously to what they saw as one more example of an unjust Allied occupation. The Allies, argued ordinary Germans and most political leaders, were repeating their mistakes from the 1920s, when a punitive peace had supposedly crippled the German nation and had paved the way for political extremism. According to one CDU politician, dismantling was "a matter of life and death for our people. At stake is the existence or extinction of our industry, and with it our entire economy."[37]

West German industrialists raised an angry voice against dismantling. In its scope, urgency, and visibility, the antidismantling campaign represented the first truly unified effort by German business leaders to halt Allied policies with a united publicity front. Not only in Germany but throughout the Western world, industrial leaders were inclined to regard dismantling as an affront to private property and economic prudence. If the Allies hoped to reconstruct Germany, argued these critics, they could not do so by destroying it.

Industry's antidismantling campaign was spearheaded by Hanns Ahrens, a chief adviser to the Allies and to German industry on questions relating to reparations.[38] From his office in Essen, Ahrens established a hot line to U.S. and British politicians and businessmen who opposed what they saw as this Morgenthauian aspect of Allied policy. Ahrens welcomed sympathetic visitors to the Ruhr, guided them on tours of factories, dined with politicians in London and Washington, and issued a stream of pamphlets decrying the Allied plans. This mass of literature presents a fascinating case study in industrial self-representation during the late 1940s. For two years West Germany was submerged under a flood of antidismantling exposés, posters, songs, and slogans, all pointing to the foolhardiness of a policy that, on one hand, declared the intention of rebuilding Germany through financial aid and, on the other hand, advocated tearing down its factories brick by brick. Like the Siemens apologias from the summer of 1945, this literature is notable for its exaggerated appraisal of a company's virtues and its bracketing or reinterpreting of the Nazi years. Every company appeared to have had a heroic past— one of selfless devotion to worker and nation. If at one time they had "grudgingly" produced for war, they were now essential to maintaining the peace and protecting the West from the Soviet menace.

One of the earliest and most interesting examples of antidismantling publicity came from the Düsseldorf chemical firm Henkel, Germany's largest manufacturer of soaps and detergents, most prominently the Persil brand of washing powder. In the fall of 1947 Henkel discovered to its dismay that it had been included on the Allied list of companies slated for partial destruction. The Allies had chosen to punish the chemical concern for its production of glycerin, a key element in the manufacture of explosives.[39] Scheduled to be destroyed were two-thirds of the machinery used for manufacturing soaps and glycerin, which the Allies considered to be unnecessary surplus capacity.[40] In the fall of 1947, the directors of Henkel launched a publicity campaign to save their company from the wrecking ball. In October they distributed *Henkel Should Not Be Dismantled!*, an eight-page brochure in English that warned of the disease, epidemics, and chaos that would ensue if the Allies dismantled soap and detergent factories.[41] "The situation is so serious," declared the leaflet, "the German population will, so to speak, suffocate in dirt if no strong counter-measures are taken."[42] Henkel presented a mass of figures on the soap industry and quoted sympathetic Allied public figures, including U.S. senator Styles Bridges, who had expressed their outrage at the dismantling policies and their potential effect on exports, employee morale, unemployment, and Allied foreign policy and trade goals. "If it is really the intention of the occupying powers not to ruin Germany," argued the pamphlet, then Henkel must be spared. "If Henkel should be dismantled, it would mean for the German people a definite loss of their faith in economic common sense and in humanity!"[43]

In the fall of 1947 all the problems that postwar West Germany faced seemed to come together in the symbol of Henkel and its production of detergents. Throughout West Germany dozens of IHKs, as well as politicians across the political spectrum, expressed their concerns that with a truncated Henkel, sanitation would rapidly deteriorate in the overrun cities and overcrowded refugee camps and that a pestilence would devour the German populace. Companies from throughout Germany and almost every industrial organization lodged protests with the bizonal authorities. The parliament of North Rhine Westphalia called an emergency session on 29 October to discuss the looming public health disaster. In the view of North Rhine Westphalia's economics minister Erik Nölting, the issue went beyond the question of material survival. "The consumption of soap may be considered rightly as the best measure of our culture, or to say it more correctly, as a measure of our civilization."[44]

The campaign did not end with this brochure. A week later, Henkel issued a second, even more dramatic appeal titled *Death by Dirt!*, which detailed the coming hygienic disaster with disturbing rhetoric and shadowy images of withered babies, grieving mothers, rows of crosses ("Crosses on children's graves! Crosses which can be prevented! Crosses which accuse!") and a skeletal grim reaper menacingly carrying his sickle. "When epidemics threaten the country," the pamphlet warned in awkward English, "there will be no halting for this scourge of mankind, and no difference between rich and poor, young and old, friend and enemy, all will be involved. The scythe of death has a good harvest. And at the end . . . chaos!"[45] Henkel had pulled out all the stops in its campaign to save itself. In the company's view, the dismantling of Henkel meant the demise of Germany. Henkel forwarded *Death by Dirt!* to British prime minister Clement Atlee, President Truman, Winston Churchill, and other high officials in both countries, pleading with them to spare the company for the sake of mankind.[46]

Unfortunately for Henkel, the Allies were in no mood for this flood of pro-

The grim reaper warns against dismantling; page from *Death by Dirt* (1947) (courtesy of the National Archives, Textual Reference, College Park, Md.)

industry literature. Still sensitive to the accusation of economic hypocrisy, the Allies responded to industry's strong-arm tactics with vigilance. While German public health officials expressed serious concern over the decrease in soap production, the British officer responsible for the dismantling of chemical industries remained unconvinced by the argument and outraged at the method of distributing this "tendentious but rather well-produced pamphlet."[47] In a confidential memo the British argued that "the publication of this expensive propaganda in English is clear evidence of Henkel's intention to carry on propaganda outside Germany.... If such a campaign is pursued, or is not immediately terminated, it will be regarded as opposition to the occupying powers and treated accordingly."[48] The British regional commissioner in Düsseldorf was instructed to reprimand the Henkel managers and to initiate an investigation into how, at a time of severe shortage, the company had managed to procure such high-quality paper for its brochures.[49] The British issued a public rebuke of Henkel and a clarification of the soap consumption in Germany, which they argued would not be affected by a reduction of ca-

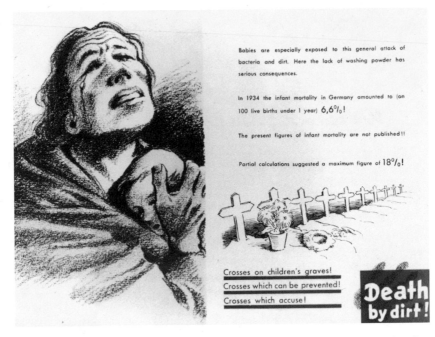

Babies are especially exposed to this general attack of bacteria and dirt. Here the lack of washing powder has serious consequences.

In 1934 the infant mortality in Germany amounted to (on 100 live births under 1 year) 6,6%!

The present figures of infant mortality are not published!!

Partial calculations suggested a maximum figure of 18%!

Crosses on children's graves!
Crosses which can be prevented!
Crosses which accuse!

Death by dirt!

Page from *Death by Dirt* (1947) (courtesy of the National Archives, Textual Reference, College Park, Md.)

pacity.[50] Henkel was forced to cease its campaign and issue a humble apology to the British authorities for its activities.[51]

The response of the British occupation to what it saw as industrial insubordination reveals the sensitivity of power relationships in early postwar Germany. While the Allies were careful not to appear too harsh, and while they always took great pains to emphasize the constructive nature of their political and economic goals, they could not countenance a crossing of boundaries between occupier and occupied. Germany was a defeated nation and had to be treated as such.

Despite the frayed nerves revealed in the Henkel case, many leaders in England and the United States in fact embraced the cause of the Düsseldorf firm. Victor Gollancz, a left-wing humanist and chairman of the Save Europe Now movement in London, and Lord Maurice Pascal Alers Hankey took up the antidismantling cause in England. A chastened Henkel, however, was now forced to report to the British authorities all private contacts with foreign sympathizers. Despite the humbling of Henkel, 1948 saw the increase of antidismantling hostility. With the escalation of the Cold War, more and more Western politicians voiced their frustration with Allied industrial policy. Hanns Ahrens lobbied on behalf of industry with the help of the

Washington-based National Council for Prevention of War as well as prominent American Quakers and conservative politicians. On his tour of Germany in 1947, former U.S. president Herbert Hoover proposed "a new economic concept in peace with New Germany," which called for an immediate stop to the removal and destruction of plants ("except direct arms plants").[52] This crescendo of disapproval culminated in 1949 in a massive protest strike and letter-writing campaign to save the steel mills of the Bochumer Verein and the Thyssen Works in Duisburg.[53] Disapproving letters poured in from throughout the world, while Thyssen introduced plans to turn the already disassembled factory into an international peace center in exchange for a cessation of dismantling.[54] Ultimately, the Allies had mixed feelings about dismantling from the start and felt that it ran counter to the aims of the Marshall Plan and economic reconstruction. By the time the Allies finally declared a halt to all dismantling in November 1949 (part of the so-called Petersberg protocols), Thyssen had witnessed the removal of 109,000 pieces of heavy machinery, of which 34,000 had been destroyed.[55] But with hindsight the picture was not so alarming. By 1949 most firms had already been removed from the dismantling list, and those companies that did lose their machinery quickly filled their empty factories with newer and more efficient equipment.[56]

Dismantling ultimately offers an example of how the Western Allies were able to indict German industry without undermining their Cold War aims. While they did destroy some factories and deliver reparations to the Soviet Union, the damage to German industry was relatively small. But the Allies were able to make a statement about German industry and its role in providing the matériel that made World War II possible. More significantly, like no other issue, dismantling bound workers and management in a common fate. The destruction of German industry meant the loss of jobs and diminished productivity, and the workers let it be known through strikes, pamphleteering, and union protests that they opposed all aspects of dismantling. Throughout the industrialists' antidismantling literature a common theme was expressed: for the sake of the workers and a new, democratic Germany, the factories must be saved. This invocation of the workers' welfare was not entirely disingenuous. Workers demonstrated a rare solidarity with the owners on this particular issue. In 1947, throughout the British zone of occupation, workers, under the threat of punishment, struck to prevent dismantling. At one point workers were even compelled at gunpoint to carry through with the destruction of their factory.[57] Admittedly, Hans Böckler, the head of the Deutscher Gewerkschaftsbund (DGB), West Germany's umbrella organization for the unions, worried that opposing dismantling could anger the Allies and jeopardize the gains the workers had achieved in the areas of codetermination. Indeed, Hanns Ahrens was quite critical of Böckler for his wavering support in the antidismantling campaign.[58] But as a whole, organized labor

"Dismantling takes away my bread and leaves me dead." An effigy hung in protest against the dismantling of the Fischer-Tropsch Works, 14 June 1949 (183/ R 77252, courtesy of Bundesarchiv, Koblenz)

and the SPD were no less outspoken than industry and the CDU, and this rare example of political and workplace unity seemed to bode well for future labor relations.

For the time being, the united front of management and workers was limited to the single issue of reparations. When it came to the theme of socialization or the redistribution of wealth, on the other hand, they occupied opposing corners. To be sure, in the ranks of industry there were progressive voices calling for a true accommodation with labor. These same industrialists had pushed through heavy industry's introduction of codetermination in the British zone in 1947.[59] But in the debate over the future of West German industry, management was not about to make further concessions to labor without a fight. Ultimately, both sides turned to the public to promote their causes, and they called on the still-potent rhetoric of class warfare to bolster their positions. And when forced to choose their most effective weapons, both sides invoked the recent past. National Socialism presented labor and management with a wealth of symbols that would be used for political purposes. But for the time being industrialists were outflanked. Not only were the labor unions rallying against industry, but the Western Allies also had one more score to settle with the defeated Germany.

Nuremberg, Denazification, and the Crafting of Memory

While deconcentration and dismantling constituted the most immediate threats to the physical survival of German industry, it was denazification that contained the potential for the deepest, most lasting material and psychological damage. For four years West Germany's industrialists, bankers, manufacturers, and middle managers were channeled through a system of holding cells and denazification courts. Many managers and owners were arrested, stripped of their positions, and then forced to retire, sit out an imposed employment ban, or find work elsewhere. In the coal industry, for example, over a thousand high-level officials had been removed from their positions by January 1946. The numbers would surely have been higher had the German economy been less dependent on these industrial experts. This purge of heavy industry coincided with (although most likely was not the cause of) such a severe decrease in coal output that the British began to fear that denazification might jeopardize the economic reconstruction of their zone, as well as the lives of the workers, who needed knowledgeable officials to regulate safety, discipline, and nutritional intake in the company. When a mining disaster killed 400 people in February 1946, the British finally decided to halt the denazification of the coal industry entirely. Hearings, however, continued into 1947 before coming to a complete halt.[60]

The British zone saw an early end to denazification, but throughout the rest of West Germany the trials of individual industrialists continued through the 1940s. These many thousands of hearings will provide future historians with a wealth of information about all aspects of industry during the Third Reich. Emerging from the few studies already conducted on regional businessmen is a picture of industrial behavior during the Third Reich that defies generalization. Individual behavior during the Nazi years ranged from outright enthusiasm and support for the Nazi Party to courageous resistance to the government's demands to purge Jewish workers. As interesting as the behavior of the industrialists is the attitude of the Allied judges who determined if company leaders were highly compromised, "fellow travelers," or totally free of the Nazi taint. What emerges is an extremely inconsistent pattern of judgment. Some individuals with questionable pasts were free to continue their careers, while some of the "smaller fish" were judged more severely.[61] The arbitrariness of denazification on all levels has evoked the criticism of both contemporaries and historians.[62]

While the denazification of thousands of businessmen was left to the discretion of local judges, the most prominent industrial directors were saved for a much more conspicuous tribunal: the courtrooms in Nuremberg. The trial of major industrialists in 1947 and 1948 is undoubtedly one of the most overlooked aspects of postwar German business history. Yet the trials represented the high-water mark of the punitive (as opposed to reconstructive) side to Allied industrial policy. In German-language literature the prosecution of officials from IG Farben, Flick, and Krupp has turned up primarily in anticapitalist polemics, while in Anglo-American historiography it has often been relegated to the status of a footnote or a passing reminder that the Americans continued their purge of the Nazi elite beyond the international Nuremberg trials of 1946.[63] But if historians have downplayed the symbolic importance of all the "successor trials" (of doctors, politicians, SS leaders, and others), big business and the rest of Germany's elites took them very seriously. Arrests and denazification triggered in the world of industry a collective despair that manifested itself not so much in industrialists mourning over the destruction of their country and their businesses, but in a loss of a bourgeois self-respect they had carried since the nineteenth century. In 1945 the world of dealmaking and smoking clubs was replaced with prisoners' stripes and shackles. Even to those who were spared actual prosecution, Nuremberg represented the culmination of this professional humiliation. In response to this collective trauma, industrialists crafted a unified interpretation of National Socialism that they hoped would save their most valued and most endangered asset: their reputations.

When the Allies arrested scores of industrialists during their initial push into Germany, and several hundred more in 1945 and 1946, company spokesmen immediately initiated intense negotiations over the fate of their imprisoned colleagues. One of the prisoners, Gustav Krupp von Bohlen und Halbach, the sole owner of Krupp until his son took over in 1943, had been slated for prosecution along with Hermann Göring and other prominent Nazis in 1946 but was deemed too ill to stand trial.[64] With no industrialist represented at the main Nuremberg trial, the Western Allies and the Soviets laid plans for a second international tribunal devoted exclusively to the prosecution of business leaders. They drew up extensive profiles of industrialists who were to be captured and tried. A list from February 1946 reads like a *Who's Who* in German business. Aside from the Krupps and Flicks and IG Farben directors, the Americans planned to prosecute heavy industrialist Hugo Stinnes Jr., the Hamburg cigarette magnate Philipp Reemstma,[65] Wilhelm Zangen from Mannesmann, VSt chairman Ernst Poensgen, and Poensgen's predecessor and former Nazi Reichstag deputy Albert Vögler, who, unbeknownst to some Allied policy makers, had taken his own life ten months before while being arrested by U.S. soldiers.[66] Tom Bower has reconstructed in detail the British insecurities that eventually led the Allies to abandon their plans for a series of international industrialist trials in favor of one French (the trial of Saar industrialist Hermann Röchling) and three U.S. prosecutions.[67] With the rapidly escalating Cold War, the prosecution of "capitalists" seemed, to many Westerners, to defy logic; an international trial, it was feared, would play into the hands of the communists.[68] In June 1946 the British Foreign Office confessed to viewing "with some misgivings the possibility of holding such a trial, if only because we fear from the scant evidence in our possession that the prosecution may be unable to secure the awarding of severe sentences of some, if not all of the industrialists concerned and because the trial may well deteriorate into a wrangle between the capitalist and communist ideologies." [69] While the Americans abandoned a full-scale assault on big business as a gesture to their nervous critics, divisions within all three Allied governments led to doubts about even the four trials that eventually did take place.[70]

On 19 April 1947 U.S. judges began hearing testimony in the trial of Friedrich Flick and four of his colleagues. They were charged with using slave labor, with plundering businesses in occupied France and the Netherlands, with the Aryanization of Jewish property, and with membership in the SS.[71] To German industry the Flick trial served as evidence of the Americans' foolhardy and hypocritical policy of economic denazification. The United States was prosecuting the very people they were calling on to nurse Germany back to economic health. Did the Allied powers not need German industrialists as frontline fighters in their global struggle against Soviet totalitarianism? Businessmen also refused to believe that the Allies could consider them as criminals cut from the same cloth as Hitler or Goebbels. Finally, they registered their belief that the trials were profoundly hypocritical. After all, they pointed out, Allied industry—from Vickers in England to Du Pont in the

United States—had obligingly supported the war effort when called upon by their governments to do so.[72] Despite such doubts industrialists also saw Nuremberg as an opportunity to take their case to the public, finally to build a united "front" against the Marxist "coffeehouse literature," which industry held responsible for propagating the Nazi/industry link.[73] For West German industry the trials in Nuremberg represented at once the worst publicity disaster imaginable and, paradoxically, the chance for an aggressive attempt at professional regeneration.

The attempts at personal self-exculpation and the company apologia went part of the way in representing the interests of big business. But Nuremberg added a new dimension to the critique of big business; now the honor of all industry was at stake. While chief prosecutor Telford Taylor insisted throughout the trials that he was not conducting a symbolic prosecution of industry or capitalism in general,[74] German big business was attuned to the reality: in Nuremberg, "every industrialist sat in the dock."[75] While German industry was hardly monolithic, in the late 1940s it was treated as such. Accordingly industrialists, for the sake of unity, put aside their differences. Throughout the trial, industrialists worked energetically behind the scenes to create a coherent interpretation of National Socialism that could then be presented to the public.

This effort at reputation damage control began in early 1946 when the Americans were sorting through mountains of documents and affidavits in preparation for their prosecution. With their colleagues and friends awaiting trial in prison, business leaders and publicists, most of whom represented the steel and coal firms of the Ruhr, took the first steps toward a unified public relations effort on behalf of all of German industry. In the fall of 1946 Wolfgang Pohle, an assistant defense attorney and member of the managing board of Mannesmann, and Dr. Walter Siemers, his colleague on the Nuremberg defense, founded with the support of heavy industry funds a document clearinghouse in Nuremberg. This archive was both to serve the immediate needs of the legal defense and to aid future historians and attorneys in their pursuit of accurate information relating to industry during the Third Reich.[76] In their search for an archival director, Pohle and Siemers turned their attention to Heinz Nagel, a small businessman and jurist who, since March of that year, had been building a collection of legal materials relating to the trial of Hermann Göring. Pohle persuaded Nagel to merge his archive with a separate collection of Nuremberg-related documents donated by the Institute for Juridical Studies at the University of Göttingen.[77]

In December 1946 Nagel opened the doors of what quickly came to be known as the Industry Office.[78] With the help of the major Ruhr firms, which forwarded their files to Nuremberg, director Nagel and his assistants gathered and cataloged unpublished and published documents that could assist in any

Friedrich Flick on trial in Nuremberg, 1947 (courtesy of the National Archives, Still Pictures, College Park, Md.)

way both the Nuremberg defendants and lesser-known businessmen during their denazification proceedings.[79] In a later profile of the archive, Nagel hinted at the solidarity that lay behind the work of the Industry Office. "The work of the archive has as its goal the gathering of legal, historical, and political documents that would help in the rehabilitation of German industrialists at home and abroad."[80] While Nagel worked at the time primarily with the legal defense, the office had as much to do with the future reputation of German business as with the immediate rehabilitation of its individual members. Throughout all of the successor trials in Nuremberg—not only those relating directly to heavy industry—Nagel was entrusted with the task of extracting from the court proceedings any piece of evidence that could affect German business adversely. While Nagel himself would eventually face resounding criticism for his sloppy and passive administration of the archive,[81] for now industry seemed to have forged its first weapon in the battle to save its public image.

This increasingly streamlined information apparatus could not, however,

Krupp defendants at Nuremberg, 1947. Alfried Krupp von Bohlen und Halbach, the owner of the firm, sits on the far left next to U.S. soldiers. (ÜF2, 16.7.8, courtesy of the Historisches Archiv Krupp, Essen)

be maintained without financial support. Because any partisan financial dealings by the firms under British trusteeship inevitably raised the suspicion of impropriety, heavy industry's contributions were never announced with great fanfare.[82] Reusch, however, did receive the permission of Heinrich Dinkelbach and the Treuhand to gather money for the Industry Office. While his own company, the GHH, shouldered most of the financial burden, Reusch was able, with some arm-twisting, to raise money from firms such as Mannesmann, Klöckner, and VSt.[83] These contributions, however, did not represent pure gestures of solidarity with the defendants. Ruhr businessmen contributed money to the Industry Office not just in defense of industry as a whole, but also as a means of protecting themselves and their own firms. Wolfgang Linz of VSt admitted to Walter Siemers that he was giving money primarily because his company was mentioned so prominently in the indictment of Flick, whose industrial enterprises had formed a cornerstone of the giant steel cartel during the war.[84] Likewise, some industrialists privately expressed resentment at having to aid Flick, who, like Gustav and Alfried Krupp von Bohlen und Halbach, had come to a greater accommodation with the Nazi regime than many industrialists could countenance (especially in Flick's toleration of the state-run Hermann Göringwerke in exchange for Reichmarschall Göring's aid in his takeover of the industrial holdings of the Jewish family Petschek). Throughout the trials, however, these challenges to industrial unity were masked in the inflated rhetoric of comradeship. If there were rifts and grudges below the surface, Reusch would not allow them to threaten the public facade of corporate solidarity.

With the establishment of a financial lifeline to Nuremberg, the Industry Office could now focus its energies on crafting a unified defense of German industry. Emerging from this collection of documents were thousands of pages of legal briefs, affidavits, and private correspondence. The first attempt by industrialists to win over the broader public also had its origins in this collection, in the form of a short manuscript called *Schwerindustrie und Politik* [Heavy industry and politics], written by August Heinrichsbauer, an industry publicist and big business lobbyist during the Weimar years.[85] With the close assistance of his colleagues, Heinrichsbauer crafted an interpretation of big business behavior that was to serve as the "foundation of a propaganda [campaign]" on behalf of German industry.[86]

The premise of this seventy-nine-page booklet was straightforward: Heavy industry could not be held responsible for the rise of Adolf Hitler. Industrialists, argued Heinrichsbauer, like all Germans had indeed made some mistakes during the waning years of the Weimar Republic. By remaining apolitical during a highly political period, industry had underestimated the menacing power of National Socialism and had not fought hard enough against Hitler. After Hitler's ascent to the chancellorship, the state began to encroach on the territory of the private economy, and industrial opposition grew stronger and more vocal. By taking a stance against the Hermann Göringwerke, by opposing the interventionist trappings of the Four Year Plan, by questioning Hitler's war of aggression, industry, argued Heinrichsbauer, had boldly challenged the Nazi dictatorship.

In short, the most common verdict of the day—that big business should bear the responsibility for the Nazi dictatorship—could not, according to Heinrichsbauer, be substantiated. "Industry does not remain infallible," he wrote. But "accusations . . . cannot be limited to heavy industry or to any particular professional group or circle of persons. They must rather be directed against all Germans and beyond them against all those officials and private authorities and agencies throughout the world, which to the last failed in their public duty."[87] In October 1948 industrial leaders from the Ruhr distributed Heinrichsbauer's tract to some of the most prominent figures in West German public life. Select members of the press as well as businessmen, church leaders, politicians, and union spokesmen were asked to study carefully and consider soberly its central arguments.

The genesis of this text is worth some detailed attention, as it bespeaks the self-conscious attempt by heavy industry to craft an interpretation of the past that would serve as a powerful public relations tool. The project began in the spring of 1947 when Hermann Reusch solicited the help of his old friend Heinrichsbauer in the rehabilitation of German industry. Reusch hoped that Heinrichsbauer, by virtue of his short-lived flirtation with National Socialism in 1932, could offer insight into the early relationship between heavy industry and the Nazi Party and directly counter the image of a Nazified business elite. Heinrichsbauer had been an active supporter of the Nazis' Reich organization leader Gregor Strasser, gathering funds from heavy industry on behalf of this seemingly more innocuous and politically moderate Nazi. With Strasser's expulsion during Hitler's consolidation of dictatorial power, Heinrichsbauer automatically became a suspicious figure to the Nazi government and to two industrialists, Wilhelm Tengelmann and Fritz Thyssen, who supported Hitler. In early July 1934 Heinrichsbauer was informed that Gregor Strasser had been one of the many political enemies murdered by the Nazis a few days earlier during the Night of the Long Knives. Fearing that his prior connection to "the opposition Nazis" might spell his own death sentence, Heinrichsbauer immediately fled the country and spent the next three years in hiding in Mexico, waiting for the political tide to turn in his favor. Jobless until 1936, Heinrichsbauer eventually returned to Germany with the help of future Reich economics minister Walter Funk and found work in a coal syndicate in Mannheim. He later spent the war years in Vienna as director of a think tank devoted to forging cultural and business ties to the southeastern European regions of the new Greater German Reich and as a coal industry adviser in Upper Silesia.[88]

In conjunction with the Flick trial and with help from Nagel and Pohle, whom he had personally consulted while serving as an incarcerated witness for the Americans,[89] Heinrichsbauer set to work in the spring of 1947 on his overtly "political" manuscript (*politische Denkschrift*)[90] that took on the assertions made by the Nuremberg prosecution. Under Reusch's direction, Heinrichsbauer began to solicit the support of Ruhr industrialists for his study.

The initial response to Heinrichsbauer's manuscript was uniformly lukewarm.[91] Ruhr industrialists were, of course, eager to support their imprisoned colleagues, whom they saw as symbols of Germany's persecution by the Allies and as a reminder of their own narrow escape from prosecution. Yet many industrialists were skeptical about supporting what their political enemies would inevitably interpret as a crude apology for big business. Certainly Heinrichsbauer's booklet was not the first apologetic work to have been passed around the circle of big business; steel patriarch Ernst Poensgen had distributed his short, exculpatory memoir to friends and colleagues in the summer of 1945. But there were doubts whether the time was opportune for a *published* explanation, especially one written by Heinrichsbauer, who personified in both Germanys the alleged financial links between Weimar business and National Socialism. Many of Heinrichsbauer's colleagues felt that a self-defense produced in business circles would merely fan the flames of hostility toward German industry and play into the hands of the communists, who eagerly waited to pounce on any further misstep by big business.[92] Ultimately, industrialists feared that in attempting to defend the honor of heavy industry, Heinrichsbauer would simply draw attention to the very claims that they desperately hoped would go away.

Clearly, despite business leaders' outrage at the public defamation of heavy industry in Nuremberg, the situation in the Ruhr was hardly conducive to an aggressive public relations campaign. Industrialists were still trying to chart a careful course between dutiful submission to the victors and a vocal defense of their own business interests. Heavy industry's dedication to the cause of collective self-defense was, consequently, always tempered by caution, and Heinrichsbauer, despite open encouragement from the GHH people, never received a wholehearted endorsement from all of his business friends. Yet with money now flowing from heavy industry to the defense's bank account in Nuremberg, Reusch and Heinrichsbauer persisted in their efforts to enlist their colleagues' help in the joint manuscript project. With the SPD's increasingly strident demands for socialization of basic industries, and the trials of IG Farben, Krupp, and Röchling around the corner, both men saw their task as urgent, and despite the lingering misgivings of their colleagues, they were gradually able to elicit the active support of the leading figures in the Ruhr.[93]

In close collaboration with Nagel, Reusch, and defense attorney Pohle, Heinrichsbauer spent the summer and autumn of 1947 preparing a working draft to be distributed to professional confidantes. Aside from Reusch and Pohle, Wilhelm Salewski, the successor to Reusch as general secretary of the WES, was particularly active during the project's conception.[94] The sparse extant correspondence dealing directly with Heinrichsbauer's early drafts offers a fascinating peek into both the social dynamics of this tight network of players that made up postwar Ruhr industry and, more importantly, their active process of memory cultivation and "retrieval" during the Flick and Krupp trials. In these discussions about the strategies of historical representation, Heinrichsbauer and his colleagues continually searched for an interpretive framework for the Nazi experience that would not only be politically effective but also contribute to the building of a new, postwar professional identity. For example, in a letter to Salewski in the summer of 1947, Heinrichsbauer touched on this latter theme of industry's self-representation, an issue that had plagued Heinrichsbauer during the preparation of his first rough draft: To what extent could or would Heinrichsbauer be speaking for all of big business when he specifically addressed *heavy* industry's relationship to the NSDAP? Might the interests of exculpating heavy industry actually be served by responding to business critics on their own terms—that is, by lumping all of German industry, as stratified as it really was, into a single-voiced mono-lith and thereby diffusing the guilt of coal and steel?[95] According to Hein-richsbauer, Hermann Reusch proposed protecting heavy industry's name by stressing that other branches of industry had accommodated Hitler at least as quickly as had heavy industry, a strategy that would involve the equaliza-tion of sins, shifting a share of complicity onto the backs of other branches of industry. By mentioning the post-1933 behavior of others (implicitly the chemical conglomerate IG Farben), heavy industry could at least relativize its own problematic relationship to the party and the regime. However, Hein-richsbauer feared that actively confessing to *any* questionable behavior on the part of industry—whatever branch—would necessarily be counterpro-ductive. Even if there was evidence that other branches worked actively with the NSDAP, Heinrichsbauer argued to Salewski, the public would in any case "throw all of German industry into one pot," in effect inferring the guilt of heavy industry from the depiction of a multibranched conciliation to Hitler.[96] He thus saw the best solution in simply emphasizing the heterogeneity of industry without discussing the sins of the "other" industries. In this fash-ion he would at least subtly challenge the common view of big business as a reactionary monolith with a sinister heavy industry at its core. Heinrichs-bauer's final version settled for a middle solution, pointing out the activities of other branches without going into great detail. While this strategy did not entirely shift assumptions of guilt away from heavy industry, it at least served as a rhetorical basis upon which to build evidence. In the fall of 1947, with this strategic dilemma still unresolved, Heinrichsbauer continued the process of amending and redrafting.

December 1947 was a busy month for heavy industry. Friedrich Flick was found guilty of three charges and sentenced to a seven-year prison term,[97] the trial of Krupp officials began, and Pohle had in his possession another draft of Heinrichsbauer's manuscript, which he intended to review personally with Reusch.[98] Over their Christmas dinner in 1947, Reusch and Pohle drew up a list of criticisms that they hoped Heinrichsbauer would address in his final version. Most of their suggestions dealt with specific factual details regard-ing the organization of industry in the 1920s, as well as questions about the funds that flowed from industry to the Nazi Party in 1932 and the relationship between Gregor Strasser and Hitler.[99] Yet Pohle raised two issues that again went straight to the broader strategy of self-representation. The first dealt with industry's cultivation of a resistance myth. In his early drafts,[100] Hein-richsbauer had apparently attempted to invoke the glory of the 1944 resisters by portraying both the pre-1933 business skepticism toward Nazism and his own fundraising efforts as an early form of anti-Nazi opposition.[101] Heinrichs-bauer hoped to depict his own behavior in 1932, which he unambiguously interpreted as a courageous attempt to bring down Hitler through Gregor Strasser, as indicative of an opposition movement within German industry. Yet if the thesis of passive and active opposition remained in keeping with the fundamental defense strategy in Nuremberg, as well as with most later apologies for German industry published in the 1950s, attorney Pohle was privately doubtful of its historical accuracy—at least for the years of Hitler's rise to and consolidation of power. "Can one really," he wrote to Heinrichsbauer, "speak of an opposition movement at the time, in the sense of its being simply a logical predecessor to the later opposition movement? To do so, one would have to find some connecting link between the entire period of 1932–37 and 1938. And even then we would need clear evidence that heavy industry actually belonged to this opposition circle."[102]

During the exchange of drafts in January 1948, another central claim— that industrialists are inherently apolitical—became a source of disagreement amongst Heinrichsbauer and his advisers. Heinrichsbauer's argument, which is still echoed today in discussions about industry and National Socialism, can be summarized as follows: With their attention focused on productivity, profit, and market fluctuations, industrialists were political creatures only to the extent that they defended their economic interests in the public arena. They ventured into politics long enough to make shortsighted pleas on behalf of business-friendly economic policies, after which they retreated into the private world of the firm. Industrialists distributed money to persons who could help them, but in the end they did not have the expertise or the inclination to indulge in the promotion of sweeping political ideologies.

While almost all apologetic writings about industry have been careful to cultivate this interpretation of business behavior during the years of National Socialism, such a position is certainly more problematic than Heinrichsbauer suggested in his December—and ultimately his final—draft. On one hand, industry wanted to be seen as having shied away from the ugly realm of politics, at most giving some money to all the parties (except the KPD) as a way of touching all bases without embracing a particular political cause. On the other hand, Heinrichsbauer wanted to drape the mantle of resistance over the Ruhr industrialists of the 1930s, portraying them as having used financial means to counter the extremism of National Socialism and to destabilize Hitler. In short, Heinrichsbauer had created an inherently paradoxical ideal type of the industrialist, that of an apolitical resister who was at once active opponent and naive political outsider. This businessman had the foresight— even the courage—to speak out against a mass movement that might affect his interests and his nation adversely, yet all the while he remained outside the realm of political activity. While this may appear to be a caricature of Heinrichsbauer's ideas, it bespeaks a very real tension within *Schwerindustrie* nd *Politik* and subsequent industrial apologies. In order to maintain his first hesis of political naïveté, Heinrichsbauer was forced to adhere to a rather narrow definition of politics as active support of and participation in a political party. But in distancing himself from this notion of politics, he unconsciously complicated and ultimately attenuated his second thesis of active opposition of industrialists within the Nazi Party.

Heinrichsbauer missed the point that his attempts to portray industrialists as true resisters would surely have been helped by a confession to being more rather than less politically engaged. What might appear to be a rather minor linguistic point about the definition of politics takes on much greater importance when considered in light of heavy industry's broader strategy of professional self-representation. In order to deconstruct what he saw as a historical myth, Heinrichsbauer had to engage in a process of reconstruction. He had to counter the image of the politicized Nazi industrialist, an image industry saw as an exaggerated anticapitalist metaphor, by fashioning an equally extreme ideal type: the detached and politically naive anti-Nazi. Both types are, of course, reductionist in their very inability to capture the broader ranges of behavior that must be discussed when studying the Nazi period. But historical reality was not what was at stake. Rather, the challenge for industry and Heinrichsbauer was to discover and manipulate a usable past—to construct an interpretive framework that would help industry fight off what it saw as the politicized use of recent history.

Pohle himself recognized the paradox inherent in the resister/outsider hybrid and its potentially unsettling effect on the defense strategy. "Up till now," he wrote Heinrichsbauer, "we have staunchly held our course [that] . . . industry is apolitical. It did nothing to help the NSDAP into the saddle; it distributed funds to *all* sides, except the KPD. Now suddenly the new line of thinking emerges that industry at the time was actively working with various currents in the party against the party leadership. To support this claim, we better have especially solid evidence." [103]

While the contradictions in Heinrichsbauer's rhetorical strategy must be highlighted, one must be cautious in interpreting this problematic conceptualization during the drafting stage as necessarily evidence of bad faith. For as Heinrichsbauer's own response to Pohle suggests, arguing that industry had indeed played a role in politics, however defined, would not necessarily delegitimate industry's claims of opposition. Yet the challenge for Heinrichsbauer lay not in employing a coherent and convincing definition of politics but in providing evidence that he and other industrialists had actually worked against Nazism, a task that proved quite difficult. Wolfgang Pohle's uneasiness with Heinrichsbauer's strategy lay less in these rhetorical contradictions per se than in the fact that Heinrichsbauer was stretching the truth considerably by talking of concerted opposition early on. Beyond the issue of resistance, Pohle questioned Heinrichsbauer's strategy of bringing *any* connection between heavy industry and the Nazis into his argument, if only to interpret it as a benign relationship that centered on Gregor Strasser.[104] Implicitly, Pohle was challenging the wisdom of trying to paint Strasser as a truly oppositional figure—or at least as a figure who would be admired by a postwar German public and a panel of U.S. judges. Strasser, after all, had still been a Nazi. Pohle gambled that it would be safer to emphasize the distance from all political movements, including Strasser's "alternative" to Hitler, than to create a questionable image of the apolitical resister working closely with the Nazi Party to undermine it from within. In effect, he urged Heinrichsbauer toward a more consistent and low-keyed rhetorical path, encouraging him to toss out the baby of resistance with the bath water of politics. Ultimately Pohle's attempts to bring order to Heinrichsbauer's interpretive hodgepodge was only partially successful. In the published version of the manuscript, Heinrichsbauer did tone down the link to actual resistance movements, even admitting that industry should have done more to fight Nazism. Yet in the final product his paradoxical formulation of an industrialist self-identity is still very much evident, with the image of resistance to and suspicion of Nazism resting uncomfortably close to claims of political impotence and lack of interest.[105]

While Heinrichsbauer's inconsistencies are indeed striking, they must ultimately be considered in the immediate historical context—Nuremberg, occupation, and the perceived threat to the survival of the market economy—that influenced their formation. Not simply a rhetorical tactic of the legal defense, the paradoxical image of the embattled and naive *Unternehmer* standing alone against the forces of a dictatorial regime became, during the early years of the Cold War, a central revisionist trope that found its very legitimation in both the "evidence" of industrial resistance during the Third Reich and the lesson of apolitical behavior in the face of the enemy. If the industrialists had fallen into the trap of political naïveté in the 1930s, all of Heinrichsbauer's colleagues agreed, it was because the communists and the unions had hypnotized the working class with their rhetoric of class struggle, wreaking havoc on an economically and politically fragile order and ultimately driving the majority of sober-minded Germans into the arms of the Nazis, who promised shelter from the red storm. By bringing a sense of immediacy to the behavior of industrialists fifteen years earlier—by portraying their anticommunism as the motivating factor behind an inability to counter National Socialism more vigorously—industry was demonstrating the hope that the fear of communism shared by the general public in the late 1940s could elicit sympathy for the dilemma faced by elites in the late 1920s and early 1930s.

The Courtroom Defense: Religion, the Worker, and *der Bürger*

In presenting this view of heavy industry, Heinrichsbauer was mirroring the defense's tactics throughout the three trials in Nuremberg and the French prosecution of Hermann Röchling. Attorneys for IG Farben argued that industry was simply a scapegoat for the misdeeds of the broader German population,[106] while Flick's lawyers maintained that "National Socialism pushed aside and condemned to impotence the economic circles. No other blame than that which has been brought against the whole German people, and against labor, too, can be brought against industry—namely, that they did not stand up in time and fight resolutely enough."[107] Rudolf Dix, Friedrich Flick's attorney, summed up this position clearly in his opening defense: "Hitler's rise to power is typically that of a pure demagogue, of a public seducer, and ultimately, of a public corrupter, a destroyer of wealth, and particularly of the influence of the leading industrial stratum. Demagogues of that type, however, ride to power on the shoulders of the masses, and not on any individual crests of the upper strata."[108] In essence, the defense attorneys in Nuremberg were, like Heinrichsbauer, making use of the increasingly potent rhetoric of totalitarianism to exculpate Germany's social and economic elites.[109] Germany's "upper strata" had been immune to the seductive appeal of Hitlerian charisma and had remained above the fray, carefully and worriedly assessing the dangers of the far Left and far Right. If they had failed to stop Hitler, it was not for lack of wanting to.

With organized labor's push for socialization and codetermination as a backdrop, the rhetorical strategies in Nuremberg assumed a pressing political immediacy. In the minds of industrialists, as long as the unions themselves were calling on the images of industrial complicity—strike busters, Nazis, and businessmen were all the same, according to them—then industrialists ought to be equally reductive in portraying the Left. Despite the SPD's and the unions' vociferous disapproval of the KPD, and despite their condemnation of industrial dismantling, businessmen depicted socialists, communists, and organized labor as the collective expression of an authoritarian tradition.

This reductive hostility to the parties on the Left was a major component of industrial mentalities before and after Hitler. Yet industrialists, much as during the 1920s, were careful to couch their attacks on labor, in particular, in terms sympathetic to the individual German worker. If the political arm of labor was to blame for both Nazism and communism, the worker remained innocent of all wrongdoing. In keeping with this view, August Heinrichsbauer's *Schwerindustrie und Politik* ends with an appeal to his readers to spare industry harsh criticism, if only for the sake of maintaining peace in the workplace and preventing the kind of disaster he felt had been unleashed by the divided Left in the 1920s and early 1930s. "Unfounded political defamation of heavy industry may lead to far-reaching consequences which could also affect the workers. The events of the last few years have all too clearly shown that, more than ever before, the destiny of all of us in Germany is insolubly welded together."[110]

In adopting such conciliatory language, industrialists were employing a time-tested rhetorical strategy designed to "enlighten" the workers and free them from the shackles of Marxist ideology and trade unionism. At Nuremberg the defendants pursued this strategy by emphasizing their labor-friendly spirit and downplaying any political free will on the part of the worker. Industrialists were not Nazis or immoral capitalists; they were socially engaged entrepreneurs who cared, first and foremost, about the welfare of their employees and their nation, both of which were vulnerable to political manipulation. Attorney Dix opened his defense of Alfried Krupp by citing the words of Cardinal Josef Frings, archbishop of Cologne, who had recently praised the Krupp firm for "great social understanding" and concern "for the welfare of their workers and employees."[111] While the company was demonized internationally, Dix argued, at home Krupp was famed for its worker-friendly policies, from company housing to high employee benefits. These repeated allusions to corporate beneficence were not, as was the case with the Siemens apology from 1945, simply attempts to portray the company in the best possible light. Protecting the worker was now cast in explicitly anticollectivist terms. Keeping the workers happy meant saving them from communism. This attempt to both appease and tame the workers became an increasingly important political weapon as the Cold War escalated in the early 1950s.

In Nuremberg one can detect the formation of an increasingly confident industrial identity. In its substance, there was little new. In their seventy-five-year-old attempt to avert a class war, industrialists had consistently argued that defending the managerial prerogative meant defending the worker. But this tried and true rhetorical tactic assumed a political and moral urgency in Nuremberg. After Auschwitz, it was imperative that the industrialist inject an even greater sense of ethical authority into his public image. One way of doing this was denying all the charges, or relativizing them against Allied wartime behavior. Another was to identify with the worker. Still another was to infuse the activities of the industrialist with a moral and religious essence. In Nuremberg, in individual denazification proceedings, and throughout the 1940s and 1950s industrialists invoked repeatedly the image of the good Christian who had served his country, his company, and technology as much out of religious conviction as out of loyalty or patriotism. "Instead of being an ambitious and ruthless industrial magnate," argued the attorney for IG Farben's chief defendant, "Dr. Krauch is an honorable Christian, a simple man, a research-worker and scientist, conscious of his responsibilities, who never committed an offense but devoted his whole life to technical and scientific progress—and this not only for the benefit of Germany but also for that of other countries, not least for that of the United States of America."[112]

This use of religion was, in part, a familiar legal tactic employed to humanize the accused. But it also reflected the substantial help that representatives of organized religion offered to the accused industrialists in Nuremberg. Ernst Klee and Frank Buscher have documented the role that the Catholic Church played in securing the release of the men convicted at Nuremberg.[113] Even the unqualifiedly anti-Nazi pastor Martin Niemöller, who had spent years in concentration camps, lent his support to Flick defendant Otto Steinbrinck.[114] The churches' support of the defendants during and after Nuremberg indicates the extent to which the Cold War, combined with anti-Allied sentiments, served to erode what were initially more widespread anticapitalist sentiments in the German political culture. Arguably, however, these clergymen and theologians were not cooperating out of any particular love of free-market economics but from a fear that their social milieu, already destabilized by war and defeat and Soviet occupation in the East, would continue to be decimated by the Western Allies. Two mass movements had destroyed their familiar bourgeois world. If industry had tolerated one of them, Nazism, it was only because, in their view, all elites had been distracted by the more serious threat, communism. But now, in a postwar world, Germany's *Bürgertum* (roughly, bourgeoisie) would overcome defeat. It would reclaim a moral space by fighting totalitarianism wherever it was found.

Historians have spent much time trying to pin a definition on this elusive concept of the *Bürgertum*. For postwar industry, it was a collective mindset, a shared elitism, and a common belief in an older, more stable world marked by traditional values under assault by modernity and mass movements. While the Nuremberg defense attempted to turn National Socialism into a tragedy for the German *Bürgertum*, another courtroom in 1948 was the scene of an equally impassioned discussion about the fate of this threatened milieu. Fritz Thyssen, the most notorious personification of industrial complicity, was undergoing a closely observed denazification proceeding in Obertaunus (Hesse).[115] As chairman of his family firm's supervisory board, Thyssen, along with Emil Kirdorf, had been Hitler's most vocal supporter in the pre-1933 ranks of big business. Much speculation and misinformation have surrounded the relationship between Thyssen and National Socialism. At stake was whether Thyssen, in his embrace of Hitler, represented German industry more generally.[116] While it is now clear that Thyssen was rather exceptional among big businessmen in his financial backing of Hitler and his view of him as an antidote to the beleaguered Weimar Republic, it is important to remember that in the 1940s—and still today—Thyssen, as one of Germany's most prominent industrialists, personified a collective big business complicity. While Thyssen eventually turned against the Nazis by 1939 and was twice imprisoned in concentration camps, after the war he would still be held accountable for the overwhelming support he had lent Hitler during his rise.

Thyssen had been responsible for organizing the Führer's notorious Düsseldorf Industry Club speech in January 1932, during which Hitler had appealed to the Ruhr industrialists for financial support.[117] While industrialists did not, as was once assumed, react particularly positively to Hitler's speech, this event became, to critics of German industry, proof of the ties between big business, high finance, and Adolf Hitler. The single speech took on such symbolic importance in the discussion of big business complicity that after 1945, industrialists, particularly those who had personally heard the speech, spent much time trying to reconstruct the circumstances surrounding it and clarifying the reception that Hitler had received.[118]

While industrialists were preoccupied with the fate of Fritz Thyssen, when it came to defending him during his denazification trial, the Ruhr was, not surprisingly, hesitant to lend an active hand to this marginalized figure. Their reticence, however, was not only due to the many grudges held against Thyssen since his overt advocacy of Nazism in the 1920s and early 1930s. There was also a tactical issue at stake. The defense in Nuremberg hinged on a disavowal of any sentimental links with Thyssen, whose connection to Nazism had caused heavy industry so much grief, and to embrace him suddenly would be entirely self-defeating. Even Thyssen's own VSt colleague Heinrich Dinkelbach was careful in his affidavit for the court to distance Thyssen from the everyday workings of the VSt. The GHH's Paul Reusch also proved unable or unwilling to testify, having expressed privately his dismay that as a Ruhr industrialist he himself was "being thrown into the same pot" as Thyssen, Kirdorf, and the reactionary publisher and erstwhile Krupp director Alfred Hugenberg, whose newspapers had provided a platform for Hitler during the rise of the Nazi Party.[119] Clearly, the cracks in the facade of business unity ran deeper than industrialists themselves cared to admit publicly.

Thyssen's closest colleagues were unwilling to lend their support to the perceived source of their woes. Yet those Germans who did testify on Thyssen's behalf produced an interpretation of German industry's past similar to that of the Nuremberg defense. The lawyers struggled to place Thyssen in a broader social and professional milieu whose moral shortcomings could not be reduced to the behavior of one individual. Ironically, in the courtroom in Obertaunus, Thyssen emerged as a sort of hero—as the quintessential entrepreneur, the worker-friendly owner, the idealist, and the religious nationalist who had thought only of his employees and his country when lending his support to Hitler. Martin Niemöller, who had met Thyssen while both were interned in Dachau in April 1945, wrote to the court to defend Germany's most controversial industrialist.[120] Catholic priests, churchmen, friends, employees, and even Jews all testified to Thyssen's piety and his tragic misguidedness in putting his faith in Hitler.[121] They portrayed him as an apolitical humanist who turned to politics when he felt that Western culture was being imperiled by an Asiatic menace. In the trial Thyssen, the putative "bankroller of the Nazis" (*Geldgeber der Nazis*), was transformed into the model of conscientious behavior and civil courage.

It is, of course, the greatest of ironies to interpret Thyssen's behavior as apolitical. Thyssen personified more than anyone the businessman-activist who lent his reputation and financial clout to a heartfelt political cause. But this obsession with—and disavowal of—politics was in no way exceptional. Indeed, industry's troubled relationship with the political can be traced back to the post–World War I years, if not before. During the early Weimar years conservatives and liberal thinkers such as Max Weber struggled to reconcile their visions of a well-educated political and bureaucratic aristocracy with the reality that industrialists possessed the power to rebuild Germany economically.[122] In Weimar, industrialists *had* to be political. In keeping with a long tradition of the *"unpolitisch"* German elite, however, most industrialists eschewed the moniker of the political activist. After both world wars, *Politik* bore especially negative connotations, having found expression in the fragile governments of the Weimar years and the totalitarian claims of the Nazis. Given this suspicion of politics, industrialists had always understood themselves as detached from politics. But after National Socialism, this self-appraisal took on an increased urgency. If the German elite was to disavow any link to Nazi crimes, it would have to call on an apolitical bourgeois tradition. But it is precisely this point that was the most problematic. For as an educated and thoughtful man, argued the prosecution, Thyssen should simply have known better. If industrialists are by definition apolitical, then they should have stayed out of politics.

Not all of Thyssen's defenders tried to portray him as apolitical. But if his goals were political, they argued, they were neither *partei-* nor *interessenpolitisch* (related neither to party nor to special interest politics) but, rather, *staatspolitisch*.[123] In other words, although Thyssen had been politically engaged, it had not been in the service of the Nazi Party but, rather, of a higher moral cause: the German state. Thyssen's flaw was loving his country too much. For this he had been punished. "There is no other German industrialist," argued the defense, "who landed in a concentration camp because of his political beliefs."[124]

To sympathetic observers of the trial, the tragedy of Fritz Thyssen mirrored that of all German elites. Thyssen had power and influence and money, but he sold his soul to Hitler in order to gain spiritual fulfillment. This view was expressed, quite clearly, in the words of Jakob Goldschmidt, a conservative Jewish banker who had emigrated to the United States in the mid-1930s. "Fritz Thyssen," he wrote,

> is of my opinion the symbol for this whole tragedy of the Germans and to a certain extent that of the world's bourgeoisie. This bourgeoisie fully recognized the dynamic forces of history, demanding and urging changes in the social structure of human society, but lacked the courage, the vision, and the ability to make the necessary decisions and compromises in time. Therefore it was caught by this gangster, Hitler, who took advantage of the historical events and the historic revolutionary context. And being caught by him there was no escape from the beginning of his satanic brutalities to the bitter end. Fritz Thyssen is a typical German bourgeois, and he has paid for his stupidity individually as much as generally, but I think that he has tried with courage to open the eyes and to clear the minds of men around the world.[125]

If it seems strange that these words emerged from the pen of a Jewish émigré, one must keep in mind the background of Goldschmidt and, more generally, the power of the *bürgerliche* ideal among many conservative German elites, whether Jewish or not. Goldschmidt had been one of the most powerful and controversial bankers in Weimar Germany. He was in close contact with a number of Ruhr industrialists who sat on the supervisory board of the Danat Bank, which Goldschmidt headed, and he financially supported the conservative publisher Hugenberg.[126] It is not surprising, based alone on industrialists' high regard for him, that Goldschmidt might defend Thyssen after the war. But more importantly, his words conveyed the feeling common among conservative social elites during and after the Third Reich that Hitler's sins did not primarily lie in his vile anti-Semitism. He was, to be sure, a racist hate-monger, but he was also a boorish rabble-rouser and a populist who despised conservative nationalists, even as he took advantage of them and their anticommunism. Hitler's disdain for social elites and their values placed conservatives like Jakob Goldschmidt and Fritz Thyssen on the same plane. Hitler sought not only to destroy the Jews but the entire social and cultural world with which they identified themselves. If "this gangster, Hitler," had managed to dupe Thyssen into supporting him, it was, according to this view, because Thyssen, like all German elites, had falsely believed that Hitler would unify rather than divide the Germans.

While after the war few industrialists, and even fewer Jews, would have openly professed an affinity with Fritz Thyssen, Goldschmidt's perspective reflected unmistakably a key element in postwar industry's self-image. To many critics, Thyssen symbolized heavy industry, heavy industry symbolized all industry, and industry stood for a discredited *Bürgertum*. As long as this reductive logic had political resonance, businessmen would have to take the legacy of Fritz Thyssen seriously. They could not ignore the symbolic importance of this single industrialist who had financed the party so enthusiastically. If they could not fully disavow a link with him, they would have to lend some plausibility to his behavior. Industrial elites, therefore, had much invested in the courtroom salvation of Thyssen, even if they did not actively contribute to the defense. Through the vehicle of Thyssen, all industrialists became patriots, men of business and science, apolitical resisters, and, in the end, victims of fascism. While this strategy was riddled with inconsistencies, it represented, nonetheless, a serviceable identity for industrialists during the Cold War years. Businessmen surveyed the damage around them and carefully cultivated this image with a combination of despair and defiance.

Organized Labor and the Politics of Industrial Guilt

By 1948 we can detect the emergence of a coherent and increasingly confident industrial self-understanding. In their defensive struggle against Allied measures, businessmen also went on the offensive, sifting selectively through the past and transferring its useful symbols into a postwar collective mentality. The "victimization" of industry during the Third Reich provided the moral underpinning for the renewal of a free-market economy and the postwar struggle against communism. Rescuing the masses from the clutches of collectivism meant reinterpreting the sins of the past and injecting an element of righteousness into German capitalism.

Despite these early examples of self-promotion, the success of any publicity campaign, many industrialists felt, would have to be measured by the reactions of the public, particularly the workers whom industry depended on during the years of economic reconstruction. But was labor ready to let bygones be bygones? In this last section, I will attempt to answer this question by demonstrating the political uses of the relationship between big business and National Socialism. I will offer an illustration of memory in action. In 1948, Germany's past was not confined to the courtroom or the partisan pamphlet. It also spilled over into the streets. The conflict with the Allies united West German industry, and businessmen would now aim their collective energies at a different and perhaps more threatening opponent: the trade unions.

On 13 April 1948 the bizonal military government, in consultation with the German-led Frankfurt Economic Council, founded an advisory board, the Committee for the Support of Steel Production, also known as the Working Committee. West Germany was at the time suffering severe shortages in all of its industrial sectors, and the Allies assembled this temporary organization to gather recommendations on how to increase steel production. Expanded steel output would mean more exports and, consequently, the import of much-needed finished goods and raw materials from abroad. After consulting industry insiders on potential appointees to the committee, the CDU's delegation in Frankfurt proposed Hermann Reusch and two other representatives of heavy industry, who were to work alongside two previously chosen British steel experts. The Allies approved the nominations without a hitch. This seemingly innocuous, three-month position was to complement Reusch's more visible and more partisan activities as head of the GHH and the Arbeitsgemeinschaft Eisen und Metall (Iron and Steel Working Group), to which he had been appointed in February.[127]

While the Allies attached no particular significance to their appointment of Reusch, organized labor did. In the words of one labor leader, the name Reusch was to the working classes like a "red rag to a bull."[128] This hostility toward Reusch centered on some antiunion comments the GHH director had made the summer before. In an affidavit for the Nuremberg prosecution, Reusch had declared that if the workers had only risen up and struck against the Nazis on 1 May 1933, then they would have dealt Hitler a severe symbolic blow and would have prevented him from consolidating his power. The unions, Reusch had implied, had wasted so much energy during the 1920s baiting the industrialists with their schemes for economic democracy that they had lost sight of the true enemy. When in 1933 it was for once the right time to take to the streets, the "class-conscious working class marched to the swastika in their May Day Parade."[129] In uttering these words, Reusch unwittingly opened a huge political can of worms. He was attempting to deflect the accusations against industry by asserting an affinity between organized labor and Nazism, between the working class and totalitarianism.

In the spring of 1948 the workers had forgotten neither Reusch's resistance to deconcentration nor, more significantly, his attempt to pin the blame for Hitler's rule on the trade unions. Upon receiving word of the Reusch appointment to the Working Committee, communist critics of industry exploded in indignation. The KPD denounced Reusch as a representative of the most reactionary elements in Germany and as a holdover from a fascist managerial tradition. The workers of the Hüttenwerk Oberhausen, who were greatly influenced by the communists' extreme rhetoric, remembered Reusch's abuse of their own Works Council director a year before, and they issued a statement condemning Reusch and calling the appointment "a challenge by the former rulers of heavy industry against the new industrial democracy." With this move, declared the workers, "the reactionary clique of Ruhr industry has moved into the front line. The heirs of Kirdorf, Thyssen and Vögler are once again taking up the reins."[130] In Oberhausen, workers spilled into the streets, striking and calling for the dismissal of Reusch.

Meanwhile, the Hüttenwerk's Works Council sent a letter to the other

German committee appointee, Paul Bleiß (originally the SPD's nominee), warning him to resign immediately or face the same personal attacks now aimed at Reusch.[131] With this flurry of activity by the KPD, West Germany's labor unions instantly recognized the opportunity to make their own political move. The DGB met for a brainstorming session and called for a general strike on 1 June unless Reusch voluntarily stepped down and made way for a labor-friendly candidate. Individual unions followed up the meeting with a flood of angry letters to the Allied occupation.[132]

The British and the Americans were caught off guard by the intensity of the response. What they had intended as a low-profile appointment to an ad hoc economic committee ballooned into the first major postwar confrontation between labor and management and the first test of the rapprochement in the Ruhr. Why had labor not been consulted? Why would Reusch, a supposed expert on coal, be chosen to advise the Allies on steel unless there was a political motive? A worker at the Hüttenwerk explained the logic of the anti-Reusch resentment: "If Reusch comes to power, than we can pack it up. The old concerns will be patched together, we'll have to return to the GHH, . . . our people on the supervisory and managerial boards will have nothing more to say, our *Arbeitsdirektor* will be sent home and with him the twenty-five other directors in the other factories, and then it's all over with socialization and codetermination."[133] According to another worker, who during the Weimar years had served as a union functionary and Works Council member, "It is like after 1918. Back then we also believed that there would be socialization. For years the socialization commission convened. Then it was too late. The political developments shifted to the right, and management won the game. Because everything remained the same, we could do nothing with the Works Councils. . . . We had no influence, and the exact same thing is happening now. Our colleagues recognize that and are fighting against it."[134] Still another worker explained that while Reusch had been appointed through "legal means," so had Hitler in January 1933, and everyone knew how that had ended. In short, Reusch had reproached labor for having offered no resistance to a tyrant in 1933, and now labor was heeding his message, applying it, ironically, against Reusch himself. Organized labor may not have acted to stop Hitler's coming to power, but it would not allow a repeat of the situation. Labor wanted to do all in its power to "avoid another 1933."[135]

Throughout April and May the British and the Americans struggled to contain the damage caused by the controversy. They asked Reusch to refrain from touring the various steel plants with the Working Committee, and they eventually canceled plant visitations altogether to avoid any provocation of the workers.[136] The state of Lower Saxony also requested that Reusch not make any appearances, as striking workers would disrupt a planned trade fair in Hanover. Meanwhile the political parties began weighing in on the debate.

The more moderate SPD, which had not initially protested the nomination, now adopted the rhetoric of its communist rivals, labeling Reusch a "monopoly capitalist" and "the leader of the group that in no way thinks to draw lessons from the past."[137] The KPD, in turn, complied and released information on Reusch's "Nazi" background and his exploitative wartime work in the ore mines of occupied Yugoslavia.[138] (Reusch had, in fact, never been a member of the NSDAP). Meanwhile the communist Freie Deutsche Jugend (Free German Youth) issued a declaration of solidarity,[139] while the SED in East Germany launched daily attacks on Reusch, labeling him industrial "Enemy Number One" among those "Nazis" still active in the economy.[140]

It was not only in Germany that the "Reusch case" was having repercussions. The joint handling of this issue also threatened to cause a rift between the Americans and the British, whose Labour government demonstrated a marked sympathy for the unions, under the directorship of the much respected Hans Böckler.[141] April and May 1948 saw a test of wills between British military governor Sir Brian Robertson, who recognized immediately the disaster the Reusch appointment represented, and U.S. military governor Lucius Clay, who, after consulting President Truman, had declared his intention to stand firm against the unions. As the strike date approached, the British secretary of state and the House of Commons began searching for an amicable settlement.[142] The British were growing increasingly frustrated with Clay, who had declared that he would consider a strike against Reusch to be a strike against the U.S. military government.[143] Clay was clearly more concerned than the British that the unions might indirectly bolster the position of the Communist Party in West Germany.

Amidst the confusion, the Allied representatives met with organized labor at the end of May in a last-ditch effort to avert a 1 June general strike, which 93 percent of the workers now supported. Both Allies saw mass action not only as detrimental to industrial production but as potentially devastating to the entire Marshall Plan, whose financial scope was to be determined by the Americans in June. At this strikingly cordial and relaxed meeting, the chairman of the Metal Workers' Union, Walter Freitag, delivered an opening statement (translated inelegantly by British note takers) that defined unequivocally the position of organized labor vis-à-vis German big business:

> The German representatives of the Trade Unions who are here today are mostly gentlemen who have grown up in the service of the steel industry in North Rhine-Westphalia. We were acquainted with the workers and employers before the first world war; we were acquainted with them during the time of the Hitler regime; we were acquainted with them after the second World War. We have come to the conclusion that it is the representatives of the employers who were responsible for the first

world war and were responsible for all the catastrophes that have accrued since. When we had come through the fearful terrors of the Nazi period, I think we may say that the unshakable will of all our people was that these gentlemen should never again be allowed to play any important part in German industry. The suffering we endured in the past, and the sufferings which the whole world had to endure as a result of this, are something which we do not wish to feel again as a burden on our people. As Trade Unionists, after the first world war we were the first among those who tried to build up a democratic and peace-loving Germany. This plan was defeated and shattered by those very gentlemen who were in supreme control of the iron and steel of Rhine and Ruhr. However tragic it may be, we welcomed the entrance of the Allied troops in 1945. You must appreciate the fact that we too have a national feeling; we too are proud of our people; but nevertheless we welcomed the entrance of the enemy troops in the year 1945; and therefore we welcomed the statements on the part of the Military Government that the Iron and Steel magnates of the Ruhr would be dispossessed of their fortunes and would never again have control over them. These were utterances which conformed very well with our own feelings and own thoughts. Unfortunately we see that today the development of events is proving very different. These very circles which were responsible for all our suffering are now trying to regain power. We do not ask for any special privileged position for the Trade Unions, but we do insist that the development of industry in Germany has got to be done on democratic lines. Therefore we should be ready to work with anybody who is no way to blame for our past misfortunes. The development that our industry is following now gives us seriously to think.[144]

Throughout the meeting, labor pursued this theme relentlessly: The appointment of Reusch spelled the end of democracy in Germany. While the unions insisted that this was a test case for democracy in Germany, the Allies pleaded for calm and for sober-minded negotiation. After several hours the meeting wound up amicably but with no mention of the impending strike.

In the meantime, industry was preparing a collective response to these developments. If labor was accusing industry of harboring Nazis, then industrialists would employ the same strategy. A dozen business organizations issued a joint letter to the Frankfurt Economic Council and Hans Böckler of the DGB, declaring their unswerving faith in Reusch and condemning the unions for using "Nazi methods" and violating the fundamental principles of democracy. The letter labeled the move against Reusch a "dictatorial power-claim" by the unions. To industry, labor's struggle was not about the "securing of a mature democracy, but about the dissolution of the totalitarian regime of

National Socialism through a totalitarian regime of the unions."[145] Industrialists also expressed among themselves a fear that the Reusch affair would have serious repercussions for international trade and for the reemergence of German industry on the world scene. It mattered little to the industrialists that, in fact, the unions themselves were declared enemies of communism. The labor unions' goal, argued an internal GHH memo, was to establish an order that "intentionally conforms to their inner-political claims to power by diminishing our ability to perform in the world market . . . and by preparing the way for a Russian/communist Final Solution."[146]

At the end of May, events came to a head when the SPD began calling for an open debate in Frankfurt over the Reusch situation. Fearing the negative publicity, the CDU withdrew its support and decided instead to "throw Reusch overboard in private."[147] On 1 June the Frankfurt Economic Council press office announced the removal of Reusch and Bleiß from the committee and the intent to search for two new nominations.[148] In response the DGB canceled its general strike. With a few hours to spare, a mass action had been averted. The unions had scored a major victory. Three days after this resolution, Generals Clay and Robertson announced that because of the controversy, they were dissolving the Working Committee altogether. While Clay offered no words of conciliation, Robertson declared his regret at not having consulted labor in the first place. He praised the unions' decision to call off the strike as a "courageous act," and he ended with the hope that the Reusch case would be "a useful lesson" to Germans as they attempted to negotiate the relationship between unions and the government.[149] Little did he know that yet another "Reusch Case" was in store.[150]

What effect did this episode have? While it is a good illustration of the political tensions of the day and of the rifts between British and U.S. labor policy, the 1948 Reusch protest did little to derail the larger process of postwar political and economic reconstruction. Indeed for contemporaries and historians since, it is overshadowed by the June 1948 currency reform. Yet the Reusch Case was an important milestone in the formation of an industrial collective identity. June 1948 marked the escalation of an already contentious relationship with the unions. While the introduction of codetermination in heavy industry had led to a calming of nerves in the Ruhr, the Reusch appointment to the Working Committee shattered this fragile peace. A few days after his dismissal, Reusch expressed privately how much the events had "shaken up" the industrialists.[151] Industrialists began using this hostility to the unions as a point of orientation, both in their struggle against communism and in their reconceptualization of their profession. By defining themselves in opposition to the unions, industrialists added another building block to their postwar self-identity and public image.

While significant with respect to labor/management relations, the events surrounding the Working Committee also demonstrated the extent to which Germans would draw on past hostilities and inflammatory terminology for economic and political purposes. To the political Left the sins of big business were perpetuated in the form of heavy industry and Hermann Reusch, who vociferously defended the managerial prerogative. For industry the evils of communism and Nazism had led to unions' demands for socialism and workplace democracy. Despite the meanness of these attacks, by conjuring up images from the past, Germans were actively confronting the consequences of their destabilized political world. By blanketing their opponents with the worst terms of opprobrium and by calling on the provocative language of totalitarianism, collectivism, and even the Final Solution, both sides were attempting to use their newfound democratic liberties and, in their view, their right to free speech to their own political advantage. By condemning each other's "fascist" tactics, labor and management were not only apportioning blame for the Nazi past but also establishing a working understanding of a new political system. In effect, they were trying to pick up where the Weimar years left off, but with a new political language. Labor was attempting to secure the gains—socialism and workplace democracy—denied to it during the 1920s, while communism was trying to discredit capitalism altogether. And industrialists were attempting to engage the widespread fear of the Left, memories of Nazism, and their own indispensability as economic leaders in the endless struggle to rebuild their national and international reputations.

I have attempted in this chapter to offer a relatively narrow but representative glimpse of German big business's self-presentation between 1946 and 1948. Although I have focused primarily on events in the Ruhr, the challenges and attitudes I have highlighted were replicated throughout all industry. For West German industry, this was a period of economic and political insecurity. Business leaders were put behind bars, companies were seized and reorganized, machinery was carried off by the ton, and the Allies and the German Left were publicizing the crimes of Germany's major firms. But it was also a time of hope and optimism. The ERP offered the prospect of economic renewal, factories were being rebuilt, and industrialists began taking comfort in the Cold War and the increasing show of solidarity by U.S. businessmen and politicians. This provisional confidence amid the chaos was manifested most clearly in the publicity activities on behalf of German industry. In a politically charged environment, where Hermann Reusch and Fritz Thyssen occupied the same symbolic space, industry recognized the need to craft a more positive self-image. In 1947 and 1948 industrialists began to coordinate their partisan publicity activities. The Heinrichsbauer piece and the dismantling literature were early examples of this cooperative work of self-portrayal that would continue into the 1950s. Industrialists exchanged drafts and comments, they attended briefings, they debated strategies over holiday dinner, and they delivered their message to the Allies and business-friendly audiences both at home and abroad. Their goal was to influence those institutions that wielded the most power—the Allies, German politicians, unions, and fellow industrialists. However, it was only with the founding of the Federal Republic that industrialists could step up their publicity work, turning for the first time to the very people they felt had brought them so much despair: "the masses."

CHAPTER THREE

Creating the New Industrialist

If the story of West Germany's Economic Miracle has a protagonist, it is surely the businessman. This, at least, is what industry wanted the public to believe in the 1950s. While West Germany's first finance minister and future chancellor, Ludwig Erhard, is credited with masterminding the country's economic recovery, it was, according to business publications, the industrialist who breathed life into his visions. He cleaned up the debris of his bombed-out factories; he founded new companies amidst the ruins; he provided jobs and prosperity for a battered nation. He put his capital on the line for the sake of the country and subordinated profit to the needs of the worker. More than anyone else, the businessman held the key to Germany's economic and spiritual renewal.

After the campaigns against Allied policies in the late 1940s, the West German public would increasingly encounter the industrialist as a self-styled and aggressively marketed ideal type. In the decades of economic recovery and prosperity in the 1950s and 1960s, *der Unternehmer* took on the status of a cultural icon. Publicists and business leaders dreamed him up, breathed life into him, and sold him to a nation hungry for symbols of success and affluence. During the first three years after the war, businessmen already tried to disseminate a new industrial ethos. But it was not until the founding of the FRG, the consolidation of the market economy, and growing economic abundance that industrialists could hope to establish a positive public image. In this regard, 1949 was a transitional year. It witnessed the end of the first phase of industrial reconstruction—when big business was purely on the defensive, struggling with the immediate manifestations of defeat and occupation—and the beginning of a second phase, when industrialists began to recognize that the revitalization of the German economy demanded more than simply pushing away the past. Defending the reputation of German industry meant recasting not only the economy but also the industrialist himself. As German business leaders surveyed their nation's economic gains and enjoyed their first tastes of political and economic democracy, they began to refine more carefully their public image through the metaphor of the *Unternehmer*.

The End of Nuremberg

In 1949 industrialists enthusiastically welcomed into the German language a new expression. Like so many others, it had originated in what Germans still lightheartedly referred to as "the New World."[1] The term was "public relations," an elusive and ill-defined concept that was to preoccupy business leaders and journalists for the next five decades. Between 1949 and 1955, industry invested public relations with an almost magical power. PR promised the salvation of free-market capitalism in Germany. It was asked to combat the forces of evil—to ward off memories of the past and to counter present political enemies. In short, public relations was to remake the reputation of capitalism in West Germany. As industrialists struggled to find meaning in a destabilized social and political order, PR became the chief tool for an assertive self-renewal.[2]

In order to understand why public relations, this "secret science from America,"[3] took on such significance for West German business, I will pick up where the last chapter left off, when industry was facing a challenge from organized labor over the Reusch appointment and Krupp's board of directors was being tried for war crimes in Nuremberg. June 1948 was a dramatic month for industry, but not only on account of these two developments. Rather, this month is etched in the collective memory of West Germans for a different reason. On the morning of 18 June West Germans awoke to find store aisles overflowing with foodstuffs and consumer goods they had not seen in years. The day before, the Allies had removed all rationing and austerity measures, and West Germany took its first step on the rapid path toward a free-market system.

The currency reform has taken on a mythical status over the last five decades.[4] In the language of the time and still today, the currency reform signaled "day one" of the "new" Germany. While the average citizen greeted the well-stocked shops with euphoric disbelief, the business world acknowledged the lifting of price controls with a sober hopefulness. With respect to their pocketbooks, many industrialists undoubtedly had reason to celebrate. While every German was to start anew from an apparently equal footing, property and factory owners found themselves in the enviable position of possessing fixed assets unaffected by the currency conversion. Industrialists were now free to invest and to earn substantial profits without Allied scrutiny. Despite this resonant victory for the free market, not everything was positive for German industry in the summer of 1948. The Krupp and IG Farben trials were still in session, the unions had just scored a major victory by defeating Hermann Reusch's nomination to the Working Committee, and socialism still held enormous promise to many Germans. Yet this greatest perceived threat to German industry—a socialized economy—had been dealt a severe blow. If businessmen still felt embattled, they also saw the tides turning slowly in their favor. In the summer of 1948, industrialists watched with a wary eye events being played out in German courtrooms. Yet they could rest assured that their prosecutors were as eager as they to place industrial denazification behind them.

This cautious optimism that accompanied the currency reform was mirrored in industry's publicity efforts. The centerpieces of industrial publicity in 1948 were the antidismantling literature and August Heinrichsbauer's *Schwerindustrie und Politik,* which industrialists planned to distribute after the verdicts in the Krupp trial were delivered in August. At the time of the currency reform in June, Heinrichsbauer was, in fact, in the middle of writing a second industry-commissioned apology for big business. This longer book was intended as the last word on industry during the Third Reich. Not only was it supposed to prove in exhaustive detail the folly of prosecuting "innocent" businessmen; it was also designed to expose the "hypocrisy" of the Americans and their entire program of "victor's justice" in Germany. By focusing not only on the three industrial trials in Nuremberg but on the entire postwar war trials program, Heinrichsbauer hoped to put an end to any talk of "Nazi industrialists."[5] As with *Schwerindustrie und Politik,* Heinrichsbauer conferred with colleagues in the business world over every aspect of this project, while Mannesmann's legal counselor and Friedrich Flick's Nuremberg defender, Wolfgang Pohle, offered regular progress reports to business leaders at the Düsseldorf Industry Club.

In June 1948 industrialists were clearly dependent on this defensive publicity strategy. In the immediate aftermath of the currency reform, however, Heinrichsbauer's colleagues began to have doubts about this longer exculpatory effort. It would be impolitic, argued business leaders, "to throw such a purely political book . . . onto the market."[6] "Industry," agreed Wolfgang Pohle, "does not want to hear anymore about the Nuremberg trials. It would like to close this chapter and devote its attention to the reconstruction."[7] Almost overnight all publicity projects that concerned business guilt, including Heinrichsbauer's completed but unpublished *Schwerindustrie und Politik* and his new book, were shelved. The decision by business elites to call off this apologetic publicity strategy indicates the optimism generated by the currency reform. While still nervous about the country's economic future, industrialists regarded the Allied move as a significant gesture in favor of big business.

Yet any sighs of relief were premature. Two weeks after Pohle's July decision to cancel the Heinrichsbauer publications, the U.S. judges announced their long-awaited verdict in the Krupp case. While the charge of having planned a war of aggression had been dismissed months earlier, Alfried Krupp and his colleagues were found guilty of employing slave labor and plundering businesses in France and the Netherlands. Krupp was stripped of all his property and business holdings and sentenced to twelve years in prison.

The Krupp judgment and the almost simultaneous IG Farben convictions, which sent nine members of the company's high-level management to prison, sent shock waves through West German industry.[8] Even more than the verdicts themselves, which unlike the Flick decision, barely considered the defense's claims of powerlessness under Hitler, the stripping of Alfried Krupp's holdings represented the most tangible affront to the institution of private property and incited industrialists to a unified expression of outrage. Immediately, industrialists in all branches rallied around Krupp and demanded that the Americans review the judgment and revise the sentence. Throughout the summer and fall of 1948, the badly shaken and now united world of German industry prepared its offensive against the legal "injustices." Under the leadership of the defense attorneys and Theo Goldschmidt, a prominent chemical industrialist and the president of the IHK Essen, businessmen bombarded the U.S. and British occupation authorities, as well as sympathetic friends within the U.S. business community, with petitions, angry denunciations, and pleas from ordinary German citizens to spare German industry its strongest and most enduring symbol: the Krupp dynasty.[9] Gen. Lucius Clay, military governor in the U.S. zone of occupation, endured the most criticism, as it was the United States alone that had tried industrialists in Nuremberg. Clay was responsible for steering all aspects of American policy in the U.S. zone,[10] and by the time he stepped down as head of the Office of the U.S. Military Government in Germany in May 1949, he had begun to question whether the imprisonment of political and economic elites would mark his legacy as essentially punitive rather than reconstructive.[11]

In September 1948 August Heinrichsbauer found himself again in demand. Pohle immediately backpedaled from his dismissal of the apologetic strategy, arguing that it was now more urgent than ever; the shock of the verdict, he predicted, "will rouse even the most lax of industrialists." [12] In response to the Krupp verdict, the West-Verlag finally hurried through the publication of *Schwerindustrie und Politik*. Business leaders rushed copies to politicians, public organizations, and the press, with an updated introduction by Heinrichsbauer. The U.S. occupation, for its part, could not be swayed by this self-exculpatory pamphlet. The U.S. consulate in Bremen forwarded a copy of the pamphlet to Washington, cautioning that the work was "in effect an apology on the part of the leading western German industrialists for the help rendered by them to the Hitler Regime."[13] Despite the transparent nature of this work, Heinrichsbauer claimed to have received positive feedback from almost every recipient of his text, despite being resoundingly criticized by socialist and communist publications and U.S. occupation officials.[14]

This spontaneous burst of anxiety over the Krupp verdict is an important event in the history of West German business. It found expression not only in letter-writing campaigns but in protest rallies, legal debates, and radio plays mocking the Americans.[15] Yet while the Krupp verdict was important as a symbol of industrial guilt and the Western Allies' determination to punish business leaders, none of the Nuremberg judgments in 1948 were able to dampen the underlying confidence among industrialists that things were beginning to go their way. Industrialists continued to pay close attention to the fate of their imprisoned colleagues and to challenge vociferously the thesis of business guilt. But in the aftermath of the currency reform, the actual long-term damage from Nuremberg was limited.

If the Krupp verdict represented only a temporary setback to industry in its quest to secure a market economy in West Germany, it was, nonetheless, a dark moment in industry's collective self-perception. Nuremberg sent a clear message that industrialists were hardly a beloved species. Winning the trust of the public—and, more importantly, convincing the world that they were reliable partners—demanded new publicity strategies. The Krupp verdict, coupled with the continued dismantling of factories, sensitized industrialists to the reality that their public face had been deeply scarred. Thus despite the sincere hope and belief at the end of 1948 that West Germany would be spared a socialist makeover, the insecurity in the business world did not disappear with the new year. But August Heinrichsbauer's apologetic efforts were finally put to rest, soon to be replaced by much grander publicity plans in a future West German state.

Corporate Publicity: West German Industry Looks to the United States

The conclusion of the Nuremberg trials spelled the end of the apologia as the foundation of industrial publicity. While big business continued to lobby the Americans for the release of the prisoners, and would still make regular use of self-defensive publications as protection against reminders of a Nazi past, industry was now considering more sophisticated, more persuasive, and more proactive steps in the defense of *die Wirtschaft*. Publicity, business leaders came to realize, had to be understood not as makeshift expressions of indignation but as the meticulous work of individuals and organizations devoting all their energies to the promotion of a positive business image. This is not to suggest that industrialists had been unable to represent their partisan interests in the public arena before 1949 — quite the contrary. The business-man, the company, the IHK, and the trade association had all been institu-tionalized expressions of business interests. Groups like the Wirtschaftspoli-tische Gesellschaft 1947, which brought together representatives of politics, business, and culture to discuss the future of the country, were also undoubt-edly a sign that business leaders had reemerged as significant players with enough clout to promote their own political and economic visions and legis-lative prescriptions.[16] Yet none of these organizations devoted themselves to publicity per se. Their orientation was one of policy and economic philoso-phy, not image.

At first glance this distinction between "professional" publicity and an age-old *Interessenvertretung* (special interest politics) may not appear significant. The activities of businessmen inside and outside their firms had always by definition been geared toward creating a business-friendly public discourse. In attempting to promote a particular product or a favorable economic envi-ronment, publicity had always been a necessary ingredient for business suc-cess in the modern age.[17] In the 1920s, industrial leaders such as Paul Reusch, Paul Silverberg, and Albert Vögler had been tireless advocates of propaganda aimed at the broader public. With their business colleagues, they devised masterful publicity tactics, sponsoring public workshops, placing probusi-ness pamphlets in office waiting rooms, and forging links with churches and schools. For decades firms and business organizations had maintained at their own disposal *Pressestellen* (press departments), which oversaw relations with local and national journalists and which traced the effects of the media on sales and on national economic policies. Before 1945, company newspapers, advertising, and an occasional promotional film had projected positive cor-porate images to the public, and the late 1940s saw the renewal of many of these established publicity methods.[18]

Yet newer attitudes and structures were still lacking in 1949. For one thing, in the absence of supraregional organizations devoted exclusively to pub-licity, all of these above-mentioned measures had a limited reach and effec-tiveness. A company newspaper spoke only to its employees. A corporate press agency maintained contact primarily with business and trade publi-cations that the general public did not read. A published apology was di-rected at limited target audiences or point men, who could confront Allied or trade union representatives personally. Yet most importantly, all these forums lacked an articulated publicity philosophy. It was not enough to speak confi-dently of propaganda blitzes and "winning the public trust" (see below). Busi-nessmen had to convey their fundamental philosophical beliefs — and their relationships to the very act of publicity — in a positive manner. They had to couch the often cynical rhetoric of public manipulation and propaganda in the lofty rhetoric of goodwill. Publicity, businessmen would soon argue, was part of a social contract between business and the public, defined by a spirit of candor, altruism, and healthy competition between society's interest groups.

Nor was it simply enough to spread the word about the advantages of a product, the dangers of communism, or the value of assertive advertising and publicity. One had to ensure that the public took industrialists seriously enough to listen to their pleas. Successful business thus depended not simply on selling quality merchandise or creating through legislation a political environment conducive to the practice and principles of free-market capitalism. It also meant one had to convince a mass audience of the virtues not simply of a product but of the producer as well.

Where was West German industry to find a model for this image-oriented and ethically minded publicity? Rather than looking to their own recent history, defined by social enmity, a cartelized economy, and elitist notions of production and consumption, industrialists, not surprisingly, looked to the United States for inspiration. West German businessmen prided themselves on the quality of their own manufactured products and their industrial ingenuity, in contrast to "trashy," mass-produced U.S. goods, but they conceded an almost romantic superiority to the United States in all matters of image making. Industrialists in the United States were so successful at advertising and marketing because, in the view of German economic elites, the U.S. public actually held businessmen in esteem. Much of the German literature on public relations adopts a tone of envy and awe, with U.S. industrialists portrayed as enjoying a permanently business-friendly national culture. These glowing appraisals were, of course, greatly exaggerated. At the end of the 1940s U.S. businessmen were hardly riding the crest of popularity, with the public composing paeans of praise to their beloved captains of finance and industry. As U.S. business approached the new decade, it was also casting about for updated publicity tools that would protect its interests and reputation against the vagaries of public opinion, the power of organized labor, and the fears of socialist ideals coming from Europe.[19] Indeed the average American could be as ambivalent as the German with regard to business.[20] U.S. business, a *Fortune* magazine article from 1950 somberly concluded, "enjoys the most tentative and precarious kind of approval."[21]

The solution to this dilemma, suggested *Fortune*, was to be found only in "good public relations." Despite the frequent use of this term in America since the 1920s, it was still easier to figure out what good public relations was not than what it actually was. It was not advertising, news releases, or "press-agentry" ("whose business was 'not the dissemination of truth, but the avoidance of its inopportune discovery.'") It was not the "propaganda and publicity" that flooded the daily newspapers, trade magazines, and billboards. Rather, argued *Fortune*, good public relations was "good performance—publicly appreciated." In other words, "business must first do a job that people can think well of, and *then* intelligently and deftly call attention to it." The process could not take place overnight. It instead entailed the gradual implanting of a probusiness sensibility in the public psyche. It meant convincing the citizens of a democracy that the corporation was not simply a profit maker but a "neighbor and a citizen."

The concepts of the corporate citizen and corporate responsibility were not, in and of themselves, new. In the 1920s, company public relations representatives had already been at work refurbishing the reputations of individual leaders (in other words, converting "John D. Rockefeller, in the public mind, from an ogre to a benefactor")[22] and overcoming William Henry Vanderbilt's famous adage that "the public be damned."[23] The calls for a "new capitalism" based on social engagement, cooperation with labor, and a Keynesian approach to fiscal policy, were also the staples of Roosevelt's New Deal response to the Great Depression. Even during and after the wartime boom, many Americans were still blaming capitalism for the misery of so many millions in the 1930s, and industrialists began to fear that a public vulnerable to socialism would declare that business be damned. After the war a lingering belief among Americans that few businessmen "have the good of the nation in mind when they make their important decisions"[24] encouraged an even greater publicity consciousness among businessmen, with the flowering of so-called outside counsels, to which corporations turned to safeguard the public trust in their companies. At the beginning of 1950 the United States was home to 500 such organizations devoted exclusively to the public image of American business. In West Germany, which was still in the throes of economic recovery, there was not one.

Public Relations Comes to Germany: The Deutsches Industrieinstitut

In 1949 Konrad Adenauer was elected the first chancellor of the FRG. At his side stood Ludwig Erhard, economics minister and mastermind of the nation's nascent social market philosophy. The advent of the new CDU-led government signaled the beginning of a decidedly more aggressive and confident period for German industry—an Americanization, if not of business per se, then of business publicity. It is not accidental that the introduction of "public relations" to the German language coincided with the founding of the FRG. Successful public relations demanded power, money, and organization. All three were possible only after the lifting of de facto occupational control and the granting of certain sovereign privileges to West Germany. Most importantly, public relations demanded a government that shared business's economic and philosophical orientation. With the founding of the FRG, West German business leaders were granted the right to establish national industrial peak organizations to serve their political interests. The BDI represented the chief industrial interest group, while the Bundesvereinigung deutscher Arbeitgeberverbände (BdA) (Federation of German Employers' Associations) concerned itself with social legislation and wage matters.[25] For fifty years the BDI and the BdA have occupied the attention of scholars seeking to understand the relationship between management and labor in the Federal Republic and the peculiar nature of power in Bonn. The focus has been both practical and political. These scholars have asked to what extent these organizations' functions and strengths were similar to those of the U.S. National Association of Manufacturers. They have explored the position of industrial pressure groups in a three-pillared corporatist/pluralist model of labor, management, and government [26] in order to determine if industrialists exercised an inordinate amount of power through their umbrella organizations.[27] Despite these important lines of inquiry into postwar Germany's political and social structures, scholars have underestimated the significance of the BDI and the BdA as part of a broader attempt by industrialists to remake themselves ideologically after the war. The BDI and the BdA were not only vehicles for a national *Wirtschaftspolitik*. They were also expressions of a cultural and social crisis. At a time when all Germans were reorienting themselves to a post-Hitler world, the founding of industrial peak organizations constituted a milestone in the attempt by big business to gain an ideological footing. The men of the BDI became prominent voices in debates not only about the economic course of the nation but also about the cultural and spiritual state of West Germany.

It is not surprising that the founding of industrial peak organizations was hardly a cause for celebration by organized labor. The BDI was derided as the reincarnation of the Reichsverband der Deutschen Industrie (RDI) and, to some, a reintroduction of the "finance capitalism" that Marxists held so culpable in Hitler's triumphs. While businessmen now had a vehicle for their own interests in the political arena, they were also open to even more scrutiny from those who looked with suspicion upon any agglomeration of industrial power.

One of the first tasks of this new industrial leadership was to neutralize assumptions that the country was in the hands of a reactionary clique of industrialists. The BDI immediately established a press department and placed at its helm none other than August Heinrichsbauer, who had been begging his business friends for employment after the shelving of his longer apologia. In 1950 Heinrichsbauer became one of a handful of individuals trying to awaken a new public relations sensibility among West Germany's economic leaders. In May 1950, in preparation for a BDI planning session on public relations, Heinrichsbauer composed and distributed with the help of Hermann Reusch a report that, much like the *Fortune* article, sought to diagnose the problems facing big business.[28] Heinrichsbauer hoped to use his "exposé" as a blueprint for a broad rethinking of industrial publicity along U.S. lines. Industrial public relations, Heinrichsbauer argued, must be conceived of first and foremost as a political counterweight to organized labor. The unions themselves had recently founded in Cologne a publicity agency called the Wirtschaftswissenschaftliches Institut der Gewerkschaften (WWI), and industry must not, argued Heinrichsbauer, waste a moment redressing this perceived imbalance in favor of labor. This struggle with the unions was not simply political. Rather, argued Heinrichsbauer, it went straight to the heart of business's own self-understanding in a democratic state, one that Heinrichsbauer himself had helped to craft over three decades.

> In public matters, the worker thinks and behaves politically. The bourgeois (der Bürger), the businessman, however, is and remains—according to its professional self-conception—more or less apolitical. The strength of the unions lies in their political function, while that of industry (die Wirtschaft) lies in the technical. . . . In a democracy, the possibility of promoting the wishes of the business world is limited. It is therefore all the more imperative to influence the voter in a "democracy." . . . But time is pressing.[29]

In this opening entreaty, one encounters instantly the familiar tropes of the early postwar years: the apolitical nature of the businessman, his self-definition through technology, and the overpoliticization of the labor unions. Most revealing, however, is Heinrichsbauer's invocation of a sociocultural category—der Bürger—to identify the businessmen, and his deep skepticism about the ability of a democratic system to protect this social and economic elite.[30] Heinrichsbauer saw the danger of democracy not only in its egalitarian tendencies, which stripped the bourgeoisie of its privileged social and moral position, but in its willingness to provide a stage for parties that embraced principles of "totality"—whether Marxist or fascist. On both the far Left and the far Right, Heinrichsbauer saw the perilous espousal of an anticapitalist, antiindividualist philosophy that democracy seemed to countenance in the name of freedom. "In the age of mass democracy," he wrote, "the influence of a determined fanatical minority cannot be underestimated."[31]

Despite this pessimism about democracy's self-protective capacities, Heinrichsbauer grudgingly conceded that it was the only viable political option for the country. With "the courage to speak the truth" (Mut zur Wahrheit), industry must use this flawed form of government to its advantage, to exploit the forum of free exchange by petitioning vigorously in favor of one's own interests. Industry must deploy the power of mass persuasion—public relations—to win the battle against the forces of collectivism. This public relations militancy, he argued, required a variety of weapons and tactics: active lobbying in conjunction with local and national elections; the creation of a central organ responsible for probusiness advertising; generous financial support of newspapers and the cultivation of personal relations with their editors; the use of radio to propagate a probusiness message; the establishment of "contact points" with universities and individual scholars; the cultivation of relations with political and cultural organizations; active church and youth work; the establishment of public relations branches abroad; the setting up of news services; and the production of industrial films that gave "a visual impression of the essence of industry" and its achievements.[32] In short, public relations involved harnessing the newest and latest technologies of communication. Its successes would be measured not only by the strength of industry's will but by the variety and sophistication of the means it employed. All branches of industry, Heinrichsbauer insisted, must work together in this. Public relations was not the responsibility of an individual firm or a business sector. It was the calling and duty of the entire *Unternehmertum*.

In 1950 August Heinrichsbauer was the leader in the realm of West German industrial public relations. In shuttling to and from Bonn and in conferring with the new governmental leaders, he offered business the experience, loyalty, and aggressiveness so essential for any successful "PR man." Yet despite, or perhaps by virtue of, his own enthusiasm, Heinrichsbauer always provoked controversy. In 1950 he was involved in a scandal that threatened to handicap severely industry's efforts to reassert itself after its disastrous years of war and defeat. In the summer of 1950 an ad hoc parliamentary subcommittee initiated an investigation into Heinrichsbauer after the weekly magazine *Der Spiegel* published a story linking the publicist to the bribery of politicians with big business funds. Heinrichsbauer was accused of having paid off members of the new parliament to vote for Bonn as the new federal capital. In 1949 the cities of Bonn and Frankfurt had been lobbying for the honor of being designated the new seat of government. With the heart of heavy industry centered in the Upper Rhine and Ruhr, many industrialists were pushing hard for Bonn, rightly seeing their own proximity to the new capital as advantageous to the exertion of political influence. For months parliamentary committee hearings on industrial graft and political corruption dragged on, ultimately failing to establish a definitive link between Heinrichsbauer, industrial funds, and bribery.

Despite these inconclusive findings, big business had been struck a serious blow. To many critics, industrial pressure groups were to remain synonymous with corruption and bribery. Yet for the nation as a whole, there was, arguably, a salutary by-product to this controversy. In this so-called Spiegel Affair of 1950 (not to be confused with the more famous Spiegel Affair of the 1960s), the country initiated a permanent dialogue about the influence of big business and the role of the pressure groups in a democracy.[33] Despite its less-than-dramatic ending, the Spiegel Affair reintroduced West Germans to an

"Money and Politics." August Heinrichsbauer on the back cover of *Der Spiegel*, 21 June 1951 (courtesy of *Der Spiegel*, Hamburg)

inhabitant of the political landscape that had been in retreat during the Nazi years: the lobbyist, as embodied in August Heinrichsbauer. Germans debated whether *Lobbyismus* was a sinister misuse of democracy or the ultimate expression of political and economic freedom. This debate would preoccupy Germans for years to come.[34]

By the middle of 1951, when *Der Spiegel* featured on its back cover the face of August Heinrichsbauer (proudly boasting his fraternity dueling scars), business leaders were starting to understand how much trouble their old-time "connection man" (*Verbindungsmann*) was causing.[35] While the problems facing big business were much greater than this one individual, it was the symbolism of Heinrichsbauer—as a personification of industry's scarred face—that represented such a danger to business interests.[36] After the Spiegel Affair, Heinrichsbauer fell out of favor with his colleagues. That postwar business had invested so much authority in this Weimar lobbyist in the first place indicates a certain naïveté, not to mention a dubious willingness to restore ex-Nazi sympathizers to positions of authority.[37] Entrusting a controversial insider with such a sensitive political function was an indication of how much rethinking still had to be done by industry in the early Federal Republic.

Despite this naive trust placed in him, Heinrichsbauer did possess the know-how and the connections so necessary to establish an industrial sphere of influence in Bonn. Business was not a popularity contest. It was about earning money and exercising political leverage. Arguably, no one individual—whether or not a former Nazi—possessed the power to single-handedly destroy or repair the reputation of German industry, and to industry it made the most sense to employ an established lobbyist who maintained close relations with the many Weimar (and some Nazi) old-timers who now filled the CDU ranks in the new federal capital.

As industry would soon discover, however, publicity and interest politics were not the same things. This very fact explains the repeated disappointments suffered by August Heinrichsbauer, who attempted to straddle two eras and two philosophies of business publicity. It was not that West Germans could not countenance any political networking and deal making. Rather, they asked industry to conduct such business openly and cleanly. Perhaps naively, West Germans chose to differentiate between the power brokering so necessary in forging an effective *Wirtschaftspolitik* and a cynical political palm greasing.

In the establishment of close relations with the new government, it was not accidental that Fritz Berg, the highly visible first president of the BDI, would succeed where the shadowy Heinrichsbauer had failed. Berg saw himself as an outsider with no glaring history of Nazism.[38] While throughout his career Berg would be accused of exerting too much influence in Bonn, he could always withstand the perpetual cries against industrial influence-peddling and "Nazi" tactics by setting himself up as the tough-minded new-comer who helped protect the nation's economic well-being.[39]

Fritz Berg's untainted reputation cannot explain the BDI's rapidly increasing political clout. The new interest group had an undeniably supportive government to work with as well. With the demise of Heinrichsbauer's influence, the BDI adopted shrewder and more pragmatic approaches to the public defense of industry, tactics that recognized an organizational distinction between politics and publicity. Behind the Fritz Bergs stood a new breed of image makers seemingly immune from the political maneuvering that the national industrial organizations were now in charge of. These were the professional public relations men, in charge not of the national *Politik* but of the concomitant *Politik der öffentlichen Meinungspflege* ("cultivating public opinion"). Many of these leaders had spent substantial time in the United States, observing firsthand the methods of U.S. business publicity.[40] But like Heinrichsbauer's, their pasts were not entirely clean.

One such person was Carl Hundhausen, the undisputed father of post-war German public relations.[41] After serving in World War I, Hundhausen studied economics and worked as a financial consultant to the Krupp concern. He spent 1927–31 in New York as an assistant treasurer of a bank on Wall Street, returning again in 1937 as marketing director of Dr. Hillers AG (a firm that produced peppermint drops) to promote his company and to study U.S. methods of publicity. During the war Hundhausen continued to work for Dr. Hillers, was active in a number of advertising organizations, and published articles for Nazi publications. Hundhausen was an active supporter of the Hitler regime; he joined the NSDAP on 1 May 1933 and later joined a number of Nazi organizations. After his 1937 trip to the United States, Hundhausen published three of the earliest German-language articles on the subject of public relations. In one, he wrote of "the Judaization of the United States" (*die Verjudung der Vereinigten Staaten*) as a potentially devastating public relations problem that affected the relationship between owners and workers in America.[42]

Despite Hundhausen's prominent Nazi credentials, in 1947 a British denazification tribunal actually acquitted him of any ideological or political affiliation with the regime, and he was free to continue his career. In 1950 Hundhausen published a book called *Werbung um öffentliches Vertrauen* (*Winning the Public Trust* in English translation), which quickly became the public relations bible of West Germany.[43] In this book and throughout his career, Hundhausen promoted public relations as the "fourth pillar" of every German company, next to production, sales, and finance. As chief articulator of this new science, Hundhausen made what some might see as a natural and predictable career move in 1950. He returned to his old company, Krupp—a firm in the greatest need of an image makeover—as head of public relations.[44]

Another eloquent promoter of West German public relations was Herbert Gross, a prominent industry publicist and cofounder after the war of *Handelsblatt*, an economic daily published in Düsseldorf. In the 1920s Gross had been affiliated with the respected Institut für Weltwirtschaft und Seeverkehr in Kiel, and in 1933 he was sent overseas, serving as the chief U.S. correspondent for the *Nachrichten für Außenhandel*, the official organ of the German Ministry of Economics. In 1940 Gross was forced to resign from the Association of Foreign Correspondents after the U.S. government accused him of having been an unregistered Nazi agent (a charge that was never proven).[45] Despite his troubles in the United States, Gross became a respected firsthand observer of the American economy, and after the war he fashioned himself as a chief spokesman for the modernization and democratization of West German business. In a 1950 essay on U.S. public relations, Gross advised his colleagues that an open political system demanded the sort of aggressive image-making that German business had so long scorned, even during the Weimar years, when industrialists were drawing inspiration from other business practices across the Atlantic. Borrowing verbatim from the 1949 *Fortune* article on public relations, Gross argued that "a true democracy without the art of persuasion is as impossible to imagine as a totalitarian state without coercion."

> In a democracy the political fate of the economy lies with the people, i.e., public opinion. Public opinion does not allow itself to be forced, but only to be persuaded—through information (*Auflklärung*), through facts. Through "public relations," industry attempts to convey on a daily basis its achievements and its concerns. It does not seek to hide or to gloss over [anything]. It takes an interest in the worries and wishes of the public and plays an active role in the resolution of community or national issues. With the politics of cards on the table (*offene Karten*), industry is an effective and active partner in public issues, like housing, art, welfare and education, etc. It accustoms the public to the fact that such problems are not simply reserved for the state bureaucracy but can also be solved by a progressive *Unternehmertum*.[46]

If Carl Hundhausen was a public relations tactician, Gross was an established philosopher of publicity. But perhaps the business world's greatest organizational asset was Fritz Hellwig, a respected publicist and business scholar who had established himself at a young age as an expert on his native Saarland's history, culture, and economy. At age eighteen Hellwig published a piece on the popular history of his home region, and at twenty-four he composed a multipaged biography of Carl Ferdinand von Stumm-Halberg, the late patriarch of a Saar steel family and one of late Imperial Germany's most vocal enemies of socialism and trade unionism.[47] During the 1930s Hellwig joined the Nazi Party and served as the managing director of Bezirksgruppe

Südwest der Eisenhüttenindustrie in Saarbrücken, giving up his duties in 1943 when called to active duty with the Wehrmacht. At the end of World War II, Hellwig found himself in a POW camp in Fort Reno, Oklahoma. During his two subsequent years of U.S. captivity, Hellwig spent much of his time with intellectual pursuits, whiling away the hours reading in the camp library and conducting lectures and workshops on culture and democracy.

At Fort Reno, Hellwig composed several articles on the intellectual history and *Geist* of Europe and the United States. His many—mostly unpublished—musings on the fate of Western civilization reveal both the widespread obsession with totalitarianism and the ambivalence many Europeans felt toward the United States, the land of both unfettered individualism and cultural vacuity.[48] While celebrating the American spirit of openness, individuality, democracy, and good humor, Hellwig expressed his fear that the U.S. democratic model, if imposed unthoughtfully on postwar Europe, would itself crack under the pressure of a socialist onslaught. Without a *geistig* reawakening, based on an imprecise combination of the U.S. pioneering spirit and the distinctly European philosophical tradition of idealism—Europe was doomed to another post–World War I scenario. To protect its precarious position between the individualist United States and the collectivist Soviet Union, Hellwig called for a strong united Europe based on a cultural and philosophical "third way" that would serve as a counterbalance to the "monopolistic" control of the emerging superpowers.[49]

In all of these early publications, Hellwig displayed a prescient interest in the interrelationship between culture, the economy, and global politics in the mass age—themes that would serve him well throughout his career as publicist and CDU politician. This many-sided concern with the issues of the day also attracted the interest of industrialists as they cast about for a person who would lead their public relations efforts. In early 1951 Hellwig was chosen as codirector (and later sole director) of industry's newest and most important public relations creation, the Deutsches Industrieinstitut.[50] Headquartered in Cologne, the DI (renamed the Institut der Deutschen Wirtschaft in the 1970s), has been for fifty years an active player in the German economy, sponsoring lectures, conducting studies and polls, and providing German industry with a devoted guardian. The DI, more than any other postwar business agency, has presided over the public image of industry by projecting a sense of purpose and unity into the diverse ranks of German business.

The origins of the DI can be located in the summer of 1950, when the public opinion polling organization the Gesellschaft für Demoskopie (Allensbacher Institut) issued a report on the popular views of big business.[51] According to the study, 60 percent of the West German public believed that the industrialist thought only about profit, while only 16 percent saw the businessman as socially engaged. Simultaneously, only half of those interviewed saw the concept of the class struggle as harmful. "From these results," concluded August Heinrichsbauer after speaking with the report's authors, "it is clear that on the one hand, the majority of the people take a very skeptical, if not entirely disapproving, stance toward industry. On the other hand they also refused to consider radical solutions."[52] It was not accidental that these sentiments came to the fore in the summer of 1950, when industry was in the midst of the debate with labor over whether to safeguard union representation on company boards in heavy industry through legislation. The hostilities between business and union leaders became intense and at times ugly, as both sides used accusations of Nazism to brand their opponents as enemies of the nation. While labor was reasserting its long-standing quest for codetermination, industry felt severely threatened by this perceived attack on private property and managerial control.

In response to the destructive Allensbach report and the heated-up political front, industrialists stepped up their publicity efforts. In the summer of 1950, industry launched a short-lived experiment called the Gesellschaft für wirtschaftliche Meinungspflege GmbH. A number of corporations, most prominently GHH, Henkel, Bayer, Hoechst, and Robert Bosch, pooled their financial resources to create a foundation whose sole purpose was to advise its members on all matters relating to corporate image, both within and outside the firm. Anniversary literature, pressure group politics, relationships to foreign business, corporate sponsorship of the arts and sports—all would be under the advisory purview of the Gesellschaft and its monthly bulletin, the *Grundsätze und Technik der öffentlichen Meinungsbildung*.[53] The most important names in West German industry lent their support to this organization: Volkmar Muthesius, a publicist who wrote on the moral underpinnings of the economy and who headed the press department of the Deutscher Industrie- und Handelstag (DIHT);[54] Ulrich Haberland, the chairman of Bayer; and Jost Henkel, Persil king and erstwhile thorn in the side of the British occupation. In the summer of 1950 industrial leaders from every branch were coming together to rethink their publicity strategies.

Despite the grand intentions behind this new creation, the Gesellschaft für wirtschaftliche Meinungspflege disappeared mysteriously almost immediately after its initiation, and in the fall of 1950 business leaders again tried to stir up enthusiasm for an organization that would channel the burgeoning public relations energies into a general staff (*Generalstab*) for all of West German industry. During a November meeting at the GHH headquarters in Oberhausen, industry unveiled its latest public relations brainchild, the Deutsche Industriegemeinschaft (DIG). Unlike the Gesellschaft für wirtschaftliche Meinungspflege, this new institute was to survive its initial trial period. Funded jointly by the BDI and the BdA, the DIG would represent the interests of all industry or business, whether the largest corporation or the smallest family-run firm.[55] In November industry circulated an appeal on behalf of its brainchild: "Germany's economic and social future, the existence of our people, . . . depends upon the production of goods, i.e., on qualitatively and quantitatively high achievements in production. . . . Productivity is an entrepreneurial achievement . . . therefore the free *Unternehmerinitiative* . . . must be defended against everything that threatens to weaken it. That is not the right but the duty of the *Unternehmer* to the public at large."[56] The DIG's appeal for support demonstrates the almost apocalyptic zeal that accompanied the codetermination debate and informed West German industry's public relations efforts more generally throughout the 1950s. Entrepreneurial creativity and productivity were portrayed as fundamentally ethical precepts, invested with the power to deflect all attackers, primarily of the socialist and communist ilk. But if its sentiments were belligerent, the new organization's methods were to be pacific. "To deepen these principles" and to "represent them to the public"—that was the task of the DIG. "With the fulfillment of its task, the DIG, like all the industrial organizations, will be prepared to work with any organization that places thoughts of community and inner social peace above the words of class war."[57]

On 15 January 1951 representatives of industry, along with leading economic writers and editors, began a two-day meeting to expand and refine the philosophy of their new public relations enterprise, now renamed the Deutsches Industrieinstitut (DI).[58] Presiding over the meeting was Carl Neumann, textile industrialist, economic publicist, and future head of the DI in the 1960s, and in attendance were some of the premier names in German industry: Wilhelm Beutler, Otto Friedrich, and Hermann Reusch of the BDI; Gerhard Erdmann and Josef Winschuh of the BdA; and Wolfgang Mansfeld, former editor-in-chief of the *Kölnischer Zeitung* and onetime publicity worker with IG Farben.[59] Future director Fritz Hellwig was not in attendance, as the industrialists were at the time setting their sights on their first choice, Wilhelm Salewski, the general secretary of the WES, who listened to the proceedings as a "guest."[60]

The DI leaders devoted their founding meeting to the theory and practice of aggressive public relations. But before they could discuss means, the participants first had to agree on the broader aims of industrial public relations. At the meeting the BdA's Josef Winschuh introduced a platform of grievances and goals, all of which reflected the class-war tone that still clearly pervaded the industrial and political culture of West Germany: (1) The industrialist must be portrayed as a "social force" in society. (2) He must also be understood as a public entity. (3) "The phantom of 'profit'" had to be destroyed. The industrialist must be understood as neither capital nor labor, but a "third force"—as the "agent, trustee, and champion of capital and the leader of those who perform the work." (4) "The phantom of the 'proletariat'" needed to be destroyed. "Not the worker, but the refugee, the academic, and the pensioner are the (truly) needy." (5) "The phantom of a 'worker majority'" must be annihilated. "The workers are in truth a minority among the people, which strives with its leadership toward dictatorship."[61]

In agreeing with Winschuh's prescriptions, the DI founders were boldly asserting the utility of public relations as a weapon against the unions and their demands for economic democracy. Public relations would expose, in industry's view, the deceitful self-victimization of organized labor and reveal to the world the true victims of German history: industrialists and their bourgeois compatriots. After laying out this basic strategy, the DI leaders then shifted their discussion to the meaning and methods of public relations. Carl Hundhausen offered his colleagues a brief genealogy of the concept in which they were now investing so much faith. Hundhausen located the origins of public relations in the first decade of the twentieth century, when U.S. industrialists organized a virulent response to the publication of Upton Sinclair's *The Jungle,* a book that, through its portrayal of the workers' misery at Chicago meatpacking plants, had been a damning missive aimed at big business. The years after World War I, Hundhausen continued, had witnessed stepped-up attacks on America's largest companies, such as Du Pont, and in response businessmen and the government together set up the Committee on Public Information designed to protect industry against further vituperation.[62]

As an indication of the siege mentality of Weimar industry, German business, Hundhausen explained, had in the 1920s tried to emulate the Americans and create a comparable organization in Berlin, only to see its plans founder due to lack of initiative. Moving into the postwar period, Hundhausen located the greatest contemporary threat to big business in the same genre in which Sinclair had launched his attack: popular literature. This was the medium that reached the most people. In the U.S. context, Hundhausen singled out Aldous Huxley as an archenemy; in Germany, it was, ironically, Ernst Jünger, the prolific novelist and conservative social commentator. Both authors, in their diverse writings, had predicted a future of collectivized workforces that, in conjunction with their machines, waged an eternal struggle against the owners.

The only way to fight off such pervasive antibusiness images, argued Hundhausen, was to inundate the public with counterimages—of benevolent managers and of "corporate citizens" who courageously protected the common weal. The techniques for propagating this image would be varied: film, radio, contact with educators and professors, and distribution of company financial reports. Equally important, argued Hundhausen, was the projection of goodwill *within* the company, including worker training schemes, increased worker input in company policy, company magazines, welcome handbooks for new employees, and company open houses, during which the workers would be exposed to the *Unternehmergeist* through speeches and discussions. In short, Hundhausen called for public relations to be accompanied by an equally new strategy borrowed from the United States: human relations. Together, public relations and human relations would win over the worker—the common man—by acknowledging a basic human reality shared by workers and owners: "Man needs recognition like daily bread."[63] Throughout the 1950s industrialists continued to flesh out this concept of human relations. Public relations, the artful defense of business interests, could not succeed without acknowledging the individual worth of the workers and enticing them into a cooperative relationship with the owners.

At this first DI meeting the founders would have preferred to focus only on defining their public relations goals. Yet they also had to resolve a nagging jurisdictional question about the new organization's relationship to its financial "parents," the BDI and the BdA. Their concern was whether the DI would serve simply as the mouthpiece for the peak industrial organization or whether it would possess greater independence. While never criticizing the need for a carefully orchestrated defense of the market economy, some business leaders, particularly those active in the local IHKs, envisioned the DI as a strictly independent agency. Volkmar Muthesius expressed elsewhere a fear that the work of image making, if subordinated to the peak organizations, would be removed from its most important factor—the *Unternehmer* himself—and forced into dependence on a bureaucratic and cloistered political organization in Bonn.[64] Public relations, he argued, should be conducted primarily on a local level. It should be in the hands of the IHKs, which could establish contacts with local press agencies, universities, and public figures.[65] If publicity needed a national forum like the DI, then this agency must vigilantly avoid becoming the mouthpiece of the BdA and the BDI. "The DI," agreed Josef Winschuh, "must not become the land fill (*Schuttabladeplatz*) for organizational propaganda but rather the spiritual center."[66]

Despite such doubts, with the most recent accusations of impropriety against August Heinrichsbauer still thick in the air, most of the DI founders acknowledged the need for top-heavy organization, if principally to avoid any secrecy or miscommunication within the ranks that would later catch industry by surprise. Every DI program, argued Hermann Reusch, must therefore be discussed openly and coordinated between the managing and supervisory boards of the BdA and the BDI. Most importantly, Reusch warned his colleagues, "Our work must be clean. We do not want to have another Spiegel trial."[67]

The Publications of the DI

The DI manifested the optimistic spirit and the renewed political activism of big business during the FRG's early years. The DI would serve as the nerve center of West German industry, regulating its vital functions and protecting its health. One of the DI's first tasks was to create a library and resource center devoted to the promotion of a new positive image for big business. The purposes of a "central collection," wrote newly chosen director Fritz Hellwig, was to provide the scholarly materials that would "influence the future image of the *Unternehmer* and *Unternehmertum*. . . . Anyone who wants to conduct scholarly and publicity work on industry or firm history will have to refer to these materials and thereby establish a personal connection with the institute."[68]

Hellwig instructed the BDI to direct its member firms to send the DI any of its publications that could service this end. Company newspapers, memorandums, customer newsletters, financial reports, prospectuses, product catalogs, advertisements, information on company social programs and benefits, anniversary publications, and stock market reports—the DI welcomed all of this.[69] The DI also lent its editorial and technical assistance to any person or event that showed promise of promoting the accomplishments of big business—trade fairs and community events, industrial organizations like Verein Deutscher Ingenieure and Verein Deutscher Eisenhüttenleute, doctoral students in economics and history, editors and journalists, and foreigners who traveled to Germany to study *innerdeutsche Probleme*.[70]

Next to gathering and cataloging these company publications, the DI also established its own publishing house in Cologne, the Deutsche Industrieverlag, which, with Wolfgang Mansfeld as its director, published dozens of books promoting free-market economics, such as the *Taschenbuch für die Wirtschaft*, a handy compendium of economic numbers and statistics that the businessman could always have at his disposal. The DI considered these publications key weapons in industry's struggle with the unions, which already employed a large publishing apparatus through the DGB and the WWI. The DI and the Deutsche Industrieverlag responded to the unions' publications *Welt der Arbeit* and the *Gewerkschaftliche Monatshefte* with three of their own weekly newsletters, the *Unternehmerbrief* [roughly, The industrialist page], the *Schnelldienst* [Express service], and the *Vortragsreihe des Deutschen Industrieinstituts* [The DI lecture series], all of which were designed to disseminate the new industrialist ethos in the business world and the broader public.[71] The *Unternehmerbrief* and *Schnelldienst* presented a collection of essays, commentaries, current event blurbs, and reviews of both pro- and antibusiness books. Distributed to firms, the press, politicians, and foreign consulates, these three publications stated that their purpose was to offer the means to propagate a business-friendly message in the public arena. In a typical issue, newsy articles about Adenauer's economic vision or political developments in both Germanys were juxtaposed with attacks on the KPD and SPD and caustic deconstructions of the Nazi/big business "myth."

In every issue of *Schnelldienst* and the *Unternehmerbrief*, the DI editors highlighted and reviewed the latest books that every industrialist should read and every company library should stock. The *Vortragsreihe*, in contrast, was understood more as a forum for the exchange of philosophical and political ideas. With lecture titles such as "The Industrialist in our Time," "Collectivism As the Crisis of the Age," "Man and Technology," and "The Categorical Imperative of the Economy," business publicists and industrialists traveled throughout Germany, preaching the new gospel of the politically, socially, and culturally responsible industrialist.[72] The DI would then reproduce the texts of these speeches several months later in the *Vortragsreihe*.

In all of these publications, industrialists made careful use of the recent past in formulating a new professional identity. National Socialism was readily invoked as the antithesis of this newly discovered industrialist spirit. In the Hitlerian "seduction" of Germany during the 1930s, industry found proof of the dangers of massification. Postwar industry's moral calling lay, then, in the revival of bourgeois values—in the protection of human freedom and individuality against further erosion by Nazilike mass movements and Marxian solutions. By vocally defending business interests, and thus Germany's *material* security, industrialists saw themselves as ultimately protecting the *moral* fiber of the Federal Republic. The lessons for Germany's second democracy were to be found in the collapse of the first one, which had seen a retreat from responsible individual leadership into a collectivist dreamworld. In elaborating on this philosophy of moral guardianship, industrialist spokesmen were expressing the basic tenets of finance minister Ludwig Erhard's "social market economy." Prosperity for everyone (*Wohlstand für Alle*) was the ultimate goal, as prosperity would make every citizen an entrepreneur on a microlevel. Hard work and frugality would bring to the German worker the most fundamental and the most precarious manifestation of Western individuality: private property.

Throughout the speeches published in the *Vortragsreihe*, one encounters time and again this conflation of the entrepreneur, the individual, and private property. Both the industrialists with their factories and the working citizens with their homes and gardens appear as the idealization of an antitotalitarian private sphere, which had been subject to encroachments by the politicized public sphere. In a speech to a gathering of small businessmen, Fritz Hellwig offered a litany of examples in which the private sphere of the firm had come under attack in recent years.[73] Hellwig relativized German industry's own Aryanization of Jewish property in the name of the *Volk* as merely one example in a long chain of attacks on the institution of private ownership in service of a public ideal. The recent Allied dismantling of German factories, the communists' confiscation of businesses in the East, the Americans' attempt to strip Alfried Krupp of his property and business holdings, and the unions' current demands for socialization of basic industries and codetermination in the workplace—all, according to Hellwig, were manifestations of a single phenomenon: the *Unternehmer*, despite his economic successes, remained an endangered species.

Overcoming this crisis, Hellwig and his colleagues argued, demanded new and aggressive public relations strategies and a "new political mission."[74] Political attacks necessarily had to be countered on their own terms, through political means. While *Politik* itself still had negative connotations to many Germans in the immediate postwar period, having found its most exaggerated expression in the total claims of the Nazis, industrialists began to argue that their future lay in a direct political confrontation with the enemy. In the age of mass politics, businessmen would be forced to refashion themselves as *politische Unternehmer*.[75] By exploiting a fear of communism and by equating the experience of Nazism with socialism, industrialists hoped to capture a moral high ground and reconstitute themselves as an ethically endowed professional elite.

It is important to point out that this reconstitution of the industrialist was a project by no means exclusive to the DI. The DI publications were only the most visible of the many newsletters and periodicals consumed by West Germany's economic elite in the spirit of a united business front. A circular called *Unternehmerinformation* arrived at the door of 269 of West Germany's largest companies, addressed to the personal attention of the company leaders. The BDI's *Mitteilungen* and *Rundschreiben* laid out the tactics of an aggressive *Wirtschaftspolitik*. The economic weeklies *Handelsblatt* and *Industriekurier* dutifully adhered to the probusiness/antilabor gospel. And probusiness journalists regularly punctuated their speeches with rallying calls like "Industrialists of the world unite!"[76]

In short, with its economic recovery, West Germany was reviving its dormant business press, which had long been essential in a country in which industry wielded enormous power. The economic press in the late 1940s and early 1950s demonstrated a deep self-consciousness and anxiety that had been a hallmark of business publishing for a long time. In considering industry's self-identity, the parallels between the late 1940s/early 1950s and the 1920s in particular are striking. While industrialists have always expressed dissatisfaction with high taxes and government intervention, after World War I, German industrialists had moved beyond these universal political critiques and into a crisis mode of sorts. They saw themselves as victims of a regulated war economy, revolutionary movements from the Left, and attempts by communists, organized labor, and Social Democrats to constrain their economic and political clout. The industrialist-as-victim motif found deep resonance in the Weimar Republic (and into the Third Reich) and ultimately contributed to the majority of industrialists showing little inclination to maintain Germany's fragile democracy on the eve of Hitler's ascension to the chancellorship.[77] But while industrialists' fears of their own extinction had been a signature business theme during the Weimar and Nazi years, the overtones of desperation and embattlement were even more apparent after 1945. With total economic devastation, the legacy of corporate criminality, and the Cold War, the fear for the actual survival of the *Unternehmer* was only magnified, and it became a ubiquitous motif of industrial public relations in the 1950s.

In attempting to diminish their perennial anxiety, businessmen cast a spotlight on themselves as the only hope for the salvation of capitalism in Germany. This soul-searching obsession with the industrialist was not simply confined to the business press. It was also reflected in a large body of scholarly and popular literature devoted to understanding this new breed of democratic capitalist. Understanding the new economy and its emerging prosperity meant analyzing the *Unternehmerpersönlichkeit* (*Unternehmer* personality).[78] A generation of Germans dusted off their old copies of Max Weber, Werner Sombart, and neoliberal hero Friedrich Hayek in order to reengage themselves with the *Unternehmer*. Business leaders consumed the words of Joseph Schumpeter, who offered the most sophisticated and articulate portrayal of the entrepreneur as the driving force behind economic innovation and progress and whose concept of democracy reserved a prominent place for political and social elites.[79] West Germany abounded with new trade schools, international business exchanges, and business administration degrees, all of which indicated the privileging of the businessman as the metaphor for the country's new economic and philosophical direction.[80]

In 1954 the newly founded Wirtschaftshochschule Mannheim approved as its inaugural doctoral dissertation a study titled, *Die Persönlichkeit des Unternehmers.*[81] Drawing on the work of Schumpeter, author Herbert Gehrig sought a sociological and psychological definition of the industrialist. He profiled eleven of Germany's most illustrious businessmen (Werner von Siemens, Alfred Krupp, August Thyssen, Emil and Walter Rathenau, Hugo Stinnes, and Robert Bosch, among others) and one American (Henry Ford) and attempted to categorize them according to type: property owner, provider of capital, employer, or manager. By delineating the distinctions and similarities among them (Alfred Krupp was an entrepreneur; Robert Bosch was social reformer; Henry Ford was both), Gehrig displayed the increasingly manifest desire to understand the industrialist primarily as an ideal type. In the 1950s hundreds of studies shared in this pursuit by tracing the history and meaning of the concept *Unternehmer* and his "world historical mission."[82] "What is the industrialist?" was one of the most frequently posed questions in the economic writing of the 1950s. The answers varied. To some he was a "demonic figure"; to others, a pioneer.[83] He was an agent of modernity. He was simultaneously an American, modeled after Henry Ford, and a quintessential German, who drew inspiration from the traditions of German handicrafts and family-run firms.

These attempts in the 1950s to consider the industrialist metaphorically bespoke postwar Germany's genuine attempt to acclimatize to democratic capitalism. On one hand, industrialists drew on their own past to discover the industrialists, inventors, and company leaders who could serve as inspirations to the postwar German youth interested in careers in business. Yet they modernized these sacred icons by infusing them with new "American" qualities: their "self-made man" status; their concern for public opinion; their philanthropic side. By inducting the Fords, Vanderbilts, and Carnegies into the pantheon of industrial giants, West German publicists and industrialists were not only acknowledging the force of the United States as a model of business success. They were also drawing on the inspiration of the U.S. *system*—free-market philosophies and industrial goodwill—as they learned the ropes of democracy.

Despite the philosophical and practical importance of this literature on the *Unternehmer,* there was something barren and uninspired about this search for a metaphorical or social scientific definition of the industrialist. It was not always immediately clear what was at stake in trying to reduce such a slippery concept to a sociological category. Despite their common attempts to offer a conceptual history of the business type, these works displayed a frustrating ahistoricism, wrenching the industrialist from his most immediate historical context—National Socialism, the Holocaust, and the mechanized terror of the recent years—in service of a decidedly static portrayal of the *Unternehmer* as the unsung hero of industrial capitalism. Too often these works degenerated into sentimental defenses of the industrialist, the eternal whipping boy (*Sündenbock*), whom socialists, communists, and unionists unjustly scorned.[84] While they attempted to historicize the disdain for the capitalist, these works rarely attempted to discover *why* industrial capitalism had preoccupied social reformers and war crimes prosecutors over the course of a century. In the end the strange mix of social science and self-pity is this literature's most salient and fascinating aspect, marking these texts as period pieces, incapable of—and indeed undesirous of—transcending the anxieties of the day (including totalitarianism and the unions' demands) for the sake of a scholarly dispassion to which they professedly adhered.

If the controversial equation of Nazism and business was deliberately missing from business leaders' treatises and disputations, in all of this literature the theme of National Socialism was nonetheless ever present, if by virtue of its very absence. By appealing to the public for a second chance, by hyperbolizing the oppression under which the capitalist had eternally suffered, by reconfiguring the *Unternehmertyp* (the Unternehmer ideal type), West German industry was both implicitly and explicitly conceding the damage to its reputation that had taken place over the last several decades. While always sparing in self-criticism, by attempting to create a *neues Unternehmerbild*, industrialists were admitting the need to start from scratch.[85]

It is ultimately this silence regarding National Socialism that is the most striking feature of much of the self-generated industrial literature of the 1950s. The bracketing of Nazism—and German business's relationship to it—reveals how real the trauma of memory was. In the obvious attempts to suppress the past, industrial public relations of the 1950s confirmed the platitude that silence spoke louder than words. Underlying the literature on the new industrialist was the public relations challenge of the century: overcoming Nazism.

Youth, Religion, and the Entrepreneurial Ethos

In the 1950s industrialists created the *Unternehmer* and infused him with an abstract essence. He was a faceless and nameless being, a diffuse bundle of attributes, a romantic wish list of positive goals for the modern businessmen: openness, aggressiveness, solidarity, honesty, political ferocity, and individualism. Yet if the new industrialist had a single, identifiable personification who, more than others, strove to embody the very type he helped create, it was lost on the broader public. One person, however, who came close to fitting this mold was Josef Winschuh, a founding member of the DI. In the three very different ideological settings of Weimar, Nazi Germany, and the Bundesrepublik, Winschuh crusaded incessantly on behalf of the *Unternehmer*, defending him against all attacks and imbuing him with a philosophical essence. The former economic editor for the *Kölnische Zeitung* in the mid-1920s, Winschuh made a short foray into national politics, entering the Reichstag in 1930 as a deputy of the Deutsche Volkspartei (German People's Party) before settling down as a freelance economic journalist. During the Nazi years, Winschuh established himself as an authority on economic and sociopolitical issues, producing voluminous articles that supported the regime's autarkic policies and factory community rhetoric without partaking of the Nazis' scurrilous dogmatism and anti-Semitic free-for-alls.[86] He produced a number of articles and books about the industrialist, including a collection of celebratory profiles of Germany's greatest entrepreneurs and a treatise on the role of the industrialist in the Nazis' "new Europe."[87] Despite his more than accommodating stance vis-à-vis the Nazis, in the fall of 1944 Goebbels's propaganda ministry began (but never completed) proceedings against Winschuh for having supposedly insulted Economics Minister Walter Funk in one of his articles and for speaking out against the Nazi expansionist economic policies.[88] After 1945 Winschuh, who had not been a party member, made much of his "between the lines" anti-Nazism. Yet the fact remains that Winschuh, through his outwardly supportive writings on Nazi economics, helped to legitimate and consolidate, wittingly or unwittingly, a criminal regime.

Like so many of his colleagues whom denazification courts had declared guilt free (*unbelastet*), Winschuh enthusiastically channeled his postwar energies into promoting democracy and decrying the collectivist mentality that he had so recently defended.[89] Transforming with ease his anticommunism before 1945 into a pro-Western democratic discourse, Winschuh became a leading spokesman of the socially and politically engaged industrialist, who was to lead the charge against all forms of totalitarianism.[90] Like Heinrichsbauer, Winschuh cast industry's public relations mission in dire class terms. "This last war," he argued at the first DI planning meeting, "threatened the secure position of the *Bürgertum* — through the losses in the East, denazification, destruction of old families, etc."[91] But despite these great privations, the economic and social elite now had an opportunity to learn from this tragedy and from its own mistakes. The "hilltop perspective" (*Hügelperspektive*) that the German bourgeoisie had occupied before had left it unarmed and unprepared for the mass uprising taking place below. The lesson industry was to derive from totalitarian mass movements was that it had to retreat from its fortress and fight for and with workers, who unwittingly carried with them the seeds of socialist destruction. Industry, argued Winschuh, had to proceed cautiously but forcefully, always with a wary eye to its supreme communist opponent. "The industrialist must wage his struggle on volcanic ground, amid his mortal enemy, Bolshevism, which seeks to exterminate the industrialist wherever it meets him."[92]

Winschuh, like his colleagues, cast this mission in deliberately foreboding terms in order to arouse his colleagues to collective action on behalf of their own calling. Yet despite the dramatic rhetoric of coming spiritual battles, Winschuh, like others, spent much of his energy trying to define this *Unternehmer* whom he was exhorting the world to defend and exalt. Winschuh drew from the trove of existing definitions. The *Unternehmer* could be the owner of a large company as well as the small businessman. He could be the holder of the controlling shares of a company as well as a high-level company executive. He could be both a member of a social elite and simply middle class. Through his participation in the BdA and the DI, Winschuh certainly had no qualms about defending the top-heavy powers of big business. Yet he actually reserved his greatest passion for his crusade on behalf of a specific breed of *Unternehmer*: the small entrepreneur lost among the masses and the large businesses that catered to them. Himself part owner of a family-run textile company in the Palatinate,[93] Winschuh in 1949 helped found the

Arbeitsgemeinschaft selbständiger Unternehmer (ASU) (Working Association of Independent Businessmen), an organization that became the spiritual home for this putatively endangered species, the small and mid-sized businessmen under attack by both the Nazis and modernity in general.[94] According to the founding principles of the ASU,

> The independent entrepreneur, the *prototype* and the most visible realization of *Unternehmertum*, possesses the greatest moral powers to influence the public without any ties to a third party. The combination of the freedom of personal decision, full responsibility, and personal risk makes him the cornerstone of all entrepreneurial thought and achievement. The independent entrepreneur is the spiritual representative (*Träger*) of an economic order, who, despite all disrupting attacks from outside, has proven himself the only one who can raise national product and secure the freedom of human choice.[95]

According to the ASU's philosophy, saving the world from the ravages of collectivism meant imbuing a new generation of West Germans with the entrepreneurial spirit and preparing it for future existential struggles. During the Adenauer years the fate of the country's youth became a national obsession. Conservative elites, churches, politicians, and sociologists were united in their belief that the regeneration of a defeated nation depended on young Germans. They placed their hopes in a generation untainted by fascism and two world wars. The desire to replenish a population ravaged by war inspired the Christian Democratic government and other social planners to initiate pronatalist policies and youth-oriented programs, while also instilling a procapitalist/anticommunist mindset in the West German family.[96] Yet in the 1950s, when prosperity was beginning to take hold, German elites were torn between their celebration of a growing consumer economy, which greatly appealed to and depended on teenagers and young adults, and widespread fears of consumerism run amok. While they represented the hope of the nation, Germany's youth, conservatives feared, were susceptible to crude U.S. pop cultural icons and "collectivist" allures from the Left—two forms of materialism that could undermine Germany's own unique position vis-à-vis "the West."[97]

I will take up this theme of consumerism, the United States, and the West in later chapters. But in the context of Winschuh's projects and the desire to consolidate a capitalist economy while maintaining German traditions, it is not surprising that the industrial community adopted much of the ambivalent rhetoric about youth. Winschuh and the ASU embarked on a campaign to instill the *Unternehmer* ethos in the society's youngest members, who represented a newer, purer Germany—the chance for a fresh start.[98] Winschuh appealed to the country's future businessmen to resist climbing the corporate ladder and instead to found their own companies or, more ideally, to take over the family firm.

In order to bring this entrepreneurial message to German youth, the ASU launched the Bundesverband Junger Unternehmer (Federation of Young Entrepreneurs). In part a response to the labor unions' *Jugendarbeit* (youth work) and the DGB's youth-directed journal *Aufwärts*, the ASU's youth federation devoted itself exclusively to inculcating the probusiness/antiunion spirit in West Germany's progeny. Its journal *Die Junge Wirtschaft* featured interviews with small businessmen; held contests, seminars, and weekend retreats; and filled its pages with entrepreneurial success stories. The magazine printed interviews with some of the more socially progressive industrial leaders, like Winschuh and Otto Friedrich, and besought West Germany's youth to aspire to similar entrepreneurial greatness.

This preoccupation in the 1950s with *Unternehmernachwuchs*—industrial regeneration—sparked the attention of Americans, who were watching to see if Germany's younger businessmen would follow in the footsteps of their older, authoritarian predecessors. In 1951 *Harvard Business Review* published Josef Winschuh's "Six Theses for Young Entrepreneurs." [99] In this widely distributed appeal to the country's future business leaders, Winschuh bemoaned the absence in West Germany of U.S.-style entrepreneurial academies that would compete with the trade unions' six training schools. He reminded those young people with a sympathetic view of labor that "the destruction of freedom of enterprise marks the beginning of a process at the end of which is the totalitarian state which will destroy even the trade union." Decrying the materialist "caste spirit" that could so easily take hold of an affluent West Germany, Winschuh called upon the young entrepreneur to give of himself— to align himself with a "third force" of educators, craftsmen, farmers, and clergymen. In short, Winschuh was calling for a revitalization of the threatened *Bürgertum*, a "broad, multifarious social middle class which has been so valuable as the cradle of good German qualities." [100]

Josef Winschuh and the ASU consistently evoked the image of a dying bourgeoisie whose regeneration depended on politics, public relations, and hard work. Perhaps most importantly, however, a *bürgerliche* revitalization demanded a spiritual and religious sensibility. In the 1950s industry turned to organized religion as a partner in the quest to infuse the nation with an entrepreneurial ethic. As Carl Schleussner reminded the founding members of the ASU, "We must not forget, that at this time of the individual's most serious spiritual torment, the Christian churches lead the difficult fight for the personal freedom of the individual human. . . . Through the practical application of Christian teaching in the factory, we hope to instill among all our workers the missing preconditions for a return to the path of faith." [101]

In the late 1940s and 1950s many West Germans accepted the self-assertions of the Catholic and Protestant Churches as the moral arbiters for the new Germany. Under the leadership of Adenauer's nominally Christian national political party, industrialists shared in the rhetoric of religious renewal. To business leaders in the 1950s, religion undergirded the new cooperative spirit with the worker; it informed the struggle against communism; it safeguarded the mores of the 1950s: work, family, and prosperity. A revival of the Christian labor movement and industrialists' active participation in organizations such as the Vereinigung für christliche Sozialpraxis indicated this comfortable merging of business and religion. The Moral Rearmament Movement (Moralische Aufrüstung) brought together hundreds of industrialists and workers from around Europe to discuss the means of reviving a "Christian-occidental" spirit of love and brotherhood in a post-Hitler world.[102] In the 1950s theologians delivered sermons at business conventions and company gatherings; clergymen assisted the leaders of the BdA, the BDI, and the ASU in drawing up speeches and drafting policy statements; labor and management regularly came together under the auspices of Catholic priests and Protestant pastors to discuss human relations and improve workplace morale.

In other countries, especially the United States, big business also turned to religion for moral validation.[103] Yet, arguably, the necessity of calling on faith to rescue capitalism was much greater in the FRG, where industry demonstrated a more genuine unease with the basic premise of free enterprise—making money—than did its American counterparts. Despite the emerging ties between Germany's neoliberal elite and U.S. conservatives, the men who could be given credit for brainstorming the Federal Republic's economic revival—Alfred Müller-Armack, Ludwig Erhard, and Wilhelm Röpke (writing in Swiss exile)—displayed an eagerness to temper the negative effects of the free market by invoking a Christian socialist tradition of state sponsorship. Even those who declared their allegiance to the "American way" partook of the pan-European search for a philosophical and economic third way between the communism of the East and the putative laissez-faire materialism of the West. Röpke had elaborated on this concept of the third way in his 1942 book, *Die Gesellschaftskrise der Gegenwart* [The contemporary crisis of society], which argued that it would not be enough to simply introduce laissez-faire ideas into a postwar Germany. The state should have the power to intervene and ensure fair play and to limit monopolies and corruption, basic services and utilities should be publicly owned, and the government should encourage artisan work and property ownership and break up large conglomerations of industrial power and property. Röpke set out to disprove that in the economy, "bigger is better." [104]

This complex relationship between a "Christianized" political culture, neoliberalism, and the social market economy has been the subject of impressive scholarship, and there is little room here to discuss the myriad implications.[105] Clearly, for many industrialists, the Economic Miracle over which they presided provoked a spiritual uneasiness, an almost surprised embarrassment that things might in fact be going their way. Unwilling to jettison their postwar economic achievements, industrialists instead asked religious leaders to devise a new philosophical justification for their worldly pursuits. They turned to prominent Catholic social scientists such as Götz Briefs and philosophers of religion like Karl Rahner to devise a moral-theological identity for the postwar industrialist. The entrepreneurial drive, the employment of workers, the furtherance of technology, the creation of wealth—all, they hoped to demonstrate, possessed a higher religious essence.[106]

These efforts to find an ethical/religious grounding for industry came together most tellingly in an organization called the Bund katholischer Unternehmer (BKU), a fascinating hybrid of Catholic antimaterialist doctrines and free-market praxis.[107] Founded in 1949 in Cologne, the BKU sought to elevate and ennoble the individualism so essential to neoliberal thinking by imbuing it with the spirit of Christian brotherhood. In this pursuit of a purified capitalism, the BKU boasted the cooperation of some of Germany's most prominent industrialists and clergymen: Franz Greiß, the president of Cologne's IHK and the BKU's long-standing leader; Cologne's Archbishop Josef Frings; and Oswald Nell-Breuning, West Germany's most respected Catholic theologian. Through their concern with Sunday work, *Familienpolitik*, property ownership, economic humanism, charity, and all aspects of business morality, the BKU members attempted to reconcile the *enrichez-vous* philosophy of free enterprise with *katholische Soziallehre* (Catholic social teachings).

In their attempts to promote a capitalism with both a human and a divine face, the ASU and the BKU called on an organic view of society in which businessman and worker were mere spiritual extensions of each other. There were, to be sure, differences in the approach of these two organizations. References to papal encyclicals were never found in the ASU's publications. And unlike the ASU and the national industrial organizations, the BKU revealed a more genuine struggle with the legacy and implications of National Socialism. Because it did not seek to disguise its ideological raison d'être, the BKU was more forthright in casting industry's identity crisis in terms of the recent past, making room for ruminations over Hitler's destructiveness and the nature of a postfascist spiritual malaise. Reeling from what they saw as the social discrediting of capitalism, the BKU members were obsessed with remoralizing the practice of business.[108] This entailed not only the promotion of a socioethical worldview but, in the words of BKU historian Klaus-Dieter Schmidt, "repairing the reputation of the Christian *Unternehmer*, which was under attack because of the behavior of many industrialists during the Weimar and especially Nazi periods."[109]

All of the organizations I have discussed thus far were expressions of industry's search for a new self-definition. They demonstrated both a particularism—the perpetuation of a Christian worldview, the defense of the small businessman, and the promotion of big business prerogatives—and a spirit of unity on behalf of all *Unternehmertum*. Certainly, not everyone in the business world was pleased about this splitting into constituent—and sometimes competitive—factions. The founding of the ASU at the end of 1949 unleashed a wave of concern in industry that the united front formed during Nuremberg would be shattered in the service of a purposeless distinction between the independent entrepreneur and the big industrialist. The *Selbständiger*, argued some, already had a home in the IHKs. Why fracture and bureaucratize the business world even more by founding a new organization? [110] Some in big business, moreover, saw the ASU as a veiled attack on West Germany's powerful CEOs, whose lingering support of cartels and big capital constituted a permanent threat to the small businessman.

Such doubts, however, were rapidly diminished as industrialists and businessmen delighted in the warm welcome given by the new government, the buying public, and Germany's global partners. The various associations settled in agreeable—if overlapping—relationship with one another, linking *das ganze Unternehmertum* in a web of philosophical, financial, and personal ties. If each had its particular view of the ideal balance between big and small business, they all seemed committed to the creation of "a moral world order" [111] based on the principles of free-market economics.

Despite the professed sense of unity in the business world, we must still account for West Germany's dual fixation with both the small businessman and large corporate success. How are we to account for the work of someone like Josef Winschuh or organizations like the DI, which stood at once for the smallest shopkeeper and the richest industrial captain? This conflation of big and small, in fact, speaks volumes about the emerging ideological thrust of the Adenauer years. In the early 1950s the "Economic Miracle," a term Germans had already begun to use a few years earlier, still remained more of a promise than a reality for most West Germans. One must distinguish between an economy that was rapidly rebuilding and one that, by the last third of the decade, could boast of being a true *Konsumgesellschaft* (consumer society) that saw the fruits of national prosperity reach the majority of Germans. [112] Nonetheless, even in the early 1950s, images and *perceptions* of material success pervaded the popular and political culture of the FRG and inspired Germans to work toward their own economic betterment. Yet with this new emphasis on material growth West Germans, ironically, felt more insecure about their spiritual orientation than ever before. They took pride in their own successes, their world-renowned entrepreneurial ingenuity, and their country's burgeoning world trade. Yet they faced this new world of affluence with considerable trepidation and, indeed, a bad conscience. While they enjoyed the fruits of this modern economy, they also, at least rhetorically, longed for a less complicated world of family and private enterprise.

With the specter of communism and the persistent reminders of its recent past, West German industrialists' hard-won gains seemed precarious. They looked back not just to the Nazi years but also to Weimar, where they saw the erasure of social hierarchies as having contributed to the revolt of the masses and the onset of fascism. Business leaders responded to these insecurities by looking back even further, calling on the symbols of a lost *bürgerliche Welt*—the self-made man, the family business, and private property. In the 1950s social commentators, led by sociologist Helmut Schelsky, began to depict the FRG as *nivellierte Mittelstandsgesellschaft* (literally, leveled out middle-class society), in which the possibilities of social mobility narrowed the economic and mental gaps between the proletarian, the shopkeeper, and the white-collar worker, thus portending the end of class society.[113] With an increased economic leveling and the disintegration of an older, elitist middle-class ideal of the "educated" and "economic" bourgeoisie (*Bildungsbürgertum* and *Wirtschaftsbürgertum*), the businessman struggled to carve out a niche among the masses.[114]

In the 1950s the very real concerns of the small businessman were thus appropriated by big business—and by the nation as a whole. Or, more accurately, West German society drew on the anxieties and inspirations of the independent entrepreneur. The small businessman and the owner of the family firm demonstrated at once a fierce free-market liberalism and a residual suspicion of big business. This is indeed the greatest irony. The independent entrepreneurs (*Selbständiger*), in contrast to some of the big business old-timers, fought tooth and nail against monopolies, cartels, and any other limits on the free market. Arguably, they felt a truer affinity with their employees than did big business, despite the latter's grand profession of solidarity in the workplace. But the universal hostility toward collectivism threw the small businessmen and the big businessmen into the same camp. Both agreed that greatness—economic or moral—began only with the individual. As demonstrated by the story of Max Grundig, who transformed his small radio shop into one of the greatest enterprises in Germany, small could always lead to large; one could rise from humble entrepreneurial beginnings to the heights of corporate success. Philosophically, then, there was in some respects very little that separated the humblest family firm from the Krupps and the Thyssens, or the ASU from the BDI. They were all, according to their own assertion, protectors of a bourgeois ethic that merged the individual and the community, money and morality.

This preoccupation with a lost *bürgerliche* world, finally, must be seen as a way that West Germans attempted to normalize the past and mitigate their postwar anxieties. While in a number of Western countries social elites were also speaking the language of moral breakdown and social leveling, the anxieties West Germans experienced in the 1950s entailed a unique set of responses to the legacy of National Socialism. German industry's soul searching reflected at once a broader anxiety about the state of capitalism in the West and a uniquely West German response to the country's moral collapse under Hitler.

By the end of 1951 West German industry had taken the initial steps toward its own regeneration and relegitimation. It had toned down (though not abandoned) its "attitude of defense, apology, and justification" in favor of a new attitude "barely known in Germany"—the offensive.[115] Through the founding of special interest organizations and the rebirth of the business press, industrialists were creating for themselves a new professional milieu suffused with an ethical, religious, and political philosophy and held together by aggressive public relations. On one hand, public relations was supposed to be distinct from the sordid work of advertising and influence peddling; it was about openness, goodwill, and the divulgence of a company's goals and philosophies to the public. On the other hand, public relations was supposed to be fiercely protective of business interests. It would avoid the antiunion mudslinging (*Dreckwerfen*) belonging to the political arena and would hold out an olive branch to the worker; yet it would fight the labor unions at every turn.

Despite its manipulative and political dimension, public relations did reflect West German industry's very real attempt to understand itself—to both justify past transgressions and find a more sophisticated and conscionable rationale for business success. The old philosophy of profit for its own sake or the Nazi image of a capitalist/racist utopia had lost all legitimacy, and industrialists were well aware of this fact. Organizations like the DI reflected the imperative of industrial self-creation and self-promotion in light of these disturbing memories. Through their various organizations, industrialists were, in their own selective way, working through the past. They were jettisoning, albeit slowly, some of their native German business philosophies of the past—a professed aloofness from politics, a lack of concern for the public, and the obsession with quality to the neglect of image—and were turning to a new place, the United States, for inspiration and for models of successful and acceptable capitalism. Industry selected out uncomfortable memories of discredited, immoral, German capitalism, which their critics felt had culminated in the Third Reich, and replaced them with a different, uncompromised capitalist tradition—namely, an American one. This did not mean that West German industrialists countenanced the wholesale imitation of U.S. business. Indeed, they profoundly feared some of the cultural implications of democracy and mass consumption that the United States represented. Their adherence to a Christian ideological strain of capitalism was evidence of this desire to distance West Germany from the crass materialism of U.S. free enterprise. Therefore even in the re-creation of the new industrialist personality, they attempted to infuse the increasingly modern, American *Unternehmer* with characteristics they saw as older or more German. If the Weimar and Nazi industrialists were unacceptable role models and the U.S. industrialists still thought too much about profit and image and too little about quality, then the postwar German industrialists would have to be a patchwork of alternative characteristics, many of which were not new at all. In the 1950s the new industrialist was, in the end, an updated version of the old one: the entrepreneur as man of labor, the industrialist as a man of science, and the factory father who loved his firm not because it earned him money but because ownership, private property, and making money comprised his religious/spiritual calling.

By the end of 1950 industrialists had begun breathing life into their new creation. Through the promise of successful public relations, political power, and a social conscience, industrialists had instilled in one another a new self-confidence and had attempted to remake the face of capitalism so badly marred by Nazism and class war rhetoric. But the success of this reinvention would ultimately have to be decided by somebody else. It was one thing to preach to the converted, but publicity demanded that industry propagate its message and sell itself. In short, industrialists now had to bring themselves — the new *Unternehmer* — to the people.

CHAPTER FOUR

Selling the New Industrialist

In examining the formative years of the Federal Republic, the historian of Germany inevitably encounters a number of contradictions. The early 1950s were a period of optimism and fear, excitement and despair. West Germans exulted in their rapidly growing economy while still bemoaning the destruction of homes, the absence of loved ones, and the loss of national unity with the founding of the East German state. Only five years removed from defeat and devastation, West Germany was born in a state of ideological, social, and cultural upheaval.[1]

With the return of democracy and freedom of expression, long-standing loyalties, insecurities, and animosities that had been buried for twelve years came rushing back to the surface of West German society. The press, the parliament, the factory, and the local pub reclaimed themselves as marketplaces for competing political visions of Germany—from working-class socialism to Catholic welfare socialism, to neoliberal laissez-fairism, to communism and even neo-Nazism. While historians have debated whether these ideological divisions were evidence of a restoration of Weimar's political culture,[2] there was at least one fundamental difference between the first democracy and the second: the *style* of politics had changed. The street fighting and bar brawling that had marked the years following World War I and the early 1930s were replaced by more orderly and less violent forms of politicking and pamphleteering. In the ideological debates of the 1950s, the stakes were still, to be sure, very high; the political and economic future of the nation was in question. In the early days of the FRG, nerves remained frayed and many scores were unsettled. In the political arena, what began as a cordial and spirited exchange could degenerate into acrimonious name-calling and character assassination, which drew their force from the lessons and language of Nazism. The growing pains of a new country would manifest themselves in youthful rebellions in the streets and in conservative fears of the new "consuming woman."[3] Yet despite these social and political changes, there seemed to be little doubt that the public saw this democracy as more stable than that created thirty years earlier.

In the early 1950s Germany's ruling party and the country's leading industrialists came together in an attempt to stabilize this chaotic ideological setting. They devoted much time and energy to overcoming the past by creating a political and economic consensus. They funded books and magazines, held forums, founded museums, and donated to charities that voiced support for free-market economics. Through the trials and transformations of the 1950s—the debate over rearmament and the compensation of Nazi victims, the belated return of imprisoned soldiers, the new role of women, and the restlessness of the youth—West Germany's elites searched for the means to repair a fragmented ideological world. They discovered their curative in Economics Minister Ludwig Erhard's "social market economy" and the figure of the reformed industrialist.

Industrialists and the Social Market Economy

To this point we have encountered the *Soziale Marktwirtschaft* in passing, as the search for a third or middle way between the poles of American laissez-faire and cutthroat competition and the Marxist state collectivism in the East. It placed the free market under the protective glance of the government. It called for savings and investment, an equal share of the tax burden, and a scaled-down, anticartelized industrial structure. It strove, in short, for an economy in its most ideal and beneficent incarnation: "capitalism with a human face."[4] While it is assumed that most West Germans supported the social market economy until it came under attack in the 1990s, in the first years of the Federal Republic this was hardly the case. The public's response to Ludwig Erhard's brainchild can be characterized, at best, as confused indifference and, at worst, as open opposition to the unleashing of economic freedoms, which many feared would lead to egotism, greed, and spiritual decline.

In 1950 the Institut für Demoskopie in Allensbach conducted two studies on West Germans' views of their country's economy. According to a public opinion poll in April, more than 50 percent of those questioned had no idea what was meant by the "social market economy," and only 12 percent could answer questions correctly about its basic tenets.[5] A second poll that year concerned popular conceptions of Germany's industrialists. The survey determined that 73 percent of the public possessed neutral sentiments about businessmen. The few people who did have strong opinions about the industrialist had, the survey suggested, carried over their preconceptions from the

Nazi or pre-Nazi years. Most Germans, the report concluded, had no recollection of any recent literature that touted the "advantages of *Unternehmertum*," and the last five years had shown little effect on opinions of big business and capitalism.[6]

The Allensbacher polls of 1950 revealed a marked apathy toward democratic capitalism in the early years of the FRG. While most West Germans were beginning to savor the first fruits of their postwar labors and most likely approved of the country's direction, few had the inclination to ponder economic and political doctrines. The quotidian pressures of family and jobs and the pragmatic demands of reconstruction left little time for reflection, and this was revealed in the polling results. With hindsight, the public's tepid (or perhaps more accurately, tacit) reception of free-market capitalism during these early years appears not only unthreatening but perhaps even *beneficial* to the maintenance of political and economic stability. Yet at the time West Germany's political and economic elites paid close attention to these polls, and they detected in this indifference a crisis in the making. Ignorance of free-market economic principles and their advantages, they argued, presented a substantial threat to the young democracy, for it left the broader masses open to socialist and communist seduction during a pivotal period in the country's formation. In designating this public apathy as dangerous, postwar elites were working through memories of the early 1930s, when the fragile Weimar Republic enjoyed few "republicans" who would support the system as it lay under siege. (They themselves had been among these critics.) With this lesson in mind, industrialists now recognized that if democracy and free enterprise were to flourish, it was not enough for the public to commit passively to their principles; the system would have to be actively defended and bolstered by a clearly articulated and widely disseminated capitalist ethos.

There was, of course, a political element to all of this. In the late 1940s and early 1950s, when the debates over codetermination and socialization dominated the headlines, economic leaders felt they had to do more than simply stave off the potential victories of organized labor and social democracy. If West Germany were to ensure the permanence of its economic order, it would have to foster not simply a state of mutual toleration but a positive relationship between the public and the economic system. An educated and sympathetic populace and a publicity-conscious *Unternehmertum* would be the only means of securing the modest gains achieved since 1945.

The first five years of the Bundesrepublik witnessed a flurry of activity aimed at securing the country's new "free" economy. Ludwig Erhard enlisted the help of all who were willing to pitch in: the IHKs, the ASU, and an organization founded in 1953 called the Action Group for the Realization of the Social Market Economy (Aktionsgemeinschaft Soziale Marktwirtschaft, or ASM), whose goal, according to A. J. Nicholls, was to achieve "the highest possible rise in the standard of living, to protect private property, preserve for the entrepreneur the freedom of decision in his enterprise, and to secure free competition based on achievement."[7] Next to the public forums, seminars, and essay contests sponsored by the ASM, the early years of the FRG witnessed an avalanche of books offering dire warnings about the collectivist alternative to capitalism. Friedrich A. Hayek's neoliberal, antitotalitarian classic from 1944, *The Road to Serfdom*, with its conflation of command economies and enslavement, is the most famous example of the alarmist, yet learned literature that influenced a generation of public figures and industrialists in Germany and the United States.[8] More often, however, these publications were directed not toward an educated audience but toward the "common man," who was seen as most in need of pro-market persuasion. The directors of industrial organizations such as the DI and the BDI regularly exchanged order forms and lists of books they wanted companies to distribute at their annual Christmas celebrations. Some of these books were scholarly publications designed to "sharpen the economic understanding" of their employees,[9] such as Herbert Gross's *Sozialismus in der Krise* [Socialism in crisis]; A. Hunold's *Wirtschaft ohne Wunder* [The economy without miracles]—a collection of essays by Hayek, Luigi Einaudi, and Wilhelm Röpke—and Goetz Brief's *Zwischen Kapitalismus und Syndikalismus* [Between capitalism and syndicalism].[10] The great majority, however, were "easily understandable and instructive" booklets aimed at popularizing the free-market economy and enticing the public toward accumulating personal wealth.[11] Typical of this genre was Ludwig Reiner's *Wir alle können besser Leben* [We can all live better], a book that was funded in part by the Regional Federation of Employer Associations (Landesvereinigung der Arbeitgeberverbände) and directed specifically at West Germany's "opinion makers," such as doctors, jurists, teachers, and factory councils.[12] The book's themes and chapter titles typify the folksy and accessible tone believed necessary to excite the public about dry economic issues: "The Pay Package and the Capitalists"; "Should We Take Money away from the Rich?"; "How Were Things Two Years Ago?"; "Why Do the Americans Live Better?"; "Never Again Unemployed?"; and "Does the Planned Economy Make You Rich or Poor?"[13] Clearly, these books were as much statements about the power of the past, specifically memories of the Great Depression and the dangers of joblessness and civil unrest, as they were optimistic defenses of a new political/economic system.

Most of these works were throwaway paperbacks, relegated to obscurity almost as quickly as they came out. A more lasting publicity effort, however, was launched in 1952 as a direct response to the 1950 Allensbacher polls and some equally unimpressive numbers two years later. In September 1952 Götz Briefs, a Cologne economist and theologian, helped interest a number of local businessmen active in the BKU in an organization called the Gemeinschaft zur Förderung des sozialen Ausgleiches (The Association for the Further-ance of Social Compromise), whose explicit goal was to promote the mar-ket economy and improve the public image of the businessman. For the next fifteen years this initiative, known popularly as *Die Waage* [The scale], inun-dated the popular press with cartoons, films, and advertisements that cele-brated the achievements of the West German economy, its industrial leaders, and the specific contribution of the ruling CDU.[14] During the height of the campaign, in the summer of 1957, *Die Waage*'s popular cartoon figures Fritz and Otto appeared in hundreds of daily newspapers in anticipation of the fed-eral elections, reminding each other in heavily didactic tones about the advan-tages of free enterprise and the dangers of the planned economy. ("Well, Otto, I think we should avoid endangering our social market economy with socialist experiments.")[15] Seven hundred West German cinemas also ran *Die Waage*'s animated, pro-CDU feature called "Behalte Deinen klaren Blick" [Keep see-ing things clearly], and two years later, satirist Loriot and poet Eugen Roth collaborated on a short *Die Waage* cartoon feature extolling the virtues of the market economy.[16] Looking back, Franz Greiß, the head of the BKU and presi-dent of the Cologne Chamber of Business and Industry, cited *Die Waage* as one of his organization's greatest contributions to the maintenance of the Federal Republic's economic stability.[17]

It is important to point out that *Die Waage* was not the brainchild of the Ruhr or "big business." The conservative and still-cartel-friendly BDI kept its distance from what it saw to be a vehicle for more neoliberal, *mittelständische* ideas, embodied in groups like the BKU and the ASU. In other words, *Die Waage* drew its inspiration not from the notion of large corporate power but from an Erhardian celebration of the individual. The BDI's aloofness and its lingering antiliberal ideas notwithstanding, *Die Waage* was not designed as a partisan campaign for small businessmen against large industrial power. The boundaries between a big business philosophy and a smaller, entrepreneurial ethos were always fluid, with both drawing on the language of individual-ism, freedom, and private property to promote themselves and their shared embrace of free-market economics. *Die Waage* therefore had a sociopolitical mission that most businessmen could support. It was aimed not only at shor-ing up support for Konrad Adenauer's administration and Ludwig Erhard's economic vision but at persuading the average citizen in both Germanys that the free market was to his or her advantage. Understandably, industrialists put their faith in any effort that might help their businesses and reputations during a turbulent period of self-questioning and reconstruction.

Yet in their attempts to "sell free enterprise" to a seemingly apathetic pub-lic, industrialists acknowledged that it was not enough simply to advocate the new economic system in which they functioned.[18] They would also have to draw attention to themselves—to the new industrialists that they were working so hard to create. While books that touted the market economy were also implicitly promoting the entrepreneur and businessman, industrialists recognized the need to showcase explicitly their calling, to revise what they saw as a historically negative judgment of the "entrepreneurial personality" (*Unternehmerpersönlichkeit*). Again inspired by the writings of Joseph Schumpeter, they portrayed the businessman and entrepreneur as the driving force behind the economy, as an innovator around whom a "cult of personality" (*Unternehmerpersönlichkeitskult*) could and indeed should grow.[19]

During the years of economic growth, what better way was there to inspire the masses than to draw attention to the men responsible for Germany's past and present economic greatness? Much as in the 1920s, when Germans looked across the Atlantic Ocean for models of economic progress and ingenuity,[20] postwar West Germans latched onto the entrepreneur as the symbol of hard work and success. The early Adenauer years can most aptly be compared to the period of rapid U.S. economic expansion in the 1890s and 1900s, when publicists and authors such as Horatio Alger helped create a folklore of capitalism through scores of novels about poor young men pulling themselves up by their bootstraps to the heights of business glory.[21] In the 1950s both West Germany and the United States witnessed a multitude of similar books devoted to inspirational, rags-to-riches tales. Herbert Zippe's *Große Unternehmer* reintroduced the West German public to five centuries of great European and American industrialists and entrepreneurs, from the Fugger and Rothschild banking families; to Alfred Krupp, Werner von Siemens, and Ferdinand Porsche; to Thomas Edison, Rockefeller, Andrew Carnegie, Ford, and Walt Disney.[22] If they were not interested in America's and Germany's great "auto kings,"[23] West Germans could engage with Karl Holdermann's biography of chemist Carl Bosch,[24] new editions of West German president Theodor Heuss's 1946 portrait of Robert Bosch, or Pierre La Mure's profile of John D. Rockefeller.[25] When they tired of reading about the great tycoons and inventors, they could immerse themselves in Gert von Klass's *Die Wollspindel*, an idyllic daily-life account of a Swabian entrepreneurial family.[26] In 1953 the DI commented on the tremendous appeal of this genre, noting with delight that West Germany's IHKs were, for example, ordering Walter Chrysler's autobiography by the thousands.[27]

Aside from such popular works, industrialists also lent their support to more highbrow presentations of the industrialist personality. In the early 1950s the DI helped the Bavarian Academy of the Sciences revive the *Neue Deutsche Biographie*, which profiled significant figures in German political, cultural, and economic life. The *NDB* was begun in the middle of the nineteenth century but had ceased regular publication during the Nazi years. In 1953 DI president Fritz Hellwig with economist Walther Däbritz organized a commission to raise industry funds to revive the *NDB* and, more specifically, to support the incorporation of profiles of businessmen into the series. Contributing financially were familiar names in business and finance: Cologne banker Robert Pferdmenges, BDI president Berg, and Ruhr industrialists Hermann Reusch, Theo Goldschmidt, Heinrich Kost, and Bayer's Ulrich Haberland, who also sat on the curatorium of the *Rheinsch-Westfälischen Wirtschaftsbiographien,* another series offering short biographies of prominent West German industrialists.[28] Also of significance was a third series called *Nekrologe aus dem rheinisch-westfälischen Industriegebiet* (1939–51), a compendium of business personalities who had left their mark on Rhenish culture and society.[29] In the preparation of all three reference sources, industrialists enlisted the expertise of some of West Germany's most respected economists and business historians, all of whom acknowledged the importance of providing role models of success and hard work.

Aside from this scholarly recognition of deceased industrialists, the death of a contemporary industrialist often inspired the writing of a biographical profile. Large and small firms used the occasion of a director's passing to highlight the company's contribution to the economic and spiritual growth of Germany. These memorial pamphlets contained wistful reminiscences not only of a late company executive and his career but also of Germany's past and present economic greatness and the unique contribution made by its entrepreneurs.

These memorializations were more than simply the creations of corporate public relations experts. They also demonstrate how industrialists constituted their calling *for themselves,* not simply for a specific audience. To be sure, selling a company through the heroization of its founder or leader made great advertising sense. Reprints of these graveside eulogies, memorial pamphlets, and words of praise from public figures were distributed on factory floors and in company publicity materials. But despite their promotional purposes, these memorials often contained genuine expressions of loss, with a loyal colleague or coworker mourning the death of the fatherly *Konzernherr.* A Henkel publication in 1953 reported the death of its head with a typical expression of deep sadness: "In his house in Hösel, our *Seniorchef* closed his eyes forever. From there the totally unexpected news reached us in the factory in the morning hours of 18 December 1952: Dr. Hugo Henkel is dead! In the factory, life stood palpably still. . . . The news was incomprehensible."[30]

More important than the sentimental nature of these pamphlets was their simultaneous mourning of a bygone industrial era defined by people like the recently deceased director. For example, on the tenth anniversary of the death of its founder Peter Klöckner in 1941, the Düsseldorf steel firm bearing his name updated and reissued a commemorative pamphlet by Volkmar Muthesius. In a new introduction in 1951, Peter Klöckner's nephew and successor, Günther Henle, waxed philosophical about the legacy of his uncle and the business age he had once represented:

> Today there is a widespread belief that the economic *Unternehmertum* already belongs to the past. Even the expression "*Unternehmertum*" has faded from use among men active in the economy. People think that the old concept is no longer timely, long since replaced by the new concept of the manager. But such views are gravely mistaken. What made us great in the past and what today has allowed the revival of our economy after the collapse of 1945 is indeed that very *Unternehmergeist* that is inseparable from a market and competitive economy. . . . Undeniably, our economic life today is organized in a way that . . . risk is no longer in the hands of the providers of capital, and that the function of the entrepreneur is entrusted to a number of personalities responsible for the leadership of a large firm. But in light of this very development, the great industrial personalities like Peter Klöckner can today serve as examples of an *Unternehmertum* that is at once levelheaded and courageous. Today anyone who helps lead a large firm has the chance and the responsibility to someday rise up to exercise a true entrepreneurial function, and it is for this very reason that he must become familiar with the very things (*Wirken*) that have brought our economy to its world position (*Weltstellung*). I hope the following booklet about Peter Klöckner will serve this purpose.[31]

Despite their difference in tone, both the Henkel and the Klöckner pieces testify not only to the widespread attraction of the entrepreneurial figure in the 1950s (or to the hope that such a figure could be *made* attractive), but to the persistence in postwar West Germany of older, more paternalist notions of the industrialist. In conjunction with this grieving over a deceased company leader was a mourning over the loss of an industrial type: the old-style company boss and factory father who was being quickly supplanted by the faceless manager. Not surprisingly, these wistful eulogies skipped effortlessly over the involvement of these firms in the National Socialist economy and war effort. The death of a company leader was hardly the occasion for soul searching about the relationship between industrial elites and National Socialism. But companies did not squander the opportunity to use the occasion to critique company structures and hierarchies under capitalism.

Indeed, the 1940s and 1950s were marked by a tremendous concern about the manager as the chief threat to the survival of the ideal of the typical Schumpetrian businessman/innovator. Even as large companies turned increasingly to directors who provided ever smaller amounts of capital, in their self-presentation they still harked back to a time when the owners and company founders were the driving force behind the firm.[32] Long after the appearance of the manager, who was already a fixture in the German economy by the 1920s, companies resisted abandoning their more romantic notions, both out of a practical recognition that the entrepreneur was simply a more appealing symbol of industrial success and out of a sincere fear that the *Unternehmer*—and the capitalist economy—were indeed endangered.

In the early 1940s, erstwhile Trotskyite and by then conservative theorist James Burnham described in his book *The Managerial Revolution* how a new class of functionaries—whether in companies or the state apparatus, whether in Nazi Germany or the Soviet Union—were wielding more and more social and political power, and how managers represented the class of the future. The West, he argued, was undergoing a sociopolitical transformation of revolutionary proportions, as capitalism was giving way not to socialism but to planned economies and centralized states populated and ruled by this new managerial elite.[33]

In the 1940s Burnham's prognosis was taken very seriously in German industrial circles, and new phrases were coined to accommodate the onset of a "manager society." "Manager" became a term of opprobrium that bore connotations of the trade union functionary, Albert Speer's wartime "kindergarten" of industry experts and technocrats, and the pencil-pushing *apparatchik* in the Soviet Union.[34] In other words, the manager came to embody a host of anxieties, from the troubled memories of Nazism and industry's role in the war economy, to the long-standing fear of the Soviet Union, to the persistent power of organized labor, to more diffuse concerns about modernity and the disappearance of the entrepreneur and the individual economic man.

Despite the pejorative and anxious use of the term, industrialists did also accommodate less politically charged meanings of "manager." Gradually in the 1950s the paranoid visions of the managerial revolution gave way to more sober attempts to understand the rapidly transforming hierarchical structures within a company.[35] For example, the common concern with *Managerkrankheit* (managerial illness) was an acknowledgment of a new personality in the firm whose workaholic lifestyle was defined by abnormally high incidences of nervous disorders and fatigue.[36] The most prominent and most celebrated businessmen in the West German economy, like Berthold Beitz of Krupp, came to resemble more closely the newer model of the manager than the older big industrialists like Rockefeller or Friedrich Flick.[37] In short, the passing of an older generation of company leaders was inevitably accompanied by the death of a powerful myth of the first industrial revolution. The "factory father," who cared as much for his firm and his family of workers as he did for profit, was a figure of yore. Yet it would take a long time before

German industrialists were to abandon a self-image so firmly rooted in the past and so much more appealing than present reality.[38]

This tendency to search for industrial role models from the past paralleled a general tendency in West Germany to revere individuals who came of age politically not in the Weimar and Nazi periods but in the pre-1914 *Kaiserreich*. That is not to say that Weimar and Nazi elites were absent from the economy and politics after 1945. Quite the contrary. A great many politicians and economists from these periods found themselves rehabilitated and professionally active in the 1950s. But in searching for usable and untainted symbols from the past, West Germans placed their hopes in their grandfathers' generation—as symbolized by Konrad Adenauer's longevity as West German chancellor (1949-63)—rather than in the generation of their wayward sons.

The *Unternehmer* and Popular Culture

Up to this point I have focused on books, pamphlets, leaflets, and brochures as the vehicle for industrialists' self-renewal. But the often contradictory representations of industrialists, entrepreneurs, and inventors were not only to be found on the printed page, and they were not only products of calculated self-promotion. In a country that was coming to define itself increasingly though images of wealth and material success, it was almost inevitable that the *Unternehmer*, in all his complexities, would penetrate the realm of popular culture independently of businessmen's careful image management.

In the 1950s a common place to find the industrialist was on the movie screen. Surveying the mainstream movies produced in West Germany after the war, we can detect clearly the public's fascination with the celluloid industrialist in his many incarnations. In the late 1940s and early 1950s the humble manufacturer, the greedy American speculator, and the elegantly sinister financier shared center screen with the tragicomic figures of the musician, the painter, the doctor, and the circus clown. The industrialist was both tragic hero and wealthy elitist. He was, most importantly, a personification of West Germany's imagined and actual economic revitalization.

The industrialist was certainly not new to the silver screen. The Nazis had used movies as a means of promoting their image of the idealized industrialist during the Third Reich. In the famous example of Veit Harlan's 1937 film *Der Herrscher* [The ruler], actor Emil Jannings played the role of a tycoon who espoused a new entrepreneurial credo in keeping with the "führer principle" (*Führerprinzip*) that was penetrating all aspects of society. Profit—indeed the potential survival of one's company, he asserted to his employees and family—must be subordinated to one's service of the "national community."[39] The industrialist remained an authoritarian figure within his own firm. But his own will would not serve the company in and of itself, nor its employees, but would be directed toward a higher spiritual goal: the maintenance of the *Volksgemeinschaft.*

After the war the celluloid industrialist was not simply the receptacle for an imposed political vision but a composite of the public's varied reactions to material success. By the late 1950s, as the promise of recovery grew into the reality of affluence, many popular films portrayed the industrialist both as a reflection of the euphoria over economic recovery and as the disenchanting underside of business success. But this ambivalence about capitalist reconstruction was evident even in the early postwar years. In *The Murderers Are among Us* (1946), the first German film to be produced after World War II, the businessman serves as the bridge between a horrifying chapter of the past that has just ended and the promise of future material glory. As an industrialist addresses a crowd about the tasks of reconstruction, the protagonist's thoughts drift back to the cruelty and destruction that he had experienced on the eastern front a short while before. Images of economic rebirth and business growth are juxtaposed with those of mass arrests and killings. The economic rebirth of the nation, the movie seemed to be presciently asserting, was not destined to be a smooth and problem-free enterprise. It was punctuated by haunting memories and a guilty conscience about the horrors that the previous boom years of the 1930s had wrought. The industrialists had one foot in the future and another in the past.[40]

This ambivalent movie portrayal of economic recovery persisted into the 1950s and manifested itself in a host of films with a businessman as the protagonist or antagonist. In the 1951 film *Das seltsame Leben des Herrn Bruggs* [The lonely life of Mr. Bruggs],[41] a humble train engineer climbs the ladder of success to become a wealthy railroad magnate, only to discover loneliness at the top. In 1955's *Nacht der Entscheidung* [Night of decision], a rich industrialist, presumed dead, returns from the war to find that he has lost his wife and his factory to another man. In numerous other films the solitary and hardworking industrialist is humanized by forces beyond his world of factory machinery and monthly sales figures: by the love of a plain and proper woman whose modesty stands in contrast to the businessman's large fortune, by an alluring movie star who offers to mother an industrialist's teenage daughter, or by the heartwarming scheming of his children, who have found in the single mother a companion for their father.[42]

Alongside these portrayals of the lonely and diligent industrialist was a more critical assessment of the businessman's inability to conform to the traditional mores of the day. He could be a lonely bachelor, or he could be a flirt and a philanderer who cheated on his wife with dancers and stewardesses. Three such movies about industrialists and extramarital affairs bore the titles *Always Innocent, When Men Cheat,* and *A Girl without Boundaries.*[43] Then there was the most famous film about businessmen and sexual improprieties,

1958's *Das Mädchen Rosemarie,* a movie (and later novel) based on the true and scandalous events surrounding the 1957 strangling death of a Frankfurt prostitute who consorted with some of the most prominent industrialists in West Germany.[44]

If the on-screen industrialist was an unassuming businessman or sexual predator, he also lived a life of joyless and calculated flamboyance, and against his strictures the creative and passionate child rebels. The industrialist's son falls in love with a pianist or a simple farm girl;[45] his daughter finds her prince charming in an insurance company lawyer or a circus clown;[46] an American tycoon's daughter falls for a homesick German ski instructor;[47] the son of a rich sawmill owner tires of his playboy lifestyle and finds spiritual renewal in his hometown.[48] In short, the entreprenuer is revealed not just as the old-style factory father who looks after his employees, but as the paterfamilias, who watches after his children but ultimately has trouble adapting to their increasingly carefree and rebellious lifestyle.

Taken together, these movies suggest that in the 1950s the industrialist was a decidedly ambiguous figure. He embodied both the elation over West Germany's economic recovery and an uneasiness with increasing affluence. He represented the hope of a stable future and the reminder of how fragile and destructive prosperity could be. He was a lonely figure at the top, watching as social norms, associated with the country's youth, changed below him. The industrialist was not unique in his ability to encapsulate the powerful postwar apprehensions. He was simply one vehicle for the expression of the many conflicted values of the period—*Heimat* (homeland), family, simplicity, wealth, and fidelity. In a culture marked by economic expansion and business success, the industrialist was a barometer of the public views about recovery, its material benefits, and its spiritual costs.

During the 1950s the power of the moving image was not lost on business leaders themselves. During the 1950s company public relations grew increasingly dependent on the so-called *Industriefilm* or *Wirtschaftsfilm,* usually a ten- to twenty-minute documentary that profiled factory production or a company's latest products. The genre had originated in the 1920s, when companies presented reenacted scenes from the factory floor as an internal training device for new employees and to introduce the company to visitors.

The 1930s saw the emergence of industrial films as documentary, advertising, and artistic creations. Professional actors and mini-plotlines were replaced with actual images of factory production, and companies employed the most modern film technology. The most acclaimed example from the Nazi years was *Mannesmann,* a profile of the Düsseldorf steel firm that demonstrated clearly the then emerging perception of the industry film as a form of avant-garde art. In February 1937 *Mannesmann* debuted at the Ufa-Pavilion at the Berlin Zoo, with a forty-piece orchestra conducted by Wolfgang Zeller providing the accompanying music and the specially composed *Mannesmann Overture*. Later that year the film achieved recognition for its "aesthetically valuable" qualities at annual film festivals in Venice and Paris.[49]

During the years following the Nazi defeat, when company publicity was rudimentary, money was scarce, and the Allies held a tight clamp on business activity, relatively few industrial films were produced. But increasingly throughout the 1950s, with the revival of the West German film industry more generally, companies began to recover a sense of the power of the visual image and musical innovation as a means of selling their products and enhancing their public image. Industrial films became professionalized, with company film departments and independent production firms recruiting young directors, artists, and musicians to create alluring portraits of corporate innovation and success. By 1960 the *Industriefilm* had become one of the most essential public relations tools at industry's disposal, with almost 200 films made annually, highlighting the newest in research, technology, production, and human relations.[50] At the *First Industrial Film Show*, held in West Berlin in 1959, the city's mayor Willy Brandt and the BDI's Fritz Berg greeted the guests with an excited acknowledgment of the indispensability of film to industrial public relations and to the artistic world of West Germany. At this exhibition dozens of documentaries about innovations in rubber, chemistry, magnetics, and sugar production competed for coveted awards for artistry, educational quality, and technical production. A documentary about U.S. business practices called *The American Look*, a short cartoon about Germany's social market economy (*Kleine Wirtschaftschronik*), and dozens of foreign films were also showcased as noncompeting features.[51] Volkswagen unveiled its *Straßen der Vernunft* [Streets of reason], which, by highlighting car production, "elucidated the positive aspects of sensible rationalization that not only make the life of the individual easier, but contribute to the prosperity of all."[52]

In all of these films the soundtrack was absolutely essential. Krupp's 1961 *Technik: Drei Studien in Jazz* sought to establish "a new relationship between images and music" by merging jazz syncopation with the visual rhythm of machinery and labor in three vignettes titled "Casting," "Forging," and "Mechanics."[53] In the 1950s conservative elites often feared that jazz would unleash a dangerously youthful abandon and a racialized sexuality, but by the 1960s industrialists obviously recognized the image of "coolness" and "modernity" that it also might bestow on their products.[54]

Through the industrial film, businessmen and companies carefully shaped and protected their public images. The industrial film was aired on television, in movie houses, and at exhibitions, and its rapid success in the late 1950s was a reminder that industrialists could no longer rely exclusively on the printed word to promote themselves and their companies; in the age of the masses, businessmen depended on new forms of mass media to propagate their message.

Industrialists did not, of course, have complete control over every documentary portrayal of German business. In 1950 the Soviet-supported film company DEFA (Deutsche Film Aktiengesellschaft) released a movie about Auschwitz and the crimes of IG Farben.[55] When the film, *Der Rat der Götter* [The revenge of the gods], began running in the Netherlands the next year, a group of Dutch doctors launched a campaign to stop Holland from importing pharmaceuticals produced by IG's successor firms (namely, Bayer). When the German ambassador to Holland expressed his frustration that the film had passed the scrutiny of the censors board, he was immediately attacked for having implied that a portrayal of Nazi crimes "damaged the reputation of the Federal Republic."[56] Although nothing came of the boycott, and West Germany's pharmaceutical firms only expanded their international markets, this minor incident did reveal the force that the industry's past exerted over the buying public, and its ability to provoke the anger of business partners abroad.

Moreover, this anecdote demonstrates the continued power of film as a political weapon. During the Third Reich, Joseph Goebbels and Leni Riefenstahl, among others, had proven the effectiveness of movies as a propaganda tool, and industry was now beginning to take advantage of them for its own purposes.[57] Indeed many of the people who produced films for the Nazis revived their careers in the 1950s.[58] This increasing reliance on films can perhaps be seen as further evidence of the "Americanization" or "modernization" of industry in the area of image making. In the age of the mass media, West German industry was forced to reconsider the means of delivering the image of economic prosperity and security. During the interwar years industry had already concerned itself with aggressive marketing and image making. But by the late 1950s, when postwar affluence really began to trickle down to the majority of Germans, the population was eager to see the latest technological and product innovations. Industrialists had to respond with the most modern technological and publicity means.

Markets, the Trade Fair, and the Ethic of Independence

In the 1950s the image of a firm and its products was an essential component of industrial public relations, as companies relied on their marketing and publicity departments to appeal to the buying public. This catering to the masses was not necessarily an indication that the public and the businessmen had abandoned their notion that quality was most important. Indeed, the advances in film and advertising drew their inspiration from the belief that the "better" German products needed a more appropriate showcase that could reach an increasingly large but still discriminating customer base. In other words, despite this overhaul in technology and marketing philosophy, the best advertisement for West German industry was still the manufactured products themselves.

It had been many decades since "Made in Germany" had first been worn as a badge of pride.[59] Since the nineteenth century, German industrialists had stressed the quality of their goods in explicit contrast to what they saw as the cheap, mass-produced merchandise from the United States.[60] German workers partook of this view themselves. As meticulous specialists—as *Facharbeiter*—they saw themselves producing wares of unsurpassable quality, in contrast to the assembly-line automatons across the Atlantic who seemed to work only for their wages with little sense of pride in the product. During the interwar years most German companies continued to focus more on quality than on volume. This does not mean that they could maintain a cavalier attitude toward images and advertising. During the Weimar and Nazi years, even when competition was reduced through a system of cartels and syndicates, there was still a need to promote a product and to outsell a competitor. But this marketing was always accompanied by a love-hate relationship with the consumer market and its echoes of American-style business methods.[61]

In the late 1940s and early 1950s, when regulatory controls were lifted and the economy expanded, industrialists continued to harbor an aversion to mass advertising. Starting in 1950, however, alongside the wave of publications about human and public relations, West German industrialists began to reflect on their own ambivalence toward the consumer and the need for mass marketing. Again they looked westward, where the Americans had already developed advertising into its own *Wissenschaftszweig* (intellectual subject area), responsible for everything from the packaging of milk cartons to the size, color, and shape of posters in company offices.[62]

Some industrialists also drew inspiration from an increasingly pervasive Erhardian, neoliberal philosophy, which prized open competition and aggressive marketing over a closed, cartelized economy. Yet despite this modernization of advertising, West German industry still resisted the notion that the image of a product was as important as its quality. Rather, it wanted to draw on the benefits of marketing techniques in order to promote a more traditional view of product quality. Advertising did not have to diminish a respect for German technological and manufacturing superiority. Indeed, it could enhance it by spreading the message farther and wider. Yet, argued many industrialists, customers had to see for themselves what had made Germany so economically great. Consequently, postwar German industry turned to the most familiar means of drawing attention to itself and its creations: the industrial and technical trade fair.

By the late 1940s, the public had already begun flocking to convention halls to peer at the most tangible manifestations of the market economy—its products. Cologne, Düsseldorf, Frankfurt, and Hanover all revived their proud traditions of the annual *Messe* (trade fair), where businessmen and politicians greeted their guests with soaring speeches about freedom, democracy, and the social market. The revived popularity of the trade fair was also fueled by competition with East Germany, which resurrected Germany's oldest *Messe* in Leipzig. By 1950 *Der Spiegel* boasted that Hanover's had become the largest trade fair in both Germanys, surpassing that year's Leipzig fair in floor space by almost 60 percent.[63] This competitive urge to trump East Germany in the realm of production must be understood in its broader Cold War context. The political tensions between communism and capitalism were reflected in marketing and product promotion and in the urge to outdo the enemy in both quality and scale of production.

Perhaps even more important than a reflection of Cold War politics, the trade fair was an indication of the increasing consumerization of West German society that marked the years of the Economic Miracle. The consumer became the driving force behind economic recovery and ultimately relied on the producers to provide the artifacts of consumption. In turn, companies conducted marketing research studies and relied on opinion polls to gauge what products the female consumer (more precisely, "the housewife"), in particular, most desired.[64]

The showcasing of German products was not limited to a domestic audience. West German industrialists brought their wares to exhibitions around the world, in Europe, Africa, Asia, and the United States.[65] In April 1949 the Museum of Science and Industry in New York, in conjunction with the U.S. Military Government in Germany, sponsored an exhibition called *Germany 49*, which highlighted the latest goods and machinery produced in the rapidly recovering West Germany and provided a buyers' guide for interested U.S. businessmen.[66]

Meanwhile at home, West Germans visited the reconstructed Deutsches Museum in Munich. The famous museum of science and technology had been badly damaged during the war, and industrialists and writers pitched in to rebuild this monument to the spirit of German innovation. In honor of the fiftieth anniversary of its founding, the DI put out a short booklet written by Eugen Roth and E. M. Cordier that offered a playful and poetic ode to German technological greatness through the story of a little boy whose father takes him to the museum and discovers the German entrepreneurial spirit.[67]

Not every German, of course, had the luxury of living near a world-class museum. However, if the Germans could not afford to travel to the big city to witness their country's latest industrial creations, then the images of prosperity would be brought to them. On 16 September 1950 a train pulled out of

Bonn's main railway station laden with brochures and booklets about West Germany's economy. The train had no destination in particular. Its purpose was to travel through the countryside until Christmas Day, bringing a message of hope and prosperity to the far corners of the young republic. In a predeparture ceremony on the railway platform, Chancellor Adenauer christened "the Marshall Plan Train," in recognition of the esteem with which many Germans held the presumed architect of their economic revival. For three months the "rolling ERP exhibition" meandered through the countryside bearing reminders that the country had come a long way from the ruins of 1945.

Of the fifteen cars that made up the *Marshall Plan Zug*, one held the particular interest of Germany's business world. It sported the freshly painted emblem of the Berlin Bear, and inside sat a scale model of West Berlin's "world famous exhibition grounds," the site of the much anticipated German Industry Exhibition of 1950. Next to this model were thousands of flyers inviting the people of West Germany to visit their former capital to see how a "free city" and "a free Germany" had pulled itself out of the ruins of war.[68] While the train made its way through the countryside, West Berlin sent a goodwill ambassador to fifty-two German cities to excite the public about what was being billed as "the largest and most representative German industry show of the postwar period."[69]

This description of the West Berlin trade fair was not off the mark. Every year starting in 1950, industrialists came to the "easternmost outpost of the western world" to remind not only the West German public but also the communist East about the benefits of the free market.[70] At the end of the Berlin blockade, East Germany and the Soviet Union had embarked on a drive to outpace the West in industrial capacity, product quality, and intellectual activity. This trade fair was part of this broader and ever escalating cultural and economic war between East and West. The BDI's Fritz Berg, who traveled to Berlin annually for the trade fair, characterized the exhibition as an "economic and moral-political" mission aimed at East German citizens. At the time, the borders between East and West Berlin were still open, and "a show like this industry exhibition," he declared to a crowd of fair visitors in 1950, "must impress upon the workers of the East that through the application of entrepreneurial initiative and liberal working conditions, the economic system of the free world brings results other than the totalitarian, bureaucratic, collectivist methods of the East."[71]

On 1 October the guest of honor, George C. Marshall, officially opened the two-week event.[72] For the price of one deutsche mark, visitors were granted access to eleven large exhibition halls, where 2,000 exhibitors showcased their newest offerings. All the symbols of the West German recovery were on display. Visitors wove their way past the latest in electronics and electrical

German Industry Exhibition, West Berlin: artist's sketch of the ERP Pavilion Hall, 8 September 1950 (F Rep. 240 Acc. 156 Nr. 35, courtesy of the Landesarchiv Berlin)

products into rooms filled with a panoply of chemicals, rubbers, paints, and dyes. When they were not staring at the leathers, furs, shoes, and textiles, they could be found admiring the newest in graphic design, paper products, typewriters, office supplies, toys, iron, tin, steel, glass, porcelain, wood, furniture, optics, building supplies, and mechanical tools. One hall was devoted exclusively to Berlin handicrafts and another to the latest developments in refrigeration, gas, and water.

The fair was not reserved only for Germany's producers. In a spirit of unity, West Berlin opened its doors to the world. A large pavilion was constructed on the Plaza of Nations to accommodate the foreign exhibitors. The French set up a booth highlighting their perfumes, champagnes, and other trappings of Gallic haute couture. The Italians displayed their food, wines, liqueurs, and textiles. The British iron and steel industry brought to Berlin the very first jet airplane, as well as models of the first jet engines, while the London Ministry of Transportation authorized the use of two red double-decker buses to shuttle guests to and from the exhibits. The George C. Marshall House held an exhibition on industry, trade, and labor in the United States, with a separate presentation on the workings of the U.S. government and American democracy.

The foreigners were not, however, in Berlin only to display their wares. Many were visitors who came simply to observe the competition or establish foreign business contacts. U.S. companies like Western Electric sent repre-

German Industry Exhibition, West Berlin: the inside of the George C. Marshall House (F Rep. 240 Acc. 156 Nr. 36, courtesy of the Landesarchiv Berlin)

sentatives to report on the event. Japanese officials were invited as honorable guests to celebrate the newly established trade relations between the two nations. In anticipation of many foreign visitors, the Kaupert Verlag prepared a German export catalog in five different languages, the first such publication since the war.

Many companies and business organizations had scheduled their meetings in West Berlin to coincide with the festivities. On 2 October Ludwig Erhard presided over a gathering called the German Global Economy Day (Deutscher Weltwirtschaftstag), which brought together the likes of economist Fritz Baade, social and economic critic Karl Thalheim, Thyssen chairman Hans-Günther Sohl, and the DGB's Hans Böckler to discuss global trade, agriculture, and food distribution. Dozens of other economic organizations traveled to West Berlin to hold their annual meetings. The BDI held a membership gathering there, while the radio industry sponsored the *Festival of Technology.* Added to the list of business organizations were the Federation of German Accredited Economists (Verband der deutschen Diplom-Volkswirte), the German Economists Congress, and the Central Federation of German Trade Representatives and Brokers.

The German Industry Exhibition also became a celebration of German cultural renewal. On the Kürfurstendam, West Berlin's main shopping thoroughfare, domestic and foreign visitors were treated to an endless stream of movies, theater, opera, variety shows, and cabarets. The Deutsche Oper, under the direction of Arthur Rother, prepared new productions of *Der Rosen-kavalier, Abraxas,* and *Tristan und Isolde.* The Hebbel Theater presented a William Saroyan play, while Shakespeare's *The Tempest* opened at the Schloß-park Theater. An art exhibition titled *The Painters at the Bauhaus* highlighted the works of Paul Klee, Lyonel Feininger, and Oskar Schlemmer, while an exhibition called *150 Masterworks of Painting from Berlin Museums* welcomed back to the former capital a collection of works by Titian, Sandro Botticelli, Albrecht Dürer, and Lucas Cranach that had been relocated to Wiesbaden during the war. Right next to the high cultural showpieces was an interna-tional boxing exhibition, a horse show, and an international soccer tourna-ment. In the fall of 1950, Berlin was demonstrating "to its foreign guests that it is not only a city of work but also of cultural enjoyment."[73] The official exhibition catalog proclaimed, "Berlin is back!"[74]

The first German Industry Exhibition came to a close on 14 October 1950. With the initiative of Economics Minister Erhard, the honorary sponsorship of Bundespresident Theodor Heuss,[75] and the input of leading business and labor leaders,[76] West Berlin had hosted a welcome-home party for German industry. When the event was over, 1,100,100 people had visited the exhibi-tion; almost half of them came from East Berlin and the Eastern zone to see "for the first time . . . what achievements the economy of the free world is capable of."[77] "For the first time," declared Ludwig Erhard, "the Federal Re-public of Germany offers a well-rounded picture of her productivity and . . . the ability and power of her economy." West Germany hoped the world would take notice of her success story, fueled by "the German entrepreneurial spirit and the diligent hands of millions of workers in the FRG."[78]

The industry exhibition in Berlin marked the triumphant return of Ger-man business. Five years after the defeat of Nazism, German business was emerging from seclusion. In the early 1950s, German businessmen were be-ginning to cultivate in one another a publicity awareness grounded in a spirit of professional self-protection and workplace morality. With the founding of the Federal Republic, West German industrialists were pulling together the disparate strands of their self-understanding into a coherent picture of hard work, religiosity, and goodwill. More importantly, they were depending in-creasingly on the public's fascination with Germany's revived productivity and the onset of conspicuous consumption as a way of blotting out the memo-ries of a more compromised incarnation of capitalism under Hitler. In other words, while the wealth witnessed in the late 1950s and 1960s still remained a fantasy rather than a reality for many, industrialists hoped that the promise of prosperity would inure the public and themselves to the Nazi past. This task, however, was not an easy one. When the self-congratulations were over and the festival lights had dimmed on the Ku'damm, industry was faced with the same uphill battle: quelling the political demands of organized labor and convincing the domestic and international public that it was worthy of their business.

The Lingering Presence of the Nazi Past

In these evocations of a sentimentalized past through biographies and eulogies, and in the trade fair's celebration of a new, free Germany, the years 1933–45 are glaringly absent. But during the early 1950s, German industrialists could not simply put the Nazi years behind them. They could not shed overnight their "Nuremberg complex" in the promise of *Gemeinwohl* (common weal) and prosperity. Indeed, there was often a hidden motive behind company biographies, which had as much to do with defending corporate reputations as with celebrating the free market and its spokesmen. In paying homage to their deceased colleagues and forefathers, industrialists recognized an opportunity both to commemorate their pasts and to "clarify" questionable aspects of a company's history. Even when they were feeling more optimistic about the future, West German businessmen still felt the urge to sell their innocence to the public. Corporate leaders commissioned respected and occasionally not-so-respected authors to compose glowing anniversary volumes and life stories, often under the pretense of scholarly impartiality. They then tried to micromanage the research and writing of these works, only to find that the desire to present a sanitized company narrative clashed with the reality of complicity with Hitler.

One of the most telling and interesting examples of this managing of memory originated from the directors of the Thyssen AG and the VSt in Duisburg, two companies whose fates had been entwined through the Weimar years, the rise of Hitler, World War II, and the Nazi defeat. In 1951 the VSt steel combine, of which Thyssen AG formed the cornerstone, was to observe the twenty-fifth anniversary of its founding. At the time the VSt faced the very real threat of dissolution; it was the number 1 target of the U.S. and CDU leadership's decartelization campaign and had been condemned for years as one of the most egregious examples of horizontal industrial combination.

When the directors came together in the fall of 1950 to discuss celebration plans, the mood was especially gloomy. The anniversary, a board member later wrote, would "give the press the opportunity for appraisals possibly of a critical or unfriendly nature."[79] The VSt directors agreed to commission a work that would commemorate twenty-five years of service to the German nation while simultaneously "countering the hostile propaganda" and the myth of the Ruhr industry's support of Hitler.[80] The project coordinator referred to the undertaking as a "twelfth-hour measure" to save the company.[81]

The VSt board cast about for a journalist who would be willing to compose this "apology for our industrial life's work" and help prevent the combine from being dissolved.[82] It quickly obtained the services of Volkmar Muthesius, whom we have already encountered as the head of the DIHT publicity department and author of the Peter Klöckner biography. Muthesius was one of the most prolific business publicists in West Germany, devoting a multidecade career to scores of company biographies, economic primers, and popular/scholarly books with titles such as *The Moral of Money, Money and Spirit*, and *What We Owe to the Market Economy*.[83] He had also been a close confidante of Ludwig Erhard since the two had met during the founding of the Wirtschaftspolitische Gesellschaft 1947 in Frankfurt. If anybody could regain the respect for the VSt, it would be Muthesius.

The directors provided the author with appropriate books and files (including copies of August Heinrichsbauer's and Ernst Poensgen's apologies from a few years earlier) and asked him to compose a fifty- to sixty-page book highlighting only the positive aspects of the firm's history. They also requested, for obvious reasons, that the volume bear only Muthesius's name as author, with no indication of its being an "official writing of the VSt."[84] Likewise they instructed Muthesius to leave out references to the more compromised Nazi industrialists, including Friedrich Flick, who had been sent to Landsberg prison for war crimes.[85] If the connection between the VSt and Flick were accentuated, argued VSt board chairman Wolfgang Linz, the public might be predisposed against the company, presuming that "if it (an alliance with Flick) happened once, it can happen again."[86]

Muthesius swiftly completed the book and sent it to the press in March 1951. But publication was delayed when Hermann Wenzel, the head of the VSt board of supervisors, aired his concern that the political climate was simply too sensitive and that such a book would be more effective after "the end of the new ordering."[87] The major industrialists had just been released from prison (see Chapter 7), and it looked as if Ruhr cartels might be able to stay intact, with most of their assets. While Alfried Krupp and Friedrich Flick were able to maintain a large part of their business empires, the VSt was not so lucky. The Allies and the government officially dissolved the cartel in 1952. Meanwhile the moment to publish the Muthesius book had come and gone. In 1955 the Droste Verlag published only 100 complimentary copies for former VSt board members.[88] Even these volumes were never distributed and were instead locked away in the safe of the VSt's legal successor, the Bergbau- und Industriewerke GmbH in Düsseldorf.[89]

In killing the Muthesius project in 1951, the Thyssen and VSt board directors were acknowledging grudgingly the crudeness of the apologia as a genre of business publicity. The book, they confessed, read unmistakably as a *Verteidigungsschrift* (a self-defense), a medium that had proved of limited value a few years earlier. Clearly, industry was still struggling with the most appropriate means of commemorating its past without coming across as too self-promoting or too blind to its own transgressions. The decision to commence and then to kill the Muthesius book reveals the tensions and pitfalls inherent in the process of directly clarifying behavior under the Nazi regime. As eager as companies were to expunge National Socialism from their corporate histories, they knew they could not do so and that broaching the theme of Nazism directly would be calling more attention to themselves than they needed. But even at this sensitive moment when the fate of the Ruhr's large companies was still being decided, industrialists simply could not totally withstand the urge to defend themselves and their companies through the commissioned corporate whitewash.

Even though industrialists like Hermann Wenzel could recognize the crudeness of these works, West German industry's self-defensive and self-promoting inclinations would never really disappear. Indeed, three years after the demise of its anniversary volume, the erstwhile VSt directors and the current Thyssen executives again tried to get a publication off the ground, this time turning to the more popular and seemingly more effective medium of biography. If industry was to confront the image of the Nazified industrialist, it would have to use some of the new lessons of publicity, highlighting the individual personality instead of defending the firm and the discredited economic system under fascism.

In 1954 the directors of Thyssen pulled together funds from a number of companies to commission a life history of VSt founder Albert Vögler, a man who had ascended from a "nameless engineer in the technical age to the general director of one of the greatest European concerns."[90] Vögler, they felt, provided the rare case of a proletarian who had risen above his origins to the heights of industrial success. The book was prepared to coincide with the tenth anniversary of Vögler's death in 1945 and, the Thyssen managers hoped, to inspire the working youth of West Germany to entrepreneurial and industrial greatness. It would also serve indirectly to exculpate the VSt and Thyssen in a way that, they acknowledged, the Muthesius book could not.

Vögler, the son of a Ruhr coal miner, was indeed a rare breed in the world of German industry. A graduate of a technical college, Vögler, with the help of steel magnate Hugo Stinnes, had climbed rapidly through the ranks of a number of companies in the Ruhr in the early 1920s. When he organized the VSt in 1926, he was already Germany's undisputed steel king, without whose approval very little could be accomplished in the Ruhr.

Vögler eventually turned to politics. In 1919 he had served in the first Reichstag after World War I as a deputy for the conservative Deutsche Volkspartei. During the last years of the Weimar Republic the anticommunist/anti-union Vögler grudgingly placed his faith in Adolf Hitler. After 1933 Vögler began to embrace more fully the Nazis and their nationalist, communitarian rhetoric, serving as VSt chair until 1935 and NSDAP representative in the

Reichstag until the end of the war. As the Allies pressed into Germany, Vögler grew depressed about the fate of his country, and in April 1945 he swallowed poison and died while being apprehended by U.S. troops.[91]

In commissioning a biography of Albert Vögler, the Thyssen managers were undoubtedly taking a great risk. They were drawing attention to one of the most controversial and criticized representatives of big business of the preceding thirty years. While Vögler had been an impressive business-man and a great supporter of science, his ignominious final years marred his legacy. In 1946 the Americans had placed the already deceased Vögler on their initial list of defendants in the industrialist trials, while communists in East and West Germany consistently identified him as one of a clique of reaction-ary businessmen who had "helped Hitler into the saddle." Despite Vögler's reputation, the Thyssen directors gambled in 1954 that the public, in its quest for dramatic stories of business success, would find inspiration in the tale of a poor boy who made good. The Vögler story would, they argued, "demon-strate to the younger generation how decisive the personality is in the course of the human life."[92]

In June 1954 the former members of the VSt supervisory board broached the idea of forming the Albert Vögler Circle of Friends (Freundeskreis Albert Vögler), which would raise funds to help publish the biography in time for the tenth anniversary of Vögler's suicide. The company received financial back-ing and encouragement from aging business personalities like Hermann von Siemens, Paul Silverberg, and some of West Germany's largest companies, such as Phoenix, Ruhrstahl, and the Bochumer Verein.[93] For an author the VSt turned to a seasoned industry publicist, Gert von Klass, whose company-commissioned biography of Krupp was at the time selling well both at home and abroad, despite being panned by the British press as a "whitewash" riddled with exaggerations and untruths.[94] Notwithstanding Klass's reputa-tion as an industry hack, Vögler's former colleagues and confidantes placed their faith in the prolific writer and enthusiastically helped him reconstruct the life and career of the VSt founder.

As part of his research, Klass arranged a visit with Friedrich Flick to gather firsthand stories from Vögler's erstwhile colleague, friend, and nemesis. It had been almost five years since Flick had been released from prison, and in that time he had rapidly sold, repurchased, and reorganized his holdings into the wealthiest industrial empire in Germany, if not in Europe.[95] Flick's rapid return to the heights of economic power was not lost on industry's critics, who saw in the rapid return of prewar and Nazi elites evidence of Adenauer's shameless coddling of fascists. Gert von Klass did not, however, count among those critics, and in December 1955 Flick welcomed the journalist into his home to talk about the past.

Klass found the seventy-two-year-old magnate suffering from bronchitis but in otherwise lively spirits. For two and a quarter hours, Flick puffed on cigars and reminisced about the glory days of the steel industry, when Hugo Stinnes had founded the Siemens-Rheinelbe-Schuckert-Union and Vögler had built up the VSt.[96] Flick spoke of his close relationship with Fritz Thyssen and his own attempt in 1936 to reprivatize the VSt, an organization Flick confessed to having greatly resented. ("You should not, however, write about this [the 1936 venture]," Flick warned Klass. "Many people would not like to hear that.") Flick was eager to defend a career that had landed him in jail, emphatically disavowing his reputation as simply a "package handler" who shuffled corporate shares and snatched up weaker companies. "I have always considered myself a true entrepreneur (*einen echten Unternehmer*)," he declared defiantly.

On a more personal note, Flick spoke poignantly of his often rocky relationship with Vögler and the latter's depression during the Nazi invasion of the Soviet Union. Flick recalled that in 1941 Vögler told him, "Herr Flick, if [the war] doesn't work out, you best take a pistol and shoot yourself and your family dead. I have made my arrangements." According to Flick, however, by 1945 Vögler, despite Germany's impending defeat, was feeling more optimistic and told Flick, "I have thought it over and I am ready to take part in the reconstruction of Germany. But I will never let myself be arrested."[97] To the shock of the Ruhr in 1945, Vögler clearly meant what he said.

By the time he spoke with Friedrich Flick, Klass had gathered most of his materials for the project, and he spent 1956 turning his notes and interviews into a biography. But the men in charge of the project were beginning to have second thoughts. The book, argued former VSt chairman Walter Rohland (1942–45) could "lead to misunderstandings."[98] Rohland took issue not only with the project itself but with Klass's portrayal of him as a onetime devotee of armaments minister Albert Speer, and he cited as an example of his insubordination the "great difficulties" he had in fact caused for Göring and the DAF's Robert Ley. He also bristled at the continued reference to himself as "Panzer-Rohland," an allusion to his close and much criticized cooperation with Albert Speer's wartime tank production.[99] "We should finally let go of this 'Panzer Rohland,'" he wrote. "As a side project, I spent two years building up and leading the tank division. But I am not a tank specialist but since 1923 an *Eisenhüttenmann* (iron industry man)."[100] Like Friedrich Flick, Rohland used the occasion of Klass's book to clarify the past and reassert his credentials as a true *Unternehmer* and not an unprincipled mogul or political opportunist.

As the Klass project proceeded, Rohland's support dwindled, and as the draft made its way through the Thyssen management, it opened more and more old wounds. Heinrich Dinkelbach went through the text line by line, striking potentially inflammatory themes, like Germany's rearmament in the

1930s.[101] Munich publisher Wilhelm Steinberg also read the manuscript and took issue with a number of points, including Klass's reference to Ernst Poensgen's seventieth birthday party thrown by the Nazi leadership and the portrayal of Vögler as a "rightist" and an "annexationist" in 1917. Steinberg was even more astonished that Klass should mention Hitler's 1932 speech before the Düsseldorf Industry Club, an event that was, to communist and socialist critics, the cornerstone of the case against German industry and which Klass apparently also took seriously. "Herr von Klass holds on to these old theses [that industry had enthusiastically received Hitler]. They are false. Vögler did not say a word that evening. Nor can you speak in any way of [Fritz] Thyssen offering 'an oath of allegiance' to the 'Führer.' All of this is a dirty legend. I was there myself that evening, and [Klass] does not, in my opinion, do Fritz Thyssen justice."[102] Clearly, even the most loyal industrial publicists like Klass could find something plausible in the notion that industrialists had lent a helping hand to Hitler.

The emendations and protestations accumulated, and Klass grew increasingly outraged by what he saw as industry's attempt to limit his authorial freedom and to sabotage his biography. When he heard a rumor that Thyssen wanted to pull the book entirely, Klass reacted viscerally.

> Over two-and-a-half years ago, I signed a contract that I have spent tremendous energy trying to fulfill. The results of these efforts have found the approval of everyone who has obtained the manuscript. I feel justified in adding that I have never abandoned my caution and restraint. In the end, however, I am a free writer who has a name and must represent it. For me, it is not a trivial matter whether or not a book that bears my name is published. I am the last person to refuse criticism when I have done something wrong. But, that being said, I do expect the consideration that my skills and achievements deserve.[103]

Klass's frustration reveals clearly the tensions inherent in a project dealing with the Nazi past. In serving as the mouthpiece for big business, economic journalists like Klass took on the almost impossible task of at once toeing a partisan line and maintaining some integrity as historian and scholar. They were asked to justify the behavior of German industry in service of the higher cause of economic freedom and political stability, but their fragile egos inevitably got in the way. It was difficult to see oneself simply as a "hired gun," which Klass ultimately was.

More importantly, Klass's experience indicates the extent to which industrial sponsors of biographies underestimated their own and their companies' compromised legacies. They naively asked industrial writers to turn controversial business figures into role models, but in doing so they, sometimes to their own surprise, were forced to face the realities of the Nazi/business relationship. It was very easy to blame the messenger when this happened. This naïveté may serve as evidence of denial or repression of memory on the part of postwar business leaders. But industrialists also knew what secrets the recent past held, and their confrontation with these realities was a conscious and painful act. The production of a corporate biography almost always resulted in crude and unconvincing self-exculpations. But the process itself reveals how much industry had truly suffered a "cognitive catastrophe" after 1945.[104]

Klass's book was finally published in 1957. It portrayed Vögler as a simple and gentle man who devoted his life not to making money but to the spiritual and cultural development of the nation's youth. "The history of his life," wrote Klass, "is a lesson book for the truly aspiring—for all who are courageous enough to reach for the stars and who nevertheless remain aware that one must never lift his feet from the solid earth."[105] In imbibing this vapid rhetoric of capitalist success, the public surely had no inkling of the expense, apprehension, and acrimony that had accompanied the book's production. It had been the result of a seven-year attempt to restore the reputation of one of Germany's most important steel firms. It put to the test industry's own ability and resolve to face the past; it posed the question of whether such a problematic figure as Vögler could serve as an inspirational figure in the 1950s. Klass and the Thyssen management felt he could. But the composition of the book brought to the surface memories that, by the mid-1950s, industry would have preferred to keep buried. In the end the biography of Albert Vögler was less of a confrontation with the past than a diplomatic truce. Klass put the facts of Vögler's career on the table—his rise to fame, his joining of the NSDAP, his suicide—and then embellished them with poetic flourishes about sacrifice and hard work and the democratic future of Germany.

In these last two chapters I have tried to show how postwar economic elites marketed not only their products but also a new economic system, the social market economy, and themselves as its embodiment. Through an increased attention to the visual image, industrialists in the 1950s provided the public with alternatives to a discredited past, marked by individual and collective guilt, personal loss, and material devastation. Through the image of the purified industrialist, West Germans were asked to forget their troubles and to invest their hopes in economic success and prosperity. The new industrialist served, in short, as an antidote to more bitter memories.

But there was a central paradox in the way industrialists remade themselves in the aftermath of Nazism. On one hand, they defended their behavior in the 1930s and during the war by retroactively moralizing it according to older, virtuous traditions. Regardless of his participation in Aryanization, Friedrich Flick remained, in his own words, an *Unternehmer* throughout the Third Reich, and Walther Rohland, despite being a devout Nazi and leader in the war economy, was, in the end, just an iron industry man. On the other hand, industrialists, business publicists, and conservative critics acknowledged that it was time to start over with a different model of capitalism.

This combination of manipulating the past and calling for a new face for capitalism revealed a deep-seated ambivalence in the West German industrial mentality. If the Weimar and Nazi industrialists had really behaved so properly, indeed, under the most trying political circumstances, then why try to reinvent the *Unternehmer?* It is clear that through the metaphor of the new industrialist, postwar businessmen were addressing their own troubled relationship to the past. These anxieties revealed themselves in the very act of industrial self-creation. In some ways the new industrialist was indeed new, demonstrating a fresh aggressiveness in politics and image making and an openness to modern, "American" business practices. But he was also old, modeled on memories of a more romantic era of small capitalism. But if the *Unternehmertyp* was, in the end, a bundle of contradictions—a hybrid created from different national and economic traditions—it was thanks to the putatively American methods of public relations that this new creation could take hold in postwar society. With its assorted publicity tools, such as films, pro-business pamphlets, and public relations departments, industry could confidently declare at the end of 1951 that the "unquestioned reign of *unternehmer-feindliche* (anti-business) slogans . . . has been broken. . . . In all important issues *Unternehmertum* has spoken and is being listened to by the public."[106]

CHAPTER FIVE

Industry, Culture, and the Decline of the West

Up to this point the new industrialist has appeared only as a creation of public relations. Threatened by the legacy of Nazism, West German businessmen reinvented themselves in order to establish a moral authority and sever their connection with a discredited past. Yet it would be a mistake to see industry only through the narrow lens of its publicity efforts. Beginning in the late 1940s, businessmen became increasingly vocal participants in larger cultural debates that were not ostensibly about image making. Motivated in part by the desire to repair their own reputations and imbue capitalism with a new legitimacy, industrialists inserted themselves into contemporary discussions about the role of culture in a fragile postfascist order and about the responsibilities of social and economic elites to their intellectual environments.[1] In the 1950s business leaders transformed the *Unternehmer* into a cultural figure, in part out of an urge to redeem themselves in the eyes of the public but also as a way of understanding themselves and their post-Hitler world. This chapter will examine the process of cultural renewal through the eyes of West Germany's economic elites. Along with social and political awareness, culture became a pillar of the new *Unternehmer* personality that would guide Germany through the vagaries of economic and moral reconstruction and help rebuild a shattered bourgeois world.

Industry and Culture before 1945

Traditionally when scholars have taken up the theme of industry and culture, they have limited their focus to patronage of the fine arts. They have invoked images of wealthy entrepreneurs and sculpture-filled villas, of tycoons sitting for family portraits, and of merchants distributing money to struggling artists in their hometowns. There is, of course, good reason for this emphasis on patron-client relations. From the rich benefactor in Renaissance Italy, to the nineteenth-century bourgeois gentleman with an increasingly disposable wealth, to the Carnegies and the Rockefellers in the United States, we encounter time and again the businessman who enters the realm of culture primarily as philanthropist or collector.

In the German context our attention is immediately drawn to the magnates of the Ruhr. The Krupps filled their family mansion, Villa Hügel, with dozens of paintings by Dutch and Italian masters. Steel industrialist Leopold Hoesch's private artworks became the foundation for the Dürener Museum. The GHH's Paul Reusch amassed a large collection of sculptures and paintings in his Württemberg estate, Katharinenhof. And August Thyssen befriended August Rodin in Paris and purchased dozens of his works, at one time vying successfully with Britain's Queen Victoria for the French sculptor's *Descent from the Cross*.[2]

In Imperial and Weimar Germany, patronage did not only entail the support of painters and sculptors and the building of private collections. The cultural life of highly industrialized cities such as Düsseldorf depended to a great deal on the financial goodwill of their leading employers and manufacturers. Emil Kirdorf, founder of the Gelsenkirchener Bergwerks AG and one of Adolf Hitler's earliest and most enthusiastic supporters, founded in 1919 the Verein der Freunde und Förderer der Düsseldorfer Akademie, which presided over the artistic life of the city. Paul Reusch and Carl Duisberg were generous backers of the Deutsches Museum in Munich.[3] In the 1920s and 1930s Germany's most respected industrial patron, Ernst Poensgen, was a tireless supporter of the cultural life of Düsseldorf. On Poensgen's seventieth birthday in 1941, the Nazis honored the industrialist's lifelong work by founding the Ernst Poensgen Stiftung, which devoted itself to the professional and intellectual edification of Germany's young entrepreneurs, technicians, and managers. In 1944 the foundation's headquarters were destroyed in a bombing raid, and the organization ceased its activities. However, in 1948 Hermann Reusch helped revive the foundation, which again became a financial lifeline for charities, cultural and sport organizations, and civic life in the Ruhr.[4]

Industrialists also contributed to academic scholarship and innovation in architecture and the applied arts. In the absence of U.S.-style charities built on private industrial fortunes, like the Carnegie and Rockefeller Foundations, Germans established a single, centralized philanthropic organization devoted to academic support. Founded in 1920, the Stifterverband für die deutsche Wissenschaft relied on the largesse of Germany's industrialists, who paid contributions into the organization without demanding control over its funding decisions.[5] Private funding also came directly from industrialists such as Stuttgart manufacturer Robert Bosch, who ostensibly out of guilt over profiting from military contracts during World War I, gave generously to the Werkbund, an organization made up of artists devoted to liberalism, humane working conditions, and industrial progress.[6]

The importance of this paternal relationship between industry, the fine arts, and scholarship, which continued into the Nazi years, cannot be overestimated. As providers of jobs and as creators of personal and national fortunes, German industrialists since the nineteenth century had enjoyed the respect (or at least the solicitations) of the intellectual and political establishment, and they responded to their status with the generous dispensation of wealth. But the pre-1945 connections between culture and industry were richer and more varied than this picture indicates. They were not only financial but also material and technological. With the rapid onset of modernization and industrialization, the applied arts—including ceramics, textile design, and miniature painting—merged with the world of manufacturing and factory production.[7] Architecture required materials produced by large-scale industry. Graphic arts, industrial and landscape design, and city planning all demanded the technical know-how and inspiration of the manufacturing world. In short, industrialization had melded the seemingly distinct realms of culture and economy.

In the 1920s Germany's adoption of Taylorist and Fordist approaches to mass production and consumption was accompanied by a kind of industrialization of culture and a reciprocal acculturation of industry. Modernist artists drew increasingly on the materials and images of factory life and *Konsumgüter* (consumer goods), while companies hired freelance artists for advertising and product design.[8] The most famous manifestation of this convergence of art and industry was the Bauhaus School of Design, which in the 1920s united the aesthetic with the practical, as mass-produced goods and architectural designs became the vehicles of an emerging collectivist aesthetic. During and after World War I, Dadaism and Expressionism also attempted to erase this boundary between the arts and mechanized "everyday life."

While in the early part of the twentieth century the techniques, images, and sensibilities of mass assembly-line production penetrated the realm of art, we must not overstate the role businessmen played in this transformation. Most industrialists spent little time, at least in their professional capacity, on intellectual matters, and to the extent that their firms engaged in cultural activities or provided raw materials for artistic undertakings, they themselves kept aloof from the broader significance of this link. To most businessmen, *Kultur* belonged to the world outside the firm. Most industrialists before 1945 still prided themselves on their practical, businesslike natures, which found little time for cerebral ruminations. This view, however, would change after the collapse of Nazism.

Industrialists and West Germany's Spiritual Renewal

After 1945 the dream of a nationalist utopia was dead for most Germans. While various social and political milieus—the churches, conservatives, communists, and socialists—clung to their specific group memories and prescriptions for the ideal moral order, West Germans in general found themselves in an intellectual and ideological vacuum. In the aftermath of Nazism and defeat, Germany's elites searched for untainted cultural symbols that could instill a sense of pride into a demoralized population. But where would they discover the ingredients of a "legitimate" postnationalist culture? Communism, at least in its Soviet incarnation, offered little to most educated Germans, who blamed the allegedly revolution-thirsty masses for having supported Hitler in Germany and now Stalin in the USSR. The far right offered even less, having spawned the Nazi movement to which the unruly throngs were ultimately drawn. In the realm of art, National Socialist aesthetics and the socialist realism of the Soviet Union further implicated both sides of the political spectrum in the crimes of totalitarianism. In the eyes of many West Germans in the 1940s and 1950s, the only untainted institution left was the church, which despite a general lack of civil courage during the Third Reich, claimed to be the body that would lead Germany's spiritual renewal.[9]

If the chief hindrances to West Germany's cultural rebirth were the totalitarian legacies of fascism and Soviet communism, then the challenge for elites was to cultivate a counterethic free from the taint of collectivism, ideology, and politics. Not only did West Germany demand a new philosophical raison d'être; it also needed leaders who would assume the responsibility of propagating a moral ethos that would bolster the country's material rebirth. Industrialists nominated themselves for this task. West Germany's business leaders, unlike the church, were able to combine an ethic of individualism, economic competition, and material success. They depicted themselves as the true embodiment of the free personality that totalitarianism sought to subdue. They traced the history of economic and political freedom and exalted themselves as the inheritors of a long history of liberal thinking. In their adherence to entrepreneurship and innovation, they portrayed themselves as the consummate nonconformists who resisted the onset of massification and social leveling. In short, they infused their economic mission—company profits and national prosperity—with a spiritual dimension: the protection of Germany and Europe's cultural essence.

Against the backdrop of the Cold War, this convergence of the economy and culture should not be surprising. Industrialists, as the guardians of the nation's material well-being, provided both the economic foundation and the philosophical justification for the war against communism. Industrialists throughout Europe and the United States saw themselves as at once the creators of wealth and the trailblazers of an ethic of Western individualism that stood in contrast to the enemy's collectivist worldview. But with a rapidly growing economy, this new self-identity actually placed businessmen in a philosophical quandary. How could West Germany's manufacturers provide basic goods and luxury items for consumers, while at the same time protecting them from the very antiindividualist, collectivist tendencies that accompanied the redistribution of wealth and the homogenization of tastes and purchasing habits? This dilemma exposed anxieties left over from the 1920s and 1930s and revealed the contradictions in postwar industry's economic and cultural philosophy: both large firms and small entrepreneurs were depending increasingly on the consumer—the "mass man"—for their business success. While producer goods like steel and coal, electronics, and dyes still represented the backbone of the West German economy, they declined somewhat in importance as the onset of mass consumer production that marked the prior two decades proceeded apace. In the increasingly affluent 1950s, particularly the latter half, when conspicuous consumption became a defining feature of West German life, companies such as Siemens, Krupp, Bayer, and BASF devoted ever more of their resources to mass-produced household and luxury goods—from radios, televisions, and ovens to cars and vinyl records. These were the artifacts of the Economic Miracle. But if the *Wirtschaftswunder* provided industrialists with increased profits, it also revived an existential paradox, one already evident before World War II but that industrialists experienced even more acutely in the 1950s. Industry was now catering to the masses, but how would it prevent the public from establishing hegemony over the country's spiritual life? These questions burdened all postwar elites, on both the Left and the Right, whose fears of collectivism (in the form of Soviet-sponsored communism) converged with fears of the collectivism inherent in mass consumer society. What these commentators often did not acknowledge in their conflation of totalitarianism and consumerism was that the latter site of "mass" activity, the marketplace, held out the notion of choice—the very thing not found in communist states.

In the 1950s industrialists struggled with these paradoxes by looking at their own profession in cultural terms. While they maintained a healthy interest in high culture and the fine arts, they now, picking up from the 1920s, expanded their notion of culture to include the images and products that they themselves were creating in their factories.[10] In short, the 1950s saw an accelerated turn to consumer or commodity culture as a legitimate object of inquiry among industrialists. The marketplace became the site of both hope and concern, as industry realized how much power it potentially wielded over the mental—and not just material—security of the German nation. As BDI managing director Gustav Stein argued, "Leading circles in the German economy must take to heart the responsibility for culture and *Menschenbil-*

dung (human development)[11] and, out of this conviction, exercise the duty and courage to influence and steer the market."[12] If they were to maintain their power over the masses, industrialists could not simply *respond* to the shifting desires and whims of the consumers. They would have to develop proactive manufacturing and marketing techniques that would save the consumers from themselves. For one critic, Hans-Joachim Sperr, a cultural editor with the *Süddeutsche Zeitung,* the key was to be found in the realm of the visual. In explicit contrast to the industrial art of the Bauhaus, which he held responsible for promoting a totalitarian ideal through mass production, Sperr called on businessmen to create an anticollectivist industrial aesthetic that would wean the public from *Massengüter* and kitsch: "From the postage stamp to the police uniform, industry's cooperation will be indispensable if the optics of German life are never again to take on collectivist characteristics." Sperr entreated industrialists and artists to forge a united visual front—to rebuild Germany's international cultural reputation and to redevelop the "German taste, which has so catastrophically disappeared," having been replaced by the "uneducated mass tastes."[13] Sperr proposed founding a journal called *Kunst und Auftrag,* which would highlight the artistic manifestations of daily life—from furniture and kitchen appliances to textiles and packing materials—while offering alternatives to a homogeneity in product design. A group of experts known as the Bundesverband der Industrieform, Sperr proposed, would work with museums to sponsor exhibits on nonconformist "building and living." "These exhibitions, if prepared with the correct propagandistic aim, could not only engage the experts at home and abroad but could exercise an inestimable influence on the public's aesthetic development (*Geschmacksbildung*)."[14] To further support these aims, an Akademie für Industrieform would fill the space once occupied by the Bauhaus and the Werkbund, albeit stripped of the leftist utopianism and the cheery progressivism that, respectively, characterized these organizations. Finally and importantly, private industry and banks, and not the "bureaucratic state," would support these new organizations.[15]

At first glance these proposals suggest the breakdown of the division between highbrow and consumer culture in industry's estimation. Industrialists had seemingly succumbed to the allures of commodity culture. Yet on a closer reading these ideas reflect the sentiments of individuals who still proudly adhered to a view of German products as quality creations designed for a select group of discriminating consumers. Indeed, the motivation behind groups such as the BDI's newly founded Arbeitskreis für industrielle Formgebung was entirely patronizing: to free the consumer industry from the "inferior, cultureless mass-produced goods" and "from dishonest, and affected (*affektgeladenen*) forms." The organization's goal, Gustav Stein elaborated further, was to replace mass kitsch with "materially true . . . , *hand-*

werklich clean, and in the truest sense beautiful and, simultaneously, useful shapes."[16] These passages make clear that industrialists, even while adapting to the structural changes in the economy and society, were struggling with the concept of consumer culture and economic egalitarianism. Notwithstanding the astounding success of companies such as Volkswagen, the symbol of both high quality and mass production, many industrialists were slow to abandon their elitist understanding of the economy. For them rebuilding West Germany meant not only selling more products but reviving a dying *bürgerliche* culture, which depended on a disdain and fear of the masses and their cultural tastes that had defined Nazi Germany.

The United States, Democracy, and the Revolt of the Masses

If commodity culture challenged the self-perception of industrial elites, this was as much due to an ambivalence about the birthplace of the consumer—the United States—as it was about Germany's own experience with mass movements. In the 1950s not just communism but also the popular and materialist culture of the United States served as the countermodels against which West Germans forged their intellectual self-understanding. Heide Fehrenbach and Ute Poiger have recently detailed West German elites' perceptions of the United States as the homeland of cultural philistinism, aesthetic vulgarity, and base popular tastes. They have looked in particular at West German youths' attraction to U.S. films, whose glorification of fast cars and loud music stood in contrast to the more sentimental German notions of homeland and a more refined European taste.[17] In the many organizations devoted to the German concept of *Heimat,* such as the Rheinische Verein für Denkmalpflege und Heimatschutz, we can see the participation of leading business leaders.[18] By protecting the most basic manifestation of bourgeois life—the traditional home—industrialists hoped to ensure the material security of a nation flanked by U.S. consumerism and Soviet collectivism.

Despite this fear of a cultural assault from across the Atlantic, industrial reactions to the United States were not uniformly hostile. Rather, America was a bundle of images, often contradictory, from which industry drew selected models and lessons. On one hand, the United States represented an unfettered individualism that business leaders saw as the antidote to the collectivism that had defined Germany's tragic and violent recent history and the current conditions in East Germany and the Soviet Bloc; America was the homeland of economic opportunity, free-market ideals, and publicity philosophies that industrialists were learning to accept. On the other hand, as the bastion of democracy, popular will, and crass consumerism, America, as an abstraction, represented cultural and political ideas that many Germans saw as anathema to their own elevated tastes and elitist sentiments.[19]

In a 1954 publication called *Unternehmer in der Politik*, Gustav Stein and Herbert Gross elaborated on this elitist suspicion of democracy in a chapter titled "Task of the New Elite."

> We live in an age of the "overtaxed (*überforderten*) voter," manifested in the continual emptying (*Entleerung*) of the economy and society by politics and the state. Democracy, in the conception of Rousseau[,] . . . certainly leads man away from absolutism but does not entirely free him. More often, it re-enslaves him through the new "peoples sovereignty," or the voting masses. National Socialism and Bolshevism are the logical consequence of the democratic principle, namely the rule of the majority of the mass. In connection with the principle of equality, democracy leads to a total politicization of life. Democracy, in its Jacobin component, is the flag-bearer for collectivism, socialism, codetermination, or for whatever form enslavement under the state takes. Democracy of this type is essentially the archenemy of liberalism, which protects the unlimited freedom of humans but holds the power of the state in check.[20]

In this passage we can witness the many hopes and anxieties that crystallized around the reintroduction of democracy in postwar Germany—fears of the total state, a disdain for the masses, a suspicion of politics, and an ambivalent embrace of liberalism and individual freedom.[21] These views were not per se new. They resonated with nineteenth-century romantic critiques of Enlightened rationality and with the emphasis in Catholic social theory on the evils that sprang from the French Revolution and the Jacobin Reign of Terror—the moment when the unruly masses were unleashed. This fear of the masses had been a common theme in European philosophy and sociology since the nineteenth century, growing into an obsession of European elites in the 1920s.[22] Yet despite these continuities between prewar and postwar thinking throughout Europe, after 1945 democracy and totalitarianism became the repositories for cultural and political anxieties that were specific to a posttotalitarian West Germany. Both political systems, many West German elites felt, unleashed a dangerous collective will that they had seen realized in Nazism and Stalinism and now in the Americanization of West Germany. Democracy and totalitarianism both laid the groundwork for a tyranny of the majority; they invited the manipulation of the public, which responded to ephemeral sensations and charismatic provocations—be they at a Nazi Party rally or a jazz concert—instead of the sober and time-tested ideals of Western humanism.[23]

This skepticism of democracy emerged not simply from a long-standing European fear of U.S. cultural hegemony but from Germans' memories of the fragile Weimar democracy, which most industrialists had rejected in the

1920s and early 1930s. If the despair generated by the Great Depression had pulled the masses toward the nationalist right, this, many West Germans believed, was the result of the flawed experiment in democratic government, which had ceded too much political power to an unruly and unsophisticated voting public. Industrialists, in promoting these views, were sharing the ideas of many intellectuals in the early postwar period. Historians such as Gerhard Ritter, Friedrich Meinecke, and Hans Rothfels blamed mass democracy for the demise of Weimar and the rise of totalitarianism.[24] In making the link between democracy and totalitarianism, postwar elites were, of course, conveniently forgetting that it was not democracy per se that had allowed the rise of Nazism but, rather, its suspension during the late Weimar years in favor of rule by emergency presidential decrees. While memories of the 1920s and early 1930s were selective, they did accompany a fear among postwar elites that democracy would again unleash the will of the masses and would lay the groundwork for a dictatorship by the communists and the unions. In short, while most industrialists ultimately welcomed a democratic form of government after the disaster of fascism, this was not without reservations and fears that this type of political organization carried within it the seeds of its own destruction.

Art Exhibitions and Cultural Patronage

Ambivalence about democracy and mass culture did not prevent many industrialists from appealing to these very forces. Both for the good of its own business and in order to remove the stigma of Nazism, industry recognized the need to promote, alongside more individualist high cultural projects, the democratic, anti-elitist images of everyday life. But this was hardly an attempt to "out-democratize" the Americans through an embrace of popular culture. Rather, it still entailed a promotion of high culture and an "undemocratic individualism"[25] as an antidote to spiritual unrest and social tensions. By instilling an appreciation of art among the people, industrialists hoped to speak to and eventually tame the masses through the visual representation of hard work and individuality.

An event sponsored by a number of Ruhr firms in 1952 reveals this urge. In recognition of the need to reawaken a respect for the once-sanctified heavy industry, and as a way of cultivating an aesthetic sensibility among factory workers and the public, the city of Düsseldorf and the WES cohosted an exhibition called *Iron and Steel*. While its stated purpose was to introduce artists to the "raw, but starkly pulsating and colorful life of the iron and steel world," it was clearly an attempt to reinvest the Ruhr with an aesthetic and cultural legitimacy.[26] A jury of businessmen and art critics convened in 1951 to choose the winners, who then created the works to be displayed the next year.[27] When the exhibition opened in 1952, painted, sculpted, and photographed images of foundries, furnaces, steelworkers, and miners greeted the visitors. For the exhibition's program, the corporate sponsors, mostly companies from throughout the Ruhr, produced advertisements touting the miraculous comeback of heavy industry after near annihilation. At a time when the Allies were still debating the status of the Ruhr, these ads tapped into a lingering nostalgia for the region's mythical, trouble-free past and present worries about its future. By asserting an affinity between industry, art, and culture, these ads, through the depiction of bronzed, axe-wielding bodies and glistening new factories, promised a future of material and cultural greatness. In his introduction to the exhibition program, WES president Wilhelm Salewski also invoked memories of a more glorious period of rapid industrialization and artistic patronage in Germany, when iron and steel stood not for tanks and cannons but for peaceful production, rapid economic growth, and cultural excellence.

The *Iron and Steel* exhibition was not a major success. It boasted few visitors and little national attention. But it did reveal the extent to which industrialists were now thinking about art and culture as tools for professional regeneration, national renewal, and public manipulation. The exhibit saw businessmen calling on the aesthetic appeal of the industrial world. They recognized the legitimating force that culture possessed, and they sought to exploit it to the advantage of their own reputations and that of West German industry. As Germans rebuilt their country after the war, they drew on a mythologized past of material success embodied in the first industrial revolution—and inserted its legacy into the unstable present. Germany's erstwhile economic greatness provided hope for those yet to benefit from the remarkable recovery of the preceding seven years. A hundred years earlier, Germany had industrialized and modernized itself faster than any Western nation, and, this exhibit asserted, it was doing so again.[28]

With their increased attention to product design and advertising, industrial trade fairs, and exhibitions like *Iron and Steel*, industrialists were demonstrating a newfound interest in the visual aspects of big business and economic success. Yet we must not see businessmen's relationship to culture as always so self-referential. Industrialists were not only interested in artistic renderings of their familiar factory world; they were also involved in broader debates about culture—from the tug-of-war between abstract and representational art, to the social and philosophical significance of visual beauty, to the potential for a nationalist aesthetics after Hitler. To a degree unimaginable before 1945, these discussions were played out at company meetings, in the economic press, on the radio, and in a number of local and national business organizations devoted to the support of museums, academies, and arts education. The Vereinigung der Freunde von Kunst und Kultur im Bergbau, for example, published a journal called *Der Anschnitt*, which reported on cultural events in the Ruhr and attempted to instill an intellectual awareness into Germany's businessmen. Local IHKs set up cultural branches and sponsored music, theater, and art exhibits. The Museumspende der westdeutschen Industrie donated hundreds of paintings to museums around the country.[29]

While these organizations exercised a decisive influence on attitudes about art, theater, patronage, and design, the most significant forum for discussions about high and low culture was the BDI's Kulturkreis (Cultural Circle). Founded in the summer of 1951 by Gustav Stein, Hermann Reusch, Bavarian textile manufacturer and BDI vice-president Otto Vogel, and twenty-four other industrialists from around Germany, the Kulturkreis is one of the most revealing and underresearched sites of industrial self-understanding after the war. The organization was premised on the view that National Socialism had left Germans in a spiritual vacuum and that the responsibility lay with German industry to guide the country toward a new cultural awareness. Conceived ostensibly as a revival of a tradition of industrial patronage of the arts (*Mäzenatentum*), the Kulturkreis, which was made up of both big businessmen such as Reusch and independent entrepreneurs like Vogel, set as its larger goal a spiritual renewal that transcended region or profession. The organization's preamble reveals the imposing presence of the recent past, the sense of unity in adversity, and a faith in the redemptive power of culture:

The catastrophe that came to Germany has forced our people to spend its entire energy eking out a material existence. An unprecedented impoverishment of its spiritual life has been the result of such a reordering of the will. One of the first endeavors that has fallen victim to this self-limitation is art. If for many people art is a nice luxury that belongs only to happy times, it becomes, in times of distress, one of life's necessities.[30]

Germany had suffered spiritually during the time of dictatorship, war, and defeat, and the Kulturkreis hoped to reintroduce artistic and intellectual greatness to a demoralized people. With annual contributions from the BDI's member firms, the Kulturkreis supported painters, sculptors, architects, musicians, and writers who did not otherwise receive funding from the state or who embodied the qualities of individualism so necessary to fend off collectivism. The organization awarded individual scholarships, raised funds for museums, sponsored exhibitions, and provided support for established writers and critics.[31]

Although the Kulturkreis, at least on paper, limited itself to these few functions, the public was not aware of it. In its first years, individuals and organizations bombarded Gustav Stein and Hermann Reusch with dramatic hardship stories and requests for financial aid that went well beyond the group's stated funding rules. These letters spoke of missing children, bombed-out homes, loved ones imprisoned in Siberia, and truncated artistic careers. Five years after the end of Nazism, these war-weary citizens were looking to industry for a little financial succor.

Yet most individuals and organizations turned to the Kulturkreis not merely out of physical want but also to gain a partner in the revival of Germany's proud cultural heritage. The German Red Cross requested donations to pay for sculptures in their new Berlin headquarters. The Ranke Society appealed for financial help for projects that, in the director's words, dealt openly and honestly with the country's past but which also corrected false stereotypes about the German people.[32] Professor Hans-Joachim Schoeps of Erlangen University wrote to Reusch asking for help in funding his new book, *Das andere Preussen* [The other Prussia], which he hoped would amend a global image of Prussians defined by "drills, polish, and barracks squares" (*Drill und Schliff und Kasernenhof*).[33] Reusch, while sympathetic to such patriotic goals, rejected them because they did not fall under the purview of the Kulturkreis.[34]

What projects did the Kulturkreis undertake in its first years? One of the earliest was the preparation of its inaugural book of the year, *Das Goldene Dach*, which, as we will see in the next chapter, sought to attract the proletariat to bourgeois living and entrepreneurial thinking. In 1952 the second publication was a study about Karl Friedrich Schinkel, the renowned Berlin architect who was to provide an example of genius, diligence, and civic and national pride. Next to these annual volumes the Kulturkreis undertook a variety of other projects designed to revive an intellectually dormant country: preservation of decaying books and manuscripts; prevention of cultural artifacts from leaving German soil; Christmas painting and sculpture sales; an annual exhibition of abstract art under the name *ars viva;* restoration of church organs; music competitions (with, on occasion, composer Carl Orff as judge); awarding prizes in literature; sponsorship of architecture and design exhibitions; and publication of *Jahresring*, a journal that excerpted poems, short stories, and essays that reflected "artistic currents of the day."[35]

Despite the diversity of these activities, it is clear that the members of the Kulturkreis, under the leadership of Hermann Reusch and Gustav Stein, devoted most of its time and resources to the fine arts, particularly painting and sculpture. Indeed the organization, as Werner Bührer has demonstrated, became the site of a long-standing debate about the social function of high art in postwar Germany. As the Kulturkreis gained in prestige and wealth, and as museums welcomed the group's generosity in expanding their collections, this internal discourse was of no minor consequence; it had the potential to affect collecting and exhibiting decisions on regional, national, and international levels. Some members of the art world criticized the Kulturkreis on ideological grounds and assumed that the group's conservative leadership necessarily rejected all modern (and especially nonrepresentational) art and clung to the traditions of "fascist art."[36] They accused the Kulturkreis of promoting a neo-*volk*ish aesthetic by favoring works that celebrated a Germanic past or that aestheticized labor and soil in a dangerously Nazilike manner. By rejecting the art of the modern world in favor of German romanticism, industrialists, critics argued, were perpetuating a long-gone nationalist ideal that should have been buried in 1945.[37]

These accusations were not entirely fair. The *Iron and Steel* exhibition itself was evidence that industrialists were not averse to artistic renderings of industrial age or "proletarian" labor. Despite the assumption among critics that the Kulturkreis was hostile to abstract art, by 1955 the organization had in fact proven itself evenly divided on the theme.[38] On one side, individuals such as Otto Vogel saw modern art (such as the works of Willi Baumeister or Julius Bissier) as anathema to the goals of rediscovering and promulgating a positive national aesthetic. They argued that people could not appreciate art and thereby help revive Germany culturally if they did not understand what they were looking at. Former IG Farben director Heinrich Gattineau, although not a Kulturkreis member, made this fear even more explicit in a letter to Hermann Reusch. Abstract art, he argued, has implicated itself time and again in the dangerous philosophies of nihilism. It set as its goal "the documentation of the spiritual disunity of . . . capitalism and the decline of the West." At a time when Germans and Europeans were trying to reconsolidate themselves along free-market lines, Gattineau suggested, it was self-defeating for industrialists to be promoting such a harmful, anticapitalist aesthetic.[39]

But while to some industrialists abstract art was impenetrable, purposeless, or even destructive, to others it was the truest manifestation of the individuality and nonconformity to which businessmen devoted so much verbal energy. Promoting modern art was, on one hand, a pragmatic response to large vacancies in this area in German museums (due to the Nazis' condemnation and removal of "degenerate art"). On the other hand, it was a defiant statement against representational art that defined not only Nazi aesthetics but also socialist realism, whose totalitarian tendencies industry's critics conveniently ignored. If, to the supporters of modern art, realism was implicated in the crimes of both Nazism and Stalinism, then it seemed only logical that industry support the very modernists who had suffered for their anticollectivist images.[40]

Despite these sometimes heated debates, art funding was never an either/ or prospect, and the Kulturkreis always cast its net widely when giving awards to artists or purchasing their works. Ironically, under the chairmanship of the conservative Reusch, who himself had little sympathy for modernism, the organization took a surprisingly friendly stance toward abstract art. Reusch, whose personal tastes ran to the likes of Caspar David Friedrich, must be given credit for not imposing his views on the group for the sake of promoting a conservative cultural politics. For the Kulturkreis chairman, giving free reign to the artistic expressions of the individual made a more powerful statement against collectivism than the cultivation of a conformist and sentimental German art. "There are," declared Reusch, "different points of departure from which one approaches the problems of culture and the tasks of *Kulturpolitik*. . . . A conservative man will wrestle with the questions of culture differently than a liberal. But what I want to make clear is that in this group, we will be active in an area where there are no differences. We who are here are all simply workers and craftsmen on the great common dome of mankind. It is up to posterity to decide if we have succeeded with our construction."[41]

Cultural Pessimism and Ideas of Decline

Industrialists' attitudes about artist patronage tell us much about the cultural debates of the 1950s and the mentalities of the country's economic elites. Yet even more revealing of industry's cultural ideals were the discussions and speeches about culture at the Kulturkreis's annual meetings, which were reprinted in journals, pamphlets, and newspapers and distributed widely. Often in the presence of West German president Theodor Heuss and other illustrious guests, speakers such as poet and art collector Carl Burckhardt, physicist Pascual Jordan, or conservative sociologist Arnold Gehlen offered their readings of mass psychology and diagnosed the crises facing West Germany's and Europe's social and economic elites.[42]

Perhaps the Kulturkreis's most influential visitor was Spanish philosopher José Ortega y Gasset, whose *Revolt of the Masses* (1930) remained a bestseller in West Germany twenty years after its initial publication.[43] Ortega was one of the most admired figures in German cultural circles in the 1950s. Before the triumph of Hitler, he had presciently foreseen the dangers inherent in mass politics, and his elitist and pessimistic premonitions still resonated with an audience that saw itself perpetually threatened by a social and spiritual *Verflachung* (leveling, or more accurately, superficialization). In his September 1953 speech to the Kulturkreis titled "Is There a European Cultural Consciousness" Ortega warned that the West was undergoing a major crisis of confidence and self-definition. A half-century of mass movements and moral weakness had severed Europe from its proud cultural heritage. Even as a post-Hitler Europe was coming together economically and politically, its individual components were drifting apart, lost without a sense of what had made the West uniquely great. In the tradition of political philosopher Claude-Henri de Saint-Simon, who a century and a half earlier had besought France's industrialists to adopt a European identity,[44] Ortega appealed to an audience of businessmen to espouse and defend the ideal of Europe (however vague this concept actually was, Ortega conceded). Despite the challenges it faced, Europe, with the help of Germany's educated and industrial elite, could, Ortega felt, survive a crisis born of world war, the dissolution of aristocratic ideas, the penetration of U.S. culture, and the onset of social egalitarianism.[45]

Five years after Ortega sounded his familiar elitist theme, Bundestag president Eugen Gerstenmaier delivered a speech to the Kulturkreis that also promoted elitist ideals as a viable alternative to communism. Gerstenmaier's September 1958 speech, "On the Meaning and Fate of the Elite in a Democracy," encapsulated the many currents of industrial self-understanding that had defined the Kulturkreis since its founding eight years earlier. He began by invoking the honor of the military opposition to Hitler, in which he himself took an active role.[46] Colonel-General Ludwig Beck and other officers and politicians like him who tried to bring down Hitler were, like the industrialists, the embodiment of the patriotism and individualism under attack by the masses. Gerstenmaier drew on the words of sociologist Karl Mannheim to declare that "the democratic mass society is *elitenfeindlich* (anti-elitist)."[47] The challenge for industrialists, then, was to maintain their own rarefied social status while making a place for the workers in the new affluent society. The rapprochement with the workers meant promising them a large piece of the pie, instilling in them *unternehmerische* thoughts, providing them with homes and gardens, and quelling their violent urges.

As both the Ortega and Gerstenmaier speeches indicate, at stake for the Kulturkreis was not simply the cultural renewal of the German nation but the survival of industrialists' own *bürgerliche* milieu in a modern world. Nazism had already struck a hard blow to the industrialists' socially stratified world; indeed, it had implicated industry in massive crimes. Now the consumers and their popular culture threatened to put the final nail in the coffin of the *Bürgertum*. In the words of one observer, "The horrible catastrophes of the last decades have not only decimated the strata of intellectual leaders in the most unfathomable way. They have also pushed them materially into the proletarian underclass."[48] Surely this was an exaggeration of the economic difficulties that social elites faced in the aftermath of World War II. Yet it is a telling statement of the elitism that underlay the cultural debates waged not only by industrialists but also by a great many conservative elites in the 1950s.[49] Economic devastation and the subsequent emergence of mass consumption had led to the irreparable breakdown of social hierarchies. The *Wohlstandsgesellschaft* had created tremendous opportunities for consumer and producer, for worker and management; but it also challenged the cherished realities of social stratification.

The Kulturkreis relied not only on famous public intellectuals to articulate its embattled elitism. In their own speeches and writings, industrialists unveiled their reading of culture through the tropes of mass psychology, social leveling, crisis, and degeneration. Otto Vogel, who was known among industrial circles for his exaggerated turns of phrase and foreboding ruminations, characterized in stark terms the crisis that Europe and the West faced:

> Will the culture of the West again be able to overcome the assault of the masses from without and within? Is the West, positioned between the new and the old world, still in and of itself a sustaining idea? Indeed is culture still in fact possible? . . . Must we fatalistically accept the dread and fear that seek to drive mankind toward the collective as the apocalyptic hoofbeats of our culture's decline? These are the questions that spring upon us from the demonic subsoil of our mechanized and depersonalized age.[50]

In the 1950s Vogel's words, while melodramatic, were in fact typical invocations of the Spenglerian language of decline. German cultural critics after the war portrayed the present as an epoch of regression, as the virtues of the West or, the Christian West (*das christliche Abendland*), were quickly withering under the assault of communism, socialism, consumerism, and U.S. popular culture. It was up to the economic elites to stem the tide of collectivism. In the despairing words of Düsseldorf banker Kurt Forberg, the spokesman for the Arbeitsgemeinschaft kultureller Organisationen Düsseldorf: "We must do something to uphold and to save from decline what we understand to be *bürgerliche* culture."[51]

It was relatively commonplace after the war to invoke the language of cultural decay—*Verfall, Zerfall, Niedergang, Untergang*[52]—so familiar to intellectuals in Western and Central Europe.[53] In some respects postwar elites were confronting the problem of modernity that intellectuals had addressed since the nineteenth century. The language of decline was remarkably similar to the Right Wing cultural criticism of Imperial and Weimar Germany. Like Julius Langbehn or Paul Lagarde a half-century earlier, postwar conservative intellectuals were engaging in a familiar "politics of cultural despair."[54] Ironically, even men of science and industry could not mask their skepticism about technology and the very process of modernization to which many of them could attribute their own business successes and fortunes.[55] This skepticism about modernity was not only limited to the Right; it also found a voice on the Left through the Frankfurt school's Western Marxist critique of mass culture.[56] Thus Gustav Stein, the secretary of the Kulturkreis, spoke for a large group of Germans across the political spectrum when he diagnosed the problems facing West Germany, where the culture-sapping forces of modernity and industrialization endangered the "working man."

Mechanization, collectivization, and massification threaten in an ever greater measure to destroy the contact of the working man with the creative substance of art and science. With all the perfection in the technical and productive area comes the threat that the human will atrophy and wither away. The creative achievements of industry and labor that lead us into the future will only be lasting if we maintain contact with the creative elements of our cultural life, which stimulate us and grant us new powers.[57]

Stein seemed to be echoing a romantic, middle-class (*mittelständische*) capitalism embodied in new organizations such as the ASU, which cast a wary glance on large-scale, modern business. Yet Stein's words were relics of cultural criticism that industrialists, shopkeepers, and independent entrepreneurs had shared since long before 1933. They were a permanent feature of Europe's cultural landscape that transcended the divisions between class and company size.

Despite the similarities between pre- and post-1945 cultural criticism, however, there were some major differences as well. First, cultural pessimism was now stripped of its communitarian features. For conservative and liberal thinkers alike, cultural renewal was no longer to be found in the community but in the individual. While, like the romantic genius, the individual was still to be grounded in a larger community, this was no longer a national, biological, or racist entity, but one based on international cooperation, collective "Atlantic" security, and a shared understanding of Western and European traditions.

Second, postwar German elites for the most part abandoned their prewar distinction between Germany, as the home of *Kultur*, and "the West" as the embodiment of *Zivilisation*. In the name of Atlantic unity and anticommunism, Germans, whether self-declared conservatives or not, began to see themselves as part of rather than in opposition to the Western traditions. To be sure, Western Marxists argued for distinctions between the positive legacy of the Enlightenment—individualism—and the negative, namely, mass society. But increasingly the political and international realities of the 1950s engendered social and cultural elites' changing ideological self-understanding, which entailed a cautious yet sincere rapprochement with the West.

A final difference between pre-1945 and postwar conservative cultural criticism was the redemptive role now attributed to the economy and its leaders. While Western Marxists credited the cultural and social crisis to capitalism, many liberal and conservative West Germans supplanted their prior nationalism with an *economic* patriotism that inevitably boded well for the standing of the businessman. If the capitalist (often portrayed as the Jewish businessman or banker) was formerly the antihero amongst cultural conservatives—indeed the very symbol of cultural and racial decadence against which they fought—after 1945 he was to be the very source of Germany's renewal. In the industrialists' view, it was up to industrialists to fill a moral space once occupied by the destroyed *Bildungsbürgertum* (educated bourgeoisie) and the Junkers, who had proven incapable of withstanding National Socialism. Now it was up to the *Wirtschaftsbürgertum* (economic bourgeoisie) to fulfill the role it had always been denied. In short, postwar cultural elites and business leaders now had the chance to rid capitalism of its negative connotations and elevate the industrialist to the level of a savior who would pull the country out of its cultural quagmire and fight the communist enemy. Next to the artist, the intellectual, the poet, and the genius stood the industrialist, imbued with a spirit of individualism and a pragmatic understanding of wealth and economic prosperity. The new *Unternehmer* would bring together the realms of the practical and the ideological, the political and the cultural. In short, the economy (as the realm of production, consumption, and free-market individualism) would serve as the basis for a new sense of citizenship after the war.[58]

The role of cultural hero was one to which industrialists happily assented. But in the industrialists' view, this privilege was not just bestowed upon them by recent political developments. Rather, industry publicists argued that there was something more fundamental in the *Kulturarbeit* of the businessman. In a 1954 article titled "Culture: Foundation of the Economy," Gustav Stein articulated how culture was, in fact, the industrialist's birthright because economic security was the foundation of all existence. Without a buoyant market economy, there would be no possibility for culture.[59] Like Saint-Simon and Auguste Comte, who had envisioned a society led by artists and industrialists, Gustav Stein saw businessmen as the promoters and defenders of the very freedoms that allowed any artistic or cultural activity to take place. They were involved in every step of the process of cultural creation. The free competition that they defended against communism and *dirigisme* was the very thing that allowed all individualists—be they artists, musicians, or entrepreneurs—to rise above the crowd. If such persons, in a leveled society, could demonstrate the unique combination of humanism and a love of freedom necessary to distinguish themselves, then it again fell to the socially and culturally responsible businessmen—gathered in groups like the Kulturkreis—to provide the material and monetary means for them to excel further. In short, it was up to industry "to exhaust all of life's possibilities in modern civilization in order to save man as a 'person' from spiritual and intellectual leveling. . . . One must do everything to arm the insecure and mistrusting man and keep him from being pulled into the undertow of collectivism."[60]

According to Gustav Stein there would be grave consequences if industry failed to seize the reins of cultural authority. Without preemptive measures, he argued, specialization and rationalization would transform individual workers into automatons, who were easy prey for Bolshevism. The human personality would be lost under the drone of factory machinery and the regulated workday, and the laboring masses would take refuge in the false god of communism. Such a renunciation of the individual ego, argued Otto Vogel elsewhere, would not only have cultural, economic, and political, but sociobiological consequences as well. "A sickness of mankind ensues when the magical forces of the individual personality, which are strong in faith, are prevented from exercising themselves, when the individual shirks his duties and abandons his mission, or when the *Volkskörper* (national body) is lacking strong-willed, powerful, self-assured, and responsible personalities."[61] Again, while this risk existed, prosperity and entrepreneurial thoughts would prevent this nightmarish scene from ever being realized. There was still time to reverse this catastrophic development. By preserving and strengthening *Unternehmertum*—the epitome of freethinking and unfettered individualism —one could resist the encroachments of modernity and collectivism and rid the national body of its democratic and egalitarian pestilence.

The above scenario of degeneration pervaded the speeches and writings of the Kulturkreis during the 1950s, especially during the first half of the decade. On one hand it reflected broader cultural discourses found throughout Western Europe after World War II. The fears of modernity and decline were not by any means exclusive to industry or to West Germany. On the other hand, the version articulated by business leaders represented an extension of West German industry's particular public relations effort. By figuring the industrialist as the victim of modernity and a national hero, industrialists were broadening their attempts to recast the *Unternehmer* beyond economic primers and pocket biographies to a new medium: culture. But while industry was intent on moving beyond Nazism with the help of *Kultur*, it did not hesitate to exploit fascist language in the process. The images of sickness, the *Volk*, and the body reveal clearly some of the continuities between Nazi and post-Nazi Germany. The persistence of *volk*ish language to characterize social and political developments exposes the success of the Nazis in transforming not only the mental but the linguistic world of Germany. That Otto Vogel's pathological visions could resonate in the business world and, indeed, in the broader public indicates the tentative nature of the break with the past and the confused political and cultural language of the day. Conservatism, although positioning itself in opposition to the freedom-crushing forces of Nazism and Stalinism, clearly still partook of established organicist tropes that had served the German Right so well before and after 1933. Clearly West Germans, both mentally and linguistically, could not transcend twelve years of National Socialism overnight.

It must be emphasized that industrialists such as Otto Vogel and Hermann Reusch, despite their frightening language, were no apologists for National Socialism. Indeed, as self-proclaimed anti-Nazis both men assumed (presumptuously) the authority to wield a Hitlerian language without fear of recrimination. Both men represented what appears to be an industrialist type who survived the Nazi years with career and reputation intact and who, therefore, had the seeming luxury to fashion himself as the champion of economic and cultural elitism. Unlike those who had been active Nazis and who had landed in jail after the war, the men who represented the Kulturkreis could afford to defend German industry with elaborate theses about the political and cultural significance of the economy. With more or less clean consciences, they countered the prevalent images of capitalism as greedy and morally pernicious with the weapon of culture and the time-tested—and in many ways discredited—tropes of cultural criticism.

Finally, one must be careful, in looking at this language of cultural pessimism, not to exaggerate its resonance after the mid-1950s. To be sure, well into the 1960s, intellectuals and cultural elites continued to publish hundreds of articles and books about the rise of the masses, the fears of communism, and the slippery slope from democracy to collectivism. But the doomsday language of cultural despair and the concerns about the arrival of the Asiatic hordes was more pronounced in the early Adenauer years. This was a time when the tensions between East and West flared into war in Korea, when Westerners feared that Stalin would dictate a communist solution to the division of Germany, and when West Germans struggled with continued calls for the democratization and socialization of the economy. These tensions found a number of outlets in the first half of the 1950s, among them ambivalence toward consumer culture, which social and economic elites at once embraced and feared. During the second half of the 1950s, when Soviet premier Nikita Khrushchev spoke of peaceful coexistence and when the promised economic affluence began reaching the average West German, some of the deeper anxieties about the consumerization of West Germany dissipated. In short, the fears associated with the early *Wirtschaftswunder* myth abated when the promised widespread abundance actually arrived in the late 1950s and 1960s.

Industrialists as Cultural Elites?

In considering the formative years of West German industry, one cannot help but marvel at the strange penetration of culture into the realm of business and economics. It was certainly not rare to see businessmen in other countries engaged in artistic and civic patronage. But how often did industrialists in other countries sprinkle their speeches about trade deficits, corporate taxes, and steel capacity with references to existentialism, nihilism, humanism, and

Beethoven? How many business leaders in the United States wrote articles about Western decline, moral degeneration, and Protestant individualism? If for the contemporary historian groups such as the Kulturkreis present a unique case study in the affinities between business and culture, contemporary observers themselves were often surprised and amused by West German industrialists' intellectual dilettantism. According to one cynical observer, industrialists, despite their best attempts to prove otherwise, "lived without an inkling of what culture meant, but not in opposition to it." They were cultural boors whose artistic tastes and cultural sensibilities leaned "more toward the spectacular."[62] But they were, admittedly, eager to learn.

The West German industrialist was never able to garner the total respect of artists and scholars as serious intellectuals. But this does not mean that they were ostracized from cultural and literary circles. Quite the contrary, in their quest to fashion themselves as a new *bürgerliche* elite, industrialists secured the help of a number of academic and public figures with whom they felt a deep affinity. The BDI, the BdA, and the Kulturkreis all curried regular favor with respected figures of West German public life who were sympathetic to the philosophical aims of industry (or at least cognizant of its political and economic power). When the DI established a number of *Arbeitskreise* (working groups) in 1951, it called on well-known intellectuals and public figures for help. Gustav Stein, banker Robert Pferdmenges, and a number of other industrialists and bankers sat next to historian Hans Rothfels and other scholars on the Arbeitskreis für Politik. On the Arbeitskreis für Meinungspflege (public opinion) Herbert Gross, Carl Neumann of the Allensbach Institut, and Hamburg cigarette magnate Philipp Reemstma sat next to playwright and poet Carl Zuckmayer.[63] On the DI's advisory council could be found, next to prominent names in banking and industry, journalists and publishers such as Marion Gräfin Dönhoff, Walter Jaenecke, and Gerd Bucerius as well as conservative sociologist Hans Freyer, freelance economic journalist Volkmar Muthesius, theologian Helmuth Thielecke, economist Alfred Müller-Armack, and Protestant bishop Hanns Lilje.[64] In short, overcoming the past and securing the future was a joint enterprise for West German elites. They all shared, in a variety of ways, a desire to rebuild a bourgeois world worn away by two world wars, a fragile Weimar democracy, and the crimes of National Socialism.

Organizations such as the Kulturkreis were, therefore, more than just ephemeral and sometimes awkward encounters between the two seemingly unrelated realms of big business and culture. Rather, they were about the self-understanding of capitalism and capitalists after Nazism. Industrial spokesmen such as Gustav Stein, Otto Vogel, and Hermann Reusch readily acknowledged that free enterprise, to compete with and defeat Marxist alternatives, would have to expand its mission and its appeal. It would have to demonstrate its ability not only to provide material comforts and economic prosperity but to safeguard the moral and spiritual fiber of the nation. If this seems a rather instrumentalized understanding of culture, it is one to which industrialists readily subscribed. The cultural training of industrialists was an openly avowed goal of organizations like the DI and the Kulturkreis, which distributed speeches to businessmen and companies in an attempt to imbue them with a political, publicity, and intellectual awareness. Flipping through the pages of the DI's *Unternehmerbrief* and the *Vortragsreihe,* one repeatedly encounters discussions of modernity and rationalization, Kant's categorical imperative, *Gesellschaft* and *Gemeinschaft,* and primarily in the 1960s, the blessings and dangers of technology.

Culture had a central role in business's self-understanding because industrialists knew how to exploit the validating force that it carried. It bestowed a gentility and refinement on those who might otherwise be seen only as doing the dirty work of making money. It injected civility and erudition into the ugly world of politics or the dry debates over *Wirtschaftspolitik.* In short, it was part of the re-creation of the *Unternehmertyp.* Culture, in its multiple forms, made the *Unternehmerpersönlichkeit* a figure worthy of reverence. Clearly then, industrialists did not engage with culture only as a means of understanding themselves or saving the West from imminent destruction. These motivations, often in their overstated form, were indeed real. But industrialists also turned to the language of culture as part of their quest for positive publicity and political leverage after National Socialism. In discussing industry and culture after Nazism, we must therefore articulate carefully the distinctions between opportunism and charity, between manipulation and ideology, between public relations and self-understanding.

CHAPTER SIX

Trade Unions, Workers, and the New Social Partnership

In the early Adenauer years industrialists were emboldened by the economic recovery of their country yet also worried about their tainted reputations and the dangers inherent in democracy and mass society. While the hopes and anxieties embodied in the "new industrialist" took many forms, they ultimately crystallized around industry's relationship to its most important constituency: West Germany's workers. Through a mixture of confrontation and conciliation, industry hoped to put an end to the class war that had haunted it since the late nineteenth century and that had been exacerbated by its assumed collaboration with the Nazis in suppressing the labor movement. In the early 1950s industrialists mobilized the figure of the *Unternehmer* in its struggle against the key unresolved workplace issue left over from the Weimar years: the introduction of codetermination, or union representation on company boards. In the course of the debates over writing codetermination into law, it became clear that industry's selective memory and self-inventions were not simply about protecting corporate reputations or engaging in cultural critiques, but about actual sociopolitical relationships and contests. Before they could win the sympathies of the broader public, industrialists hoped to diminish the real power of organized labor, and they approached their task with a vengeance. Yet after the uproar over codetermination had died down, industrialists began using more pacific means of normalizing a worker-manager relationship once so fraught. They employed the stylized figure of the new industrialist and the promise of prosperity to coax workers to lay down their arms and join in the euphoria sparked by the country's economic successes.[1]

The Struggle over Codetermination

When the first German Industry Exhibition ended in Berlin in October 1950, West German industry occupied a strong position politically. A business-friendly Adenauer government was reinforced by a network of interest organizations and lobbyists who moved freely through the corridors of power in Bonn. Individual industrialists like the BDI's Fritz Berg and representatives of industrial pressure groups were able to go directly to Adenauer to ask for favors and advise the chancellor and his party on economic matters.[2] Yet despite this renewed political clout and an ever expanding economy, a huge shadow hung over German industry. It took the form of the labor unions' demands for codetermination in the workplace. For a U.S. audience it is difficult to convey the drama surrounding this theme, yet codetermination was in fact one of the most significant and disputed issues in postwar West Germany.[3] I have alluded to its basic feature in earlier chapters—the unions' desire for a more participatory role in companies or, ideally (and more dangerously in management's estimation), actual representation on company supervisory and managerial boards.

The latter version, known in German as *paritätische betriebliche Mitbestimmung,* was at the center of the negotiations in 1950. In 1947 Ruhr industrialists had already witnessed the British occupation's brokered introduction of this form of codetermination in the coal and steel industry. This negotiated settlement provided for equal labor and capital representation on the supervisory board and a worker director on the management board. After the founding of the Federal Republic, the DGB began to lobby the Adenauer government to enshrine into national law the codetermination that already existed through Allied fiat in the heavy industrial firms of British zone. When the BDI and BdA attempted to block such legislation in 1950, and indeed to roll back the 1947 model, the DGB used the threat of strikes to force Adenauer to the negotiating table with labor and management. The fruit of these rancorous talks was the codetermination law of February 1951, which applied a limited codetermination only to coal and steel firms with 1,000 or more employees. The law was seen as a victory for industry, which had staved off a more sweeping introduction of workplace democracy. Following on the heels of this law was the equally contested *Betriebsverfassungsgesetz* (Work Constitution Act) of 1952, essentially a very watered-down version of codetermination that established a Works Council, which possessed a consulting role in matters of human relations and company welfare policy. A series of mass gatherings and warning strikes against this law revealed workers' displeasure with these partial concessions to economic democracy.

In the literature on codetermination, these negotiations and protests in the early 1950s have been analyzed in political, economic, and social terms. They

Eighty thousand workers gather in Frankfurt on 20 May 1952 in a warning strike against the Works Constitution Bill, which the unions felt was a half-hearted governmental response to their codetermination demands (183/ 14387/ 2N, courtesy of Bundesarchiv, Koblenz)

have been rightly portrayed as a resumption of the struggles for economic democracy during the Weimar years and an early post–World War II test of whether business leaders were ready to shed their older, antidemocratic clothes. But historians have all but ignored the extent to which the broader discussions about culture and the Nazi past penetrated the debate over economic democracy. In a sometimes vicious media war, industry, labor unions, and politicians invoked the memories and the language of National Socialism and cultural decline in order to demoralize and discredit their opponent and to demonstrate how its political and economic objectives would accelerate the nation's spiritual erosion. The industrialists portrayed the unions as a clique of power-hungry functionaries who were duping the workers into submission, much as Hitler, in their view, had done in the 1930s. In turn the DGB, the SPD, and the communists showed a remarkable unity in reminding the public of the role that industry had purportedly played in supporting the Nazis in 1932 and conspiring to crush labor after Hitler's *Machtergreifung*.[4] While the communists were most strident in their invocation of industry's "fascist tradition," the labor unions, the Social Democrats, and the left wing of the CDU (in contrast to the Adenauer government) all agreed that codetermination would be the cornerstone of what the DGB referred to as the "reordering of the German economy."[5]

If we take a closer look at one event in the fall of 1950, we can witness clearly the bitterness and paranoia that shaped this debate about codetermination. On 5 November the BDI sponsored its first annual membership meeting. Fresh from the euphoria of the German Industry Exhibition in Berlin a month earlier, businessmen from around Germany gathered to celebrate what had been dubbed the Day of the *Unternehmer*. Five thousand company owners, managers, and buyers packed Cologne's trade fair pavilion to celebrate West Germany's economic achievements over the preceding five years and to demonstrate that "business is ready to fight for its rights and its freedom."[6] Ludwig Erhard, Fritz Berg, and Alexander Menne, the chairman of the Arbeitsgemeinschaft Chemische Industrie, spoke in turn about the blessings and responsibilities of free enterprise.

Their uplifting words, however, were overshadowed by the more uncomfortable theme of codetermination. At the time the metalworkers' union IG Metall was building up support for a protest strike against the owners' intransigence, and the industrialists were using their BDI meeting as a sounding board for their views against union demands. While BDI president Fritz Berg's words represented a particularly powerful attack on the unions,[7] the evening belonged to the organization's vice-president, Otto Vogel, who delivered a speech brimming with bombast and antiunion invective. Vogel's speech is worth close attention, as it encapsulated industry's philosophical and cultural argument against codetermination. Vogel portrayed the clash between management and labor as part of a Manichean struggle between good and evil, between the "Orient and the Occident," between the sacred tenets of Western civilization—individuality, freedom, and private property—and the forces of Asiatic barbarism. "It concerns our planet!" Vogel insisted. "Today it is no longer about Germany, France, America, England or any other state. Today it is about our planetary consciousness—about all of mankind, which is rent asunder by two powerful ideologies. . . . Today we find ourselves again in the midst of a struggle. It is exactly the same as if Xerxes wandered towards Europe or if Stalin with his fifth columns . . . declared war on us."[8]

After this dramatic introduction, Vogel traced the lineage of the Western concepts of property and freedom and the individual, from Homer and Socrates to the present-day businessman. He portrayed the industrialist as the culmination of a 2,000-year struggle to defend the basic tenets of liberty and individual worth against all attackers. The Christian Occident (*Abendland*) had always taken on all those who sought to destroy its cultural greatness— from Hannibal to Ghengis Khan to the Ottoman Turks. But now the enemy was to be found at much closer quarters. "Today, Gentlemen, we are in a much more difficult situation. . . . For the first time in this struggle of freedom and property against slavery, of the market economy against the collective, the enemy is not only coming from the East—from outside—but from deep within the ranks of our people. . . . At the suitable moment, it will lead . . . Western humanity into a horrific *Sklavendasein* (slave existence)."[9]

The immediate enemy was the trade unions. The only way to stop their campaign of collectivism and codetermination, Vogel concluded, was to marshal the energies of West Germany's industrialists, "this daring group of men who create for the *Volk* the basis of life though their will and through the common labor of its working people." The German industrialist, Vogel argued, occupied the front line in a major *Kulturkampf* (cultural struggle).[10] He had to launch a preemptive strike against the do-nothing "union functionaries," who, with their reckless thirst for dictatorial power, threatened to bury two millennia of Western culture and hurl the world into darkness. Together with a freedom-loving United States, all of Europe must fight the forces of totalitarianism to the end and, through victory, create a truce between the *Unternehmer* and the worker. To complete the struggle, Vogel concluded to thunderous applause, industry must "draw upon our own will. . . . God give us the strength to do so."[11]

Otto Vogel's speech to his colleagues depicted industry in the midst of a mortal struggle. But what exactly did codetermination represent that incited industrialists to compare the unions repeatedly to Stalin and Hitler and the negotiations to a crusade or a *Kulturkampf?* The answer can be found in the dozens of pleas, manifestos, studies, and tirades that circulated through the world of industry and labor in the early 1950s. Some of these documents were sober discussions of the economy and labor's goals. Yet most reflected the tone of "Democracy in Danger!" a two-page leaflet that argued that the unions, in their attempt to rid the owners of their *Herr im Hause* mentalities, were waging war against the most sacred of Western rights: private property.[12] A company belonged to its owners, not its workers, and through their demands for codetermination, argued the flyer, the unions were trying to reverse a centuries-old social compact. The owners and the stockholders provided the capital, and they alone possessed the right to decide how their property would be used. A single union representative on a managerial or supervisory board could, in an attempt to politicize an otherwise docile labor force, block major managerial decisions and bring a company to its knees.

The case laid out in "Democracy in Danger!" not only invoked the abstract rights of the owners and management. It also questioned the right of the labor unions to speak for all of West Germany's *Schaffende* (producers). While most industrialists grudgingly acknowledged the unions as the political mouthpiece of skilled factory labor, they did not welcome their attempts to represent all workers, especially the lower middle class. What about the *Selbständige* (independent), the document asked—the baker, the shoemaker, the tailor, or the architect? What about the teacher, the small businessman, or the artist not represented by the unions? They too were part of the *Volkskörper* (national body), and they had a right to represent themselves in a free democracy, without the union bosses professing to be speaking for labor. In presenting this argument, industry was posturing as the true defender of the worker. The audacity of the unions lay not only in their codetermination demands but in their original sin of presuming to represent the country's labor force. In the end, argued industry, it was the entrepreneurs and the employers—not the union bosses—who provided for the worker, both materially and psychologically.

The greatest danger of codetermination, however, according to "Democracy in Danger!" was that it would usher into West Germany the forces of communism. Codetermination was not simply a harmless quest for workplace rights; it was a plan hatched "by the Politburo in Moscow" to destroy the Federal Republic. A law introducing *economic* democracy would mean the end of *political* democracy. From the moment codetermination was in place, practically nothing could take place, in either politics or economics, without the approval of the union headquarters (*Gewerkschaftszentrale*). In the entire economic and political history, argued the piece, there had never been such a concentration of power, not even in the totalism of the Nazi regime. Moreover, the dangers lay not only with the unions or the Soviet Union but also with West Germany's Social Democratic Party. Social democracy, in industry's estimation, was the godfather of codetermination and, as such, desired nothing less than the "dictatorship of the proletariat" and thus the end of democracy. The SPD's support of codetermination, industry argued, exposed German socialism as the forerunner of communism and thus anything but democratic. The day that codetermination took effect would be seen by future generations as the trade unions' and the SPD's "day of *Machtergreifung.*"[13]

How seriously are we to take the ominous prognostications of "Democracy in Danger!" and its litany of enemies who threatened West German and European civilization? Clearly we must recognize them as an example of the often inflated political rhetoric prevalent during the Cold War, when two world systems—communism and "the free world"—were poised against each other. In this heated international context, industry's apocalyptic verbiage was a genuine statement of anguish over the prospects of the unions' penetration into the ranks of management. Yet these words were also meant to be provocative, to rouse the industrialists to a heightened indignation against a law that many truly found objectionable, while at the same time undermining the authority of the entire political Left—from socialism to communism. Forged in a rhetorical style reminiscent of Hitler or Goebbels, they also aimed to scare the public into an antiunion frenzy, and for a short while they succeeded in fomenting a debate, although not always to industry's advantage.

In November all the major newspapers covered the BDI's Day of the *Unternehmer*, and they reported Vogel's speech as the culmination of the event. Three days after the gathering, the NWDR (Northwest German Radio) broadcast Vogel's diatribe to its evening audience. The reaction was swift and divided. Letters and phone calls poured into the radio station and newspapers and to Otto Vogel himself. A short-lived public debate was unleashed.

Supporters, mostly fellow industrialists or disaffected union members, praised Vogel for having delivered a "masterpiece."[14] Finally, somebody had demonstrated "civil courage" by bravely taking on "the wasp's nest of union bossocracy" (*Wespennest der Gewerkschaftsbonzokratie*).[15] In the letters of support, a deep-seated disdain for the unions came to the fore. The unions, wrote one Vogel defender, are "the gravediggers of the German *Volk*, the forerunners for all forms of political and economic terror, a state within a state with no ideals other than class hate and class struggle."[16] Representatives of the nationalist Right, which responded euphorically to Vogel's words, shared this sentiment. Hans Polzer, editor of the magazine *Das Volk*, a self-designated successor to Goebbels's *Das Reich* and an alternative to the "one-sided representation of the errors of the past," wrote to Vogel, thanking him for his courageous thoughts and his contribution to the struggle by the "war generation" to rediscover its "self-worth" through a glorious German past.[17]

Vogel's critics—and there were many—drew on memories of National Socialism to argue their case. A self-declared union functionary described to Vogel in an open letter how this sort of visceral antilabor hostility had led to his own imprisonment in a concentration camp seventeen years earlier.[18] Others took grave offense at Vogel's assertion that DAF leader Robert Ley served as the "idol" of the unions. If anyone, they argued, it was Vogel who followed in the footsteps of the Nazi labor chief. Finally, socialists and communists presented Vogel as a prime example of a "renazification" of West German public life. Yet whether or not they saw him as an unreformed Nazi, all of Vogel's critics agreed that the BDI vice-president had delivered a destructive blow to the cause of social peace in West Germany. Respected NWDR commentator Peter von Zahn criticized the tone of the entire BDI gathering. "The corporals of the social order" had delivered their message with a "drill sergeant's tone" (*im Kasernenhofton*).[19] Another critic likened Vogel to an "elephant in the social porcelain shop."[20] The time for a cooperative reconstruction of the nation, the DGB's *Welt der Arbeit* declared, was now over.[21]

November and December saw a flurry of activity directed at Vogel. The Christian unions protested his behavior in a letter. In Vogel's home city of Augsburg, the DGB issued an urgent appeal for mass action (with a convenient play on Vogel's surname): "Employees, arm yourselves against the *Raub-Vogel* (predator)."[22] DGB chief Hans Böckler suggested that the negotiations over codetermination might cease altogether. Even some BDI members were unnerved by their colleague's provocative behavior. At a time when industry was trying to negotiate peaceably with the unions, such inflammatory language could only escalate tensions and harm the chances for compromise. Hermann Reusch, while praising his colleague, acknowledged that not all industrialists were pleased with the severity of Vogel's tone.[23] Otto Friedrich, obviously disheartened by the speech, called Vogel's words "excessively harsh." The Hamburg industrialist, however, did muster some diplomatic (if halfhearted) praise for his colleague for having brought the codetermination debate to a head.[24]

Clearly, in invoking terms like "seizure of power" and "dictatorship of the proletariat," industrialists were consciously and cleverly exploiting the past, which they knew had a tremendous power in the present political setting. They were turning these symbols not only against the unions but against the Social Democrats, who despite some industrialists' claims, always had a deep antipathy toward the Communist Party and totalitarianism. If it appeared rather disingenuous to lump socialists with communists and Nazis or to blame organized labor for the rise of Hitler, we cannot forget that this manipulation of memory—of class war and the opprobrium of National Socialism—was common in the confused political and ideological landscape of postwar Germany, where memories of Nazi persecution were raw and fears of communism were real and deep-seated. This rhetorical manipulation was also a conscious strategy employed by both sides. To the industrialists, Adolf Hitler and his cohort had destroyed the fragile Weimar democracy, and now union men such as Hans Böckler threatened to do the same. By setting themselves up as the only defenders of democracy (their own ambivalence about democracy notwithstanding) and by demonstrating a slippery slope from codetermination to Stalinism, industrialists could tap into the public's very real fear of totalitarianism. For labor, in turn, it was the Hermann Reusches and Otto Vogels who followed in the footsteps of Hitler and Himmler. It mattered little that neither man had been an avid Nazi. Their deep conservatism and their reactionary posturing vis-à-vis labor consolidated their credentials as fascist union-busters.

Despite rumors of protest strikes and mass action, the furor over Otto Vogel's comments died down relatively quickly as negotiations over codetermination proceeded apace, culminating in the February 1951 Codetermination Act, which gave labor a limited voice on heavy industry company boards. The exaggerated drama of 1950 was now to be followed by more sober negotiations over the Works Constitution Act and an eventual retreat by the unions in their quest for true economic democracy in favor of a campaign for a larger wage packet and company welfare measures. Yet while the short-lived hostility surrounding the Vogel affair was to give way to relative social harmony in the 1950s, it was not before the unions had exposed the BDI leadership—

or at least prominent members of it—as anything but the conciliatory and repentant lot that labor had hoped it had become. West Germany's leading industrialists, with personal prodding from Konrad Adenauer, acceded to some of the unions' codetermination demands, but labor did not readily forgive management for what it saw as the blatant and political misuse of the Nazi legacy. While they could dismiss with relative ease industry's turgid rhetoric of degeneration and decline, they saw turning the theme of Nazism against labor as unpardonable.

Many industrialists themselves also felt this sort of language did more harm than good and were henceforth careful to keep people like Vogel on a short leash.[25] But resentment lingered. When the BDI's Kulturkreis appointed Vogel to its board in September 1951, some industrialists expressed their displeasure at having their organization represented by such a controversial figure, one who might stymie attempts to cooperate with the unions on matters of cultural as well as social policy.[26]

The Vogel incident demonstrates a convergence of the many themes that preoccupied West German elites at the beginning of the 1950s. Business fears of union power intersected with broader fears of communism, which in turn drew their force from the memory and experience of National Socialism. At the crossroads of culture and politics, of ideology and economics, and of the past and the present, stood the debate over codetermination. While people like Otto Vogel and Hermann Reusch tried to appear progressive, modern, or avant-garde in their aesthetic tastes, the same was not true of their views of social legislation or economic democracy. To them democracy, in its positive incarnation, unleashed a romantic spirit of individualism—of the artist, the musician, and the industrialist—and protected a liberal political order in which these figures flourished. In its negative form, however, it was the foundation of an automated and atomized society and mass politics. It brought inflated bureaucracies, codetermination, and political terror, and it was the harbinger of cultural decline. In short, in the early 1950s, culture and codetermination jointly embodied the industrialists' broader preoccupations—the public relations disaster of Nazism, the loss of prestige, the need to reinvent and relegitimize capitalism, the threats of totalitarianism, the dangers inherent in democracy, and the fear of the masses and degeneration. All of these developments had threatened the revered social position of Germany's *Bürgertum* and, by extension, its industrialists.

Yet this explosion of symbolic language was not only about self-understanding and overcoming the past; it was also about skillfully maneuvering the legacy of Nazism and the tensions of the Cold War for a present political purpose. In its calculated strategies for containing the unions, industry was demonstrating how far it was from a gut-wrenching and penitent *Vergangenheitsbewältigung* (coming to terms with the past). But it also laid the groundwork for a rapprochement of sorts, based on the heady talk of good-will and harmony. Industrialists, after demonstrating their hostility to unions and diffusing the broader issue of economic democracy, set out to pick up the pieces and prove their loyalty to the working man and woman.

The *Unternehmer* and the Worker

After codetermination became a fait accompli, West German industry sought to repair the damage wrought by its antiunion rhetoric. As long as people like Otto Vogel represented the public face of German industry, this would remain a difficult task. As long as *die Wirtschaft* positioned itself in direct opposition to organized labor, the businessman as a type would remain a controversial figure, pursued by the language of capitalist exploitation and the memory of Nazi crimes. He could remake himself as a patron of the arts or an entrepreneurial folk hero, but from the perspective of the "man on the street," the industrialist had to do more than simply tout himself as a reformed business and cultural leader. As the Vogel episode makes clear, using the figure of the *Unternehmer* to promote the market economy entailed considerable risk, namely, the further disenchantment of those segments of the populace already unfavorably predisposed toward big business.

This dilemma was not lost on industrialists themselves. With the self-conscious emergence of public relations in West Germany came a discussion of whether it was wise to draw explicit attention to the *Unternehmer* as the representative of the posttotalitarian political and economic system. It became increasingly clear to industry that it could not win the sympathies of the worker by bullying the labor unions or indulging in narcissistic self-adulation, especially at a time when it lacked the respect of a large segment of the public. The growing skepticism about this approach was evident when, in 1953, the DI announced its plans to sponsor a *Woche des Unternehmertums* (a week of business/entrepreneurial activities), during which the country would acknowledge the achievements of the industrialist and entrepreneur. After receiving the announcement of the event, a number of industrialists expressed reservations about orienting public relations so overwhelmingly around the *Unternehmer* concept. Typical were the thoughts of Bavarian textile manufacturer Wolfgang Dummer:

> The thought of focusing industry's publicity activities extensively on the concept of the *Unternehmer* is, in and of itself, not new, and holding an "*Unternehmer* Week" is therefore understandable. I, however, have always been of the opinion that this type of publicity is pointless. The *freie Unternehmer* is, in the end, only possible in a free economy, and it seems to me much more important to center publicity around the free

economy and the methods according to which it functions. In doing so, one would simultaneously help the industrialist gain in recognition and prestige. But in contrast, the perpetual references to the *Unternehmer* seem to me unlikely to resonate among the broader population. A "Week of the *Unternehmer*" would achieve little sympathy and would only give the impression that we are conducting the politics of class and privilege, even though we intend the very opposite.[27]

In a certain sense, Dummer was touching on a reality that industry publicists had acknowledged since the founding of the FRG: that the fate of the businessman was wedded to that of the new social market economy and that what was good for one was good for the other. In the literature on the social market economy, industry certainly highlighted not just the businessman but the system in which he functioned.

Yet Dummer's reservations also reflected more directly on the risky nature of any publicity enterprise that featured the businessman as the centerpiece. It was unwise for industry to promote itself in a climate still marked by ambivalence toward the rich man, the magnate, the tycoon. West German industrialists had to avoid the impression that they were simply out to promote their own interests—as a "producer class" that had little concern for the common people, except in their capacity to work for the profit of the firm. Dummer's alternative plan was to recast the Week of the *Unternehmer* as the Week of the Free Economy, which would relegate the controversial figure of the industrialist into the background but still draw attention to his achievements. But Dummer also feared the public would see through such a transparent rhetorical maneuver; it knew that "the free economy" was a euphemism for business interests. Dummer therefore also suggested taking advantage of the more egalitarian rhetoric to be found in what he saw as an American style of public relations. If industry could not avoid drawing attention to the *Unternehmer*, it should do so not as the means of promoting the partisan interests of the business elite but as a way of reminding the public that "every capable, diligent, and intelligent man can make a successful career in the economy and especially in industry."[28] In other words, the challenge was to avoid touting ad nauseum the achievements of industry and instead to invite the worker to join in the successes. Here was the crux of the new approach to public relations that was to emerge throughout the 1950s and coincide with the mass of literature on the *Unternehmer:* The industrialist was still considered by some to be an unsavory figure; he therefore had to be reglamorized and equipped not simply with an appreciation of high culture or a respect for the power of public relations, but with more widely appealing features with which the worker could identify or strive to imitate. If the old-style industrialist was selfish, pampered, and elitist, the new industrialist was down-to-earth, hard working, and compassionate—in short, an incarnation of the worker. The boundaries between worker and industrialist were to be, if not actually, at least symbolically erased as a means of selling the new social market economy.

Human Relations and the Language of Conciliation

Industry surely faced a dilemma in implementing such a strategy of projection and identification, particularly in light of the lingering class-war language that had come to the fore in the codetermination debate. Yet industrialists understood the damaging power of rhetoric, which took the form of antibusiness slogans like "monopoly capitalism," "finance capitalism," and "concern lords." They therefore found the solution to their dilemma also in the realm of language. In the late 1940s and early 1950s a calculated conflation of the worker and the industrialist began to assume a number of linguistic forms. Conciliatory phrases such as *Partnerschaft* (partnership), *Gemeinschaftsdenken* (community thinking), *Zusammengehörigkeitsgefühl* (feeling of togetherness), and *Solidaritätsbewußtsein* (solidarity consciousness) emerged from the lips of even the most authoritarian business leaders. The most notable linguistic development was the substitution of *Mitarbeiter* (coworker) —and later, *Arbeitnehmer* (employee)—for *Arbeiter* (worker) in popular and business language. While "the worker" was associated with an inharmonious past, when the proletariat was considered a downtrodden and revolutionary underclass, the "coworker" was one among equals, along with the shareholders rooting for, profiting from, and taking pride in the financial successes of the company. This lexical transformation marked an attempt by both management and labor to abandon more ideological rhetoric in favor of an egalitarian—or at least communitarian—concept of work.

Such a purposeful recasting of work and the worker had already been the hallmark of Weimar and Nazi politics and labor policies, embodied in the creation of workers' parties, the concept of the *Betriebsgemeinschaft* (factory community), and the struggle for the "soul of the worker."[29] Some of the features of this factory community had been developed before 1933 by a group of young industrial psychologists and labor experts associated with DINTA (German Institute for Technical Labor Training), who sought to maximize the productivity and happiness of the worker through the promotion of ideal factory conditions and leisure programs.[30] After 1933 the Nazis added an ideological and authoritarian element to the Weimar studies on worker contentment and on Fordism, Taylorism, and "psychotechnics." The National Socialist plant utopia was supposed to be sustained by a harmony of form, matter, and ideology. Modernized machines and remodeled workrooms were combined with a beautified decor, perfected lighting, ample breaks and vacation time (as promoted by the Strength through Joy programs), careful ideological training, and obedience to hard work and efficiency.[31] But while the Nazis applied their communal ethos toward a racist and sometimes (at least in their early rhetoric) anticapitalist end, after the war the language of workplace amity was now used to solidify the country's embrace of free markets and individual liberties. There were certainly continuities between these visions, particularly in the shared hostility to the power of organized labor. The factory was still the site of natural hierarchies, conformity to stringent rules, and deference to authority, and fostering a sense of belonging to the company was still as much about defusing workers' demands for a decision-making role in the company as it was about goodwill on the factory floor. Yet in the years after World War II, the desire both to pacify and to befriend the worker was more widespread, more coordinated, and arguably more genuine. Argued the BKU's Franz Greiß, "After having forgotten for over 100 years to define people as part of the firm, we have suddenly 'discovered' *die Menschen.*"[32]

This emphasis on the worker as human being was articulated in the newly Germanized concept of human relations. A detailed recounting of the origins and propagation of this important concept is beyond the scope of this chapter.[33] It is important to note, however, that the notion of the worker as something more than a piece of machinery or an extension of the owner's capital again predated the 1950s. In the 1920s, in both America and Europe, the social organization of labor and *Betriebspsychologie* were rapidly developing areas of research that gave much attention to worker satisfaction, motivation, and free-time activity as essential factors in productivity.[34] But after World War II, the new science of human relations was fleshed out in a series of studies, magazines, and journals. These discussions usually dovetailed with the theme of public relations.[35] The two were considered to be extensions of each other. Effective public relations began within the firm and then projected itself outward. If workers were cared for, productivity and contentment would increase, and both would ultimately reflect well on the company.

Once again the United States was the acknowledged home to these ideas of public manipulation; it served as the model of what was once a purer and freer capitalism and, to some industrialists, a more humane one (at least superficially) than the German version. U.S. industrialists were presumably better at treating workers as human beings, having learned this approach in courses on industrial psychology, managerial methods, and business organization. Clearly, as with public relations, however, this humanity of human relations was, in West German industry's estimation, as much appearance as reality. The United States was still, according to the familiar generalization, the home of unbridled competition and economic Darwinism, which stood in contrast to the professedly more merciful—or at least more honest—paternalism of old, or the reformed third way capitalism embodied in the social market economy.

Yet West German industry, despite doubts about the depth of U.S. businessmen's benevolence, was eager to learn from these modern developments. Like public relations, the new art of human relations did not take hold overnight. Many older industrialists felt that rigid hierarchies were simply too deeply ingrained in the German workplace culture to be tampered with. Yet, ironically, some of the same men who subscribed to a more authoritarian "German" tradition of *Menschenführung* (human leadership) were also the most open to U.S. methods of public and human relations. For both concepts, despite their professions of egalitarianism and openness, were in some ways about manipulation and propaganda, albeit executed with varying degrees of moral conviction and expertise.[36] They emanated from the top down—from management to labor—and as such, they could be placed neatly into the *Herr im Hause* mental framework of people like Hermann Reusch, who adhered to a traditional view of workplace authority and decision-making rights while subscribing eagerly to the *language* of conciliation. The new talk of social partnership was therefore never about democratizing the workplace but, rather, about holding out a rhetorical olive branch to the workers and offering some tangible concessions to improve their lives and, more cynically, ensure their docility. Today the references to labor and management are interchangeable with the benign concept of *soziale Partner* (social partners), but in the early 1950s the transformation bore the marks of both openness to the workers' needs and an ingrained hostility to their political demands.

Workers' Publications and the Economic Miracle

At the time of their inception in the early 1950s, these new ideas of partnership and human relations were disseminated through a variety of media. One was a series of periodicals on industrial management, such as Munich publisher Wilhelm Steinebach's 1949 magazine venture *Mensch und Arbeit* [Man and work], which was directed more at the manager than at the worker. Another was the new employee and visitor manuals, which presented a brief history of the company and showcased the many benefits allotted to the worker. Yet the chief means of displaying industry's new consideration of the worker was the *Werkszeitung*, or company newspaper, which many firms had introduced in the 1920s and revived in the late 1940s and early 1950s as a tangible expression of their eagerness to enhance the life of the *Mitarbeiter* not simply on the factory floor but in his or her life outside the company.

In 1951 approximately 200 West German firms put out a company magazine for their workers. Two years later, West Germany could boast 400 such *Werkszeitschriften/zeitungen*, bearing such apt titles as *You and Your Work* [*Röchling*], *Echo of Work* [*Hüttenwerk Oberhausen*], *Work and Me, Work and Us, My Work, Our Work, Work and Man, Work and Leisure, Work and Home,* and *Work and Life.*[37] Next to these individual company publications, a number of *überbetriebliche* (industrywide) journals and magazines were distributed to smaller companies that could not afford their own publications. Many of these were trade specific, as evidenced by their titles, such as *The Shoe and Leather Post, Stones and Earth, The Spindle,* and *The Papermaker.*[38] Yet others were simply about the working person in the new Federal Republic.

Industrialists articulated a clear purpose for the magazines. In the strikingly fascistic-sounding words of the BKU's Franz Greiß, the company magazine was to be the chief vehicle for a renewed understanding of the factory as *Lebensraum für die Werktätigen* (living space for the working person). The factory, he argued, was a microcosm of the social world in which the worker was permanently embedded. Leisure was simply an extension of the factory and the factory an extension of life. The company magazine, suggested Greiß, was to express the totality of worker existence. In contrast to those publications originating from the ranks of organized labor,[39] the "factory paper" would present up-to-date, colorful, and alluring articles and pictures, not for the partisan interests of labor but for the health of the entire company organism. In Greiß's crude formulation, "the *Werkszeitung* needs to be interesting without having to bring in naked women."[40]

This quest to integrate the worker into a business-friendly, organic community was not only expressed in the company magazine and newspaper. In conjunction with the founding of the FRG and the debate over codetermination, industry began proposing in earnest the publication of more widely distributed weeklies and monthlies, to be read by a broader readership of working men and their families. An industry-sponsored publication in 1949 called *Nach Feierabend*, which was designed to follow in the vein of the popular nineteenth-century weekly *Die Gartenlaube,* was a short-lived failure. September 1950 saw the first issue of *Heim und Werk*, another ill-fated magazine sponsored by Rhenish industrialists with the aim of "deepening social understanding and social peace" through images of diligence and a comfortable home life.[41] Meanwhile the DI also tried its hand at peaceful factory coexistence with the successful *Der Mitarbeiterbrief,* a workers' newsletter distributed on factory floors.[42]

The most effective example of this genre, however, was *Das Fenster,* the first volume of which hit the newsstands in April 1952. The magazine's subtitle, *Bilder und Berichte von Mensch und Zeit* [Pictures and reports of people and the times], did not immediately betray the partisan slant of the magazine. Nor did the first issue's colorful features on Eskimo women, honest communication in the workplace, the daily life of a hausfrau, and a fictional adventure story taking place in the Himalayas. However in a mass mailing to company executives a few months after the launching of the magazine, the publisher, while (falsely) disavowing any financial link to industry,[43] made clear his broader probusiness goals:

> *Das Fenster* is the only illustrated magazine working FOR the relaxation of sociopolitical tensions, the principle of the market economy, and free entrepreneurial initiative, and AGAINST socialization and the welfare state, the supremacy of the unions, and a deepening of social conflicts. . . . Many of your employees and your visitors may be of a different opinion. Subscribe to *Das Fenster* and place copies in hallways, waiting rooms, and cafeterias. By doing so you can offer to dissenters—and above all to . . . the younger generation who [is] being one-sidedly influenced—a clear overview of the sociopolitical situation in Germany.[44]

More than any other weekly, *Das Fenster* propagated a new capitalist folklore from the business point of view—prosperity, leisure, conservative values, and the desire of each worker to become his or her own *Unternehmer*. Articles on work and home life, anticommunism, and mass consumption were complemented by profiles of legendary industrialists (such as Rudolf Diesel) and interviews with prominent business leaders (such as Otto Friedrich, in an article titled "Was ist ein Unternehmer?").[45] Almost every contribution seemed to be an advertisement for the Protestant work ethic; working hard and making money were portrayed as the highest calling. In a 1954 article called "We Need More Millionaires," Volkmar Muthesius made a case for this materialist sensibility:

> The fact that there are rich people means nothing more than that anyone can become rich if he is sufficiently capable and resourceful, talented, and industrious. Most well-off people started small. The history of the economy is the history of the social ascendance of small people, who, through prudence, cleverness, and an iron diligence, attain prosperity and prestige. Not everyone can become a Gottlieb Daimler, a Robert Bosch, or a Henry Ford. . . . But we all have plenty of examples among our friends and neighbors of men who started with a vendor's tray and became a wholesaler . . . or an electrical fitter who became a manufacturer of electrotechnical products, with hundreds of workers and a large fortune.[46]

Muthesius's attitude was ubiquitous during a time of increasing prosperity. It all began with the little man—the entrepreneur—and greatness followed. West Germany's rapid economic recovery spawned a number of such myths that explained and legitimated this economic rebirth. The most famous narrative was, of course, that of the Economic Miracle. Importantly, the *Wirtschaftswunder* was not a creation of *post facto* reminiscence, when West Germans looked back wistfully to the comfortable and conservative 1950s. Rather, it was a contemporary invention consciously embraced by West Germans of all ilk. Nor was the Economic Miracle simply the rhetorical by-product of economic success. Rather, the story of West Germany's almost magical rebirth was actively imagined, scripted, and propagated, often by businessmen and firms who recognized the power that a post-Hitler national myth would have in securing the free market and taming the working classes.

It is ironic that part of what sustained the Economic Miracle was West Germans' repeated disavowal of its literal meaning. A number of publications argued emphatically that economic success, in contrast to the idea of a miracle, could *not* be credited to some supernatural force but, rather, to the blood, sweat, and tears of the West Germans themselves. A 1953 book called *Das Deutsche Wunder* [The German miracle] was a clear example of this dialectic of affirmation and denial. Through pictures and words the book traced the revival of German industry since 1945—from defeat to dismantling, to the Marshall Plan, to the ECSC. The BdA, the BDI, and the DI all recommended the book highly to its member firms as proof, the title notwithstanding, that in fact "no 'German Miracle' had taken place but rather that the reconstruction was the result of German hard work and the partnership of the industrialists and the employees."[47] *Das Deutsche Wunder* employed the myth of the miracle in order to undo it—to credit both German industry and its workforce with the nation's economic successes.

Another attempt to both invoke and deny the "miraculous" quality of West Germany's recovery and to invite the *Mitarbeiter* to partake of the revival was an industry-commissioned book by Heinrich Hauser, a prolific novelist and essayist who had lived an eclectic life as a physician, a deck hand on a large sailing ship, a publicist for a traveling circus, a refugee from Nazi Germany, and a gardener at the University of Chicago.[48] Hauser published numerous works about his private voyages and the German economy and culture. In 1951 industrialists called on Hauser to tell the inspirational story of how German industry had risen from the ashes of defeat and dismantling to its present state of prosperity.[49] Through the images of labor and management working hand in hand, industry hoped to overcome the persistent perception of the unreformed businessman—to prove to the worker that "the coming type of industrialist was no longer the capitalist in the old sense."[50] During the book's formative stages, Hauser appealed for the help of industrialists from around Germany, promising to deliver a work of utmost political significance. By contrasting the dazzling economic reconstruction of Germany to the initial U.S. plans in 1944 to pastoralize the country, Hauser hoped to tap into both the workers' and the industrialists' shared sense of resentment at Allied occupation and denazification and thereby awaken in them a common sympathy for the plight of private enterprise.

Hauser and his publisher Wilhelm Steinebach petitioned IHKs to forward to them stirring tales of the economic recovery of their member firms, from which Hauser could then choose the most inspiring stories to highlight in his final draft. Hauser discussed with industrialists his rhetorical and marketing strategies. In the age of mass readership, how would they reach the worker, who "whether he knows it or not" is on a course toward Marxism? All agreed that the worker's contribution to economic recovery must be emphasized alongside the celebration of industrial ingenuity. Yet more important even than this fundamental strategy of flattery would be the book's style. The publication, Hauser argued, had to appeal to the "man on the street." The only way to keep the attention of the average worker, he concluded, was to make a book about German industry read "like a detective novel," replete with riveting language and colorful pictures.[51]

Selling a positive public image in the age of the masses also demanded a careful marketing strategy. Rather than simply flooding bookstores with Hauser's publication, industrialists thought it wiser to order copies and distribute them to their workers on the factory floor. While the industrialists deemed this a clever propaganda move, they hoped that the workers would perceive it as a magnanimous gesture on the part of the bosses. Industry saw the young workers, in particular, as its most important target, as they would be more receptive to the entrepreneurial thinking than the politically hardened, antimanagement old-timers. Hauser's publisher and local IHKs advertised the book accordingly as the perfect gift for the teenager. Whether as a birthday or Christmas present or as a reward to a student who had just passed his or her exams, Hauser's book was intended to serve as an effective means of neutralizing the collectivist tendencies of working youth. In 1952 the book appeared under the title *Unser Schicksal: Deutsche Industrie* [Our fate: German industry].[52] With this colorful paean to the utopian spirit of the factory community, Hauser had composed the poetry of the *Wirtschaftswunder*. Images of an industrial wasteland—dismantled factories, bombed-out towns, and starving workers—give way to vivid descriptions of roaring furnaces and sweaty, muscle-bound miners happily leading the charge toward economic rebirth.

Another book embracing the same strategy of persuasion was Eberhard Schulz's, *Das goldene Dach* [The golden roof].[53] Commissioned as the first Book of the Year by the Kulturkreis, *Das goldene Dach* set out to pacify the worker through the promise of owning a home. Eberhard Schulz had published widely on architectural and urban design, and through his visual and textual celebration of the postwar housing settlements that had sprung up around the Ruhr factories, as they had during the 1880s and 1890s, industry hoped to take another step toward winning back the worker. Like Hauser's project, *Das goldene Dach* is striking in its use of utopian imagery as a means of taming a potentially violent working class. In the industrial settlement, the worker family would finally realize its bourgeois dreams of material comfort. During the day the husband would work around the corner in the steel factory while the wife protected hearth and home. As "the soul of the house" she would, aside from her motherly duties, prepare fruit baskets, tend the garden, visit the local hairdresser, and prepare meals for her husband, all against the backdrop of the factory smokestack.[54] Through this existence the worker family would breathe in the "perfume of freedom" and would reject the "collectivist" alternative offered by the trade unions and Soviet communism.[55] More importantly, the worker would assume a moral status equal to that of the industrialist. The distinction between manager and employees would be erased in this utopian realm. In the struggle against communism, the class boundaries of the West would dissolve, as the common enjoyment of private property would amalgamate all West Germans into a single, collective mindset dominated by the masculine hero of the *Unternehmer*.

This new creation would embody not just the entrepreneurial ethos of the Adenauer years or stand as a symbol of anticommunism; he would also help to secure a "proper" sexual division of labor that had been disrupted through the upheavals of war and destruction. During the Nazi and postwar years, women had entered the factory, and so-called *Trümmerfrauen*, or "rubble women," had cleaned up the wreckage of bombed-out cities. In the Adenauer years, just as during Weimar, the strong and independent woman represented a threat to the conservative mores of the country's elites. The image presented by Hauser of the working man and the dutiful housewife reflected, therefore, a desire not simply to consolidate a procapitalist mindset but to restore the concomitant gender relations that many elites saw as a necessary component of a stable and prosperous West.[56]

Again it is important to highlight not simply this text but also the extent to which business leaders engineered its construction. Hermann Reusch and Gustav Stein, the cochairs of the Kulturkreis, corresponded often with fellow members of the circle about both the broad interpretive strategies Schulz should employ and more specific rhetorical tactics.[57] For example, Reusch warned Schulz to refrain from using particular turns of phrase that might distract the working class from the positive achievements of German industry. By mentioning too often words like "Krupp" or "slavery" (as in "Slavery of Technology," one of the original chapter titles), for instance, Schulz risked evoking negatively politicized associations with the recent past.[58] Through the introduction of a benevolent paternalism into the factory, industrialists could calm the revolutionary tendencies of the workers. They then would also finally succeed in drawing a curtain between themselves and National Socialism. By establishing themselves as antitotalitarian freedom-fighters and socially engaged "factory fathers" *(Betriebsväter)*, industrialists calculated that they would bury once and for all the myth of the amoral profiteer who would sell his soul to any political cause if it was "good for the business."

With hindsight these words might appear as hackneyed and cynical tools of managerial manipulation. But they were also juxtaposed with practical solutions for keeping working people in the fold of freedom and market economics. In the summer of 1953 the IHK Essen launched a major propaganda action known as "Auch Du sollst besitzen" (You too should own property), which aimed at enticing workers toward "property and capital accumulation" and away from collectivism. As part of the publicity blitz, the IHK Essen, with the help of Gert von Klass, prepared a million copies of a short brochure that emphasized that the security of one's family could only be maintained through ownership of property. The booklet, available for 30 pfennig at kiosks and bookstores, mapped out the three ways to own property: personal savings, help from the company, and tax breaks from the state. To further promote this message, the IHK Essen also used the press and radio to unleash "a flood of enlightening articles, speeches, and advertisements." It prepared posters, short films, and special exhibitions. "The entire campaign," argued the coordinator, should contribute to the view of the "private economy as the solution to social problems."[59]

"Auch Du sollst besitzen" was one of many such campaigns on behalf of hard work and private ownership. Yet physical labor and property accumulation were not enough. They were to be complemented by an education that would consolidate the ideological underpinnings of free enterprise and private ownership. If industrialists wanted to maintain peace in the workplace and thereby their own hegemonic position in society, they would ultimately have to pass on the cultural—and not just materialist—values to which they themselves adhered. The combination of *Eigentumsbildung* (private acquisition of property) and *Persönlichkeitsbildung* (personality development) would eventually lead to the "deproletarianization" of the working class.[60] According to Gustav Stein, it was up to companies to hire directors and managers who displayed *Persönlichkeitswerte* (personality value), the rare combination of cultural awareness and economic expertise. The company man of the future must not only be an expert in engineering, management, or "tax laws"; he must also be well-versed in world literature, which imparts eternal values and "independent" *(selbständige)* thoughts. After this cultural awareness was successfully imbued in the individual manager, it would then suffuse throughout the firm, creating a company ethos that was firmly grounded in notions of freedom and self-worth, but that also maintained social hierarchies.[61]

By the mid-1950s this cultural "trickle down" from industrialist to worker was, arguably, taking place, as companies began taking active measures to inculcate the new posttotalitarian ideals into the workers. The reality was that many Social Democratic workers did not really need training in anti-totalitarian ideals. They were critical of industrialists, but they were also viru-lently anticommunist. Nonetheless, managers feared that socialists, by defi-nition, were impressionable to communism, and they took active measures to prevent a collectivist infiltration of their firms. Companies constructed libraries and reading rooms; they founded in-house choirs and orchestras; they sponsored group visits to concerts and the theater; they financed lecture evenings and continuing education courses. And for the "central problem of social renewal—the support of the family," companies were building homes and work settlements. All of this comprised a collective effort to demonstrate to the masses that hard work was not a "soulless" enterprise—that it was "an achievement for the preservation of the way of life of Western man."[62] Ultimately, culture and the mores of the *Unternehmer* were to converge in the home, where the comforts of bourgeois domesticity and a male-centered nuclear family would anchor the worker securely in a free-market economy. According to the advertisement for *Das goldene Dach*, "The cultural tasks of industry are directed toward the personality of the working person. Only in a healthy and attractive home can it develop. Industry's greatest tradition of settlements must be continued. The single-family home is the realm where culture and affluence unfold. Far from the ideas of collectivism, the worker experiences a happy family and personal security. It is here that self-help pre-vails over the welfare state."[63]

At first glance, these harmonious prescriptions for the worker—turning the mass man into his own industrialist, creating a nation of *Unternehmer*, granting a house and a garden to everyone, protecting the family and the male breadwinner, and forging a society educated in liberal humanism—are diffi-cult to square with the elitism and antiunion posturing described earlier in the chapter. Were not these democratic, egalitarian ideals the very things that industrialists resisted? In a way they were, and thus we arrive at a seeming paradox of early West German industry: the sincerely held belief in social peace and progress, on one hand, and on the other, the industrialists' stub-born clinging to older paternalist notions that entailed the inviolability of owner and managerial control and a lingering fear of mass worker unrest. On closer examination, however, industrialists' ideas about the worker are not so contradictory. Anchoring the worker in a secure job and home and mol-lifying him with economic comfort and family stability has been a universal desire that transcends postwar Germany. Yet it also echoes the particular con-servatism of the Adenauer years, marked by politicians, sociologists, and the general public's embrace of the now clichéd, but ultimately accurate, *Kinder, Küche, Kirche* (children, kitchen, and church).[64] In short, in the early 1950s industrialists, like most West Germans, were sincerely bent on overcoming a past marked by social strife. Yet they hoped to accomplish this on their own terms and by any means—with carrots, sticks, and the conflicting projections of optimism and paranoia.

Despite the offensive posturing and cultural pessimism of people like Otto Vogel, it would be facile to see the emerging language of social harmony only as public relations gambits by ex-Nazis or embattled conservatives. The 1950s did witness the metamorphosis of industrial attitudes about labor/manager relations. The abandonment of hostile, antiunion notions was a slow but forward process. In the early 1950s industrialists were still beginning to let down their guard, and they demonstrated a willingness to learn, albeit selectively, from their past mistakes. But we must also be careful, in light of these very real gains on the part of workers, not to overstate industrialists' openness to economic democracy in the early 1950s. If we look closely at the language of cultural and social solidarity, we discover that much of it was a political strategy—one that still bore the residue of a National Socialist labor utopianism and an antiunion hostility.

Ultimately, industry's shift from a combative to a conciliatory strategy reflects its increasing confidence. In 1950 the BDI and other organizations employed culture, antiunion fighting words, and the figure of the heroic industrialist to wage long-standing political battles. Yet industry's vocal anti-labor posturing belonged to a passing phase of industry/labor relations. Otto Vogel's speech in Cologne was perhaps little more than a parting shot at the unions—a final nod to the authoritarian "class struggle from above"[65]—before industry embarked on the path of peaceful social reconstruction.

After the passing of the *Betriebsverfassungsgesetz* in 1952, which gave the work councils a consultative voice in companies, the remnants of an older antagonism began to disappear, and businessmen now applied Germany's cultural pride and a reformed self-image toward the new social partnership. Importantly, the DGB shifted its strategy as well, eventually abandoning its more confrontational demands for workplace democracy and focusing instead on the quest for higher wages and better working conditions. Businessmen perceived the emergence of what has come to be known as "consensus capitalism" as a victory, and they grew emboldened in their use of the *Unternehmer* and the allures of self-enrichment as an incentive for worker pacifism.[66] But despite industry's increasing confidence and publicity caginess, it could no longer ignore the worker, as either an image or a reality. Through the story of rags to riches, industrialists acknowledged the worker as a hero in his (and sometimes her) own right. The worker was, in short, the mirror image of the industrialist and as such could not be shut out from the economic recovery. Without his other half—*der Mitarbeiter*—the new *Unternehmer* would remain malformed and incomplete.

CHAPTER SEVEN

Krupp, the United States, and the Salvation of West German Industry

In the preceding four chapters we have seen how after 1949 West German industry maneuvered more self-assuredly through the vagaries of economic and political reconstruction. Businessmen set up public relations organizations, they took part in the cultural and political discussions of the day, and they asserted themselves against perceived threats from organized labor. In short, industry assumed a confident and increasingly secure position in the young Federal Republic. Yet despite industrialists' growing optimism about their country's future, the Nazi past maintained a powerful presence after 1949. It defined the parameters of political discourses, it served as the catalyst for industry's image makeover, and it weighed heavily on the individual and collective psyches of West Germany's social and economic elite. Industrialists, like other elites, saw the Nazi years as obstructing the path to West Germany's psychic recovery. While they often attempted to ignore or navigate around this roadblock, they never abandoned their hopes of removing it entirely. Ironically, as the successes of German industry in domestic and international markets increased, businessmen became more aware of National Socialism's persistence as a theme. As individual companies and business organizations branched outward, they brought into each new market a publicity apparatus that could influence not only the purchasing habits of foreign consumers and business partners but their attitudes toward West Germany and its past.

Nowhere was this pattern more evident than with respect to the United States. In the early 1950s German industrialists solicited the help of sections of the U.S. public both to engage with West Germany economically and to bury the "myth" of German industrial complicity with Adolf Hitler. In particular, America's conservative intellectuals and business leaders rallied behind German industry in a demonstration of camaraderie and in a concerted effort to protect the capitalist West against the menace of collectivism at the height of the Cold War. These Americans saw themselves as part of an international milieu of businessmen and conservatives who understood one another and the necessities of the day. They drew on their pre-Hitler contacts, their affinities as "men of business," and their professed disdain for Nazism in order to forgive German capitalism for any misdeeds in the service of the united struggle against totalitarianism.

The first half of this chapter traces the developments in industry following the conviction of Alfried Krupp von Bohlen und Halbach and other businessmen in Nuremberg in 1948. Against the backdrop of rapid political and economic changes, most notably the formation of the ECSC and the Korean War, it follows the Krupp company's attempts to secure the release of its managers from prison and to defend its reputation at home. The second half of this chapter focuses on West German industry's attempt to ingratiate itself to an English-speaking public. In order to repair their image overseas, businessmen called on a number of prominent U.S. and British conservatives to plead the cause of West German industry. Their efforts culminated in an apologetic work by Louis Lochner, a prize-winning journalist who, in the words of one industry insider, was the "first person after the war to write for the purpose of saving the honor of German industrialists."[1]

Krupp and the Campaign for Amnesty

On 31 January 1951 U.S. High Commissioner for Germany John McCloy made an announcement that delighted the West German business community. After much deliberation McCloy had decided to grant amnesty to dozens of industrialists, politicians, doctors, and Nazi officials who had been found guilty in Nuremberg and who now sat in Landsberg prison.[2] Among those affected by this sweeping declaration were Alfried Krupp von Bohlen und Halbach, who had spent almost six years in detention and prison since his arrest, and eight of his colleagues on the Krupp board of directors. Friedrich Flick, the steel magnate convicted in a separate trial, had already been released in August 1950 for good behavior. By the mid-1950s Flick and Krupp had reclaimed their companies and personal holdings and had established a forceful presence on the political and economic scene. It is believed that they became the two richest men in Europe, in control of large empires of steelworks, shipyards, and manufacturing ventures. German industrialists' assurances to the contrary, the leading positions in German industry were again filled with people who had been deeply involved in the Nazi regime.[3]

The granting of clemency to industrialists and a number of other individuals convicted of war crimes is a familiar and still controversial theme. It has served both as the object of serious scholarship and as the centerpiece of more polemical attacks against Adenauer, the United States, and West Germany.[4] It has been used as proof that denazification was badly flawed, as evidence of capitalism's pervasive and pernicious force, and as a sign that the U.S. high commissioner was willing to coddle ex-Nazis. Most historians agree on a number of factors influencing the clemency decisions in 1951: the powerful effect that the Cold War exercised on U.S., and certainly McCloy's, thinking; the desire to appease a German public highly critical of Nuremberg and the concept of collective guilt; and McCloy's own belief that many of the sentences had been arbitrarily harsh.[5] For whatever reasons, John McCloy did make it clear that the United States was willing to accept the rehabilitation of individuals with questionable personal pasts. The majority of West Germans approved of the commissioner's decision, which they saw both as America's acknowledgment of the "injustice" of Nuremberg and, even more so, as a sign that the United States now needed West Germany as a Cold War ally.[6]

Business leaders had not stood idly waiting for this encouraging moment. In the two and a half years separating the last Nuremberg convictions and the release of Krupp in 1951, industrialists were not only waxing philosophical about culture or shoring up their political position vis-à-vis the unions. These years were also marked by frenetic activity on the part of industry, and West German elites more generally, to reverse the effects of the Nuremberg trials. Dozens of industrialists, Nazi doctors, high-ranking politicians, and SS and military leaders were serving long prison terms or were awaiting the carrying out of their death sentences. With the founding of the FRG, the U.S. military government led by Gen. Lucius Clay was replaced by a civilian American administration under McCloy, who immediately faced loud demands to release the Landsberg prisoners and commute death sentences. In a conscious show of unity, industrialists, politicians, jurists, and church leaders came together to challenge the concept of collective guilt embodied in Nuremberg.[7]

One of their first steps after the final verdicts in 1949 was the establishment of a central Coordination Office to direct the campaign on behalf of the Landsberg prisoners. In the summer of 1949 Eduard Wahl, CDU politician and former legal counsel for the IG Farben defense team, founded what came to be known as the Heidelberger Juristenkreis (Heidelberg jurists' circle), which was mainly comprised of fellow Nuremberg defense attorneys and church leaders.[8] Aside from preparing a document called the "Memorandum about the Necessity of a General Amnesty," which called on the Americans to reconsider the imprisonment of industrialists and political and military leaders,[9] the Heidelberger Juristenkreis also helped write and distribute, with the financial support of IG Farben, a 164-page document known as the Protestant Church's War Criminal Memorandum (Kriegsverbrecher-Denkschrift der EKD). This and other documents made a favorable impression on McCloy, who began to question the wisdom of maintaining the retributive features of

U.S. policy—as embodied in the Nuremberg prosecutions—while trying to build a trusting and cooperative relationship with the West German public.

While industrialists were contributing to the joint efforts on behalf of the convicted, they were also focusing on the specific circumstances of their imprisoned business colleagues. After the Krupp verdicts, for example, individual industrialists, companies, and business organizations sent numerous appeals to McCloy's predecessor, Clay and, eventually, to the U.S. Supreme Court to reconsider the convictions. Neither, however, would countenance a reversal of the Nuremberg decisions.[10]

In light of these rebuffs, industrialists decided to focus not only on legal issues but on the physical and mental comfort of their imprisoned colleagues. In 1949, for example, the Association of German Steel Industry Employers (Verein deutscher Eisenhüttenleute) pressed the director of Landsberg prison to provide the inmates with some meaningful work with which to pass the time.[11] The organization was able to secure some positive results: Krupp executive Eduard Houdremont was granted time off from physical labor to prepare the second edition of his book *Manual on Special Steels Science*,[12] while Landsberg prison director Colonel Graham appointed another Krupp director, Fritz von Bülow, as his personal secretary and "letter writer."[13] In another show of solidarity, Hermann Reusch, chairman of the Association of German Steel Industry Employers, distributed a circular to his colleagues proposing that they "send more frequent letters to cheer up the gentlemen incarcerated in Landsberg prison."[14] This seemingly harmless request caused a small stir. A labor union representative got a copy of this memorandum and passed it on to the Office of the U.S. High Commissioner for Germany (HICOG), perhaps out of concern that Reusch was conspiring in some way with his colleagues. While there was nothing to these suspicions, the Americans found the documents quite illuminating. "The circular and minutes," wrote a HICOG official, "are highly significant since they reveal that the Ruhr steel barons will identify themselves with those of their number which were convicted as Nazi offenders and shows [sic] they are still making an effort to keep the convicted Nazis within the innermost circle of the limited group which controls the powerful iron and steel industry."[15] This statement reveals inter alia the extent to which the U.S. government and the West German unions still had misgivings about German industry. They may have been ready to entrust the economy to Germany's businessmen, but they were under no illusion that mentalities had changed overnight.[16]

In the opinion of a HICOG official, this document spoke volumes about Ruhr industrialists' intentions, yet it also had something to say about the state of U.S. and labor union attitudes in the early 1950s: clearly industry was not yet to be trusted, not even behind bars. This habitual distrust is further evidenced by a detailed U.S. State Department report from late 1951 that traced the political backgrounds of the leading men of heavy industry. The report was conducted in response to popular literature about former Nazis "getting back into power."[17] The study ranked current board members in the Ruhr as either former "active Nazis," "nominal Nazis," "non-Nazis," or "anti-Nazis." While the newer companies, with union members on their boards, fared well in the study, the report concluded that "a good number of the 'bigger Nazis' are still about and have by no means abandoned their interests in the industry."[18] Americans were prepared to hand over the reins of the economy to German industry, but not without reservations about the past behavior and present attitudes of its leaders.

Taking the Legal Case to the Public

While German industrialists were able to obtain some minor concessions regarding the treatment of the prisoners, their chief goal still remained the release of their colleagues. Their most potent strategy, therefore, entailed demonstrating that the law was on their side. If they could prove that the U.S. judges had committed legal errors, in both the establishment and the conduct of the war crimes tribunals, then business leaders could perhaps challenge the *moral* validity of Nuremberg and eventually secure the release of their men. Industry therefore relied less on emotional appeals, which were finding little sympathy among U.S. officials, and more on the fine points of international and American law.

In particular, lawyers and legal scholars outlined the case against the Krupp decision, which had resulted in the greatest number of guilty verdicts and which constituted the most visible challenge to the West German business establishment. Their arguments rested on the belief that the tribunal improperly relied on ex post facto law by applying U.S. jurisprudence to acts that had not been crimes on German soil. They also complained that, even when applying U.S. law, the judges refused to allow American lawyers to represent German defendants. In effect they forced German lawyers to learn U.S. jurisprudence overnight. These critiques also questioned the absence of legal precedents, disputed a host of procedural decisions by the judges, fumed over the January 1948 jailing of Krupp's attorneys for contempt of court, and disputed the charges of slave labor and spoliation, which lawyers claimed had been committed by other countries during the war.[19]

Perhaps the most interesting and elaborate legal treatise originated from the Krupp firm. In the fall of 1949 Krupp defense attorney and Heidelberger Juristenkreis member Otto Kranzbühler prepared a short manuscript titled "Drei Amerikaner richten Krupp" [Three Americans convict Krupp], which argued against the Nuremberg verdict in familiar legal terms.[20] When Tilo Freiherr von Wilmowsky, former deputy chairman (*stellvertretender Vorsitzen-*

der) of the company's supervisory board, read the piece, he persuaded Kranz-bühler to expand it into a book-length work dealing with the issue of Krupp's guilt or innocence.[21] The study, they decided, would be reworked by a legal scholar but would bear the name of Wilmowsky, whose reputation, in sharp contrast to his company's, had emerged from the Nazi years intact, if not enhanced.

For followers of the fate of German industry's "royal family," Wilmow-sky was a familiar name. Best known as the uncle of Alfried Krupp by mar-riage, Baron Wilmowsky himself possessed an illustrious lineage. He was the grandson of Kaiser Wilhelm I's last adviser, the son of a cabinet minister for Wilhelm II, and the husband of Barbara Krupp, whose father, Fritz, had headed the firm during its glory days during the *Kaiserreich*.

During the Nazi years Wilmowsky joined the Nazi Party, but as a devout Christian, conservative, and monarchist he had maintained links to the men who formed the underground resistance against Hitler. After the failed assas-sination attempt in July 1944, the Gestapo arrested Wilmowsky and prose-cuted him for having consorted with the bomb plotters, as well as for criticiz-ing the SS, for helping Jews to emigrate from Germany, and for patronizing the Lutheran Church. Although he had not, in fact, known beforehand about the assassination attempt, Wilmowsky was found guilty and was sent to Sachsenhausen concentration camp with his wife, where the two remained until the end of the war.[22]

When Wilmowsky and Kranzbühler agreed to prepare a book, they real-ized that they would have to proceed cautiously. The Allies were at the time still considering breaking up the company, and neither man wanted to anger the people who controlled their fate. But they ultimately considered the book to be a proactive step that would clarify the peaceful nature of the firm with-out provoking the Americans. As a sign of this caution, they, besides designat-ing Wilmowsky as author, changed the original provocative title to the less anti-American "Krupp, Victim of a Myth." In order to convert Kranzbühler's dry legal argument into readable prose, they also hired Ernst Rudolf Huber as a ghostwriter.[23] Huber, in 1950 a professor of law at Freiburg University, had been a devoted Nazi and one of the leading National Socialist legal experts, having enshrined Hitler's *Führerprinzip* in *The Constitutional Law of the Greater German Reich*.[24] Krupp also called on the services of August Heinrichsbauer, lobbyist and erstwhile apologist for big business, to provide contacts within industry and to clarify historical details, especially about the company's re-lationship to German rearmament in the 1920s and 1930s.[25] Given Krupp's attempts to avoid controversy at this stage, it is stunning that the firm would employ the services of two controversial figures, especially the Nazi scholar Huber. This perhaps testifies to industrialists' stubborn unwillingness to ac-knowledge how much damage their reputations had and could still suffer. But

Krupp was aware enough of Huber's controversial writings during the Nazi years to keep the ghostwriter entirely behind the scenes.

The book was completed in the spring of 1950, bearing its final revised title, *Warum wurde Krupp verurteilt?* [Why was Krupp convicted?], a phrasing that the company hoped would appear less polemical and thus more appealing to German and U.S. readers. The book began by drawing on the power of the resister defense carefully honed during Nuremberg. The preface reminded the readers that the "author" Wilmowsky had been an opponent and prisoner of the regime and thus had no stake in exonerating those truly guilty of atrocities. It then argued that from an American, German, "Christian," and legal standpoint, the Krupp trial had been a disaster. The prosecution had turned Krupp and industry into a symbol of other people's complicity, it had misapplied international law, and it had not recognized the impotence of industrialists in the total state, especially with regard to slave labor. In short, it had not understood that in Nazi Germany, "*der Staat befiehlt der Wirtschaft*" (the state commanded the economy).[26] Finally, the book leveled a tu quoque charge: before blaming Krupp for having plundered and destroyed property, the Americans should have looked at their own policies during and after the war. The Morgenthau Plan, property confiscation, and dismantling were proof, argued the book, that the Americans were still caught up in a "war psychosis."[27]

As evidenced by the letters to Wilmowsky, many segments of German society, especially the business world, welcomed the publication of *Warum wurde Krupp verurteilt?* The book gave readers an opportunity to express their rage against Nuremberg, an event that, in the words of one reader, was "worse than a crime. . . . It was an irreparable blunder."[28] Max Ilgner, defendant in the IG Farben case, expressed his regret that his own company had not written a similar book; perhaps *Warum,* he told Wilmowsky, would serve as a model for such an undertaking.[29] Konrad Adenauer himself read the book thoroughly and passed on to Wilmowsky his opinion that Krupp had been gravely wronged; the chancellor gave his assurances that he would support the family and firm in any way possible in their quest for rehabilitation.[30]

Over the next two years, various plans to translate the book into English were also adopted but were ultimately abandoned. The German publication of *Warum* did, however, get some attention in the United States and England, particularly after Wilmowsky, with the assistance of the German General Consulate in New York, distributed free copies, along with an apologetic pamphlet written by Kranzbühler titled *A Short Survey of the Krupp Trial,* to businessmen, senators, publishers, university and public libraries, law schools, and political science and German departments.[31] Some U.S. magazines and organizations did review the book favorably. The Federation of American Citizens of German Descent, not surprisingly, welcomed the appearance of a work that separated itself from the typically anti-German fare.[32] The *New Statesmen and Nation* also gave a positive review to Wilmowsky. When in the next issue there appeared a letter to the editor criticizing this review—citing industry's shameful use of slave labor—Wilmowsky wrote his own editorial, outlining in detail his arrest and imprisonment in the "notorious concentration camp Sachsenhausen" and insisting that "the use of POWs and foreign workers was the sad but unavoidable result of a total mass war."[33]

Like most public relations projects, *Warum wurde Krupp verurteilt?* was designed to appeal to both a German and an American public, as well as to company employees and unionized workers in West Germany who still harbored suspicions of big business.[34] Its most important aim, however, was to secure the release of imprisoned Krupp officials. In this regard, Krupp directors received encouraging news as they were making the final revisions to the book in March. High Commissioner McCloy announced the formation of a clemency board to review the sentences handed down in Nuremberg.[35] The Advisory Board on Clemency for War Criminals (also known as the Peck Panel, after chairman David W. Peck, a New York Supreme Court justice) was slated to consider the Krupp case in June, after which it would offer recommendations to McCloy about possibly commuting sentences or granting amnesty.[36] Wilmowsky spoke with his imprisoned nephew and his lawyers, and they decided that by hurrying the publication of *Warum*, they might in fact influence the three-man clemency board in favor of Alfried.[37] But the book's author wondered in private whether his legal treatise would have such a salutary effect. Declared ghostwriter Huber,

> I cannot begin to guess how the American side will receive this book. I do, however, believe that, as it stands, it avoids wording that could in any way be interpreted as a challenge. Certainly the danger exists that certain groups in America will denounce any criticism from Germany as a symptom of a much ballyhooed German "nationalism." . . . Yet it is equally our task to speak up for what we with good conscience believe is right and just, even if one tries to avoid . . . polemics. I am not without hope that our piece will have a positive effect on the Clemency Board.[38]

In June 1950 *Warum wurde Krupp verurteilt?* reached the Peck Panel just as it took up Alfried Krupp's case.[39] It is not, however, known if the three Americans ever read the book—or if they could read German at all. But that hardly seemed to matter. The book would soon spawn a larger transatlantic project on behalf of West German industry. Moreover, within two months the clemency panel would issue recommendations to Commissioner McCloy that were very favorable to the Landsberg prisoners. However, two other events preceding the announcement that summer did more to influence U.S. attitudes about German industry than this self-serving legal treatise. The first was the unveiling of the Schuman Plan in May 1950, and the second was the outbreak of the Korean War.

International Developments and the Amnesty of German Industrialists

The Schuman Plan, named after French foreign minister Robert Schuman, was the culmination of a multiyear Allied discussion about the fate of German heavy industry.[40] Various plans had ranged from deconcentration to nationalization to internationalization to the establishment of a customs union between France and West Germany. The plan eventually ratified in April 1951 created the ECSC, in essence a pooling agreement between heavy industry in France, West Germany, Italy, and the Benelux countries. A jointly administered "high authority" in Luxembourg was made responsible for regulating and coordinating the production and export of six countries' coal and steel. The Coal and Steel Community did not become a giant European steel cartel that divvied up markets and fixed prices. Rather, it lifted tariffs while, in effect, leveling the playing field for French heavy industry, which had long been overshadowed by the Ruhr.

Most of West German industry threw its support behind the Schuman Plan, which, to the Americans, was a hopeful sign that German industry was now committed to peaceful competition and cooperation with its neighbors. For their part, when faced with the choice of dissolution and liquidation or existence within a regulated community, industrialists happily chose the latter. Yet a week after the announcement of the plan, German industry learned some bad news. The Allies unveiled Law No. 27, which called for the liquidation and recombination of the Ruhr's largest companies and which controlled the steel output of each company. As much as Western policy makers had delighted in the show of solidarity around the Schuman Plan, they would not abandon their intention to break the traditional power of German heavy industry. Industrialists bitterly resented Law No. 27, primarily on the grounds that it went against the spirit of the Schuman Plan, which called for the revival, not the destruction, of German industry.[41]

If these two proposals appear contradictory, they nonetheless reflected the Allies' ambivalence about the revival of the West German economy. On one hand, the United States, France, and Britain wanted to welcome industry into a community of democratic economies. The Ruhr would again produce for Europe and the world. On the other hand, Germany had once proven itself incapable of adhering to the standards of international cooperation and peace, and the Allies were not going to pretend they had forgotten about Hitler's aggressive imperialist aims. High Commissioner McCloy did not disguise this ambivalence when on 16 June 1950 he spoke to a group of fifty Ruhr industrialists and bankers in Düsseldorf about U.S. views of West German business.

With events moving rapidly in the Ruhr, this was to be McCloy's "state of the union" speech to industry, perhaps the most significant address to Germany's businessmen since the end of the war. McCloy began by congratulating industry on West Germany's rapid recovery since the Marshall Plan and the currency reform. (Industrial output, according to McCloy, had reached 104 percent of its 1936 levels).[42] Despite such cause for celebration, McCloy warned his listeners to avoid complacency. Unemployment was still high, the country depended on foreign aid, exports lagged far behind imports, and investment needed to increase. In reference to the burgeoning *Osthandel* (trade with Eastern bloc countries) and U.S. fears about German economic relations with the Soviet bloc, McCloy reminded the audience that West German trade lay "not in the East but in the West." Finally, West German industry, McCloy argued, still faced a major psychological barrier:

> To be perfectly frank, this development [the revival of the Ruhr] causes serious doubts in the minds of many people. For many other countries, the Ruhr is a symbol of industrial capacity devoted to aggression and its rebuilding creates concern for their security. Looking at the past, they wonder whether these factories and foundries will be used in the future for peace or for aggression. . . . For Germany itself, the re-growth of industry is certain to raise serious questions. Many Germans are concerned lest their economy be dominated again by a small group who will use their concentrated power to control German political and social life. The question is: will the men managing the industries of the Ruhr use their influence to support a liberal, democratic German state? Or will they use it to stifle progressive elements and to aid men and policies that in the past led Germany to destruction and have caused so much misery in the world? In short, Ruhr industry faces the task of winning the confidence of the German people and the people of the world. You and others like you, therefore, have a tremendous opportunity and responsibility. Your actions and your attitudes can ensure that the resources of German industry are dedicated to a new and peaceful development of Europe; your actions can contribute greatly to the creation of a genuinely democratic society and state in Germany.[43]

Commissioner McCloy's speech was a notably blunt commentary on the challenges facing West German industry. While it acknowledged the many problems German business faced, with respect to both its economy and its international image, it was tactful and restrained, especially when broaching the issue of German business guilt. Clearly, whatever McCloy felt about German industry's relationship to Hitler, he would not let it come to the surface or mute his overall optimism. His audience seemed unruffled by his admonitions, expressing enthusiasm for the Schuman Plan and gratitude for the support the United States had shown. Yet certain observers were secretly fearful. Much of the old guard still resented Washington's punitive treatment of German industry, both its prosecution of business leaders and its steering the economy so dramatically away from a cartel tradition that they still cherished.

These lingering resentments came to the surface during the question-and-answer period after McCloy's speech, when Theo Goldschmidt, president of the IHK Essen and a fierce defender of Ruhr interests, stood up to complain about excessive taxes and the high cost of absorbing refugees from the East. The mood in the room quickly changed. An animated McCloy jettisoned his rhetorical caution and angrily chastised Goldschmidt for harping on U.S. "failures."

> Don't forget that America's high taxes are the result of German aggression. Don't forget who started this war. Whether or not you gentlemen here are responsible personally for it, remember the war and all the misery that followed it—including your own—was born and bred in German soil and you must accept the responsibility. . . . Why didn't you mention the Marshall Plan? Why didn't you mention the aid we are giving the refugees while you stall? Why don't you recall how the occupied countries lived under your occupation? . . . Don't weep in your beer. Think of the good things as they come to you.[44]

A chastened Goldschmidt took his seat, while a hush descended over the room. Then resounding applause followed. The Ruhr elite, out of either shock or politeness, seemed to be countenancing the condemnation of their influential colleague.

What is so interesting about this speech—and its dramatic end—is that it reflects all the tensions and contradictions in the U.S. view of West German industry. It was at once cordial and upbeat, suspicious and accusatory. But it also made clear that there was no turning back or giving in to the antibusiness sentiments expressed by some members of the U.S. and West German public. His doubts notwithstanding, John McCloy saw West German industry as the best hope for a peaceful and prosperous Europe. But it had to be contained within a democratic system of checks and balances and constantly reminded of its compromised past.

Whatever lingering doubts McCloy had about the revival of the Ruhr were greatly tested when, nine days after his speech in Düsseldorf, North Korean troops crossed the thirty-eighth parallel and entered South Korea. Throughout the West the outbreak of the Korean War unleashed a sense of panic. There was talk of communist agitation in West Germany and Russian troop concentrations on the East German border. Rumors circulated about food rationing and the flight of U.S. military personnel from Germany. Stories spread of the rapid remilitarization of West Germany, the revival of the army, and the reactivation of Wehrmacht generals and officers.[45] In light of such concerns, the Korean War seemed to bode ill for industry. It restored negative memories of an aggressive military and economic powerhouse, and it fed into the emerging debate in 1950 on the rearmament of West Germany. At a time when they were trying to regain the trust of the world, industrialists did not readily welcome images of tanks rolling off the Krupp assembly lines and German rockets flying eastward.[46]

In fact, however, the Korean War had more positive than negative implications for German industry. For one, it increased demand in the West for raw materials and finished goods to support the war effort. West German industrial output increased, and a new phase of economic growth was initiated. Both as a response to war demands and as a gesture to industry in the quest to get the Schuman Plan ratified, the Allies announced in October 1950 that they had lifted their limitations on steel production. The war thus seemed to be ushering West Germany and its economy fully into the Western fold. On a psychological level, too, the Korean War did not simply stir up old fears about German industrial and military might; it also seemed to provide evidence of what industrialists had taken great pains to prove: that they were indispensable in the fight against communism.[47] For their part, German industrialists, given the accusations about past complicity, were always extremely cautious about publicly supporting the rearmament of West Germany. The debate over rearmament was accompanied by public demands for the release of military leaders still in prison, and given the explosiveness of this theme, industrialists were wise to stay as far from this debate as possible. On the rare occasion that they entered the fray, business spokesmen like Fritz Berg and industrial publications consistently forswore any urge among industrialists to expand their businesses into military contracting.[48]

The Korean War and the Schuman Plan provided industrialists with a difficult choice with respect to lobbying for the amnesty of their colleagues. Either they could step up their campaign on behalf of the convicted industrialists while international events were going their way, or they could soft-pedal in anticipation of a positive announcement by the clemency board. In effect, the events of the summer of 1950 forced industry to decide in which direction to take its public relations. Those who subscribed to more vigilant tactics argued that industry should draw up a new set of resolutions regarding the Nuremberg judgments and continue to push its legal case vigorously. But Otto Kranzbühler, who seemed to be calling the shots, rejected this idea. Industry had bombarded the Americans enough, and now it would be better to employ more indirect means. He saw one such opportunity at the church congress (*Kirchentag*) to be held in Essen in late August, where a captive audience of local workers and sympathetic clergymen planned to pay homage to the city and its chief employer, Krupp. It was to be a show of solidarity by

Germany's employees and managers. In anticipation, Kranzbühler contacted the event coordinators and asked that the speakers, such as Hanover's bishop Hanns Lilje, highlight the firm's history of social achievements and, in particular, the fact that there had never been a strike at Krupp. He also asked the speakers to link the imprisonment of Alfried Krupp to the most controversial topic of the day: industrial codetermination. Both, argued Kranzbühler, posed a grave threat to the morale of the Essen workers and, thus, the productivity of the Ruhr.[49] By linking Alfried Krupp's imprisonment to the ostensibly more political issue of codetermination, Kranzbühler was cleverly manipulating the sentiments of the workers, who were sympathetic to their imprisoned owner's cause while, at the same time, taking advantage of the anticodetermination sentiments of a number of occupation officials.

On 25 August the Beauftragte für das Evangelische Männerwerk des Kirchenkreises Essen sponsored its gathering. The speakers dutifully portrayed Alfried Krupp as a provider and protector against the dangerous influence of "the masses." In a talk titled "Man in the Collective," one speaker quoted the imprisoned Krupp verbatim: "I am saying this for the whole world to hear: there is in Essen a mass—tens of thousands of Kruppianer. But these Kruppianer are not mass men. And we will do everything to make sure that they do not gradually become mass men through privation, and that the large family of Kruppianer will reunite for the peaceful work of reconstruction— the family of Kruppianer with the Krupp family."[50]

Three days after these words were uttered, the "Krupp family" received the news it had been waiting for. The Advisory Board on Clemency for War Criminals had submitted its report, and it was the panel's conclusion that Alfried Krupp's sentence and the confiscation of his personal fortune and industrial holdings were unduly harsh in light of the decisions against other industrialists. The panel recommended a reduction of his sentence and the return of his property. It made no recommendations on the IG Farben and Flick defendants, as they were soon to be released for good behavior.

While the Peck Panel's decisions have often been portrayed as an overly solicitous gesture to West German elites, they did not let the Landsberg defendants off the hook entirely. As Thomas Schwartz has written, the panel "sought to appease all sides by combining a strong defense of the Nuremberg principles with a wide-ranging leniency."[51] It did not challenge, for example, the thesis presented at Nuremberg that institutions and professions—the SS, industry, and doctors—had conspired to realize National Socialism's aims. Nor did it accept the defense's arguments about the impropriety of U.S. law in a German context. But when it came to individual cases, the panel did believe that many of the men who were now imprisoned had possessed a relatively low position in the Nazi government or corporate hierarchy and that the sentences had been applied unevenly.

McCloy was not obligated to accept these recommendations, but he ultimately did so, both out of conviction and for practical reasons. On 31 January 1951 he announced that he was releasing the industrialists and dozens of other prisoners convicted in the Nuremberg trials.[52] He returned Alfried Krupp's property and holdings on the grounds that their confiscation was "generally repugnant to American concepts of justice."[53] On 3 February West German industry breathed a sigh of relief as the prisoners left Landsberg and returned home. While the public and political debates over the amnesty for other prisoners would continue through the 1950s, for industry the Nuremberg nightmare seemed to be over.

In granting amnesty to Krupp and his colleagues, McCloy, as Schwartz has rightly argued, grossly underestimated the extent to which industry had been involved in Nazi crimes. For example, he bought into industry's incorrect claim that Alfried Krupp was a lowly official tried in lieu of his sick father, Gustav, and he also accepted too readily the defense's contention that companies had been forced to use slave labor. Critics of McCloy's decision have long assumed that the Korean War and the desire to rearm Germany against the communists induced McCloy to free the "capitalists" and put them back to work. But McCloy, while indeed a staunch anticommunist, vehemently denied that Korea, the Cold War, and the rearmament debates had anything to do with the release of Krupp.[54] His decision was, he insisted, based solely on legal and humanitarian considerations. There is indeed no direct evidence that the debates in 1950 over remilitarization and the public pressure for the release of military officers influenced McCloy's decisions regarding industrialists. But Korea and the rapidly escalating tensions with the Soviet Union had certainly fostered hysteria about the security of Western Europe that could only have worked to the industrialists' advantage. Whether or not he would concede as much, John McCloy was responding to the political mood of the day, which saw little use in perpetuating a punitive relationship to Germany during the Cold War. McCloy felt that the fight against Soviet communism demanded Western unity, industrial strength, and eventually West German participation in an Atlantic defense force.

The immediate aftermath of Krupp's release is an oft-told story. The British press was outraged, while West Germans were ecstatic over McCloy's decision. "The liberation of Alfried Krupp," wrote a VSt director to McCloy, "has rejoiced our economic leaders."[55] The now notorious photos of Alfried Krupp hosting a celebratory champagne brunch after his release unleashed a furious response among international observers as well as U.S. occupation officials, who bristled at this tasteless display of self-indulgence following their gesture of goodwill. In reality the Krupp firm itself had not planned this champagne breakfast. It was an unexpected and unrequested gift from the hotel to which Krupp retired after his release. The Krupp management itself was furious and probably predicted a negative U.S. reaction. The Americans were indeed so unsettled that they sent Günter Henle to investigate this public relations blunder. Wrote a HICOG employee to Henle,

> It was unfortunate that this publicity was attached to Mr. Krupp's departure from Landsberg. Such are the incidents which create a bad atmosphere, although they are of course not intentional. Somewhere, somehow, something went wrong and Mr. Krupp was badly advised. That such matters can be handled in a discreet manner without publicity is proven by the discharge of Mr. Flick, who left Landsberg practically unnoticed and whose name has been kept out of the public limelight ever since. However, the less said about this matter from here on will be the best for all concerned.[56]

The Krupp fiasco was one more reminder of the Western Allies' lingering suspicions of German big business. To be sure, since the end of World War II, the Allies had been offering mixed signals about their willingness to countenance assertiveness on the part of Germany's businessmen. Occasionally they would allow a public relations initiative or a self-promoting measure, but they were easily angered by any show of disrespect or tactlessness by the vanquished. Clearly, postwar industrial recovery involved a series of gambles and tests, and West Germany's economic elites would still have to proceed with caution if they were to regain the complete trust of the Allies.

Six years had passed since the end of the war, and industry had made many strides in its attempt to secure a new legitimacy in the eyes of the Western Allies and the West German public. Yet memories of industrial behavior and, more importantly, actual mentalities *within* industry could not disappear or transform themselves overnight. Most company leaders had joined the Nazi Party and had supported, tacitly or actively, the Nazis' economic aims, and this the Americans would not easily forget.[57] Yet despite lingering concerns, by the beginning of 1951 the United States also made it clear that it was on the side of West German industry. Industry now had to reckon with a tougher customer, one that held even more power over the future of German industry: the American public.

U.S. Conservatives and the Rescue of German Industry

After the release of the Landsberg prisoners at the beginning of 1951, West German industry faced important decisions about how to approach the lingering issue of corporate guilt under Nazism. Most industrialists felt that the fight against the "myth" of business complicity should continue. The attacks on German industry were still occurring, and they were coming not only from the labor unions and the East German press but from across the English Channel and the Atlantic in a spate of scholarly and popular works about Germany. In the words of a VSt official in 1950, the chief culprit was America's implicitly Jewish "immigrants," who were perpetuating the view "that Ruhr industry was of the same heart and mind as the NSDAP."[58] It is not clear to which immigrants he was referring, but the 1950s had indeed begun with a number of books in English calling attention to the past and present situation of German industry. In 1950 James Stewart Martin, the former head of the Decartelization Branch of the U.S. Military Government, published *All Honorable Men*, which narrated in extremely disgruntled terms the author's vain efforts to prevent German industry from regaining its pre-1945 strength. Martin drew on the familiar theme that the Nazis' rise and consolidation of power was the handiwork of big business and that industry's postwar resistance to change signaled the endurance of Nazi mentalities. In 1950 West German industrialists read Martin's book with great curiosity about the "mentality of the American deconcentration fanatics," as well as with considerable concern about Martin's "destructive judgments about German industry."[59] They passed the book on to one another and compiled lists of specific passages that could in any way be damaging to their interests.[60]

All Honorable Men was just one of dozens of books from the early 1950s that criticized the "return to power" of industrialists and militarists.[61] Despite a stream of critical publications, German industrialists were encouraged by the appearance of a few books that resisted the more damning clichés about industry. They took heart at the publication of Norman J. G. Pounds's *The Ruhr,* which according to Tilo Wilmowsky, avoided the trap of blaming German industrialists for Hitler.[62] They also passed around other books that criticized U.S. occupation policies more generally. Victor Gollancz, the British reconciliationist publisher, wrote *In Darkest Germany* about his visit to a malnourished and disease-ridden Germany in 1946.[63] The book displayed photographs of sick and emaciated Germans, thus drawing an implicit comparison between the fate of Germans under the occupation and that of Germany's victims before 1945. Other books espousing an open sympathy for Germany were U.S. conservative Freda Utley's *High Cost of Vengeance*, Montgomery Belgion's *Victors' Justice,* and Lord Maurice Pascal Alers Hankey's *Politics, Trials, and Errors*—all damning assessments of the American occupation, its war trials program, and its industrial and food policies in West Germany.[64] These books were not best-sellers. But they represented a unified voice of dissent at a time when most literature was overwhelmingly critical of Germany. More importantly, they were all, with the exception of Pounds's book, issued by a single U.S. publisher, Henry Regnery, who took upon himself the task of representing what he saw as a downtrodden and unfairly maligned nation. Regnery was one of postwar America's most important conservative voices and the sponsor of West German industry's definitive answer to its critics.

Through Regnery we can witness the emergence of a conservative intellectual sensibility that stretched across the Atlantic and encompassed social and economic elites in Western Europe and the United States. The descendant of German Catholic farmers in Wisconsin, the son of a Chicago textile magnate, an exchange student in Nazi Germany, and a former student of economist Joseph Schumpeter at Harvard, Regnery seemed almost naturally predisposed toward German business. After writing a number of articles critical of the Democratic Party and its punitive policies toward Germany, Regnery inaugurated his own publishing company in the late 1940s with three books that foreshadowed a lifelong preoccupation with Germany. Next to the Utley, Gollancz, and Belgion publications, three of his earliest titles, Regnery also published Hans Rothfels's *The German Opposition to Hitler* and, later, an array of works by prominent German conservatives such as Ernst Jünger, Friedrich Georg Jünger, Konrad Adenauer, and neoliberal economist Wilhelm Röpke, who would become a regular foreign contributor to the *National Review* in the mid-1950s.[65] Despite Regnery's interest in Germany, his most famous "discoveries" were William F. Buckley Jr., whose first book, *God and Man at Yale*, lashed out at liberal academic elites and their failure to inculcate a spirit of Christian individualism in their students, and Russell Kirk, whose *The Conservative Mind* became the bible of postwar U.S. conservatism.[66] By 1950, when German industry learned of him, Regnery had established himself as America's foremost conservative publisher who, in the words of Krupp attorney Otto Kranzbühler, also published German-friendly books "as a hobby."[67]

Regnery's connection to West German industry began with a letter from Tilo von Wilmowsky. In June 1950 Alfried Krupp's uncle asked Henry Regnery to publish an English translation of *Warum wurde Krupp verurteilt?*[68] Regnery rejected the book on the grounds that it would not sell well in translation, but he did express his support for a project that would take on the Nuremberg trials and the thesis of big business guilt more generally. Wilmowsky, while disappointed with the rejection of "his" book, was in fact already drawing up plans for a more exhaustive study of the Nuremberg industrialist trials and the behavior of German industry during the Nazi years.[69] As we have seen, industry had taken on such projects before. But this, in its final form, would be different. It would be written in English, it would be widely distributed, and it would carry the weight of two continents and numerous influential backers and advisers, most notably Krupp and Regnery.

From the time of the project's inception until its publication in 1954 in the form of Louis Lochner's *Tycoons and Tyrant*, four years would pass. During this period Wilmowsky gathered around him some of the most influential names in West German politics, as well as an impressive list of supportive Americans. Some of the more prominent names are worth mentioning. Former German chancellor Heinrich Brüning, who in 1950 was winding down an eleven-year teaching stint at Harvard in preparation for a move to the University of Cologne, was privy to the project from the outset.[70] Brüning's successor as chancellor in 1932, Franz von Papen, who had recently been released from prison and whose autobiography was, at the time, selling well, also offered his assistance.[71] From the world of German politics there was, finally, Herbert von Dirksen, the former German ambassador to Moscow, Tokyo, and London, who used his old connections to secure support among pro-German Britons for a study that, in Wilmowsky's words, would clear the "rubble" in industry's way.[72]

When Wilmowsky broached his latest book idea to his friends and colleagues, he encountered, as had become usual, a mixture of support and concern about the project's scope and timing. Rather than doing a study on the guilt or innocence of German industry, Dirksen suggested, it would be "psychologically better" to commission a "neutral investigation of industrialists in the total state and in total war."[73] The head of the Siemens archive echoed these reservations: "Would it not be timely to follow [the Wilmowsky book] with a more general investigation into the political activities and influences of industry in this era and in different countries?"[74] Clearly both men had in mind a comparative history of the Nazi and Allied economies during World War II. If they could reveal industry/state cooperation as a universal phenomenon during times of war, then the behavior of Germany's industrialists—fulfilling arms contracts, employing POWs and forced labor, and plundering—would, they hoped, be relativized and perhaps even humanized. The behavior of German business would no longer be considered sui generis but, rather, the expression of a universal readiness to support one's country while its citizens were fighting and dying at the front. Moreover, with the announcement of the Schuman Plan, Dirksen felt such a book would be politically expedient.[75] What better moment, when the eyes of the world were on German industry, to prove itself worthy of international trust and put an end to the "Nuremberg Complex"?[76]

Heinrich Brüning, in contrast, expressed doubts about whether the time was ripe for an English publication, especially when things *were* going better for big business. Montgomery Belgion, in response to Dirksen's suggestions, doubted that the English-speaking public paid any attention to the Schuman Plan, let alone German business. "My own feeling," he wrote to Dirksen, "is that such a book . . . would not appeal to the general public unless it could be cast in the form of a dramatic story, and that would require on the part of the author a rare combination of gifts—an understanding of the problems of large-scale business and also an ability to give the exposition of them a kind of magic touch. I do not myself know of any English or American writer who possesses that combination."[77]

Most of Wilmowsky's colleagues within German industry were doubtful at first. They remembered well the brisk beginnings and abrupt endings to earlier projects defending industry. Flick officials were especially wary of such an undertaking. In June 1950 their boss was still in prison, and Friedrich Flick personally expressed a fear that a book about industry would jeopardize his tenuous position with the Allies, who were considering his early release. Another opponent of the project was Hermann Reusch, who had been so active in the Heinrichsbauer apology in 1948. Only a publication in *Time* or *Life* magazine, the GHH director argued, would reach enough readers to have any effect.[78] Finally, Wolfgang Pohle, the former legal counsel for Flick, was leery of another venture into the publicity unknown. He recalled his own aborted efforts with Heinrichsbauer and a more recent attempt by honorary professor Kurt Hesse of the Frankfurt Academy for World Trade to write about the industry trials.[79] After spending two nights reading through Hesse's finished manuscript with representatives of the Klöckner company, Pohle determined that the work had to be entirely rewritten. The project was eventually declared an "absolute failure" (*absoluter Mißerfolg*) and abandoned entirely.[80] Finally there was the problem of funding. Allied Law No. 27 held the iron and steel companies of the Ruhr in a state of liquidation, and this made obtaining funding from heavy industry an extremely difficult process, one that demanded constant circumspection and humble solicitation of the authorities. Any new project, wrote Pohle, would therefore have to rely heavily on funds from the chemical and the machine tools industries, which controlled their own financial fates.[81]

As in the past, however, doubts gave way to cautious support. As the events of the summer of 1950 played out, business leaders detected a friendlier climate for an investigation into the "defamation of business" (*Wirtschafts-Diffamierung*).[82] In June the Allies had opened the West German economy to overseas investment. In August the clemency board had made its recommendations regarding Krupp, and Friedrich Flick had been released from prison. Finally Wilmowsky's primary contact in the United States, former editor of the *Berliner Tageblatt* and Regnery copyeditor Paul Scheffer, predicted enthusiasm in the U.S. business community.[83] With the support of the Americans, the project might indeed have a chance. That summer the battle lines were being drawn in the codetermination debate, and industry could use the support of U.S. business, which found codetermination anathema to its own labor traditions and principles. By February 1951, when Krupp was released from prison, Wilmowsky could happily report that the four companies tried for war crimes (IG Farben, Krupp, Flick, and Röchling) all supported his idea.[84]

Despite the now unified support of West German business, two essential ingredients were still missing: an author and a publisher. As to the latter, Montgomery Belgion had been doing some footwork. He spoke with the head of the University of Chicago Press, who welcomed the project in principle but feared low sales. Despite his rejection, the editor did express his willingness to help find a writer and perhaps defray some of the book's expenses. Belgion also turned to Yale University Press, whose editor was Eugene Davidson, a Germany specialist and editor on the board of the conservative journal *Human Events* with Regnery.[85] Davidson reported encouraging words from the university's economics department, as well as his own belief that while it would not sell well to the mass public, a study of the war economy would find great support in academic circles. This conception of the book differed markedly from that of Wilmowsky, who had envisioned the book not as a piece of dispassionate scholarship per se but as a potential best-seller.[86] If the book was supposed to reach as broad an audience as possible, somebody who wrote in a popular style was needed. Given these sentiments, it should not be surprising that Wilmowsky held the more suitable Henry Regnery in reserve should Yale withdraw its support.

A year had passed since its inception, and the project was moving slowly forward. But it still needed an author. Wilmowsky solicited the advice of Marion Gräfin Dönhoff, a descendent of an old Prussian noble family with an anti-Nazi record, a journalist on the liberal *Die Zeit,* and an occasional contributor to *Human Events.*[87] Dönhoff was unable to come up with any authors. At IG Farben's request, Wilmowsky then offered Montgomery Belgion the job, but the latter demurred, preferring to continue serving as a project adviser rather than author.[88] Over the course of 1950 and 1951 the list of potential authors grew to include some of the most prominent (mostly conservative) names in U.S., British, and German letters: Allen Dulles, former Office of Strategic Services representative in Switzerland with connections to Germany, soon to be named director of the Central Intelligence Agency, and author of a 1947 book on the anti-Nazi resistance, *Germany's Underground;*[89] novelist and erstwhile big business critic Sinclair Lewis; Harry Elmer Barnes, formerly of the revisionist school of U.S. history during the 1920s; Götz Briefs, an émigré social scientist teaching at the New School for Social Research; Arnold Wolfers, former president of the Politische Hochschule in Berlin until 1933 and professor at Yale; Armin Mohler, a conservative young Swiss writer whose dissertation, "Die Konservative Gegen-Revolution, 1819–1933," had just been published by *Warum* publisher Friedrich Vorwerk;[90] Vivian Stranders, professor at the University of London and publisher of the anti-Soviet *The Bulwark* in London;[91] and finally William Henry Chamberlin, historian of Russia, former correspondent in Moscow, and author of the virulently anticommunist *America's Second Crusade,* which Henry Regnery published in 1950 as his "first revisionist work."[92]

None of these authors worked out, and after a long and fruitless search, Wilmowsky and Scheffer finally came up with the name of Louis Lochner.

Louis Lochner and two other U.S. correspondents interview Adolf Hitler in Berchtesgaden, Bavaria, 1932. Lochner is on the far right. (X3, 20669, courtesy of State Historical Society of Wisconsin)

Lochner was a journalist who had just edited and written the introduction to Regnery's newest publication, the memoirs of Lochner's close friend and confidante Prince Louis Ferdinand of Hohenzollern, who aside from being the grandson of Kaiser Wilhelm II and would-be heir to the German throne, had worked as a mechanic at Ford's Michigan plant in the early 1930s.[93] Lochner, however, had even stronger credentials than his friendship with a royal scion. He was a Pulitzer Prize–winning journalist, a pacifist, an expert on Germany, and a proven business advocate. He was the editor of Joseph Goebbels's diaries and a biographer of Henry Ford, of the violinist Fritz Kreisler, and, later, of Herbert Hoover.[94] As head of Berlin's Associated Press office in the 1930s, Lochner had closely followed the rise of Hitler and the consolidation of his regime. For a time he had even been held in a Nazi detention camp and had, like Wilmowsky, maintained close ties with the men who were later murdered following the July 1944 plot against Hitler.[95] An anti-Nazi fluent in German, staunchly anticommunist, and friendly with some of the most prominent figures in German public life, Lochner seemed perfect for the job.[96] Regnery rightly predicted that Lochner would grab at a chance to be of service to his old contacts in the German political and economic establishment. "Standing before me is the greatest challenge of my not entirely uneventful

The Salvation of West German Industry   221

life!" wrote an excited Lochner to Wilmowsky upon accepting the latter's formal offer to write the book.[97] Wilmowsky had found his author. When Yale learned that Lochner and not one of their own economics professors had been offered the book, they withdrew their support. The project was now squarely in Regnery's hands.

The next step was to secure funding. Regnery and Wilmowsky originally considered turning solely to U.S. backers, such as foundations or private philanthropists. Eugene Davidson had recommended the Social Science Research Council,[98] while Robert Hutchins, the recently retired chancellor of the University of Chicago, suggested that Regnery speak with the Ford Foundation, an organization that Hutchins served as adviser on German matters.[99] While the Ford Foundation would never underwrite a publisher, suggested Hutchins, it might indeed grant a fellowship to the Foundation for Foreign Affairs, which Regnery and Eugene Davidson codirected in Washington. The latter foundation, Hutchins pointed out, could then forward funds to Regnery and Lochner.

Lochner and Regnery were dissatisfied with these options. It would take at least six months to get a decision from the Ford Foundation, and Lochner was eager to start on the project immediately. They therefore turned instead to the people who had the most to gain from this project: West Germany's industrialists. In October Alfried Krupp met with his lawyers to discuss the feasibility of his firm's funding part of the Lochner project. After much discussion they decided that Krupp would give an initial advance of $10,000 to the project, which Regnery would eventually pay back from the book's royalties, and a $6,000 travel account for Lochner after his arrival in Germany. All this, however, was made contingent on other West German companies pitching in. Krupp asked Theo Goldschmidt to solicit other firms for contributions. Over the course of the next year, and with the active involvement of the DI and the BDI, Krupp managed to raise the appropriate funds.[100] In March 1952, a few months before Lochner's arrival in Germany, Kranzbühler received the approval of the economics ministry in Bonn for the transfer of funds to Regnery.[101]

These arrangements, even though approved by Bonn, were not risk free. Wilmowsky warned that while the impetus and much of the money was coming from German industry, all parties involved must pretend that the project had originated in the United States. "We must find a way to avoid any impression that the book is a plea financed by the German side. We do have certain reservations about making an official contribution to the publisher. We must find instead a cover-address (*Deckaddresse*) in the U.S. . . . to which the payment is transferred." [102]

Regnery and Scheffer disagreed vehemently with Wilmowsky's surreptitious approach. "The Ruhr has a right to be heard," Scheffer declared, and it should not feel the need to proceed under cover, at least with regard to money. Moreover, such financial secretiveness, argued Scheffer, could have serious repercussions. "In an extreme case . . . it could lead to an investigation by the Senate or the House, which seems to be in vogue today. It would be uncomfortable, to say the least, if it emerged that we represented the project's origins exactly opposite to the actual facts." [103] This is not to say that Scheffer advocated open discussion of the impending project. "It would not be fatal, but nonetheless damaging," he wrote, "if the plan was introduced to the public not through your people or the publisher, but through a third party."

Such a "leak" almost became reality. Scheffer and Lochner were unnerved when they learned that Heinrich Brüning had told Prince Louis Ferdinand about the book during a conversation at Harvard. Nevertheless, "the secret," Scheffer reassured himself and Lochner, "is in good hands with these men." [104] Despite such concerns about secrecy, Scheffer could not hide his excitement. The book, he argued, would be of high political significance and would help West Germany earn the respect of U.S. policy makers.[105] Indeed, he effused, it might turn out to be among the most significant books of the preceding two decades.[106]

By the spring of 1952 the project had begun to take shape. Lochner revealed his plans to the excited press director for the German Diplomatic Mission in Washington,[107] while Lochner's friend and fellow international journalist Dorothy Thompson briefed a group of enthusiastic U.S. businessmen about the impending trip.[108] Back in Germany some of the biggest names in German industry were also preparing for the journalist's arrival. Heinz Nagel, who had built a large document archive for the Nuremberg defense, was readying his collection for the months of research ahead.[109] In February Wolfgang Pohle and Wilmowsky held a meeting at the Düsseldorf Industry Club to inform their colleagues of the latest developments.[110]

At the meeting, despite general support, they encountered a few lingering doubts. Some people still questioned the necessity of the project, while others took issue with the choice of Lochner as author. In a letter to BDI president Fritz Berg about the meeting, Wilmowsky also revealed a third worry: "that through this investigation, contributions of the German industrialists to the NSDAP could be uncovered." [111]

In July 1952, after two years of preparations and several small setbacks, Lochner finally flew to Germany to begin his project on German industry and Nazism.[112] Upon his arrival, he met with Krupp's legal advisers for a brainstorming session. He then immersed himself in the papers of the Industry Office, while archivist Nagel arranged interviews with industrialists around the Ruhr. When he was not reading through musty files at the IHK Essen, Lochner was traveling around the country looking for people with stories to tell. From July 1952 until February 1953 he established contact with hundreds of company leaders and public figures, many of whom he had met and befriended during his years in Berlin. He spoke with chemical executives, textile manufacturers, managers of electrical firms, shipping magnates, banking executives, and the head of the Zeppelin works.[113] He met with economists, lawyers, archivists, and company secretaries. August Heinrichsbauer, Hans Ficker,[114] and Kurt Hesse told him individually of their failed attempts to write the definitive defense of German industry.[115] Hermann and Paul Reusch recounted for Lochner their removal from the GHH board for anti-Nazi insubordination in 1942.[116] Ludwig Kastl, the former executive director of the RDI, welcomed Lochner to his farm in Bavaria and told of his and RDI president Gustav Krupp's disdain for the Nazis. Ferdinand Porsche Jr. gave Lochner documents purportedly demonstrating that Hitler had betrayed his father, the founder of Volkswagen. According to the young Porsche, even after Hitler committed himself to war in 1937, the Führer had assured his father at a personal meeting that his aims for Germany and Volkswagen were purely peaceful.[117] Volkswagen became one of the most important military contractors and employers of compulsory labor during World War II.

One of Lochner's most interesting meetings was with Walter Rohland, the former managing director of the VSt and the former deputy leader of the Iron Industry Group, a compulsory trade organization formed by the Nazis during the war. The controversial and often vilified Rohland explained over several bottles of wine that he had in fact *protected* industry by cooperating with the Nazis. If he had not joined the NSDAP in 1933, the criminal elements would have ruled the party. If he had not accepted the position of a deputy führer of the Iron Industry Group, he would have jeopardized his future in industry and, worse, "politicians would [have been] installed as leaders of our organization." As nightfall descended and his discussion with Lochner drew to a close, Rohland concluded with a bitter complaint about the destruction of his family estate by Allied bombs. With that act, "the account with the Jews is settled" (*Damit geht die Rechnung mit den Juden auf*), Rohland declared as he accompanied a shocked Lochner and his cohort Heinz Nagel to the door. Outside, the two men sadly confirmed to each other that they had not misheard their host. Rohland had, as Lochner later observed, equated genocide with the destruction of his garden.[118]

As a bizarre aside, when *Tycoons and Tyrant*, which included direct quotes from Rohland, was finally published, Rohland wrote to Lochner claiming never to have met the journalist. Lochner wrote back to Rohland reminding him of the exact date and time of their interview and the fact that they had drunk a lot of wine. He also reiterated his shock at Rohland's equation of the murder of Jews with the destruction of the industrialist's property. Rohland wrote back to Lochner and profusely apologized for having forgotten the interview from three years earlier, and he explained that by his Jewish comment he had only meant that the "victimization" of Germans was part of the price to pay for what happened to the Jews. His own Jewish friends, insisted Rohland, were of the same opinion. "The score is settled," they purportedly told Rohland with outstretched hands.[119]

That summer and fall Lochner spoke with old journalistic acquaintances, including Marion Dönhoff, Paul Sethe from the *Franfurter Allgemeine Zeitung*, and Friedrich Stampfer from the SPD's *Vorwärts*. He also traveled to Bonn and Frankfurt to apprise members of the West German government and the U.S. High Commission of the project. While in Bonn, he interviewed Economics Minister Ludwig Erhard and Rüdiger Schmidt of the Economics Ministry. Paul Löbe, former Reichstag president sent to a concentration camp after Hitler came to power, spoke with Lochner about the waning years of the SPD before the party's suppression in 1933. John McCloy met with him on a number of occasions to talk about this and a different project Lochner was carrying out for the State Department. Finally, Lochner met with some of the most influential politicians in Germany: West Berlin mayor Ernst Reuter, SPD *Bundestag* member Carlo Schmid, State Secretary Walter Hallstein, Finance Minister Fritz Schäffer, FRG president Theodor Heuss, and Chancellor Konrad Adenauer.

In December 1952, with the bulk of his research behind him, Lochner sat down with Otto Kranzbühler and Krupp director Fritz von Bülow to update his backers on his travels and findings during his six months in Germany. Kranzbühler was particularly curious about what Lochner had learned about the most contested issues regarding industrial complicity: the claim that big business had financed Hitler's rise and that it had provided Hitler "with a platform for acquiring respectability."[120] Lochner had certainly spent much time wrestling with these themes. Former German chancellor Franz von Papen had sent Lochner copies of exchanges he had recently been carrying out with his predecessor Brüning about the fateful years before Hitler's ascension.[121] At the Düsseldorf Industry Club, Lochner had spoken at length with some of the men who, twenty years earlier, had listened in the same building to Adolf Hitler's half-baked economic theories and his fulminations against communism. Some told Lochner of the enthusiastic response granted to Hitler after his 1932 speech, while most denied that the industrialists had been impressed at all.[122]

Despite this impressive research, Kranzbühler discovered to his dismay that Lochner still did not have the story straight regarding the funding of the NSDAP. "Herr Lochner was still not clear as to whether [industry] had financed Hitler before the *Machtergreifung*," wrote a surprised Kranzbühler to Wilmowsky. The Krupp attorney was forced to remind the journalist again that "aside from the support of Thyssen and Kirdorf, there is no evidence of significant support from industry circles." He also referred Lochner to a book by an unnamed Dutch writer arguing that *American* banks rather than German industry had funded Hitler before 1933. But whoever funded whom, Kranzbühler maintained, one should, in the end, not make too much of the financial issue, since according to Nazi propaganda minister Joseph Goebbels's diary, which Lochner himself had edited and published in English, party coffers were empty at the time of Hitler's ascent to the chancellorship.[123]

At this point we must examine why German industry was so interested in the years prior to 1933. Industry was, of course, responding in part to the priorities of its Marxist critics who saw National Socialists as the servants of capital. These critics focused on the last years of Weimar as a tumultuous period when "finance capitalism" naturally paved the way for a fascist victory. A rather different explanation of fascism appeared in the United States, where some elites embraced a Jeffersonian ideal according to which powerful big business interests marked the ruin of the shopkeeper, the entrepreneur, and the farmer. In examining Germany they saw Weimar as the culmination of this process whereby industrial modernization and economic concentration had forced the disgruntled lower middle class into the arms of the Nazis. Even those who did not identify per se with an ideological critique of big business focused on the last years of Weimar as a time when German elites still could freely direct the fate of their country. Politicians and industrialists were faced with a seemingly clear option of supporting the forces of authoritarian and rightist dictatorship or defending a shaky but nonetheless democratic order. They made the wrong choice, and National Socialism was the catastrophic result.

Not only critics of big business but industrialists themselves devoted the bulk of their attention to the Weimar years. This can be explained in part by postwar German elites' fatalistic view of the Nazi years. According to most postwar corporate apologias, after 1933 there were few possibilities of resisting Hitler. The Third Reich acquired a momentum of its own, fueled by the intoxicated masses and drawing in everyone, including its "apolitical" economic elites. After Hitler came to power, so this interpretation continued, events spiraled to their natural end, and the moments of choice for industry became fewer and farther between. In the view of postwar industry, the true questions of guilt or innocence did indeed lie in the final years of the Weimar Republic, a time when industry felt it *could* demonstrate successfully that it had not collectively funded or embraced Hitler.

In privileging industry's pre-1933 attitudes and behavior, industry's critics paradoxically gave businessmen the opportunity to downplay or justify their concessions to the Nazi regime after 1933. With the fear of Soviet communism as the backdrop, after the war industrialists could argue to the public with greater ease that the forces of the total state took away all free will. Industrial cooperation with the state was simply the inevitable result of living under a totalitarian regime. Ironically, however, by insisting that they had had little *Handlungsspielraum* (room to maneuver) under Hitler, industrialists were actually acknowledging that their behavior after 1933 was damning on a collective level. By keeping the emphasis of the discussion on events before 1933, industrialists took refuge in the memories of a less threatening time— before they had joined the party, before they dismissed their Jewish employees, and before *Kristallnacht*, war, and mass murder—in short, before their own, albeit "undesired" and "forced" complicity.

Importantly, this emphasis on the Weimar years did not by any means preclude a discussion of behavior after the Nazi takeover; it simply elevated Weimar to the first and most important order of business. With respect to the years after 1933, industrialists offered Lochner what were by then well-honed images of impotence, resistance, and victimhood. If the industrialists had no choice when it came to matters of racial policy and rearmament, they did manage, in their words, to commit acts of everyday defiance—from the avoidance of the expression "Heil Hitler" to criticizing the Nazis at board meetings, to resisting divorcing a Jewish wife, to providing extra rations or better-quality food to forced laborers, to refusing to carry out Hitler's self-sabotage orders in the spring of 1945. Lochner came away from his research with a number of such examples of everyday *Resistenz*.[124]

These examples of defiance, which had obviously been ineffectual challenges to the regime, are not necessarily postwar inventions or embellishments. The reality of life in Nazi Germany was such that cooperation, indifference, or a general sense of impotence *could* be combined with local or selective acts of disobedience. By claiming to have spoken out against a particular policy or to have selectively resisted some aspect of the regime, one was not necessarily claiming to be a hero. But the contradictions and tensions in this notion of opposition do become significant when we consider how often industrialists granted equal status to both forms of behavior—impotence and resistance. Industrialists saw themselves both as the object of forced measures and as courageous challengers of the Nazi government.

Despite claims otherwise, industrialists behaved politically and opportunistically during the Third Reich. As men accustomed to wielding tremendous social and economic power, they joined the Nazi Party to avoid being shut out of political developments. Especially in 1940, as Germany racked up military successes, industrialists made peace with the regime in order, among other reasons, to have some voice in postvictory decision making. They were not about to sit out the "thousand-year Reich." After defeat, however, industrialists were loath to concede their pragmatism or to portray themselves in such amoral (or immoral) terms. They tried to recast their self-interest as ethical behavior, usually with unconvincing results. Thus we encounter somebody like Walter Rohland paradoxically insisting that his decision to cooperate with the Nazis was at once a freely chosen attempt to avert the worst aspects of the regime and a response to a dictatorial fiat.

There was, of course, a real resistance movement during the Nazi years, and it behooved industry and Lochner to look for connections between big business and the better-documented examples of underground activity. Lochner did not lose any time hooking up with his old acquaintances who had been connected with the 1944 attempt on Hitler's life. He met with Otto John, the then head of the Bundesamt für Verfassungsschutz (Federal Office for the Protection of the Constitution) and one of only two anti-Hitler bomb plotters to survive the postattack purge. Otto John had been the Madrid representative of Lufthansa and had arranged secret meetings between members of the Kreisauer Kreis, Ludwig Beck, and "successor to the German throne" (*Thronfolger*) Prince Louis Ferdinand, who explained to Lochner his own involvement with the underground.[125] Lochner also met with émigré professor Hans Rothfels, who briefed the author on the German resistance to Hitler and his view that, in Abbott Gleason's words, "it was precisely the conservatives who had opposed Hitler, that avatar of modernity and mass politics."[126]

Lochner did find that some industrialists had been involved in the underground movement. Ewald Löser, a Krupp director, had been chosen by the resistance to be the first finance minister after the coup d'état. He was arrested in July 1944 but was spared execution.[127] Robert Bosch, the Württemberg industrialist who stood noticeably apart from his colleagues by embracing liberal-democratic principles, conspired against the Nazis. Aside from providing financial help for emigrating Jews (not ipso facto an example of resistance), Bosch had been an active member of the anti-Hitler Goerdeler Kreis until his death in early 1942.[128] There are other examples of resistance that were not connected to the German underground per se. The Bavarian machine tools firm M.A.N. had, at 4 percent, the lowest number of company employees as Nazi Party members, and the firm was generally hostile to party demands.[129] As recent films and books have made clear, there were also pockets of resistance and heroism among managers and entrepreneurs in occupied Europe, Oskar Schindler and Berthold Beitz being the most prominent examples.

Despite these links to the underground and the few instances of individual heroism, one can in no way speak of a collective resistance movement on the part of industry. In his book Lochner himself had to concede the absence of verifiable resistance in German industry. But unwilling to rule out more anonymous acts of "rebellion," Lochner had to rely on the clumsy and unconvincing argument that "in judging the attitude of a population in a totalitarian state, it is essential to avoid drawing conclusions from the lack of external evidence as to the existence or non-existence of active opposition to tyranny."[130]

More important than whether or not industrialists can be included in the ranks of resistance is the fact that in the 1950s, people like Lochner were actively trying to find these links. The reasons for this go beyond the mere desire to portray businessmen as anti-Nazis. The legacy of the 1944 resistance was quite controversial in West Germany. There was no widespread approval of executed resisters like Claus Schenk von Stauffenberg and Helmuth von Moltke. Indeed, books like Karl Strolin's *Verräter oder Patrioten?* [Traitors or patriots?] reveal the ambivalence on the part of many Germans who themselves had not challenged Nazism.[131] Many people felt that the men of July 1944 had undermined their country while Germans soldiers were dying in a two-front war. Probably a good many industrialists shared this view, if only privately. If the resistance served to remind them of their own inactivity, industrialists publicly embraced the conservative ideas that the *Widerstand* represented. It is well known, for example, that Carl Goerdeler and his associates were anything but democrats. They envisioned a post-Hitler monarchical order that espoused God and country and even certain limitations on the rights of Jews.[132] Whether or not individual businessmen were aware of or subscribed to every value espoused by the resistance, they probably detected a class-based kinship between themselves and the military and political elites who conspired against Hitler. These men of 1944 had resisted, if sometimes late and rather selectively, the temptations of the Nazi utopia. They were, in their own estimation, the "other Germany"—still patriotic, still embracing traditional bourgeois values, but virulently anti-Hitler. At least this is what Tilo von Wilmowsky and Louis Lochner hoped to demonstrate.

Krupp and Louis Lochner's *Tycoons and Tyrant*

In February 1953 Lochner began writing his book. It was now to encompass not only the Weimar and Nazi years but also the first seven years of West Germany. In preparation for his final chapter, called "Whither German Industry?" Lochner had carried out research on the Morgenthau Plan, disarmament, the Schuman Plan, the industrialist trials, and the Moral Rearmament Movement. By extending his discussion into the Adenauer years, Lochner hoped to make the case that industry, despite some mistakes in the past, was now fully trustworthy. But as Lochner was working at his home in Essen, events across town served as a reminder of how hard this task would be. On 4 March 1953 Alfried Krupp signed the so-called Mehlem Treaty, in which he agreed to sell, at full value, his coal- and steel-producing enterprises and renounce any future production of either.[133] This was the culmination of drawn-out negotiations with the Allies over the breakup of Krupp concerns. Krupp had apparently given up forever the very thing that had made his company great: steel. This dramatic concession catapulted Krupp back into the international headlines, and the firm was now even more intent on improving its reputation across the Atlantic.[134] A public relations rush ensued. Alfried Krupp granted newspaper and radio interviews, a second edition of *Warum wurde Krupp verurteilt?* was issued, and Lochner proofread Gert von Klass's *Die drei Ringe*, an apologetic history of the Krupp firm that appeared in bookstores in the fall, accompanied by two shorter manuscripts for use on radio programs. Meanwhile, Berthold Beitz, Alfried Krupp's chosen plenipotentiary and public representative, took over the everyday management of the firm in November.

This media blitz only drew the firm further into the spotlight, and in the summer of 1953 the Krupp office in Bonn proposed a number of ways to improve its corporate image in the ever important United States. In a set of memos, the firm recommended, for example, producing films about Krupp's contributions to West German reconstruction.[135] Pamphlets with titles such as *What Do German Firms Do for Their Workers?* would have special sections devoted to Krupp. The firm would invite American journalists to Essen for tours of the Villa Hügel, the Krupp family's huge and gloomy Victorian residence. The Roy Bernard Co., the New York–based public relations firm representing the West German government, prepared pro-Krupp propaganda for Adenauer's visit to the United States later that year. Finally, the summer memo stated, the company would "station a man in Congress in Washington to work continually on the senators and thereby exercise a decisive influence on the speakers. He must in particular get along well with the general secretaries [*sic*] of the various committees."[136] But at the top of the list of public relations measures stood the Lochner book. As Krupp publicity director Carl Hundhausen wrote to Berthold Beitz the next year, "There is no better advocate (*Anwalt*) for Krupp than Lochner."[137]

In April 1953 Lochner sent his finished draft to Wilmowsky and the Krupp lawyers, who were at the time helping colleague August von Knieriem, the head of IG Farben's legal department, with his own book about German industry.[138] The Krupp officials passed around Lochner's manuscript to other industrialists for approval,[139] while Heinrich Brüning offered to go over the piece with a fine-tooth comb.[140] Lochner himself distributed copies to the German consulates in Washington and Chicago, and both expressed their enthusiasm.[141] Meanwhile, in anticipation of the book's success, Krupp officials had already begun searching for a German translator. For representatives of West German industry and politics, Lochner had risen to the occasion.

In October 1954, after a year of delays, Louis Lochner's *Tycoons and Tyrant: German Industry from Hitler to Adenauer* was finally published. Some reviews were positive. Hans Kohn argued in the *New York Times* that Lochner had proven his case that industry was not to blame for Nazi crimes.[142] But most reviews were critical of the book's familiar and problematic motifs: the industrialist as victim, the industrialist as anti-Nazi resister, and the indus-

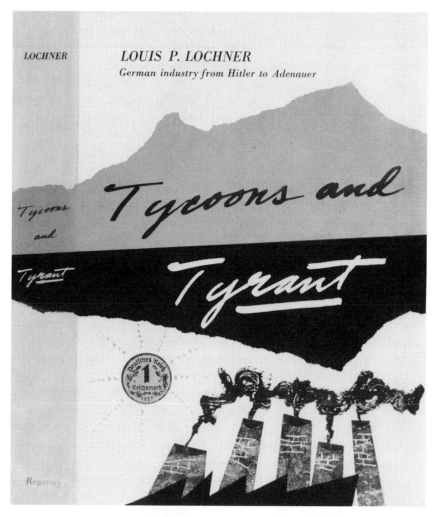

Dust Jacket of Louis P. Lochner's *Tycoons and Tyrant* (1954) (courtesy of Regnery Publishing, Washington, D.C.)

trialist as the moral conscience of the new Germany.[143] The *Nation* accused Lochner of misunderstanding the "sociology of fascism."[144] Oscar Schnabel, the former Austrian consul general in Amsterdam, wrote in the *New Leader* that the book was an "ardent defense rather than an impartial judgment. It excuses whatever can be excused, and, where excuses are impossible, it pleads mitigating circumstances."[145] A year later a German translation encountered both praise and even harsher criticism than the English edition.[146] Business-friendly journalist Herbert Gross praised Lochner for "avoiding propagandistic whitewashing,"[147] and Chancellor Adenauer wrote to Lochner to congratulate him on producing an "objective and courageous" book that would help build friendly relations between Americans and Germans.[148] The East German press, however, called the book an "attempt by an American history-falsifier to hush-up the blood guilt of German industrial lords."[149]

Lochner had indeed painted a one-sided picture of German industry, once crushed under the Nazi heel but coming to life with renewed energy and courage. In Lochner's view Germany's industrialists had not behaved perfectly; some had even supported the Nazis. But according to Lochner, Germany's economic leaders had been caught in the unenviable position of choosing between opposition and the survival of their firms. Some had managed both, but most had simply been businessmen protecting all that they had built up. Lochner's concluding message was unmistakable: Regardless of the historical complexities, now was the chance to rebuild Germany. Let the industrialists go about their tasks unencumbered.

Tycoons and Tyrant did not captivate the American public. Lochner himself attributed this fact to poor advertising and a personal falling-out with Regnery (by the time the book came out, the two were no longer on speaking terms).[150] Regardless of the book's poor sales, we must nonetheless ask why U.S. conservatives and Cold War liberals like Lochner and conservative-nationalists in Germany had perceived this project as so essential to the rehabilitation of West Germany. This question goes to the heart of German-American business and cultural relations during the years of the Cold War. As early as 1945 Americans had grown concerned that holding Germany's capitalists co-responsible for the crimes of Nazism would be tantamount to supporting the Soviet Union's ideological campaign against private enterprise. The debate in the U.S. Congress over industrial denazification and dismantling was always conducted in pragmatic terms. To what extent could the West afford to sacrifice Germany's economic future at the altar of moral justice and accountability? By 1948 the answer was clear. In Nuremberg the United States had subscribed to big business crimes, but now it was time to move on and rebuild. Probusiness Americans like Lochner and Regnery would embrace any effort that helped establish West Germany as a prosperous bulwark against communism, even if it meant forgiving past misdeeds of German business.[151]

Yet we can attribute this urge to salvage German industry's reputation not only to the politics of the Cold War but to the self-conception and self-perception of intellectual and business elites on both sides of the Atlantic. Lochner's project was part of a much broader effort in both countries to promote the industrialist as the embodiment of core Western values that had been threatened by Nazism, war, and big government. The businessman stood for a tradition of freedom, hard work, sacrifice, family, and private property. In the Nazis' wartime direction of German industry, in the East

Germans' and Soviets' seizure of factories, and in the replacement of the traditional owner and entrepreneur by the technocratic manager, U.S. conservatives like James Burnham recognized the signs of a dangerous global phenomenon by no means limited to totalitarian settings. According to Burnham, the erosion of economic and political freedom by repressive regimes was, in fact, akin to the New Deal's regulatory control of U.S. business.[152] In all industrialized societies, the faceless manager with no stake in a company threatened to supplant the true businessman, who put his own capital at risk and who alone bore responsibility for his company's direction. To U.S. conservatives, protecting the reputation of German industry and portraying it as the eternal victim of much broader hostile forces, including Nazism, was therefore as much a critique of the political and ideological status quo in the United States as it was an attempt to salvage the economy of Western Europe.

In West Germany, however, the flood of encouragement for Lochner can be attributed not only to a conservative, Cold War sensibility but to the peculiar politics of West German memory. For unlike in the United States, where the battle against communism also defined the mood of the 1950s, postwar Germany's antitotalitarian raison d'être was simultaneously always predicated on an assessment of guilt and responsibility under Nazism.[153] By railing against the latest version of totalitarian rule in the Soviet Union, Germans could at once relativize their experience of Nazism against a more universal phenomenon of modern state terror and control. By portraying Hitler and Stalin as two sides of the same coin, West Germany hoped to demonstrate contrition for past sins not by anguished breast-beating but through a devoted rallying against all manifestations of totalitarian evil, past, present, and future.

In the late 1940s and 1950s many West German intellectuals, politicians, church leaders, and businessmen shared a common self-perception. Standing between Hitler's small entourage of criminals and the misguided and hypnotized masses, they were "the other Germany" (*das andere Deutschland*), embodied in a proud tradition of bourgeois elitism unshaken by the total claims of the Nazis and embodied in the *Widerstand* against Hitler. Educated, humanistic, patriotic, and apolitical, Germany's economic and social elites heralded themselves as leaders of their country's spiritual revival. They alone could provide postwar Germany with an alternative past, a clean conscience, and a model for ideological renewal.

In this context Lochner's project must be understood as an open call to Germany's social elites to arise and claim their nation's past and future. It is not accidental that the industrialist occupied center stage in this crusade. For more than any other figure, I have tried to show, it was the industrialist who claimed to address both the practical demands of economic reconstruction and the need to discover an uncompromised political and spiritual tradition in Germany. To Lochner and his friends in Germany and the United States, big business alone could keep this bourgeois tradition alive. Imbued with a devotion to democracy, individuality, diligence, progress, and equality, industry was to move Germany beyond the experience of National Socialism. Unlike the military or the bureaucracy, the private sector could remain confident that it had not been directly involved in the Nazi government itself. Yet as long as the Americans and the Soviets saw big business as bearing substantial responsibility for the most heinous crimes, Germany's cultural and economic renewal would remain endangered. In order to proceed with the business of reconstruction, Germany's establishment turned to Lochner with high hopes. By moralizing the industrialist, Lochner would reactivate the spirit of bourgeois elitism, and thereby remoralize Germany.

Well into the 1950s, West German businessmen had not abandoned their desire to address the subject of Nazism and to challenge assertions about industrial complicity. Despite growing optimism about the economic health of the Federal Republic, the men of big business were still looking over their shoulders. They were haunted by the past, and they stopped more than occasionally to confront their demons. This collective and, more importantly, selective *Vergangenheitsbewältigung* came to involve the work of many individuals in West Germany, the United Kingdom, and the United States. In the late 1940s and early 1950s, industrialists reestablished prewar social and economic networks with the hope of normalizing their relationship to the rest of the world and to their own pasts. These networks spanned a broad range of professional orientations and personal histories. Not every participant in this transatlantic dialogue held the same views about religion or nation or the responsibility of Germany to its recent past. Some were devout Catholics, some were Lutherans, and others were Jews. There were figures with blatant records of collaboration and individuals who had demonstrated courage during the Third Reich. There was even the self-avowed socialist Victor Gollancz, who saw the nonpunitive resuscitation of the German economy as a most desirable goal. What did unify this diverse group was a sincere conviction that Germany had a long and rich tradition that had been held hostage from 1933 through 1945 and that it was again threatened by Bolshevism. Reviving Germany's cultural and economic greatness meant propagating this particular view of the Nazi years. It was essential not only for the spiritual well-being of the West but for its physical security as well.

Despite the varied purposes and origins of those who made this case, this was an essentially conservative enterprise. The West German economy—and by extension the reputation and well-being of its leaders—was the basis of the struggle not only against the forces of collectivist evil but against the tendencies of mass society that threatened to erode more timeless Western values:

work, private property, God, and country. That West Germany and the United States in the 1950s embraced such views—and that they were grounded in economic progress and material wealth—is not a new observation. Historians have long been interested in how Americans and Europeans worked together to revive the West German economy and to create a democratic-capitalist West upheld by conservative values and an antitotalitarian philosophy. But the calculated solidarity, the tireless raising of funds, the intricate public relations apparatus, the busy exchange of letters, and the involvement of dozens of figures from all walks of life does demonstrate to a surprising degree how cooperatively and meticulously postwar Germans and Americans engaged in the politics of the past. Accounting for industrial behavior, usurping the status of victim and resister, discussing the nature of terror and totalitarianism—these moments of reflection were not passive events or coincidental motifs that accompanied economic rebuilding. They were carefully created, packaged, and sold in service of an "Occidental" moral ethic that would accompany an ascending West German market economy.

The New Industrialist and West German Memory

This book has profiled West German industry's self-presentation over a ten-year period, from the defeat of Nazism in 1945 to the middle of the 1950s, when the Federal Republic enjoyed growing international respect as a free-market liberal democracy. During these years businessmen, economists, publicists, politicians, and theologians created a social romance of capitalism to accompany the country's emerging prosperity.[1] The protagonist of this tale was the *Unternehmer,* who appeared in various guises: as the venture capitalist, the family manufacturer, the genius inventor, and the benevolent company manager. Despite a long history of defending his achievements, the industrialist, according to this postwar narrative, had faced his greatest challenge from 1918 to 1945, when he was flanked by enemies on either side—communism on the left and National Socialism on the right. During the Weimar and Nazi years, the industrialist battled both opponents at once, never losing sight of his true goal: freedom for the entrepreneur and for humankind. By the time this story ends in the mid-1950s, the *Unternehmer* has defeated one mortal enemy, Nazism, and has triumphantly led his country from the ruins of war to the promise of unparalleled abundance. Freedom, diligence, and private property have prevailed. Now with the help of the entire Western world, the businessman is poised for the final struggle against communism and the completion of his "world historical mission."[2]

At first glance this story may appear as an overblown metaphor for the serious issues that West German businessmen faced as they negotiated their new surroundings. Rebuilding the economy was surely about much more than this gushing apotheosis of the industrialist and entrepreneur. Yet in the 1950s and beyond, multiple versions of this narrative appeared in countless books, speeches, and articles. The story of the Economic Miracle and its heroic business leaders accompanied the demanding work of actual postwar economic

236

reconstruction and the building of a West German state. It simultaneously addressed the need to inspire a war-weary country toward prosperity and provide a philosophical defense of capitalism during the Cold War. In the late 1940s and 1950s this multipurpose discourse was, to be sure, not limited to West Germany; it was present in Western Europe and especially the United States as well. During the years when communism and capitalism squared off against each other, the lionizing of free enterprise and its leaders was not unique to the Federal Republic.

As I have argued, however, industry's postwar self-fashioning was about more than Cold War ideologies or popular mythologies of material success evident during other times and in other national contexts. In its particular West German form, it was about overcoming a history of class conflict, economic upheaval, and the relationship of big business to war and genocide. Reeling from accusations of complicity in Hitler's crimes and from the perceived dangers of socialization and codetermination, industrialists in the 1950s called on older, validating motifs of capitalism—the rags to riches tale, the Protestant work ethic, and the avuncular factory owner—and recast them for contemporary political and publicity purposes. They turned the standard account of the rise of capitalism into a tale about the benefits of freedom, the horrors of Nazism and collectivism, and the eternal innocence of big business. In reaction to the Marxist worldview, according to which capitalist greed leads to global enslavement and eventual self-destruction, industry presented a sanitized and moralized parable of the market and its leaders. This West German industrialist no longer lived by the law of the jungle, in piracy, war, advertising, and trade; nor did he make Faustian pacts with the devil, sacrificing spiritual purity for material gain. Rather, he was the true embodiment of the central values and mores that defined Western society and that were under assault by totalitarianism.

In the 1950s the "new industrialist" was not only a response to industry's publicity crisis arising out of complicity with National Socialism. The reworked image of the businessman—victim of the Nazis and defender of the culture and economy—converged with other legitimating narratives that accompanied West Germany's reconstruction. Recent scholarship has demonstrated how different group narratives in the FRG were universalized into official national narratives. West Germans drew inspiration and power from the hardships of women and the fortitude of the "rubble women" who cleaned up Germany's bombed-out cities. The late-returning war veteran came to symbolize the national sense of victimization and the difficulties of moving beyond Nazism. The "consuming woman" became a metaphor for the country's economic rebirth and a displaced post-Hitler nationalism. Anxieties over the past and present were channeled into concerns over the fate of the country's youth and the influence of U.S. popular culture.[3]

To this list must be added the industrialist, who was perhaps the most visible symbol of the postwar Economic Miracle. The self-proclaimed provider of prosperity and freedom, *Der Unternehmer*, perhaps like no other figure, embodied the many contradictions of Konrad Adenauer's Germany. The Federal Republic and its industrialists were at once conservative and progressive, and socially oriented and militantly committed to free enterprise; they celebrated the flowering of a post-Nazi individualistic *Geist* and the security provided only by a continued devotion to the *Gemeinschaft*—family, neighborhood, church, and a supranational European defense community. Finally, they looked to U.S. cultural and business models with both excitement and deep apprehension. In the 1950s the industrialist came to mirror West Germany's conflicted hopes and ideals.

The industrialist, to be sure, did not have an exclusive hold on the public's imagination. Rather, his success story intersected with and, indeed, depended on the other national narratives and social realities mentioned above. The masculine *Unternehmer* was nurtured by a doting 1950s housewife; he was no longer the authoritarian Herr in his factory but the democratic family father in a comfortable home; his company's financial success relied on the economic power exercised by the consuming bourgeois woman;[4] the ex-soldier was transformed into a factory worker who relied on the company management to reintroduce him to a social world beyond the battlefield. In short, the West German economy of the 1950s served as the site for cultural, political, and social regeneration.

Despite the ubiquity of the *Unternehmer* ethos, from its appearance in the rubble of Berlin to its propagation on factory floors, we may still question what effect the reinvention of the businessman actually had on corporate reputations and on West German society more broadly. By the mid-1950s business leaders certainly had regained more authority as they settled into an economically and socially hegemonic position. The unions had scaled back their demands for economic democracy in favor of wage and benefits issues, and they had toned down their anticapitalist rhetoric in order to create a united front against communism. In 1953 the probusiness CDU had achieved a resounding victory over the SPD and other parties, indicating a public mandate for the continuance of Adenauer and Erhard's economic, social, and foreign policies. The Communist Party was outlawed in 1956, and by 1959 the SPD had also dropped all Marxist language from its party platform. If one surveys the pages of industrial publications in the latter half of the 1950s, one is struck by the powerful effect of these political developments on industrial perceptions. The tone of DI publications, *Handelsblatt*, and *Industriekurier* grew increasingly placid and sanguine, as industry aimed its most strident attacks less at "internal enemies" and more at the GDR and the Soviet Union.

Despite these victories for West German business, throughout the 1950s

Preview of the film *Krupp Today: People and Their Factory* at the Deutsches Museum, Munich, 17 November 1960 (ÜF2, 10.14.2, SA, courtesy of the Historisches Archiv Krupp, Essen)

the leaders of the DI expressed the concern that industry's efforts at "mass psychological influence" were not really working—that they were, in effect, still preaching to the converted via business-friendly propaganda. Industrialists were not the only ones to wonder whether the public was really listening. In 1955 *Der Spiegel* conducted a poll to discover what "Herr X thinks of the industrialist." The liberal weekly determined that most people did not spend a lot of time thinking about him; they were certainly unable to define the concept of *Unternehmer* with any precision. (It was, indeed, an imprecise concept.)[5] While a similar poll five years earlier had provoked concern among industrialists about public apathy, such results were now interpreted positively. Public indifference to the industrialists, big business had discovered, could now be portrayed as a testament to the subtlety and skill of its propaganda. By mid-decade most of the public seemed to have dropped *all* preconceptions— thus its negative ones—of the industrialist, and this was welcome news to big business. Economic growth was being taken for granted, and this was a sign, at the very least, that the pro-market literature was not *counter*productive. The figure of the *Unternehmer* and industry's publicity efforts both drew force from and fed into the FRG's national discourse of prosperity in the 1950s. In light of these gains, business leaders grew only more convinced of the indispensability of public relations. In 1958 they helped found the Deutsche Public Relations Gesellschaft, and by the 1970s major universities such as Erlangen had established chairs in public relations.[6] What began in 1949 as an exotic concept from across the Atlantic is now a permanent feature of German society.

Despite industry's growing confidence and a gradual pacification of the workforce, all was not totally well for big business after the mid-1950s. The mutual recriminations and the politics of the past never did disappear from the social and economic scene. They continued to manifest themselves, albeit more occasionally, in documents like former IG Farben attorney August von Knieriem's 1959 book *The Nuremberg Trials,* another Regnery publication about the "innocence" of German industry with respect to forced labor,[7] and the DI's 1963 *Die Legende von Hitler und der Industrie,* a pamphlet published to coincide with the thirtieth anniversary of Hitler's "seizure of power" that again denied links between Nazism and industry. In response to this latter text, the DGB put out its own *Hitler und die Industrie,* which purported to document industrial complicity in the rise of Hitler.[8]

These occasional flare-ups between the self-avowed social partners, however, were not limited to the printed page. The year 1955 began, for example, on a note of controversy when the loose-tongued Hermann Reusch told a gathering of GHH shareholders in January that the 1951 introduction of co-determination in the iron and steel industry had been attained through the union's "brutal blackmail" tactics. Much as they had seven years before, the unions reacted with outrage to this antilabor utterance. Almost a million miners, with the support of the DGB, laid down their work in protest. Articles and radio commentaries about Reusch's "Nazi past" again circulated around the country, while the industrialists reexamined the implications of codetermination and argued that the unions were violating the free speech of a businessman. Before the debate died down, Chancellor Adenauer had stepped in to condemn Reusch's comments, and the business world had again been forced to confront the theme of industrial complicity, with conservative industrialists railing against the power of the unions and more liberal-minded leaders scrambling to contain the damage.[9]

This event reveals that beneath the increasingly calm surface of 1950s West Germany, social relations were still fragile, and memories of past hostilities and perceived transgressions were still raw. The legacy of class warfare exercised a powerful influence over workers and management, even during a relatively peaceful period in industrial relations. The Reusch affair of 1955 also reveals the actual and symbolic power that businessmen still possessed. Authoritarian industrial leaders such as Reusch, even as their ranks were thinning, continued to personify industry at large, and the opinions of one individual could reflect badly on all of industry. Likewise, the return of Alfried

Krupp and Friedrich Flick to positions of wealth and influence was the source of tremendous suspicion that the much-heralded economic and social new beginning had in fact never taken place.[10] A drawn-out debate over the rearmament of West Germany throughout the 1950s continued to trigger reminders of Germany's previous rearmament in the 1930s, the eager participation of industry, and the horrifying war that followed.[11] Finally, the gradual reconcentration of West German industry and banking (the latter taking place in 1957) in the late 1950s and 1960s, despite the passage of anticartel legislation, was a major blow to U.S. deconcentration efforts, and these developments further deepened suspicions that West Germany had failed to break cleanly with its illiberal and fascist past. Despite some industrialists' professed devotion to free markets and "Americanized" business structures, the West German economy, some historians have argued, did indeed come to resemble its old corporatist/dirigiste self.[12] While in the 1970s many foreign observers came to admire the "German model" of corporatism, the close relationship between industry, banking, and government has remained a highly contested theme to this day in Germany.

It is important, too, that the direct accusations of corporate complicity in Nazi crimes did not simply disappear as national prosperity increased. The country's economic hard times may have been over by mid-decade, but in some ways German industry was only beginning to feel the direct financial consequences of its past.[13] In 1954 and continuing through the early 1960s, the Claims Conference, an organization that represented former Jewish victims of National Socialism, began seeking compensation for former slave laborers. The Claims Conference appealed to West Germany's largest companies, among them IG Farben, Krupp, Siemens, Flick, and Rheinmetall, to acknowledge their past crimes by helping survivors of their wartime factories.[14] But the process was not so easy. Bitter negotiations and industrial recalcitrance culminated in each case with rather meager settlements paid by German companies and distributed to Jewish survivors. During these negotiations industry stuck to its standard claim that the state and the SS were to blame for any hardships suffered by forced workers; indeed, companies were to be credited for mitigating harsh circumstances. In the aftermath of each settlement, U.S. public relations consultants helped German industry to portray these payments not as confessions of guilt but as willing and selfless expressions of generosity.[15] Clearly, in the 1950s and 1960s, industry was unwilling to confront honestly business involvement in mass crimes.

Since the early 1950s industrialists, to be sure, have made gradual attempts to replace bad memories with good deeds. With the founding of family and corporate foundations and charities, we can witness the desire by industrialists to foster national and international goodwill. Krupp, Thyssen, and Volkswagen have all supported a variety of worthy causes, from studies on the environment to endowed university chairs in Germany and abroad. Industrialists can certainly point to the past fifty years during which the business community has abandoned its authoritarian relationship to labor and come to terms with industrial and political democracy. This has not taken away criticisms of big business opportunism, from setting up chemical plants in Iraq and Libya to selling arms to rogue nations.[16] There is, some would charge, a cynical aspect to corporate beneficence. When Friedrich Flick's grandson donated a large sum of money to Oxford University in the mid-1990s, his offer was attacked as a hollow attempt to whitewash a maligned family name. Amid a storm of controversy, Oxford was forced to return the gift, but not before the story of industrial complicity during the Third Reich was again reexamined by the international media.[17]

This long-standing scrutiny of German business has gradually shaken industrialists out of their comfortable denial, especially with respect to the Nazi period. Indeed, with the establishment of the compensation fund in 1999, more and more companies are admitting that their firms were deeply involved in the Nazi war economy and the exploitation of innocent civilians. With the end of the Cold War and the diminished fear of ideological repercussions, companies, to their credit, are now allowing scholars into their archives to research all aspects of their pasts.[18] However, much as during the early postwar years, there is still an element of desperation in this new openness. Negotiations over compensations are predicated on a cessation of future lawsuits, and some companies probably hope that once their behavior during the Third Reich is revealed, they can move on and put the past behind them. This, however, will not be so easy, especially as the picture of industrial complicity grows bleaker and more complicated the closer one looks.

From this picture of industrial attitudes after World War II, one may draw some final conclusions about the idea of collective memory that originally informed this study. This book has argued that, in contrast to persistent assumptions, West Germans did not and could not escape the memory of National Socialism during the immediate postwar years. For industrial leaders, memory took the form of public relations. It manifested itself both in attempts to deny corporate criminality and in business leaders' collective rethinking about democracy, mass society, economic recovery, and labor relations. Industry's paradoxical urge at once to bury the recent past and to salvage and remake it reveals both the dangerous and the emancipatory power of memory during the years of economic reconstruction. In their fervent desire to overcome the Nazi/business link (both its myths and its horrifying realities), West German industry ultimately recognized an opportunity to reinvent itself—to refurbish its damaged image and, by extension, the image of West Germany—during the tumultuous years of rebuilding.

Through the creation of self-exonerating company narratives or through the use of Nazi terminology to fight its political opponents, West German industry in the 1950s faced the past when it chose to. Industrialists recognized the utility of the past in contemporary political and ideological contests, and they consciously used fears of collectivism to justify their own questionable behavior under Nazism and to position themselves as the very people that would help the country prevent a return to totalitarianism. Admittedly, businessmen, along with most West Germans, were mostly silent about the mass murder of Jews and other minorities. In the first decade after World War II, memory was rarely about struggling with the Nazis' genocidal policies as such. But this often calculated silence could be counterproductive. When a publication showcased only the putatively admirable aspects of a company's history or a personal past, it excluded the more compromising themes relating to the Holocaust, and this absence simply drew more attention to the images of corporate misdeeds industrialists were working so hard to overcome. Not only with hindsight but in the minds of industry's critics at the time, the stubborn silence about the most damning aspects of industrial behavior was as revealing and incriminating as the attempts to address the theme through apologetics and self-pity. Silence, to invoke the old convention, did often speak louder than words.

This deliberate use of the Nazi legacy does not mean that industrialists were pure opportunists who used memories of totalitarianism and fears of communism simply to save themselves and their businesses. Like most West Germans in the 1940s and 1950s, company leaders were genuinely concerned that their country's economy might go the way of East Germany if they did not aggressively defend the free market. They truly believed, in the words of Louis Lochner, that "every 'capitalist' . . . is doomed once the commies take over." [19] But industrialists' very real fears of "collectivism" and their personal (if usually mistaken) conviction that their firms acted honorably under Nazism does not negate the fact that memory was an opportunity as much as a curse. Whether by clumsily and frantically confronting accusations of guilt or more meticulously fashioning a new industrial personality, industrialists carefully mined the recent past for exculpatory and aggrandizing examples of corporate morality that would be serviceable after the war.

The example of corporate publicity ultimately elucidates the conscious and deliberate components of postwar memory. When looking at Siemens's 1945 corporate history or the writing of a biography of Albert Vögler, we can witness memory as an intentional and collective process often aimed at a target audience—be it the public or a member of one's own professional and national group. By looking at the behind-the-scenes workings of public relations, we can see the convergence of language and agency. We can witness the decision by a company executive to delete a word or phrase that could be incriminating to a firm. In the margins of a rough draft or in correspondence we can observe firsthand how industrialists bristled at the mention of a name, like Friedrich Flick, that would evoke negative associations. We can watch the lexical transformation of potentially damaging terminology, as "slave labor" gives way to "forced labor," "foreign labor," or the more innocuous "guest labor" or "manpower."[20]

By revealing collective mentalities and ideologies through acts of creation, embellishment, and obfuscation, I have de-emphasized the tortured face of memory. In the case of postwar West Germany, collective memory was not to be found in anguished confessions of guilt or in the achievement of some psychic closure, by which past misdeeds are publicly confessed and privately expiated. Rather, memory was about the very public presentation and manipulation of symbols, lessons, and experiences. This process, to be sure, had a psychological component: the self-worth of the individual and his or her desire for protection against accusations of guilt. But this survival mechanism was bound up inseparably with shared political, economic, and professional needs.

One may return to Maurice Halbwachs's model of collective memory to elucidate West Germany's confrontation with National Socialism as a fundamentally social process, as an open dialogue with one's contemporaries and with "the public." All individuals, groups, and nations have pasts that are remembered, articulated, contested, and forgotten for a variety of contemporary social and political reasons.[21] Memory does not exist in a vacuum. It manifests itself as conscious processes of selection, as the strategic choices of language, and as the studious presentation of symbols and stories from the past and their marketing—and manipulation—in the present.

In the end, by focusing specifically on West Germany and the economy, I have tried to challenge the prevailing categories of "coming to terms" and "working through," which measure memory solely in terms of a "successful" or "unsuccessful" end (either groups and individuals achieve total psychological closure *or* they are in a state of denial). With these rigid standards as their guidelines, it is not surprising that historians have seen the Adenauer years as devoid of memory—of a total "overcoming." More specifically, as long as West Germans failed to struggle openly with their country's culpability in the Holocaust, memory has rather easily been depicted as absent in the early postwar years. But the memory of National Socialism more broadly *was* at work in West Germany, and it revealed itself in every facet of life—in politics, education, social relations and social policy, culture, and as I have shown, the economy. In West Germany memories of Nazism were at once diffuse and selective, traumatic and defiant. But they were always there, even when West Germans preferred that they would simply go away.

Notes

ABBREVIATIONS

In addition to the abbreviations used in the text, the following abbreviations are used in the notes.

ACDP	Archiv für Christlich-Demokratische Politik an der Konrad Adenauer Stiftung, Sankt Augustin
ASU	Library of the Arbeitsgemeinschaft selbständiger Unternehmer, Bonn
Augsburg	Papers of the Industrie- und Handelskammer für Augsburg und Schwaben, Augsburg
BAK	Bundesarchiv, Koblenz
BAL	Bayer-Archiv, Leverkusen
BC	Private Papers of Dr. Werner Bührer, Technische-Universität, Munich
BfP	Bibliothek Institut für Publizistik, Frei Universität, Berlin
BKU	Library of the Bund Katholischer Unternehmer, Cologne
Böckler	DGB-Archiv in der Hans Böckler Stiftung, Düsseldorf
CC	Office of the Conference on Jewish Material Claims against Germany, Frankfurt am Main
Degussa	Degussa Archiv, Frankfurt am Main
HHSA	Hessisches Hauptstaatsarchiv, Wiesbaden
HstA	Nordrhein-Westfälisches Hauptstaatsarchiv, Düsseldorf
IfZ	Institut für Zeitgeschichte, Munich
IW	Library of the Institut der Deutschen Wirtschaft, Cologne
IWW	Library of the Institut der Weltwirtschaft, Kiel
KA	Historisches Archiv Krupp, Essen
LAB	Landesarchiv, Berlin
Mannesmann	Mannesmann-Archiv, Düsseldorf
NARA	National Archives Records Administration, College Park, Md.
NL	Nachlass (private papers)

PRO	Public Record Office, London
RC	Paul-Jürgen Reusch Private Collection, Backnang
RWWA	Rheinisch-Westfälisches Wirtschaftsarchiv, Cologne
SA	Siemens-Archiv, Munich
Stiftung	Stiftung Archiv für Massenparteien- und Organisationen der ehemaligen DDR, Berlin
Thyssen	Archiv der Thyssen AG, Duisburg
VDMA	Verband Deutscher Maschinen- und Anlagenbauverein
VVN	Vereinigung der Verfolgten des Naziregimes Files
Wisconsin	State Historical Society of Wisconsin, Madison

INTRODUCTION

1 A settlement was reached in December 1999 and ratified by the German parliament in July 2000. More than 5,000 firms have now pledged contributions to the fund, and the numbers will surely increase. As of January 2001, however, German industry, to much criticism, was still trying to find enough contributors to reach their promised contribution of 5 billion deutsche marks.

2 Historians, politicians, industrialists, and attorneys are now struggling with the distinction between "slave labor" and "forced labor." There is by no means consensus on how the terms should be differentiated, but in recent discussions the category of "slave laborers" has come to include all Jews who worked in death camps, concentration camps, and other work camps in Nazi-occupied Europe. In most cases, industry's use of slave laborers was in keeping with the SS's intention to eventually work Jews to death. "Forced laborers," on the other hand, includes POWs and any civilian who was compelled to leave his or her home in order to work for Nazi Germany. Some historians reject the term "slave labor" altogether.

3 "German Companies set up Fund for Slave Laborers under Nazis," *New York Times*, 17 February 1999.

4 Ibid.

5 The German government, which was itself a major employer of forced labor during the Third Reich, is providing half of the money, while German industry is providing the other 5 billion deutsche marks.

6 By using the term "legitimation crisis," I am not referring to a crisis of "advanced" or "late" capitalism, as scholars such as Jürgen Habermas would later argue in the 1960s and 1970s; see Habermas, *Legitimation Crisis*, 1–31.

7 See Marchand, *Creating the Corporate Soul*, 7–47.

8 Berghahn, *Americanisation*, 2; quote is from Ralf Dahrendorf, "Eine neue deutsche Obersicht," *Die Neue Gesellschaft* (1962): 25.

9 Our knowledge is, however, slowly improving. See, e.g., Hayse, "Recasting West German Elites," and Erker et al., *Deutsche Unternehmer*.

10 See the standard studies on industrial mentalities: Koehne, *Das Selbstbild deutscher Unternehmer* and *Unternehmertum im Wandel*; Redlich, *Der Unternehmer*; Hartmann, *Authority and Organization*.

11 The important literature on memory is too extensive to list. For some recent

studies, see Gillis, "Memory and Identity"; Hutton, *History As an Art of Memory;* Huyssen, *Twilight Memories;* Irwin-Zarecka, *Frames of Remembrance;* Le Goff, *History and Memory;* Matsuda, *Memory of the Modern;* Nora, *Realms of Memory;* and Roth, *Ironist's Cage.*

12 On a comparative study of "coming to terms with the past" in East and West Germany, see Herf, *Divided Memory.*

13 Mitscherlich and Mitscherlich, *Unfähigkeit zu trauern.*

14 This view of the Adenauer years as marked by a flight from the past is now undergoing revision. See Frei, *Vergangenheitspolitik;* Brochhagen, *Nach Nürnberg;* and the more polemical Kittel, *Legende von der "Zweiten Schuld."*

15 Halbwachs, *On Collective Memory.*

16 On Freud and Halbwachs, see Hutton, *History As an Art of Memory,* 59-68. For more on "collective" memory per se as a theoretical problem, see Confino, "Collective Memory and Cultural History," and Crane, "Writing the Individual Back into Collective Memory."

17 For more recent studies on public commemoration in Germany, see, for example, Koshar, *Germany's Transient Pasts;* Confino, *Nation as a Local Metaphor;* and Rosenfeld, *Munich and Memory.* On West German memory more generally, see Maier, *Unmasterable Past,* and Hartman, *Bitburg.*

18 For the purposes of this study, I will not be considering bankers, who, while intimately linked to the business world, do not, as such, constitute industrialists.

19 On the divisions within German industry, see Feldman, "Social and Economic Policies of German Big Business," and Hayes, "Industrial Factionalism."

20 There are multiple words in German, for example, *Fabrikant, Industrielle(r), Unternehmer, Geschäftsmann,* etc.

21 For a generational approach to changing industrial attitudes, see Berghahn, *Americanisation,* 40-71.

22 On the political power of industry in postwar West Germany, see Prowe, "Foundations of West German Democracy" and "Economic Democracy"; also Abelshauser, "First Post-liberal Nation."

23 Friedman, *Capitalism and Freedom,* 133.

24 For significant studies on industry during the Third Reich, see Erker, *Industrie-Eliten;* Gall and Pohl, *Unternehmen;* Hayes *Industry and Ideology;* Gillingham, *Industry and Politics;* Mollin, *Monatkonzerne und "Drittes Reich";* Schweitzer, *Big Business;* and Blaich, *Wirtschaft und Rüstung.*

25 For a good summary of the relationship between fascism and capitalism and the debates it has engendered, see Kershaw, *Nazi Dictatorship,* 42-50, and Geary, "Industrial Elite."

26 An extreme example of this view from East Germany is Pätzold and Weissbecker, *Geschichte der NSDAP;* also Czichon, *Wer verhalf Hitler zur Macht?*

27 For a tendentious book representing this position, see Pool and Pool, *Who Financed Hitler?*

28 On the political behavior of German industrialists during Weimar, see Henry A. Turner, *German Big Business;* Neebe, *Grossindustrie;* Weisbrod, *Schwerindustrie in der Weimarer Republik;* and Geary, "Industrial Elite."

29 On the Industry Club speech, see Henry A. Turner, *German Big Business*, 204–19. On party finances, see ibid., 291–304.

30 See Neebe, *Grossindustrie*, and Geary, "Industrial Elite."

31 See Gillingham, *Industry and Politics*, esp. 112–38.

32 On the survival of market mechanisms in Nazi Germany, see James, *German Slump*, 343–419, and Kershaw, *Nazi Dictatorship*, 42–60. For one of many contemporaries' reflections on the survival of capitalism in Nazi Germany, see Neumann, *Behemoth*, 221–54.

33 Kater, "Heinrich Himmler's Circle of Friends."

34 Balabkins, *Germany under Direct Controls*, 48.

35 On *Wehrwirtschaftsführer*, see Erker, *Industrie-Eliten*, 96–101.

36 On the individual perspective of one industrialist, see Hayes, "Fritz Roessler and Nazism."

37 On business executives' treatment of fellow Jewish board members, see Hayes, *Industry and Ideology*, e.g., 90–94, and James, "Deutsche Bank," 293–308.

38 On the expulsion of Jews from the economy, see Ludwig, *Boykott, Enteignung, Mord*. On the removal of Jewish board members from company managerial and supervisory boards, see the specific case of Oscar Altmann, who was forced to retire from the *Aufsichtsrat* (company supervisory board) of Mannesmann in 1936 and emigrated to Brazil. See correspondences regarding Altmann's retirement in 1936, file M20.017, Mannesmann.

39 On state planning and the diminishing power of economic leaders, see Mason, "Primacy of Politics." On the Four Year Plan, see Petzina, *Autarkiepolitik im Dritten Reich;* Hallgarten and Radkau, *Deutsche Industrie und Politik*, 250–69; and Deist et al., *Ursachen und Voraussetzungen*, 329–67.

40 On the Hermann Göringwerke, see, as an introduction, Gillingham, *Industry and Politics*, 60–61, and Schweitzer, *Big Business*, 539–42.

41 For a detailed study of the economy during World War II, see Herbst, *Der Totale Krieg*, and Deist et al., *Ursachen und Voraussetzungen*, 211–637.

42 On SS enterprises, see the account of Nazi armaments minister Albert Speer: Speer, *Infiltration*. For recent literature, see Naasner, *Neue Machtzentren*, esp. 234–40. On the use of concentration camp labor in these SS enterprises, see Erik Schulte, "SS-Unternehmen."

43 On industrialists' ability to make their own corporate decisions during the war, see Astrid Gehrig, *Nationalsozialistische Rüstungspolitik*, 195–301.

44 On the theme of Aryanization, see Wojak and Hayes, *"Arisierung"*; Barkai, "German Entrepreneurs and Jewish Policy" and *From Boycott to Annihilation*, 69–77; and Hayes, "Big Business and 'Aryanization'" and "Profits and Persecution." For an example of how one industrialist, Kurt Hermann, profited from Aryanization, see "Diamanten für den Reichsmarschall," *Der Spiegel*, 17 February 1997, 44–58.

45 See Herbst, *Der Totale Krieg*, 130–50.

46 For an introduction to this complex theme of forced and slave labor in all of its manifestations, see, esp., Herbert, *Hitler's Foreign Workers; Sklavenarbeit im KZ;* and Ferencz, *Less Than Slaves*.

47 See Hayes, *Industry and Ideology*, 347–58.

48 Herbert, *Hitler's Foreign Workers*, 382–96.

49 On forced labor and racial hierarchies, see Langbein, "Arbeit im KZ-System."

50 On the often brutal treatment of forced and slave laborers in service of the war effort, see Ferencz, *Less Than Slaves*, 88–96, and Gregor, *Daimler-Benz*, 150–217. On the punishment of foreign workers, see Herbert, *Hitler's Foreign Workers*, 117–18.

51 On one company's desire to prepare for the postwar period, see Gregor, *Daimler-Benz*, e.g., 192.

52 On industrial complicity and profits, see Simpson, *Splendid Blond Beast*.

CHAPTER ONE

1 On the material and human destruction in Germany, see Backer, *Priming the German Economy*, 31–59. On the destruction of Siemens, see Plettner, *Abenteuer Elektro-Technik*, 30. Recent studies have tempered some of the exaggerated depictions of total industrial devastation. See Backer, *Decision to Divide Germany*, 109–10.

2 On the ability of German industry to rebuild quickly after the war, see Gregor, *Daimler-Benz*, 251.

3 Many aspects of the firm's pre-1945 history have been well researched: electro-technology, company culture, worker relations, and the political stance of the company during the *Kaiserreich*, Weimar, and the Third Reich. For an exhaustive presentation of Siemens as a case study in modernization and bureaucratization, see Kocka, *Unternehmensverwaltung und Angestelltenschaft*. On Siemens in the 1930s, see Homburg, *Rationalisierung und Industriearbeit*, esp. chap. 10, on company social policies. Only a few studies have focused on the company during and after 1945. See Plettner, *Abenteuer Elektro-Technik*, and Henke, *Amerikanische Besetzung*, e.g. 455–59, 755.

4 Declaration issued by the supervisory and management boards and the work councils of SSW and S&H, 12 October 1947, 7500-1, SA.

5 For most of its history, Siemens was comprised of a parent company, Siemens & Halske, and Siemens-Schuckertwerke, which was the largest of the firm's many subsidiaries. The two companies officially merged into Siemens AG in 1969.

6 For a guide to some of these testimonies and company reports, see "Aktenverzeichnis über im Siemensarchiv vorhandene Dokumente und Aufzeichnungen über die Ereignisse und Folgererscheinungen des Jahres 1945," 60/Li 187, SA.

7 Feldenkirchen, *Siemens* (1995), 216. In using Feldenkirchen's study, one should keep in mind that the author wrote his book in his capacity as director of the Siemens archive. While one may assume that his evidence is accurate, and he does not overlook the issue of Siemens's use of forced and slave labor, he buries most of this controversial material in his lengthy footnotes. The book reads as a scholarly, but often biased account of a firm whose record during the war was much more disturbing than the text of the book suggests. Unfortunately, the foreword to the recent English translation (not written by Feldenkirchen) reads as a whitewash of the Nazi years. See Feldenkirchen, *Siemens* (1999), xiv–xvi.

8 "Tagebuch-Aufzeichnungen von Dr. Dietrich Müller-Hillebrand über den Zusammenbruch in Berlin-Siemensstadt, 1945," entry from 4 April 1945, 51/Lm
  136, SA.

9 Henke, *Amerikanische Besetzung*, 457.

10 Georg Siemens, in his official company history from the early 1950s, offers a fascinating, if melodramatic and biased, portrayal of these suicides. He depicts these
  managerial deaths in heroic, militantly anti-Soviet terms. Suicide was a better
  fate than slavery under the conditions of "Asiatic" savageness. See Georg Siemens,
  History, 280. On the depiction of Soviet atrocities, such as rape, in postwar Germany, see Naimark, *Russians in Germany*, and Heineman, "Hour of the Woman."
  On industrialists' suicides in 1945, see "Nun habt ihr Frieden und könnt arbeiten,"
  Frankfurter Allgemeine Zeitung, 29 April 1995, 15.

11 See Henke, *Amerikanische Besetzung*, 457.

12 Plettner, *Abenteuer Elektro-Technik*, 32; Henke, *Amerikanische Besetzung*, 457.

13 These two directors, Professor Gustav Hertz and Dr. Hans Kerschbaum, respectively, returned many years later from detention in the USSR; see Plettner, *Abenteuer Elektro-Technik*, 32.

14 Ibid.

15 On Bingel and Buol, see ibid.; also Georg Siemens, *History*, 278–79. Robert von
  Siemens, head of the Scientific and Technical Central Office of SSW, died along
  with Bingel in Landsberg. See Henke, *Amerikanische Besetzung*, 457. Also see Eric
  Scobel to Wolf-Dietrich von Witzleben, 24 June 1946, and Fritz Jessen to Dr. Heil-
  pern, Office of the U.S. Chief of Counsel, Berlin Delegation, 14 August 1946, NL
  Jessen, 11/La 200, SA.

16 Müller-Hillebrand, diary entries dated 7–13 June but corresponding to the following week, 51/Lm 136, SA. On dismantling in the Soviet zone, see Naimark,
  Russians in Germany, 178–83.

17 On the Soviet policy of taking "trophies" and the extensive damage wrought by
  these reparations, see Naimark, *Russians in Germany*, 166–70, and Clay, *Decision in
  Germany*, 120–24.

18 See Plettner, *Abenteuer Elektro-Technik*, 33, and Georg Siemens, *History*, 281.

19 See Feldenkirchen, *Siemens* (1995), 215.

20 Witzleben to Frenzel and Leipersberger, 29 June 1945, 7539, SA.

21 Plettner, *Abenteuer Elektro-Technik*, 28. Hermann von Siemens was arrested not in
  his capacity as head of Siemens but as a member of the Deutsche Bank supervisory
  board. He was replaced by his cousin Ernst von Siemens. See Feldenkirchen, *Siemens* (1995), 212.

22 On Witzleben's career, see Feldenkirchen, *Siemens* (1995), 213. The "war criminal"
  Witzleben is also profiled in V280/97 and "Wo sind die Hitlerschen Wehrwirtschaftsführer?," B46/V280, Stiftung.

23 Feldenkirchen, *Siemens* (1995), 216.

24 Georg Siemens, *History*, 282.

25 Name unclear (probably Witzleben's assistant) to Frenzel, 13 July 1945, 7539, SA.

26 Ibid.

27 Ibid.

28 On Siemens's use of forced and slave labor, see Feldenkirchen, *Siemens* (1995), 204–12; Ferencz, *Less Than Slaves*, 117–18; Sachse, "Zwangsarbeit"; Siegel, "Doppelte Rationalisierung"; and Max Stein, "Report on the Employment of Slave Work," CC; see also "Sklavenarbeit bei Siemens" in same file.

29 Feldenkirchen, *Siemens* (1995), 205. Carola Sachse places the figure at 1,300 by October 1940. See further figures in Sachse, "Zwangsarbeit."

30 Feldenkirchen, *Siemens* (1995), 163.

31 Georg Siemens emphasizes only the "humanitarian" aspect; see Georg Siemens, *History*, 269.

32 Feldenkirchen, *Siemens* (1995), 163. On the attempt to inspire in foreign workers a German devotion to "skill . . . justice, incorruptibility, and cleanliness," see Witzleben's memorandum "Ausländische Arbeitskräfte," 21 July 1942, 11/La 176, SA. This letter was attached to a company report on forced labor (see below) ostensibly in order to document the "humanity" with which Siemens directors had treated their foreign labor.

33 Feldenkirchen, *Siemens* (1995), 550.

34 Ibid., 201–6.

35 Ferencz, *Less Than Slaves*, 118; Feldenkirchen, *Siemens* (1995), 207–8.

36 Feldenkirchen, *Siemens* (1995), 206; Sachse, "Zwangsarbeit"; 5; Arndt, "Frauenkonzentrationslager Ravensbrück." See also the testimonies of former prison inmates now deposited in the archive of the Mahn- und Gedenkstätte Ravensbrück in Fürstenburg, Germany.

37 Max Stein, "Report on the Employment of Slave Work," 26, CC.

38 On the resistance of German and foreign laborers in industrial factories, see Herbert, *Hitler's Foreign Workers*, 326–58.

39 Quotes from Berghahn, *Modern Germany*, 189–90.

40 On West Germany's unions after 1945 and during the early Adenauer years, see Markovits, *Politics of the West German Trade Unions*, 61–83.

41 Quoted from Berghahn and Karsten, *Industrial Relations*, 172–73.

42 On Dirks, Kogon, and the *Frankfurter Hefte*, see Hermand, *Kultur im Wiederaufbau*, 57–60.

43 On Benkert, see Georg Siemens, *History*, 209, and Plettner, *Abenteuer Elektro-Technik*, 50–51. On Pohlmann, see "Schützen SPD-Betriebsräte bei Siemens Kriegsverbrecher?," *Vorwärts*, 5 September 1946, 1, and Georg Siemens, *History*, 51. Pohlmann had been a top engineer in the Siemens laboratories.

44 Delius, *Unsere Siemens-Welt*, 30.

45 "Siemens—ein Kriegsverbrecherbetrieb," *Neues Deutschland*, 15 December 1946, 5. On the company's portrayal of Benkert, see Georg Siemens, *History*, 208.

46 This document, "Über den Ausländereinsatz," is mentioned in *Neues Deutschland*, 17 December 1946, untitled article clipping in V279/35 VVN, folder 1—Siemens, Stiftung. On the document, see Feldenkirchen, *Siemens* (1995), 201–14, 547–59. Also, a document circulated by the SED quotes a Siemens protocol from 13 June 1944, which refers to Benkert's meeting with SS-Standartenführer Maurer regarding the forced employment of 2,000 Hungarian Jews. See "Bewiesene Schuld!," B45/V279/39, Stiftung.

47 Witzleben is listed as a *Wehrwirtschaftsführer* in Erker, *Industrie-Eliten*, 96–101.

48 Feldenkirchen, *Siemens* (1995), 213.

49 Ibid., 559.

50 Witzleben to Frenzel, 12 July 1945, 7539, SA. Carl Knott had been actively involved in Siemens's forced labor program. After the war he was tried and found guilty, only later to be rehabilitated. See Feldenkirchen, *Siemens* (1995), 214.

51 Witzleben chose as his replacement Fritz Jessen, who would take over as chairman "provided that he is also not arrested." See Witzleben to Frenzel, 12 July 1945, 7539, SA.

52 On Krupp's arrest, see Manchester, *Arms of Krupp*, 578–80.

53 Zangen was interned from 12 July 1945 until 10 November 1945. See Zangen, *Aus Meinem Leben*, and "Einkommensentschädigung unserer inhaftiert bezw. interniert gewesenen Vorstandsmitglieder," Hauptverwaltung, Mannesmann-röhren-Werke to Treuhandverwaltung im Auftrage der North German Iron and Steel Control, 13 February 1948, B109/5764, BAK.

54 On the arrest of other industrialists and Thyssen's trial, see Chapter 2.

55 "Streng vertraulich! Zur Frage der 'Kriegsverbrechereigenschaft' von Siemens," Jessen to Witzleben et al., 6 July 1945, NL Jessen, 11/La 176, SA.

56 Feldenkirchen, *Siemens* (1995), 153.

57 Max Stein, "Report on the Employment of Slave Work," 1, CC.

58 Jessen to Witzleben, 7 July 1945, NL Jessen, 11/La 176, SA.

59 Feldenkirchen, *Siemens* (1995), 558 n. 173.

60 Ibid., 212. Max Stein reports that Bingel donated to Himmler's SS fund a gift of 100,000 reichsmarks on behalf of Siemens; see Max Stein, "Report on the Employment of Slave Work," 3, CC.

61 Pentz to Witzleben, 1 August 1945, NL Jessen, 11/La 176, SA.

62 The two working titles were "Die Haltung des Hauses Siemens während des Hitler-Regimes" and "Das Haus Siemens: Sein Geist, seine politische Haltung und heutige Lage; Eine Denkschrift, Sommer 1945," NL Jessen, 11/La 176, SA.

63 "Die Haltung des Hauses Siemens," 2, NL Jessen, 11/La 176, SA.

64 Ibid., 3.

65 See Werner von Siemens, *Lebenserinnerungen.*

66 On Siemens's work and family policy and "social rationalization," see Sachse, *Siemens*, 95–257, and Siegel and Freyberg, *Industrielle Rationalisierung*, 287–424.

67 In fact, in the 1930s Siemens had given up one such subsidiary, the Siemens-Apparate-und-Maschinen GmbH in Berlin Spandau because, among other reasons, it had involved a "technology that is foreign to our own real specialty in electro-technical matters" (qtd. from James, "Deutsche Bank," 346).

68 "Die Haltung des Hauses Siemens," 8, NL Jessen, 11/La 176, SA.

69 Ibid., 12.

70 On C. F. von Siemens and Weimar politics, see Jones, "Carl Friedrich von Siemens."

71 Ibid., 14.

72 Ibid., 13.

73 This was the French company Outillage électrique Silex S.A., which sold 3,200 of its shares to Siemens in 1941 at 500 franks a share, but whose director stayed in control.

74 "Die Haltung des Hauses Siemens," 18, NL Jessen, 11/La 176, SA.

75 See Erker, *Industrie-Eliten*, 46–53.

76 "Die Haltung des Hauses Siemens," 14, NL Jessen, 11/La 176, SA.

77 This is translated from the German "Einsatz ausländischer Zivilarbeiter, Kriegsgefangene, Juden und KZ-Häftlinge im Hauses Siemens," NL Jessen, 11/La 176, SA. The arguments were previewed in a section of "Die Haltung des Hauses Siemens," ibid.

78 "Einsatz ausländischer Zivilarbeiter," 3, NL Jessen, 11/La 176, SA.

79 Ibid., 40.

80 Sachse, "Zwangsarbeit," 4.

81 Ibid., 3.

82 "Einsatz ausländischer Zivilarbeiter," 19, 40, NL Jessen, 11/La 176, SA.

83 See conversation with Fritz Groote regarding vegetable deliveries to the Haselhorst camp, in Investigative Committee Papers, NL Jessen, 11/La 176, SA.

84 Ibid.

85 Dr. Simon to the Directors of S&H, esp. Witzleben, 11 October 1945, 7539, SA.

86 Witzleben to Pentz, 24 August 1945, NL Jessen, 11/La 176, SA.

87 For example, Pentz asked, "Is there any documentary evidence that C. F. Siemens instructed that Siemens were not to make 'war profits?'" See Pentz to Jessen, 22 August 1945, NL Jessen, 11/La 176, SA.

88 "Bemerkungen zur Denkschrift-Stand vom 20. August 1945," NL Jessen, 11/La 176, SA.

89 Ibid. For a list of the managerial board members who belonged to the Nazi Party, see Feldenkirchen, *Siemens* (1995), 558 n. 170.

90 For one expression of this view in the 1940s, see Ritter, *Corrupting Influence of Power*.

91 Witzleben to Jessen, 9 September 1945, NL Jessen, 11/La 176, SA.

92 Firmenleitung to Heilpern, 10 September 1946, NL Jessen, 11/La 200, SA.

93 Ferencz, *Less Than Slaves*, 120.

94 *Greuelpropaganda über den Siemens-Konzern*, sent from Pentz to O'Sheah, 8 April 1947, NL Jessen, 11/La 176, SA.

95 O'Sheah to Pentz, 15 May 1947, NL Jessen, 11/La 176, SA.

96 SSW and S&H Directors to *Deutsche Volkszeitung*, 7 August 1945, NL Jessen, 11/La 176, SA.

97 On Potsdam and the "thorny problem" of reparations, see Backer, *Priming the German Economy*, 60–89.

98 On British policies in occupied Germany, see the many articles in Ian Turner, *British Occupation Policy*, and Scharf and Schröder, *Deutschlandspolitik Grossbritanniens;* also Roseman, *Recasting the Ruhr.*

99 On the French zone of occupation, see Willis, *French in Germany.*

100 On the Soviets' relative lack of concern about Nazis in postwar industry, see Nai-

mark, *Russians in Germany*, 191–92. On their views of industry's collective guilt, see ibid., 183–86.

101 See Collins, *Business Response to Keynes*, 27–73.

102 Fones-Wolf, *Selling Free Enterprise*, 23–57.

103 On the attempts to break the monopolistic power of German companies, see Martin, *All Honorable Men*. Martin was in charge of the Economic Division of the Office of the U.S. Military Government in Germany. On Martin and decartelization, see Berghahn, *Americanisation*, 91–110, and Greiner, *Morgenthau Legende*, 274–89.

104 On the Morgenthau Plan, see Berghahn, *Americanisation*, 88–89, and Greiner, *Morgenthau Legende*. For a lengthier discussion of these policy transitions regarding industry, see Backer, *Priming the German Economy*, and Gillingham, *Coal, Steel, and the Rebirth of Europe*.

105 Schwartz, *America's Germany*, 21.

106 Stokes, *Divide and Prosper*.

107 On the evolution of positions regarding JCS 1067, see Kindleberger, "Toward the Marshall Plan," and Backer, *Priming the German Economy*, 21–30.

108 On Levels of Industry plans, see Backer, *Decision to Divide Germany*, 96–99, and Gillingham, *Coal, Steel, and the Rebirth of Europe*, 107–8.

109 For an exhaustive handling of this issue by the British Control Commission, see FO 1039/147, PRO.

110 On political parties in the British zone, see Marshall, *Origins of Post-War German Politics*, 1–33, 154–81. On grassroots politics in the Soviet zone, see Naimark, *Russians in Germany*, chap. 5. For an introduction to British occupation policies regarding German industry, see Ian Turner, "British Policy toward Germany Industry." On the formation of political parties on the grassroots level in the U.S. zone, see Boehling, *Question of Priorities*, 156–209.

111 The SPD was still active in the Western zones of occupation, however, and its newspaper *Vorwärts* regularly reported stories about business guilt, although it was less vituperative in its attacks on Siemens and other segments of "monopoly capitalism."

112 "Krupp an KZ Auschwitz beteiligt: Siemens lieferte die Vergassungsanlage," *Deutsche Volkszeitung*, 5 August 1945.

113 Springer to Witzleben, 6 August 1945, NL Jessen, 11/La 176, SA.

114 Siemens SSW and Siemens S&H Directors to *Deutsche Volkszeitung*, 7 August 1945, NL Jessen, 11/La 176, SA.

115 Witzleben to Lyne, 28 August 1948, NL Jessen, 11/La 176, SA.

116 Ibid.

117 For another expression of the outrage, shock, and worry that industrialists felt at being treated as common criminals, see Sohl, *Notizen*, 98–107.

118 Witzleben to Lyne, 28 August 1948, NL Jessen, 11/La 176, SA.

119 For declarations against Benkert as a former Nazi and "reactionary war monger" (*Reaktionäre Kriegshetzer*), see "Siemens-Belegschaft gegen Konzerne," *Deutsche Volkszeitung*, 28 September 1945. On the December 1945 vote, see *Vorwärts*, 9 September 1947. The above articles from communist and socialist newspapers and

those that follow can be found in the VVN newspaper clipping files, V280/144, Stiftung.

120 Siemens, alleged *Neues Deutschland*, had helped to organize "Spanish Nazism" and had supported the Argentinean dictatorship in the 1930s by providing fascist fifth columns on both continents with weapons and propaganda material; see Albert Norden, "Siemenskonzern organisiert spanischen Nazismus," *Neues Deutschland*, 19 October 1946. Fritz Jessen's name shows up in this regard in a fascinating 180-page British document from 1944 or 1945 titled "Memorandum for G-2 SCHAEF-130 Key German Businessmen Linked with German Espionage," in FO 1031/56, PRO. This document profiles German businessmen and their firms' activities in Latin America, including all types of economic intelligence, disruptive propaganda, clandestine political organization, and paramilitary action. There also appears to have been some link between Siemens and the funding of the Nazi "Brown Houses" in South America. See H. F. Mayer to Witzleben, 30 October 1945, 7543-1, SA.

121 U.S. Military Law No. 8 made it illegal for companies to retain as managers or owners former Nazi Party members who were not successfully denazified. See Clay, *Decision in Germany*, 68.

122 Laskey, Director, German Political Branch of the Control Commission, Berlin, to H. Reade-Jahn, Berlin Economic and Social Council of the Control Commission of CC, Berlin, 14 January 1947, FO 1039/148 (file on the denazification of Siemens), PRO.

123 Reade-Jahn to Laskey, 31 January 1947, FO 1039/148, PRO.

124 Lt. Colonel Fletcher of Economic Branch of the Military Government to Reade-Jahn, 6 February 1947, FO 1039/148, PRO.

125 Memos from 2, 6, 10 February 1947 regarding Law No. 52, 7536, SA.

126 "Wer ist Fritz Jessen?," *Vorwärts*, 7 February 1947.

127 The decision came down on 25 February 1947. See the company's summary of the judgment in 7536, SA, and the "Bekanntmachung" from 8 April 1947 in same file.

128 Plettner, *Abenteuer Elektro-Technik*, 50.

129 Bekanntmachung von Witzleben, 31 March 1947, 7536, SA.

130 Plettner, *Abenteuer Elektro-Technik*, 40.

131 See Office of Military Government U.S. (OMGUS), Report on Investigation of Siemens & Halske AG, 5 vols., 10 April 1946, RG 94, NARA.

132 The Poensgen manuscript can be found in NL Jessen, 11/La 166, SA, and in almost every company archive in the Rhine-Ruhr area. See VS/4146, Thyssen, for more extensive discussions regarding this manuscript. Klaus-Dietmar Henke has hypothesized that the text was actually written by Walter Rohland, Poensgen's VSt successor and highly compromised mouthpiece for the Nazis' industrial policies. See Henke, *Amerikanische Besetzung*, 522-27.

133 Other companies prepared reports on their forced labor programs. See, e.g., the report by Herr Zapf, head of the "Fremdarbeiterabteilung" of Daimler-Benz AG during the war, titled "Mercedes-Stern und Fremdarbeiter 1941-1945." I thank Dr. Neil Gregor for providing me a copy of this report.

134 See Gregor, *Daimler-Benz*, 175–217.

135 See, e.g., Moeller, "War Stories."

CHAPTER TWO

1 For details of the arrests in the British zone, see, e.g., an official report on the arrest of forty-two members of the Rhine/Westphalia Coal Syndicate, 18 September 1945, FO 371/46722, PRO. Also see Henke, *Amerikanische Besetzung*, 523, and Hetzer, "Unternehmer und leitende Angestellte." For partial lists of the arrested industrialists, see B109/5764, BAK. For personal accounts of arrest and internment, see, e.g., Henle, *Three Spheres*, 56–61, and Sohl, *Notizen* 98–108. On the psychological impact of these arrests on German industrialists, see Hartewig, "Die 'alliierte Besatzungsmacht,'" and Plato, "Lebenswelten und politische Orientierung."

2 Companies did not always have an easy time accommodating industrialists who sought their old positions after returning from prison. For discussions about whether industrialists should receive back pay for their time behind barbed wire, see "Gutachtliche Stellungnahme zu der Frage, ob und welche Ansprüche diejenigen Mitglieder des Vorstandes von Bergwerksgesellschaften und von Unternehmen der Eisen- und Stahlindustrie aus ihren Dienstvertragen haben, die auf Anordnung der Militär-Regierung interniert gewesen sind," 17 October 1947, A1472, Thyssen.

3 The arrests of German industrialists took place simultaneously, but more sporadically, throughout the U.S. and French zones, and again in the British zone in 1946, accompanied by the detention of leading figures in banking in January. See James, "Deutsche Bank."

4 Henle, *Three Spheres*, 58.

5 *Neue Rheinische Zeitung*, 5 December 1945.

6 Industrialists in the British zone were transferred to several different camps, including Staumühle and Recklinghausen. On the network of British internment camps, see Wember, *Umerziehung im Lager*.

7 See Henle, *Three Spheres*, 45–61.

8 Ibid., 67. Henle made this comment during a debate in the Frankfurt Economic Council when Communist delegate Friedrich Rische "once again played his old record equating the iron and steel industry with war criminals." If in public industrialists were critical of this blanket condemnation of heavy industry, in private they often expressed their belief that "nobody in industry has a clean *Fragebogen* (questionnaire)." Quoted in letter from Paul Reusch to Hermann Reusch, 13 March 1946, RC.

9 See Berghahn, *Americanisation*, 61.

10 Haberland had been on the IG Farben defendants list but escaped prosecution at the last minute. See WO 309/1457, PRO. On the grooming of Haberland for a postwar directorial position, see Stokes, *Divide and Prosper*, 83–85.

11 On the arrest and internment of Kellermann, see newspaper clippings and memos in NL Hermann Reusch, 4001016/5, RWWA, and scattered correspondences in RC.

12 On the rebirth of the IHKs, see Rainer Schulze, "Representation of Interests."

13 On the formation of industrial organizations under Allied occupation, see Berghahn, *Americanisation*, 64, and Rainer Schulze, "Unternehmerische Interessenvertretung"; also Plumpe, "Unternehmerverbände und industrielle Interessenpolitik."

14 See Henke, *Amerikanische Besetzung*, 523, 567, and Henle, *Three Spheres*, 55.

15 On the discussion of who was to represent heavy industry to the Allies, see "Niederschrift über die Besprechung des 'Notkreises,'" 20 December 1945, Salewski Papers, BC.

16 On the Vereinigung, see Berghahn, *Americanisation*, 64.

17 On the council at Minden, see scattered correspondences in NL Frowein, BAK. On the Economic Council in Frankfurt (Wirtschaftsrat), see Nicholls, *Freedom with Responsibility*, 178–79, 214–17.

18 Berghahn, *Americanisation*, 182.

19 Hermann Reusch to Paul Reusch, 6 May 1946, RC.

20 On the conflicts that arose over the interpretation and implementation of deconcentration, see Berghahn, *Americanisation*, 89–96, and Diegmann, "American Deconcentration Policy in the Ruhr Coal Industry."

21 On the dissolution of IG Farben, see Stokes, *Divide and Prosper*.

22 On 1 March 1947 the Hüttenwerk Oberhausen AG came into existence.

23 Notes of a meeting between three board members of the GHH and the *Vorstand* of the Hüttenwerk Oberhausen AG, 20 March 1947, B109/5884, BAK.

24 Ibid.

25 Berghahn, *Americanisation*, 97. Apparently the Allies were equally suspicious of Dinkelbach, who catered to the wishes of both the Allies and his friends in German industry. In early 1948 one U.S. official referred to Dinkelbach as "an opportunist who has known how to adapt himself to changing conditions and ingratiate himself with the powers-that-be, regardless of principles." See American Consulate in Bremen to the U.S. Secretary of State, confidential, 30 January 1948, RG 84 4/61/42/7, box 6, Bremen Consulate General Confidential Files, 1946–48, NARA.

26 Treuhand to Reusch, regarding the conversation of 16 June 1947, B109/5718, BAK.

27 "In der Angelegenheit Dr. Reusch," undated, B109/5718, BAK.

28 "Akten-Notiz, betr: Angelegenheit Dr. Reusch," Potthoff Collection, 101/6, Böckler.

29 Reusch to indecipherable name, 27 February 1947, B109/5884, BAK.

30 Notiz to Herr Meiner, 21 June 1947, B109/5884, BAK.

31 "Akten-Notiz, Betr: Angelegenheit Dr. Reusch," Potthoff Collection, 101/6, Böckler.

32 See Chapter 6 for a more extensive discussion of codetermination.

33 On the 1947 codetermination debates in the Ruhr, see Berghahn, *Americanisation*, 203–30.

34 On the public's and politicians' harsh views of the Allies, see Foschepoth, "German Reaction to Defeat and Occupation," and Marshall, "German Attitudes."

35 See http://cnn.com/SPECIALS/cold.war/episodes/03/documents/marshall.plan; for introductory essays on the ERP, see Maier, *Marshall Plan*.

36 Of the 682 plants listed for dismantling, 496 were in the heavily industrialized

British zone and 186 in the U.S. zone. See Balabkins, *Germany under Direct Controls*, 24.

37 Quoted from Foschepoth, "German Reaction to Defeat and Occupation."

38 Ahrens, *Demontage*, 80–81.

39 C. G. Wickham on behalf of Director General of the Chemical Industry Branch of the Industry Division to Mr. Prentice, Deputy Chief of the Industry Division, 3 November 1947, FO 1013/1216, PRO.

40 Report sent from Oberstadtdirektor Döss to the Public Health Authority, n.d., FO 1013/1216, PRO.

41 *Henkel Should Not Be Dismantled!*, with cover letter to the British Foreign Office, 18 October 1947, FO 1013/1216, PRO. See same document with cover letter from Henkel to President Truman, 6 November 1947, in RG 59, 862.60/11-1647, box 6800, NARA.

42 *Henkel Should Not Be Dismantled!*, supplement 4, FO 1013/1216, PRO.

43 Ibid. (no supplement).

44 Ibid.

45 *Death by Dirt!*, RG 59, 862.60/11-1647, box 6800, NARA. This pamphlet is also on display at the Haus der Geschichte der Bundesrepublik Deutschland museum, Bonn.

46 In-house memo from Jost Henkel, 19 December 1947, FO 1013/1216, PRO. Winston Churchill wrote back to Henkel, arguing that he also opposed dismantling in principle but did not find evidence that the reparations against Henkel would affect available washing materials. See P. W. Hodgens on behalf of Churchill to Henkel, 17 November 1947, ibid.

47 Hodgens to Woel, 10 January 1948, FO 1013/1216, PRO.

48 Confidential Telegram, Berlin to Düsseldorf, 2 December 1947, FO 1013/1216, PRO. The British also expressed concern over the public relations tactics of the Westfälische Drahtindustrie of Hamm.

49 See "Notes of meeting held in Regional Commissioner's Office," with members of the Henkel family, the board members, and the Works Council, 4 December 1947, FO 1013/1216, PRO. It was eventually determined that Henkel had used its leftover stock of heavy poster paper purchased in 1938. See the report on the paper investigation, 12 December 1947, FO 1013/1216, PRO.

50 Press Release, 4 December 1947, FO 1013/1216, PRO.

51 Henkel to Nölting, 12 April 1948, FO 1013/1216, PRO. Henkel insisted that the distribution of this pamphlet had been modest. Two hundred and fifty copies had been distributed in England, and sixty in Germany. See Jost Henkel to Nölting, 12 April 1948, FO 1013/1216, PRO.

52 See Best, *Herbert Hoover*, 298–300.

53 For a contemporary example of the VSt's and Thyssen's antidismantling publicity, see *Zur Frage der Demontagen*. On the VSt's and Thyssen's reaction to dismantling, see Treue and Uebbing, *Feuer verlöschen nie*, 138–56.

54 Another widely distributed piece of protest publicity was Emmet, *Zerstörung auf unsere Kosten*.

55 Treue and Uebbing, *Feuer verlöschen nie*, 151. On the Petersberg protocols, see

Schwartz, *America's Germany*, 82–83, and Lademacher, "Zur Bedeutung des Petersberger Abkommens."

56 On the modernization of factories through dismantling, see Berghahn, *Americanisation*, 82.

57 Marshall, "German Attitudes," 667.

58 Ahrens, *Demontage*, 106–8.

59 See Berghahn and Karsten, *Industrial Relations*, 178–79.

60 On this and other mining disasters, see the report by the North German Coal Control, "The Denazification of the Coal Industry in the British Occupied Zone of Germany," 10 October 1946, FO 1051/535, PRO. For more information on the denazification of the coal industry, see occupation reports in FO 1039/147 and FO 1046/52, PRO, and Roseman, *Recasting the Ruhr*, 39–41.

61 See Bräutigam et al., "Drei württembergische Unternehmer."

62 For critical perspectives on denazification, see Solomon, *Questionaire*, and Fürstenau, *Entnazifizierung*.

63 See Buscher, *U.S. War Crimes Trial Program*. In this otherwise fine study of the "successor trials" and West Germans' reaction to them, Buscher hardly mentions industrialists.

64 On the debate over whether to try Gustav Krupp and/or his son Alfried, see memorandums in FO 1019/101, PRO. See also Taylor, *Anatomy of the Nuremberg Trials*, 89–94.

65 On Reemstma's putative link with Göring, see Reemstma to Zangen, 6 August 1947, M18.174, Mannesmann.

66 For these U.S. recommendations and the British criticisms of them, see FO 371/57503 and 371/47584–5, PRO. On the extradition of industrialists from the British to the U.S. zone, see WO 309/1455, 1456, PRO.

67 Bower, *Pledge Betrayed*, 287–354, and " 'Alle deutschen Industriellen.' "

68 Not surprisingly, the Soviet Union did not know quite what to make of this strange phenomenon of capitalists prosecuting capitalists. While they approved of the trials of Krupp and Flick, they were not pleased that the United States was conducting them. See V279/38 in VVN-Zeitungsausschnitte betr. Kriegsverbrecherprozess gegen Krupp, 1945–49, Stiftung.

69 Foreign Office to A. Duff Cooper, D.S.O, Paris, 21 June 1946, FO 371/57584, PRO.

70 The pretrial interrogations of industrialists comprise thousands of pages. See RG 238, Pre-Trial Interrogations, NARA. The British had serious misgivings about releasing some industrialists and bankers to testify in Nuremberg. To their annoyance, the Americans demanded the extradition of the Deutsche Bank's Hermann Joseph Abs, who was at the time providing valuable help to the British Finance Division in Düsseldorf, and Willy Schlieker, the steel and shipping magnate who in 1946 was serving as a consultant to the British on heavy industry matters. See WO 309/1455, PRO.

71 On the disputes surrounding the legal legitimacy of the industrialist trials, see Jung, *Rechtsprobleme*. On the career of Friedrich Flick, see Jung, *Rechtsprobleme;* Ogger, *Friedrich Flick der Grosse;* and Stallbaumer, "Strictly Business?"

72 For industrialists' attempts to relativize their behavior, in particular their use of

forced labor, see Wolfgang Pohle's speech to an unnamed industrial organization, NL Pohle, RWN 218, HstA.

73 Walter Pfeiffer to Wilhelm Salewski, 28 July 1947, Wirtschaftsvereinigung Eisen und Stahl-Press Department, P2103, IW.

74 "The men in the box are not symbols. . . . The individual defendants in this case are not being prosecuted for the sins of others, or because the name 'Krupp' has acquired over the years a sinister sheen" (*Trials of War Criminals*, vol. 9, opening statement of the prosecution).

75 Quoted from Tom Bower article title.

76 Pohle to Reusch, 19 February 1949, NL Hermann Reusch, 40010145/166, RWWA.

77 Throughout the trials the Nagel Office received the bulk of its documents from Göttingen. Later, as heavy industry debated the fate of Nagel and his office, the university asked that the collection be returned. See Pohle to Reusch, 19 February 1949, NL Hermann Reusch, 40010145/166, RWWA; see also, e.g., Pohle to Hartens, 6 July 1948, BC.

78 Also known as Nagel Information Service or simply the Nagel Office. For information on the Nagel Office, see "Nagel Informationsdienst, 1948–1964," Industrie- und Handelskammer Essen Collection, 28-117-3, RWWA, and Wiesen, "Overcoming Nazism."

79 On this process of information gathering, see, e.g., Nagel to Wecker, 2 March 1949, and other letters in file VSt/1422, Thyssen.

80 "Bericht Dr. Nagel über die Arbeiten des Nürnberger Archives," NL Hermann Reusch, 40010145/166, RWWA. Modified versions of this report are also in IHK Essen Collection, 28-117-3, RWWA.

81 Pohle to Reusch, 19 February 1949, NL Hermann Reusch, 40010145/166, RWWA.

82 See Reusch to Linz, 23 March, 1 April 1947, NL Hermann Reusch, 40010145/164, RWWA. For the receipts of the wire transfers from Mannesmann to Siemers in Nuremberg, see M.20.227, Bd 8, Mannesmann. See B109/170, BAK, for the Treuhand's internal paperwork regarding these transactions.

83 On Reusch's fundraising efforts, see Wiesen, "Overcoming Nazism."

84 Swept up in the monopolist spirit of the day, Flick willingly entered his firm Charlottenhütte into the VSt during the depression. See Jung, *Rechtsprobleme*, 26. For more on the VSt's thoughts about the trial, see NL Dinkelbach, A9050, Thyssen, esp. Fritz Wecker of the Legal Department to Wolfgang Linz, 19 June 1947.

85 Heinrichsbauer, *Schwerindustrie und Politik*.

86 Hermann Reusch to Paul Reusch, 10 November 1947, RC.

87 Heinrichsbauer, *Schwerindustrie und Politik*, 78–79. Translation taken from English-version manuscript in IW. This English version is not, however, an exact translation of the German publication, as it leaves out the key passage above that distributes blame for Hitler to *Personen in der ganzen weiten Welt*, a phrase whose relativizing tone would not have been received kindly by an English-speaking readership. I have thus supplemented the English translation with the more complete wording from the original German text.

88 This information is based in part on a conversation with Dr. Jürgen Heinrichs-

bauer, 14 February 1995, Cologne. On Heinrichsbauer before 1933, see Neebe, *Grossindustrie*, 117–19, and Henry A. Turner, *German Big Business*, 148–49. On Heinrichsbauer's career in Vienna, see Orlow, *Nazis in the Balkans*, 145.

89 While Heinrichsbauer's testimony can be found in RG 238, T301, NI series (microfilm), National Archives, Washington, D.C., as well as in the Stiftung Westfälisches Wirtschaftsarchiv, Dortmund, the most accessible collection of his testimony is in the Nuremberg prosecution file "August Heinrichsbauer," 1239/53, IfZ.

90 This is Heinrichsbauer's expression. Throughout his letters, he and Pohle emphasized the role this publication would play in influencing political decisions in the Ruhr and internationally.

91 Conversation with Dr. Jürgen Heinrichsbauer, 14 February 1995, Cologne.

92 For a sense of how closely East Germany was watching the behavior of "monopoly capitalists" like Hermann Reusch, see "Listen und biographische Angaben von ehemaligen Wirtschaftsführern während Faschismus," V279/95, Stiftung. The SED, not surprisingly, followed the industrialist trials and their aftermath very carefully. See V280/90, Stiftung, on the release of Flick and Krupp from prison in 1950 and 1951.

93 Röchling, the industrial leader of the Saarland, was tried and prosecuted by a French military tribunal made up of French, Polish, Dutch, and Belgian judges. For a newspaper clipping file on Röchling, see V279/35, Stiftung.

94 In the summer of 1948 Dr. Karl Jarres of Klöckner, Dr. Hermann Wenzel of VSt, and Dr. Ludwig Kastl were also reviewing drafts. See Heinrichsbauer to Salewski, 6 September 1947, NL Hermann Reusch, 40010145/147, RWWA.

95 On the stratification of the business world, see Hayes, "Industrial Factionalism."

96 Heinrichsbauer to Salewski, 6 September 1947, NL Hermann Reusch, 40010145/147, RWWA. See also Heinrichsbauer's two letters to Salewski on 17 and 20 September 1947, BC.

97 Flick was found guilty of employing slave labor, plundering, and complicity with the SS.

98 Pohle to Reusch, 12 December 1947, NL Hermann Reusch, 40010145/148, RWWA.

99 Pohle to Heinrichsbauer, 5 January 1948, NL Hermann Reusch, 40010145/148, RWWA. The same letter can be found in M20.227, Mannesmann, with more pages of criticisms that do not appear in the Reusch files.

100 Having been unable to locate an actual copy of either the fall or the December rough drafts, I am relying on the exchange of comments and suggestions that once accompanied these now missing drafts.

101 On the political stance of industrialists vis-à-vis the Nazi regime, see Erker, *Industrie-Eliten*, 32–40.

102 Pohle to Heinrichsbauer, 5 January 1948, NL Hermann Reusch, 40010145/148, RWWA.

103 Ibid.

104 On Gregor Strasser's relationship to Heinrichsbauer, see Stachura, *Gregor Strasser*, e.g., 93, 118, and Henry A. Turner, *German Big Business*, esp. 148–49.

105 With all of its problems, the pamphlet remains a valuable source of information

on heavy industry during the Weimar Republic. Neebe considers it a useful, if "tendentious" source. See Neebe, *Grossindustrie*, 207.

106 *Trials of War Criminals*, opening defense of Hermann Schmitz, 7:221.

107 Ibid., opening defense of Friedrich Flick, 6:127. The quotation, taken from a pamphlet by Bernhard Skrotzki, was read aloud in court.

108 *Trials of War Criminals*, opening defense of Friedrich Flick, 6:123.

109 On the concept and history of totalitarianism, see Gleason, *Totalitarianism*.

110 Heinrichsbauer, *Schwerindustrie und Politik*, 68.

111 *Trials of War Criminals*, opening defense of Krupp, 9:132.

112 Ibid., opening defense of Karl Krauch, 7:210.

113 On the Catholic Church and industry, see Buscher, *U.S. War Crimes Trial Program*, 91–113; Klee, *Persilscheine und Falsche Pässe*, 61–82; and Brochhagen, *Nach Nürnberg*, 35–7.

114 Niemöller portrayed Otto Steinbrinck as a good Christian and an internal enemy of Nazism, despite his having "paid consideration to the state, since the state took control of the government and the entire economy." See affidavit of Pastor Martin Niemöller, 9 August 1947, *Trials of War Criminals*, 6:340.

115 On the denazification of Fritz Thyssen, see the Spruchkammerakte zu Fritz Thyssen (Thyssen files), ABT, 520/FZ #6626, files 1–20, HHSA.

116 On the career of Fritz Thyssen, see Henry A. Turner, "Fritz Thyssen und 'I Paid Hitler' "; also see the Americans' multipaged intelligence report on Thyssen from 4 September 1945, FO 1078/29, PRO.

117 See Introduction and Henry A. Turner, *German Big Business*, 214–17.

118 See Salewski to Karl Jarres, 6 May 1947, and to H. Reusch, 7 May 1947, BC.

119 Paul Reusch to Hermann Reusch, 24 October 1947, RC. See also Paul Reusch to Spruchkammer Obertaunus, 14 August 1948, Thyssen files, folder 6, HHSA.

120 Niemöller to Herr Albrecht, Vorstizer der Spruchkammer, 24 July 1948, Thyssen files, folder 6, HHSA.

121 On Thyssen's "civil courage," see the testimony of Carl Christian Schmidt, a German of Jewish decent, 10 March 1948, and the testimony of a Jewish employee, Eduard Herzog, regarding Thyssen's intervention on his behalf, 7 September 1948, Thyssen files, folder 6, HHSA.

122 Struve, *Elites against Democracy*, 145.

123 Paul Karrenbrock, "Der Fall Thyssen: Ein Beitrag zum Verständnis und zur Überwindung des Nationalsozialismus," in Thyssen files, folder 20, HHSA. Karrenbrock, the former head of the Institut für Ständewesen in Düsseldorf, was hardly the ideal defense witness, having proven his Nazi credentials in a book on the "Jewish Question." See Karrenbrock, *Lösung der Judenfrage*. On the state in German political philosophy, see Vollrath, "Perspectives of Political Thought."

124 From the defense's written response to the indictment, 27 June 1948, Thyssen files, folder 20, HHSA.

125 Jakob Goldschmidt to Louis Lochner, 5 August 1946, Lochner Papers, reel 8, Wisconsin. The awkward English is Goldschmidt's.

126 On Goldschmidt's career and ideas, see Feldman, "Jakob Goldschmidt."

127 Berghahn, *Americanisation*, 65.

128 Minutes of the meeting between U.S., British, and German labor representatives, 27 May 1948, FO 1030/108, PRO.

129 From Hermann Reusch's Affidavit, 28 July 1947, Oberhausen, NL Hermann Reusch, 40010145/164, RWWA:

> Adolf Hitler would probably have seen greater troubles if the economic leaders had responded to him with a definitive "No." But that sort of definitive expression of opinion was, as I have just shown, in no way possible. In contrast, however, Adolf Hitler could have under no circumstances persisted if "*nicht am 1. Mai 1933 die gesamte klassenbewusste Arbeiterschaft den Maiumzug hinter den Hakenkreuzfahnen mitgemacht hätte* (see above)," and if, after the seizure of the union buildings, the class conscious working class had conducted a general strike, which at the time would not have represented a risk. This general strike would have undoubtedly caused more damage to the National Socialist *Machtergreifung* than industry's legendary millions in contributions, which is still today unproven, could have served it.

130 Anonymous report "Protest against Reusch," 13 April 1948, from Oberhausen, FO 1030/108, PRO.

131 Hüttenwerk Works Council to Dr. Bleiß of the Verwaltung für Wirtschaft in Minden, 13 April 1948, Potthoff Collection, 101/6, Böckler.

132 See, e.g., the declaration of the Metal Workers Union, 14 April 1948, Potthoff Collection, 101/6, Böckler.

133 Heinrich Mertens, "Das politische Ärgernis. Eine Meinung zum Fall Reusch," 16 April 1948, Potthoff Collection, 101/6, Böckler.

134 Ibid.

135 Bergmann of DGB, Low Saxony District, to Hans Böckler, 3 June 1948, Potthoff Collection, 101/6, Böckler.

136 Bishop to Macready, 1 May 1948, FO 1030/108, PRO.

137 "Dr. H. Reusch und der Stahl-Ausschuß," in *Sopade Informationsdienst,* 4 May 1948, in Potthoff Collection, 101/6, Böckler.

138 "Ein ungeheurer Schaden für das deutsche Volk," *Freiheit,* 18 May 1948, in Potthoff Collection, 101/6, Böckler.

139 F. Delheim of FDJ (Freie Deutsche Jugend), Bezirk Niederrhein, to DGB Vorstand, 31 May 1948, Potthoff Collection, 101/6, Böckler.

140 "Industrielle Kriegsverbrecher in der westdeutschen Wirtschaft," 1950, V280/97, Stiftung. Reusch was followed in rank by Hermann Josef Abs of the Deutsche Bank.

141 See files FO 1051/426 and FO 1051/130, PRO, on the British support of the unions' position.

142 No date, memo, FO 1030/108, PRO.

143 Manpower division of British Control Commission to Robertson's secretary, 31 May 1948, FO 1030/108, PRO.

144 Minutes of the meeting between the Americans, the British, and German labor representatives, 27 May 1948, FO 1030/108, PRO. The awkward wording of this passage is drawn verbatim from the original minutes taken in English.

145 Various trade organizations to Koehler, Erhard, Böckler, and Dr. Spiecker, chairman of the Länderrat, 31 May 1948, NL Hermann Reusch, 40010148/8, RWWA.

146 No author, "Confidential, only for personal perusal!," distributed to the GHH Vorstand, 23 June 1948, NL Hermann Reusch, 40010148/8, RWWA.

147 Macready to Bishop, 31 May 1948, FO 1030/108, PRO.

148 Press office announcement, Frankfurt Economic Council, 1 June 1948, FO 1030/108, PRO.

149 Text of General Robertson's press conference, 4 June 1948, FO 1030/108, PRO. For more information on the Reusch case from the British perspective, see FO 371/70586-7, and FO 371/70592-3, PRO.

150 See Conclusion.

151 Reusch to Frowein, 4 June 1948, NL Hermann Reusch, 40010145/187, RWWA.

CHAPTER THREE

1 "Public Relations," in the newsletter of the Bayerische Hypotheken-und Wechselbank, April 1953, NL Vogel, box 146, Augsburg.

2 During the 1950s, industrialists circulated among themselves a mass of pamphlets, books, and letters about public relations and the United States. See, e.g., Mörtzsch, *Offenheit macht sich bezahlt,* and the periodical *Informationsbrief für Innerbetriebliche Beziehungen und Public Relations.* On the history of public relations in West Germany, see Binder, *Entstehung unternehmerischer Public Relations;* Rühl, *Public Relations der Gewerkschaften;* and Lehming, *Carl Hundhausen.*

3 "Public Relations," NL Vogel, box 146, Augsburg.

4 On the memories and mythology of the currency reform, see Grube and Richter, *Das Wirtschaftswunder,* and Buchheim, "Währungsreform 1948 in Westdeutschland."

5 See Wiesen, "Overcoming Nazism."

6 Pohle to Heinrichsbauer, 20 July 1948, M20.277, Mannesmann.

7 Ibid.

8 On the IG Farben verdicts, see Hayes, *Industry and Ideology,* 378-79. On the trial itself, see the sensationalistic DuBois, *Generals in Grey Suits.* For a clear statement of industry's frustration over the IG Farben verdict, see Menne, *Nürnberger Urteil gegen die IG Farbenindustrie.* On the Krupp verdict, see Pohle's speech (undated) to fellow industrialists, NL Pohle, RWN 218, HstA.

9 Almost every industrial organization in West Germany raised an angry voice against the verdict. For a small sample of the extensive correspondence and letters of protest that followed the announcement of the Krupp verdict and sentence, see the papers of the Industrie und Handelskammer Düsseldorf, 400-2, #2, RWWA.

10 On Lucius Clay, see Clay, *Decision in Germany,* and Henke, *Amerikanische Besetzung,* 975-85.

11 Schwartz, *America's Germany,* 156-58.

12 Pohle to Heinrichsbauer, 2 August 1948, M20.277, Mannesmann.

13 See Bührer, "Return to Normality," 139.

14 Heinrichsbauer also resumed writing his second book. It was, however, never com-

pleted. On the fate of this longer project and the criticisms of *Schwerindustrie und Politik*, see Wiesen, "Overcoming Nazism."

15 See, e.g., Hellmuth Dix, "Die Urteile in den Nürnberger Wirtschaftsprozessen," *Neue Juristische Wochenschrift* 17 (1949), and R. R. Stroth, "The Flick Verdict: Review of one of the Nuremberg industrial cases," circular dated 26 August 1948, NL Hermann Reusch, 40010145/166, RWWA. Also see Taylor, "Krupp Trial" and *Anatomy of the Nuremberg Trials.*

16 See Wirtschaftspolitische Gesellschaft, *Deutsche Initiative.*

17 On the postwar history of economic publishing, in contrast to public relations, see *Wege der Wirtschaftspublizistik.* I thank Ms. Sabine Pudor for her kind assistance.

18 For example, Mannesmann produced an elaborate "factual and artistic" film profile of itself in 1935. See Wessel, *Kontinuität im Wandel*, 222.

19 On U.S. business's fears of socialism and the dangerous effects of public cynicism, see editorial "Big Business Is Still in Trouble."

20 On postwar U.S. ideas about business and labor, see Collins, *Business Response to Keynes*, 113–72.

21 "Big Business Is Still in Trouble."

22 Ibid.

23 See Cutlip, *Public Relations History*, 188. On public relations in the United States from the turn of the century until the end of World War II, see Marchand, *Creating the Corporate Soul.*

24 Roper, "Public Looks at Big Business."

25 The original name of the BDI was the Ausschuß für Wirtschaftsfragen der industriellen Verbände. On the history of the BDI, see Braunthal, *Federation of German Industry in Politics;* Bührer, "Unternehmerverbände nach den beiden Weltkriegen"; and Tornow, "Die deutschen Unternehmerverbände."

26 On corporatism in postwar West Germany, see Prowe, "Foundations of West German Democracy" and "Economic Democracy," and Abelshauser, "First Postliberal Nation."

27 On the political influence of the BdA, see Bunn, "Federation of German Employers' Associations," and Eschenburg, *Herrschaft der Verbände?* For an introduction to German industrial *Interessenvertretung*, see Overy, "State and Industry in Germany."

28 Hermann Reusch to Fritz Berg, 30 May 1950, NL Hermann Reusch, 40010146/306, RWWA.

29 August Heinrichsbauer, "Die Organisation der Public Relations in der Wirtschaft" (early 1950), NL Hermann Reusch, 40010146/306, RWWA, and scattered documents in NL Vogel, box 146, Augsburg.

30 On conservatives' suspicion of democracy after World War II, see Grebing, *Konservative gegen die Demokratie*, 83–261, and Schildt, *Konservatismus in Deutschland*, 211–52.

31 Heinrichsbauer to Wilhelm Beutler, 16 January 1950, NL Hermann Reusch, 40010145/306, RWWA.

32 August Heinrichsbauer, "Die Organisation der Public Relations in der Wirtschaft," NL Hermann Reusch, 40010146/306, RWWA.

33 On the background of and hearings related to the Spiegel Affair, see various related articles in *Der Spiegel*, 27 September 1950, and subsequent issues throughout October 1950.

34 August Heinrichsbauer's troubled career in industry culminated in 1968 when the publicist sued novelist Michael Mansfeld for having portrayed him as a postwar lobbyist with prior Nazi ties. See Michael Mansfeld, *Bonn Koblenzer Straße* (Munich: Desch, 1967), and "Der Beleidigte Lobbyist," *Capital*, March 1968, 12–15.

35 Back cover of *Der Spiegel*, 20 June 1951, with heading "Geld und Politik."

36 On the fallout from the Spiegel Affair and industrialists' reactions, see NL Hermann Reusch, 40010145/152 and 40010145/153, RWWA, esp. Günter Henle to Otto Seeling, 2 November 1950, in latter file. Many businessmen were angry that such a controversial figure had been given any responsibilities in the realm of campaign contributions.

37 On the question of continuity and restoration after 1945, see as introductions Grebing, "Demokratie ohne Demokraten?," and Schwarz, "Modernisierung oder Restauration?"

38 This was not entirely the case. Berg had been involved in the wartime planning of bicycle production. On Berg's career, see Berghahn, *Americanisation*, 70.

39 For an example of the many articles examining the power of Fritz Berg, see the cover article "Berg, der Interessen-Bündler," *Der Spiegel*, 2 November 1960, 24–41. For a collection of Berg's own writings and speeches, see Berg, *Westdeutsche Wirtschaft*.

40 On transatlantic business relations after 1945, see Link, *Contribution of Trade Unions*, and Vaubel, *Unternehmer gehen zur Schule* and *Zusammenbruch und Wiederaufbau*.

41 On the career of Hundhausen, see Lehming, *Carl Hundhausen*.

42 Carl Hundhausen, "Public Relations," *Zeitschrift für Betriebswirtschaft* 15, no. 1 (1938): 48–61. Quote from Lehming, *Carl Hundhausen*, 28.

43 Hundhausen, *Werbung um öffentliches Vertrauen*.

44 On Hundhausen, see Flieger and Ronnenberger, *Public Relations Anfänge*.

45 "Press Group Ousts 2 As Nazi Agents," *New York Times*, 3 January 1941, 5.

46 Herbert Gross, *Die Pflege der öffentlichen Meinung durch das amerikanische Unternehmertum* (1950), NL Hermann Reusch, 40010145/306, RWWA.

47 Hellwig, *Carl Ferdinand Freiherr von Stumm-Halberg*.

48 See, e.g., Fritz Hellwig, "Amerika und Europa-Die geistige Begegnung," *Kulturspiegel: die Zeitschrift der deutschen Kriegsgefangenlager in Großbritannien*, October 1946, 27–48. On Hellwig's publications and early career, see NL Hellwig, file 003/2, ACDP. Also see conversation with Dr. Fritz Hellwig, 3 February 1995, Bonn-Bad Godesberg.

49 Fritz Hellwig, "Europa zwischen den Mächten," *Die Brücke für Verständigung und Friede* (Zeitschrift der Studenten von Wilton Park Training Centre), NL Hellwig, 003/2, ACDP. On the cultural and intellectual activities of German POWs in the United States, see Robin, *Barbed-Wire College*, and Smith, *War for the German Mind*.

50 When the first choice, the WES's Wilhelm Salewski, declined an offer to take over

the DI's helm, the BdA and BDI turned to Hellwig, who at the time was working as an independent financial adviser in Düsseldorf and as an adviser to the CDU leadership and the party's finance committee in Bonn. While expressing reservations about giving up his activities with the CDU and his active role in the WES's Arbeitskreis für Fragen der Neuordnung, Hellwig agreed to take over the DI's day-to-day operations as managing director (along with Otto Mejer). August Heinrichsbauer coveted Hellwig's position. Wrote Hermann Reusch later, "He was of the opinion that he was the suited leader of the DI, which would have been impossible after the Spiegel Affair" (Hermann Reusch to F. Gummert, 26 February 1955, NL Hermann Reusch, 40010145/173, RWWA).

51 Institut für Demoskopie (Gesellschaft zum studium der öffentlichen Meinung, M.B.H), *Unternehmer und Öffentlichkeit* (Allensbach, 1950), in IW.

52 Heinrichsbauer Aktenvermerk, 28 June 1950, NL Hermann Reusch, 40010146/306, RWWA.

53 "Entwurf einer Abonnements-Einladung" (Frankfurt am Main, 1949), NL Hermann Reusch, 40010145/306, RWWA.

54 The DIHT was the IHKs' supraregional umbrella organization. Muthesius, a former editor with the *Berliner Tageblatt* and the *Deutsche Zeitung*, was, in the early 1950s, the head of an organization called the Gesellschaft für wirtschaftliche Beratung in Frankfurt.

55 On the funding of the DI, see, e.g., Carl Neumann to Otto Vogel, 26 May 1951, NL Vogel, box 204, Augsburg.

56 "Aufruf zur Bildung der 'Deutschen Industriegemeinschaft'" (ca. November 1950), NL Hermann Reusch, 40010146/306, RWWA.

57 Ibid.

58 "Notizen über Oestrich 15./16.1.51, 'Gründung des Deutschen Industrie-Instituts,'" NL Hermann Reusch, 40010146/307, RWWA.

59 See Mansfeld's polemic against the unions and their attempts to "manipulate the masses" against industry: Wolfgang Mansfeld, *Unternehmer und öffentliche Meinung* (Cologne, 1951), in the papers of the DIHT (B156), file 169, BAK. This file contains extensive materials on the DIHT and public relations.

60 On Salewski, see Bührer, *Ruhrstahl und Europa*, esp. 41–52.

61 "Notizen über Oestrich 15./16.1.51, 'Gründung des Deutschen Industrie-Instituts,'" NL Hermann Reusch, 40010146/307, RWWA.

62 On the Committee on Public Information, see Marchand, *Creating the Corporate Soul*, 89–90.

63 DIHT Rundschreiben betr. Public and Human Relations, Nr. 22/51, 23 April 1952, NL Vogel, box 146, Augsburg.

64 Niederschrift über die Sitzung des Hauptausschüßes des DIHTs, 3 March 1950, NL Vogel, box 126, Augsburg.

65 Dr. Horst Dilthey, "Exposé über Public Relations," 25 May 1951, NL Vogel, box 146, Augsburg.

66 Josef Winschuh in "Notizen," NL Hermann Reusch, 40010146/307, RWWA.

67 Reusch, in ibid.

68 Mejer and Hellwig to Vogel, 14 December 1951, NL Vogel, box 204, Augsburg.

69 Wilhelm Beutler and Gustav Stein to BDI Presidium, Vorstand, and Geschäftsführer, 11 May 1951, NL Vogel, box 204, Augsburg.

70 See Jahresbericht des DI, 1951/52, NL Vogel, box 204, Augsburg.

71 The DI also launched the *Rundfunkspiegel des Deutschen Industrieinstituts,* which summarized and reprinted radio programs or news items of interest to industry.

72 See, respectively, Hans Mosberg, "Der Unternehmer in unserer Zeit," *Vortragsreihe des Deutschen Industrieinstituts,* 4 August 1952; Fritz Gruenagel, "Kollektivismus als Krise der Zeit," *Vortragsreihe,* 6 October 1952; Ernst Schrewe, "Mensch und Technik," *Vortragsreihe,* 15 October 1951; and Otto Seeling, "Kategorischer Imperativ der Wirtschaft," *Vortragsreihe,* 21 January 1952. All of these publications and other publications of the DI can be found in the IW.

73 Hellwig, "Die Echte Unternehmer in der Marktwirtschaft."

74 Stein and Gross, *Unternehmer in der Politik,* 111.

75 See title of Berghahn and Friedrich, *Otto A. Friedrich.*

76 "Unternehmer aller Länder vereinigt Euch!," in *Der Unternehmer in unserer Zeit,* by Ernst Schrewe (speech held in October 1949 in front of *Verbände* and IHK press departments in Württemberg-Baden), in 69/1877, IW.

77 See Feldman, "Politische Kultur und Wirtschaft," and Bührer, "Unternehmerverbände nach den beiden Weltkriegen."

78 See Fritz Hellwig, "Die Einheit der Unternehmerpersönlichkeit," *Vortragsreihe,* 9 July 1951.

79 See Schumpeter, *Kapitalismus, Sozialismus, und Demokratie.* For a good summary of Schumpeter's philosophy of the entrepreneur, see Peter Mathias, "Entrepreneurs, Managers, and Business Men."

80 The literature on the *Typologie des Unternehmers* is not only a product of the 1950s. Still today, business scholars pursue this interest in classifying and defining the industrialist; see *Der Unternehmer im Wandel der Zeiten.*

81 Herbert Gehrig, *Persönlichkeit des Unternehmers.*

82 Silberschmidt, *Bedeutung des Unternehmers,* 16.

83 Schumpeter used the term "demonic" in reference to the entrepreneur's behavior, which was at once creative and innovative but also depended on the destruction of competition.

84 For 1950s studies of the *Unternehmer,* see Otto Friedrich, *Leitbild des Unternehmers,* and Flender, *Stunde des Unternehmers.* For a study of the industrialist as an internal whipping boy, see Andreae and Freudenfeld, *Sündenbock Unternehmer?*

85 Winschuh, *Das neue Unternehmerbild.*

86 For an extensive collection of Winschuh's published and unpublished articles, including an unfinished manuscript from the late 1940s called "Die Sittliche Würde der Wirtschaft" [The ethical value of the economy], see NL Winschuh, 1223/12, 14, BAK.

87 Winschuh, *Männer, Traditionen, Signale* and *Der Unternehmer im neuen Europa.*

88 The investigation came to a halt with the end of the war. See NL Winschuh, 1223/1, BAK.

89 Another such industrialist was Heinrich Krumm, who, as a loyal Nazi and head

of the Ludwig Krumm AG, penned a speech called "Der Unternehmer im neuen Deutschland" in 1941. After the war, Krumm wrote about industrialists' democratic calling. See his self-serving "wartime" diary, re-created after the war: Krumm, *Tagebuch eines deutschen Unternehmers.* Copy housed in IWW.

90 Both Winschuh and Fritz Hellwig presented talks called "Das neue Unternehmerbild" at a business retreat in 1954. See *Vortragsreihe,* July–December 1954. Both were reprinted in *Beitrag zur Förderung des Unternehmernachwuchses* (1. Baden Bädener Unternehmerseminar vom 13. Juni bis 3. Juli 1954) (Bergisch Gladbach, 1954), no page numbers. For a collection of materials relating to Winschuh's work on the public image of the industrialist, see NL Winschuh, 1223/84, BAK.

91 Winschuh, in "Notizen über Oestrich 15./16.1.51, 'Gründung des Deutschen Industrie-Instituts," NL Hermann Reusch, 40010146/307, RWWA.

92 Josef Winschuh, "Unternehmertum und Bürgertum," *Vortragsreihe,* 2 July 1951.

93 J. J. Marx, Tuch- und Filztuchfabrik in Lambrecht, Pfalz.

94 Roughly the equivalent of the National Federation of Independent Businesses (NFIB) in the United States. Both the NFIB and the ASU publish a magazine called, respectively, *The Entrepreneur* and *Der Unternehmer.* (The ASU's chief organ was originally called *Die Aussprache*). On the founding of the ASU, see the papers of Curt Becker, I-162, file 161/1, ACDP. See also "ASU, Porträt eines Unternehmerverbandes," *Handelsblatt,* 23 March 1982, 19.

95 Advertisement for the ASU in Walter Eckhardt, *Entwurf eines Ertrags- und Einkommenssteuergesetzes,* issue no. 2 of the *Selbständige Unternehmer* series (Frankfurt: ASU, 1981), in ASU library.

96 On pronatalism during the Adenauer years, see Moeller, *Protecting Motherhood,* 213-14, and Heineman, *What Difference Does a Husband Make?,* 147-49.

97 See Mitchell, "Materialism and Secularism."

98 For a collection of Winschuh's numerous speeches to young businessmen, see NL Winschuh, 1223/80, BAK.

99 Winschuh, "Young Businessmen." This is a translation of Winschuh's *Ansprache an den jungen Unternehmer* (Frankfurt: Lutzeyer, 1950).

100 Winschuh, "Young Businessmen." On the "third force," see also Theodor Büchner, "Unternehmer und Dritte Kraft," *Junge Wirtschaft* 7 (July 1954): 158-60. On the concept of *Bürgertum* after 1945, see Siegrist, "Ende der Bürgerlichkeit?," and Lepsius, *Interessen, Ideen, und Institutionen,* 153-69.

101 From welcoming speech by Carl Schleussner, in the "Erste Arbeitstagung und erweiterte Gründungsversammlung" (30 September 1949, Wiesbaden), NL Becker, file 161/1, ACDP.

102 Based in Caux, Switzerland, with branches in Oxford and Düsseldorf, the movement published a newsletter, the *Merkblatt Caux,* which reached many industrialists. In 1951 the BDI's managing director Gustav Stein encouraged his colleagues to attend a ten-day conference in Caux. See Gustav Stein to BDI Vorstand, 7 September 1951, NL Vogel, box 203, Augsburg.

103 On business and religion in the United States, see Fones-Wolf, *Selling Free Enterprise,* 218-54.

104 On Röpke, see Nicholls, *Freedom with Responsibility,* e.g., 90-101.

105 See ibid., chap. 11; Ambrosius, *Durchsetzung der sozialen Marktwirtschaft*, 14–37; and Berghahn, "Ideas into Politics."

106 See, e.g., Gustav Grundlach, "Der Unternehmer in christlicher Schau," speech delivered at the BDI/IHK-sponsored "Unternehmer-Seminar" (subtitled "Betriebsführer Gespräche"), 14 June to 2 July 1954, in NL Becker, I-162-055/1, ACDP, and Rahner, "Der Unternehmer und die Religion." I thank Roman Siebenbrock of the Karl Rahner Society for a copy of the latter article.

107 See Greiß and Lohmann, *Gründung des Bundes Katholischer Unternehmer*, and Schmidt, *Soziale Gerechtigkeit*.

108 This was a perpetual concern of the BKU's. See Peter Werhahn, *Die moralische Bewältigung des wirtschaftlichen Fortschritts*, #9 of the BKU's *Schriftenreihe* (Cologne: BKU, 1964), in BKU library.

109 Despite their clear attempt to distance themselves from Nazism, the original founders themselves were burdened in the 1950s by the assumptions that industry had been the "stirrups" (*Steigbügelhalter*) of Nazism. See Schmidt, *Soziale Gerechtigkeit*, 21.

110 For a good expression of these worries, see Rundschreiben to members of DIHT Vorstand regarding the ASU, 19 January 1950, NL Vogel, box 125, Augsburg. At the founding meeting of the ASU, the participants had trouble defining *selbständig*; did not every industrialist deem himself independent? See "Erste Arbeitstagung und erweiterte Gründungsversammlung" (30 September 1949, Wiesbaden), NL Becker, 161/1, ACDP.

111 "Manifest der selbständiger Unternehmer," *Die Aussprache* 3, no. 6 (June 1953): 77–78.

112 On the transformation of West Germany into a consumer society by the end of the 1950s, see Wildt, "Privater Konsum."

113 On the concept of the *nivellierte Mittelstandsgesellschaft*, see Schelsky's 1953 essay, " 'Nivellierte Mittelstandsgesellschaft,' " and Mooser, "Arbeiter, Angestellte, und Frauen."

114 On the cultural and political self-understanding of military and industrial elites, see Negt, "In Erwartung der autoritären Leistungsgesellschaft."

115 Herbert Gross, "Unternehmer und Öffentlichkeit," *Hamburger Allgemeine Zeitung*, 8 March 1950.

CHAPTER FOUR

1 For important studies of this period, see Heineman, *What Difference Does a Husband Make?*; Moeller, *Protecting Motherhood*; Fehrenbach, *Cinema in Democratizing Germany*; and Schildt, *Moderne Zeiten*.

2 See Grebing, "Demokratie ohne Demokraten?"

3 On youth rebelliousness, see Poiger, *Jazz, Rock, and Rebels*, 71–105; on the consuming woman, see Carter, *How German Is She?*

4 On the Freiburg school of economists who promoted a *mittelständisch*, anticartel philosophy combining economic freedom and social order (often called "ordoliberalism"), see Hentschel, *Ludwig Erhard*, 60–73.

5 Nicholls, *Freedom with Responsibility,* 298.

6 Institut für Demoskopie (Gesellschaft zum studium der öffentlichen Meinung, M.B.H), *Unternehmer und Öffentlichkeit* (Allensbach, 1950), in IW.

7 Nicholls, *Freedom with Responsibility,* 298. On the founding of the ASM, see *Entscheidung für die Freiheit,* Aktionsgemeinschaft soziale Marktwirtschaft, Tagungsprotokoll (Bad Nauheim/Ludwigsburg: Vita-Verlag, 1953).

8 Hayek, *Road to Serfdom.*

9 Wolfgang Mansfeld to DI curatorium, 12 November 1953, NL Vogel, box 205, Augsburg. See, e.g., Schleussner, *Fibel der sozialen Marktwirtschaft.*

10 Gross, *Sozialismus in der Krise;* Hunold, *Wirtschaft ohne Wunder;* Briefs, *Zwischen Kapitalismus und Syndikalismus.*

11 Hans-Otto Wesemann, *Die Verbraucher hat das Wort* (1953), discussed in letter from Mansfeld of Deutsche Industrieverlag to Kuratorium, 12 November 1953, NL Vogel, box 205, Augsburg.

12 Reiner, *Wir alle können besser leben.*

13 These titles are cited in Rundschreiben #12 of the DIHT's Pressestelle, 12 August 1953, B156/169, BAK.

14 The first advertisement, "Aufklärung über die Erfolge der Marktwirtschaft," appeared on 5 October 1952 in 545 daily and weekly newspapers, with a total of 12 million copies printed. On the history of *Die Waage,* see Schindelbeck and Ilgen, *"Haste Was, Biste Was!"*

15 Schmidt, *Soziale Gerechtigkeit,* 48.

16 Ibid.

17 Greiß, "Erhards soziale Marktwirtschaft"; Nicholls, *Freedom with Responsibility,* 296. In the early years of this publicity blitz, the BKU always worked anonymously behind the scenes.

18 Fones-Wolf, *Selling Free Enterprise.*

19 Among the author's many writings on the subject, see Schumpeter, *Essays.*

20 See Nolan, *Visions of Modernity.*

21 For an engaging discussion of the entrepreneurial ethos during this period, see Rossiter, *Conservatism in America,* 128–62.

22 Zippe, *Große Unternehmer;* see also Wagenfuhr, *Schöpferische Wirtschaft.*

23 Seherr-Thoss, *Zwei Männer—Ein Stein;* Frankenburg, *Porsche.*

24 Holdermann, *Im Banne der Chemie.*

25 La Mure, *König der Nacht.*

26 Klass, *Die Wollspindel.*

27 Wolfgang Mansfeld of the Deutsche Industrieverlag to the DI curatorium and editorial board, 1 April 1953, NL Vogel, box 204, Augsburg. See Walter Chrysler, *Mein Weg und Aufstieg: Vom Schlosser zum Autokönig* (translation of Chrysler, *Life of an American Workman*). As in the 1920s, the United States and Germany were obsessed in the 1950s with the great automobile entrepreneurs, especially Henry Ford. On Germany and Fordism, see Nolan, *Visions of Modernity,* 30–57.

28 On industrialists' participation in the publication of *Neue Deutsche Biographie* and *Rheinisch-Westfälischen Wirtschaftsbiographien,* see NL Haberland, file 271/1.1.64, BAL.

29 Directing this project was Fritz Pudor, a respected economic publicist and activist on behalf of the FRG's displaced German Polish population. Pudor's firm was the West-Verlag in Essen, which had published August Heinrichsbauer's *Schwerindustrie und Politik* in 1948.

30 *Gedenkschrift für Hugo Henkel* (Düsseldorf: Henkel, 1953).

31 *Vorwort zu der Schrift von Muthesius über Peter Klöckner*, NL Henle, 1384/488, BAK.

32 For the classic study on how the U.S. economy came to depend on managers, see Chandler, *Visible Hand*, e.g., 484–500.

33 Burnham, *Managerial Revolution*. On Burnham, see Diggins, *Up from Communism*, 303–37.

34 Terms such as *Parteibuch-Industrielle*, *Funktionärs-Manager*, and *Techniker-Unternehmer* were used pejoratively to refer to young engineers and businessmen who made up Albert Speer's so-called kindergarten of industrialists who worked with the armaments ministry. See Erker, *Industrie-Eliten*, 26–32.

35 See "Und noch einmal: Der Manager," *Unternehmerbrief*, 15 May 1952, 4. Among the countless books on the theme of the manager, see, e.g., Schlenzka, *Unternehmer, Direktoren, Manager*, and Domaniewski, *Intellectual Capitalism*, esp. 17–48.

36 "Managerkrankheit-Gespenst oder Wirklichkeit?," *Anlage zum Unternehmerbrief*, 16 July 1953, 1. On the theme of manager sickness, see Alfred Angst to the board members of the Augsburg IHK, 23 November 1955, NL Vogel, box 148, Augsburg. Angst reminds the businessmen to eat well, to exercise often (e.g., hiking and jumping rope), and to get eight hours of sleep; otherwise they will risk dying twenty years younger than expected. On work and fatigue, see Rabinbach, *Human Motor*, e.g., 219–37.

37 The generational aspect of this theme can be seen in 1969's Rosenthal Affair, in which porcelain industrialist and manager Philipp Rosenthal insulted Friedrich Flick and his older generation of big capitalists. His comments sparked an angry response within industry circles. See Berghahn and Friedrich, *Otto A. Friedrich*, 329–32.

38 Despite its lingering status among an older generation of businessmen as a term of opprobrium, "manager" is now a value-free term in common usage. See, e.g., the widely read *Manager* magazine in Germany.

39 "To serve the national community—that has to be the goal of every business leader who takes his responsibilities seriously. That is the guiding principle for my work, and everything else must submit to it, without question, even if I run this business into the ground because of it" (qtd. from Kreimeier, *Ufa Story*, 261). On this credo, see also James, "Deutsche Bank," 282.

40 On *Die Mörder sind unter uns*, see Fehrenbach, *Cinema in Democratizing Germany*, 59.

41 This was the original, not exactly literal, English translation given the film upon its release. The following English subtitles are a combination of my own translations and the translations given if released in the United States. Much of this information is drawn from Helt and Helt, *West German Cinema*.

42 For the last three story lines, see, respectively, *Vor Sonnenuntergang* [Before sundown] (1956); *Mein Mann, das Wirtschaftswunder* [My husband, the economic miracle] (1960); and *Alle Tag ist kein Sonntag* [Every day's not Sunday] (1959).

43 *Unschuld in Tausend Nöten* (1951), *Wenn Männer Schwindeln* (1950), and *Mädchen ohne Grenzen* (1955).

44 *Das Mädchen Rosemarie* (1958), and Kuby, *Das Mädchen Rosemarie*.

45 Respectively, *Ich hab mein Herz in Heidelberg verloren* [I left my heart in Heidelberg] (1952), and *Veronika, die Magd* [Veronika, the maid] (1951).

46 Respectively, *Es begann um Mitternacht* [It began at midnight] (1950), and *Artistenblut* [Performing blood] (1949).

47 *Pulverschnee nach Übersee* [Powder snow export] (1956).

48 *Wilde Wasser* [Wild water] (1962).

49 Wessel, "Überlieferung von Filmquellen" and *Kontinuität im Wandel*, 22.

50 See the series *Der Deutsche Industriefilm*, published by the DI (1960-).

51 See the catalog *Industriefilmtage Berlin 1959* (12-14 September 1959, Kongreßhalle Berlin). For a discussion of the implications of the industrial film for big business, see "Industriefilme werben um Vertrauen," *Handelsblatt*, 10 September 1959, 7.

52 *Industriefilmtage Berlin 1959* (12-14 September 1959, Kongreßhalle Berlin).

53 See *Filmkatalog der DIZ (Deutsche Industriefilm-Zentrale) in der deutschen Industrie-Verlags GmbH* (Cologne, 1963), in IWW. This work from 1961 received a prize for best educational film for youth, National Industriefilmtage, Berlin, 1961, as well as a music and dance prize in Valencia, Spain.

54 On Germans' ambivalent view of jazz in the 1950s, see Poiger, *Jazz, Rock, and Rebels*.

55 See Fabian, *Der Rat der Götter*.

56 See short report "Götter" in *Der Spiegel*, 7 November 1951, 4.

57 Hilmar Hoffmann, *Triumph of Propaganda*.

58 Fehrenbach, *Cinema in Democratizing Germany*, 59.

59 The term can be traced back to 1887, when the British coined the expression as an anti-German "protectionist stigma." See Head, *"Made in Germany,"* chap. 2 and quote from back cover; see also Williams, *Made in Germany*.

60 On Germans' belief in the superiority of their products, see Kugler, "Vor der Werkstatt zum Fließband," and Nolan, *Visions of Modernity*, 58-82.

61 On marketing and on industry's ambivalence toward consumption in the Weimar period, see Nolan, *Visions of Modernity*, 50-54. On consumption and views of the United States during the Third Reich, see Schäfer, *Gespaltene Bewusstsein*, 114-62.

62 Roman Musiel, "Die Bedeutung der Werbung im Wirtschaftsleben," *VDI-Nachrichten*, 22 June 1950.

63 *Der Spiegel*, 11 May 1950, 22.

64 See Carter, *How German Is She?*, 88-91. On consumption in West and East Germany during the Cold War, see Pence, "Labours of Consumption."

65 See Glouchevitch, *Juggernaut*, 46-51.

66 *Germany 49*, Industry Show, New York Museum of Science and Industry, RCA building, 9-24 April 1949 (New York: Exhibition Committee for the German Industrial Show, 1949).

67 Eugen Roth and E. M. Cordier, *Unser Deutsches Museum* (Cologne: Deutsches Industrieinstitut, 1952), in NL Vogel, box 205, Augsburg. On industrialists' contributions to the museum and the DI's publication of this booklet, see "Anträge auf

Förderung 1953," NL Vogel, box 205, Augsburg. For the prewar link between the museum and industry, see Herzog, *Paul Reusch und das Deutsche Museum.*

68 Deutsche Industrie Ausstellung, Berlin, 1–15 October 1950, Press Information Materials, Report #14, 28 August 1950, LAB. See invitation *Berlin ladet Sie ein,* in same collection.

69 Pressestelle der Deutschen Industrieausstellung, #1, 2 August 1950, A1019, LAB.

70 See the various publications relating to the Berlin Industry Exhibition, such as *Jährlich Einmal in Berlin* (1953), A1019, and *Schaufenster der Welt* (1954), ser. 30, in LAB.

71 Fritz Berg, "Wirtschaftsbau durch Gemeinschaftsarbeit," speech held on 19 September 1952 at the opening of the Deutsche Industrieausstellung in Berlin, *Vortragsreihe,* 22 September 1952.

72 See *Deutsche Industrieausstellung Berlin 1950: Veranstalter, Berliner Ausstellungen, Eigenbetrieb Gross-Berlin* (Berlin: Berliner Ausstellungen, 1950), in A1019, LAB.

73 Pressestelle der Deutschen Industrieausstellung, #13, 26 August 1950, A1019, LAB.

74 Ibid., #33, 17 October 1950.

75 Chancellor Adenauer was slated to visit the event but canceled at the last moment. His inability to attend was criticized by the SPD's Kurt Schumacher. See *Der Spiegel,* 11 October 1950, 31.

76 Labor and management, big business and small business, and governmental officials came together to organize the event. Ludwig Erhard, Fritz Berg, Hans Böckler, and West Berlin mayor Ernst Reuter sat on the honorary exhibition presidium. Also active in preparation for the events were DIHT president Alfred Peterson and Richard Uhlmeyer, the president of the Central Federation of German Handcrafts.

77 Pressestelle der Deutschen Industrieausstellung, #33, 17 October 1950, A1019, LAB.

78 Ludwig Erhard in Pressestelle der Deutschen Industrieausstellung, #18, 8 September 1950, A1019, LAB.

79 Wolfgang Homburg to Sohl, Linz, Schwede, and Seelig, 5 March 1951, VSt/3057, Thyssen.

80 Daub to Homburg, 26 October 1951, VSt/3057, Thyssen.

81 Ibid., 27 January 1951.

82 Erwin Daub to Hermann Wenzel, 5 October 1950, VSt/3057, Thyssen.

83 See, e.g., Muthesius, *Moral des Geldes, Geld und Geist,* and *Was wir der Marktwirtschaft verdanken.*

84 Erwin Daub to Hermann Wenzel, 5 October 1950, VSt/3057, Thyssen.

85 Hermann Wenzel to VSt Vorstand (confidential), 1 March 1951, VSt/3057, Thyssen. Muthesius, in the final text, does refer to Flick.

86 Wolfgang Linz to Schwede, Seelig, Sohl, 10 March 1951, VSt/3057, Thyssen.

87 Notiz from 18 March 1951, VS/3057, Thyssen.

88 See Volkmar Muthesius, "Schicksal eines Montan-Konzernes (Als Manuskript gedrückt für interne Zwecke anläßlich des 25 Jährige Jubiläums der VSAG)." Unpublished copy #41 in Thyssen.

89 Muthesius himself never received a copy of his own book until 1955, when the

press department of the BDI gave him one. See Muthesius to Homburg, 12 December 1955, VS/3057, Thyssen.

90 Dust jacket of Klass, *Albert Vögler*.

91 On Vögler's suicide, see Henke, *Amerikanische Besetzung*, 476-78; on Vögler in the 1920s, see Feldman, *Hugo Stinnes*, e.g., 586-693, and Henry A. Turner, *German Big Business*.

92 Minutes of the meeting of the Freundeskreis Albert Vögler in Gelsenberg/Essen, 11 November 1954, A/8943, Thyssen.

93 See list of contributions in A/8943, Thyssen.

94 Klass, *Die drei Ringe*.

95 On Flick's financial transactions and holdings in the early 1950s, see Pritzkoleit, *Wem gehört Deutschland?*, 317-23.

96 On Stinnes, see Feldman, *Hugo Stinnes*. On the Rheinelbe firm, see ibid., 816-17.

97 For a summary of the conversation with Flick, see Aktennotiz, 8 December 1955, betr. Biographie Albert Vögler. Besprechung mit Herrn Dr. Friedrich Flick am 7. December 1955 in Düsseldorf, A/8943, Thyssen.

98 Wilhelm Steinberg to Heinrich Dinkelbach, 4 March 1957, A/8943, Thyssen.

99 See Speer, *Inside the Third Reich*, 564-65. On Walter Rohland, see his self-exculpatory autobiography, *Bewegte Zeiten*.

100 Rohland to Dr. Jur. W. Huber, 25 February 1957, A/8943, Thyssen.

101 Dinkelbach to Klass, 27 March 1957, A/8943, Thyssen.

102 Steinberg to Dinkelbach, 25 March 1957, A/8943, Thyssen. On the speech, see Henry A. Turner, "Fritz Thyssen und 'I Paid Hitler.'"

103 Klass to Ludwig Holle, 22 March 1957, A/8943, Thyssen.

104 Political theorist Karl W. Deutsch's term referring to the 1930s. Quoted from Feldman, "Politische Kultur und Wirtschaft," 1.

105 Klass, *Albert Vögler*, 14.

106 Jahresbericht des DI, 1951/52, NL Vogel, box 204, Augsburg.

CHAPTER FIVE

1 In this chapter I use the term "culture" loosely, mostly as a reflection of industrialists' own broad and imprecise understanding of the concept. "Culture" will appear as an umbrella term for "high culture," "art," "spirit," and intellectual activity more generally. On culture in West Germany, see Glaser, *Rubble Years;* Pommerin, *Culture in the Federal Republic;* and Doering-Manteuffel, "Kultur der 50er Jahre."

2 See Wilhelm Salewski, "Eisenindustrielle als Förderer der Kunst," in catalog for the exhibition *Eisen und Stahl* (Düsseldorf, 1952), and Gustav Stein, *Unternehmer als Förderer der Kunst*.

3 *Carl Duisberg, ein Mäzen des Deutschen Museums: zum 25. Todestag am 19. März 1960* (Munich: Vorstand des Deutschen Museums, 1960). See also Herzog, *Paul Reusch und das Deutsche Museum*, and *Deutsches Museum: Abhandlung und Berichte* (1967): 5-14.

4 See Anlage zur Niederschrift über die 1. Ausschuss-Sitzung der Ernst Poensgen Stiftung, 2 February 1942, NL Hermann Reusch, 400101460/1, RWWA.

5 See Winfried Schulze, *Der Stifterverband,* 153–58.

6 On the history of the Werkbund, see Campbell, *German Werkbund.* On German industry and the Werkbund, see Jefferies, *Politics and Culture in Wilhelmine Germany,* chaps. 3–4.

7 For a general study on the relationship between art and industry, see Eells, *Corporation and the Arts.*

8 On product design in the 1950s, see Gerd Selle, "Produktdesign der 50er Jahre."

9 See Mitchell, "Materialism and Secularism."

10 Articles from the 1950s about the relationship between art and industry are too numerous to cite. As an example, see "Die Kunst—Partner des Unternehmers," in *Unternehmerbrief des DI* 4, no. 20 (20 May 1954): 1–2, and Werner Berndt, "Umsturz im Weltbild der Industrie," unpublished manuscript in NL Hermann Reusch, 40010146/612, RWWA.

11 The term *Menschenbildung* made a regular appearance in the speeches of the Kulturkreis. See, e.g., Hermann Reusch "Die Formung des Menschenbildes in der Kultur der Gegenwart," NL Hermann Reusch, 40010146/612, RWWA.

12 Gustav Stein, "Kultur-Fundament der Wirtschaft."

13 Sperr to Reusch, 4 November 1951, NL Hermann Reusch, 40010146/608, RWWA.

14 Ibid.

15 Ibid.

16 Gustav Stein, "Kultur-Fundament der Wirtschaft."

17 See Fehrenbach, *Cinema in Democratizing Germany,* 151–67.

18 In English: The Rhenish Society for the Preservation of Monuments and the Protection of Homeland. See Gustav Stein to Hermann Reusch, 9 February 1954, NL Hermann Reusch, 40010146/520, RWWA. On the history of architectural preservation in Germany and the involvement of social elites in the construction of monuments, see Koshar, *Germany's Transient Pasts.*

19 On the transfer of U.S. democratic ideals to West Germany, see Merritt, *Democracy Imposed.* On German and U.S. views of democracy in the immediate postwar years, see Boehling, *Question of Priorities.*

20 Stein and Gross, *Unternehmer in der Politik,* 165.

21 On conservative critiques of democracy before Nazism, see, e.g., Struve, *Elites against Democracy,* pt. 3.

22 On one thinker's, namely Oswald Spengler's, views of the masses, see ibid., 252–69.

23 On cultural pessimism and the ambivalence toward democracy after 1945, see Hermand, *Kultur im Wiederaufbau,* 221–62; Schildt, *Moderne Zeiten,* 303–50, and "Ende der Ideologien?"; and Lenk, "Zum westdeutschen Konservatismus."

24 Ritter, *Corrupting Influence of Power;* Meinecke, *German Catastrophe;* Rothfels, *German Opposition to Hitler.*

25 "Undemokratische Individualismus," *Unternehmerbrief,* 6 May 1954.

26 Wilhelm Salewski, "Eisenindustrielle als Förderer der Kunst," in catalog for the exhibition *Eisen und Stahl* (Düsseldorf, 1952).

27 See "Die Jury stellt aus" and other documents relating to the exhibition, in Treuhand papers, B109/1373, BAK.

28 For other attempts to promote the Ruhr at home and abroad through art, see NL Hermann Reusch, 40010146/618, RWWA. In one project, eighty sketches of Ruhr factory life by painter Richard Gessner were gathered in a publication titled *Das malerische Ruhrrevier*. The BDI's cultural circle (see below) also considered the promotion of books on the history of mining and heavy industry.

29 See NL Vogel, box 177, Augsburg.

30 From the *Satzung des Kulturkreises im Bundesverband der deutschen Industrie, e.V.* (1951), NL Hermann Reusch, 40010146/616, RWWA. Hermann Reusch elaborated on these sentiments when he paid homage to the icons of German culture who had brought inner peace to the Germans during their time of need. It gave Reusch a supreme feeling of "inner security during the hours of catastrophe during the last war to gaze upon a painting of Dürer, Grünewald, Philipp Otto Runge or Caspar David Friedrich" or to listen to "a symphony of Beethoven, Schubert, or Richard Strauss" (from undated *Frankfurter Allgemeine Zeitung* article, in NL Hermann Reusch, 40010146/609, RWWA).

31 One of the few scholarly studies of the Kulturkreis is Bührer, "Der Kulturkreis im Bundesverband der deutschen Industrie." See also the BDI publication *Dokumentation über die zehnjährige Tätigkeit des Kulturkreises im Bundesverband der Deutschen Industrie* (BDI, 1961), in IW. For a list of the Kulturkreis's original members, see "Mitglieder des Kulturkreises . . . ," NL Hermann Reusch, 40010146/608, RWWA. The group included the familiar heavy industry names of Theo Goldschmidt, Otto Wolff von Amerongen, Hans Günther Sohl, and Jost Henkel and a number of other textile and chemical industrialists, like Erich Konrad from Bayer AG.

32 Prof. Dr. G. A. Rein of the Ranke Gesellschaft to August Heinrichsbauer, 19 October 1951, NL Hermann Reusch, 40010146/609, RWWA. Note the reappearance of August Heinrichsbauer, German industry's grand apologist, as a behind-the-scenes Kulturkreis administrator.

33 Prof. Dr. Hans-Joachim Schoeps to Reusch, 25 October 1951, NL Hermann Reusch, 40010146/608, RWWA.

34 For Hermann Reusch's numerous speeches about industry, art, and culture, see the many Kulturkreis files in NL Hermann Reusch, files 40010146/608–40010146/619, RWWA.

35 *Mitteilungen des BDI*, 10 November 1954, 15. This series can be found in the IW library.

36 For a clear statement of these divisions and their cultural implications, see the Bund für freie und angewandte Kunst's appeal, "An die Freunde und Gegner der gegenständlichen Kunst," NL Hermann Reusch, 40010146/616, RWWA.

37 See "Opponierende Mäzene," *Das Feuilleton*, 30 November 1953. See industrialists' response to this criticism, e.g., Bernhard Sprengel to Reusch, NL Hermann Reusch, 26 January 1954, 40010146/620, RWWA. For other criticism, see "Industrie als Mäzen," *Die Kunst*, January 1954, in same file.

38 On the Kulturkreis's views on representational and nonrepresentational art, see Reusch to Richard Freudenberg, 26 January 1954, NL Hermann Reusch, 40010146/620, RWWA.

39 Heinrich Gattineau to Hermann Reusch, 28 September 1953, NL Hermann Reusch, 40010146/618, RWWA.

40 Some industrialists had already defied the Nazi aesthetic during the Third Reich. Bahlsen, the Hanoverian cookie manufacturing family, secretly built up its own "degenerate art" collection and donated it to the Hanover Museum of Art after the war.

41 Hermann Reusch's introductory speech at the Kulturkreis's founding meeting, "Warum Kulturkreis im Bundesverband der deutschen Industrie?" See also "Bericht über die konstituierende Sitzung des Kulturkreises des Bundesverbandes der Deutschen Industrie," both in NL Hermann Reusch, 40010146/608, RWWA.

42 See Berghahn, *Unternehmer und Politik*, 236. See, e.g., Otto Friedrich, "Der Freiheitsbegriff in der europäischen Wirtschaft und Kultur," summarized in *Mitteilungen des BDI*, 10 September 1955, 23.

43 Ortega y Gasset, *Revolt of the Masses*. On Germans' reception of Ortega in the 1950s, see Schildt, *Zwischen Abendland und Amerika*, 90–100.

44 See Saint-Simon, "Letter to the Industrialists."

45 Ortega y Gasset, "Gibt es ein Europäisches Kulturbewußtsein?," *Kulturkreis im BDI, Jahrestagung, München 28.–30. September 1953*, in IW.

46 See Schlabrendorff, *Eugen Gerstenmaier im Dritten Reich*, 30–43.

47 Eugen Gerstenmaier, "Vom Sinn und Schicksal der Elite in der Demokratie," delivered on 9 September 1958 to the annual Kulturkreis Mitgliederversammlung. Copy in I-288/006/6, ACDP.

48 Dr. Uebe to Reusch, 3 September 1951, NL Hermann Reusch, 40010146/608, RWWA.

49 See Schildt, *Konservatismus in Deutschland*, 211–52.

50 From Otto Vogel, introduction to pamphlet accompanying the *Fugger und Welser* exhibit, Augsburg, 1950, in NL Vogel, box 12, Augsburg. Also reprinted in Bührer, *Die Adenauer-Ära*, 115–16.

51 Forberg to Reusch, 21 August 1951, NL Hermann Reusch, 40010146/608, RWWA.

52 See, e.g., Hermann Reusch's speech "Kulturverlust heißt Untergang," NL Hermann Reusch, 40010146/616, RWWA.

53 See Herman, *Idea of Decline*.

54 Stern, *Politics of Cultural Despair*.

55 On postwar cultural pessimism and technology, see Herf, "Belated Pessimism."

56 See Horkheimer and Adorno, *Dialectic of Enlightenment*, 120–67.

57 Gustav Stein, "Unternehmer nach 1945."

58 On the economy, consumption, and citizenship (particularly female citizenship), see Carter, *How German Is She?*, 79–82.

59 Gustav Stein, "Kultur-Fundament der Wirtschaft."

60 Ibid.

61 Otto Vogel, introduction to pamphlet accompanying the *Fugger und Welser* exhibit, Augsburg, 1950, in NL Vogel, box 12, Augsburg.

62 "Industry As a Patron of Art: The 'Kulturkreis' Paves the Way for Artists," *Deutsche Korrespondenz*, 19 March 1955.

63 Fritz Hellwig to DI Kuratorium, 8 October 1951, NL Hermann Reusch, 40010146/309, RWWA.

64 List of DI Beirat members, NL Hermann Reusch, 40010146/309, RWWA.

CHAPTER SIX

1 On the postwar relationship between West German industrialists and workers, and the influence of the United States in particular, see Wiesen, "Coming to Terms."

2 Berghahn, *Americanisation*, 188–89.

3 For an introduction to the theme of codetermination and economic democracy in Weimar and West Germany, see ibid., 203–30; Berghahn and Karsten, *Industrial Relations*, 148–91; Thum, *Wirtschaftsdemokratie und Mitbestimmung*; and Markovits, *Politics of the West German Trade Unions*.

4 See, for example, the 1951 speech delivered by DGB chief Christian Fette in San Francisco, NL Hermann Reusch, 40010146/143, RWWA.

5 Berghahn, *Americanisation*, 223.

6 "Tag des Unternehmers," Rundschreiben of the VDMA, Landesgruppe Nord, 21 October 1950, VDMA (VI-003), file -077/6, ACDP.

7 See Berghahn, *Americanisation*, 226–27.

8 "Ansprache von Herrn Vizepräsident Otto A. H. Vogel auf der Kungebung des Bundesverbandes der Deutschen Industrie am 8. November 1950 in der Messehalle zu Köln," NL Vogel, box 251, Augsburg.

9 Ibid. Vogel was likely inspired by Friedrich Hayek, whose *Road to Serfdom* was the quintessential statement on totalitarianism and command economics. See Gleason, *Totalitarianism*, 64–67.

10 As a Bavarian Catholic, Otto Vogel was well aware of the persistent power of the term *Kulturkampf* (referring to Bismarck's campaign against Germany's Catholics in the 1870s).

11 "Ansprache von Herrn Vizepräsident Otto A. H. Vogel auf der Kungebung des Bundesverbandes der Deutschen Industrie am 8. November 1950 in der Messehalle zu Köln," NL Vogel, box 251, Augsburg.

12 "Demokratie in Gefahr," NL Vogel, box 251, Augsburg.

13 Ibid.

14 V. Leder to Vogel, 21 January 1950, NL Vogel, box 252, Augsburg.

15 Albert Gayler to Vogel, 4 January 1951, NL Vogel, box 252, Augsburg.

16 Dipl-Ing. H. C. Bremer to Vogel, 10 November 1950, NL Vogel, box 252, Augsburg.

17 See Hans Polzer, "Projekt F" (proposal for the magazine *Das Volk*), and Polzer to Vogel, 10 November 1950, NL Vogel, box 252, Augsburg.

18 Karl Grzmehle, of the DGB, Bremerhaven and Wesermarsch branch, to Vogel, undated open letter, NL Vogel, box 252, Augsburg.

19 Quote from "Von Vogel bis Ehrich-Die Reaktion in Bewegung," *Welt der Arbeit*, 1 December 1950. This and the following articles relating to Vogel's statements can be found in NL Vogel, box 252, Augsburg.

20 Gert Spindler, "Elefanten im Sozialporzellanladen," *Der Fortschritt*, 23 November 1950.

21 See "Rückfall in die Unkultur," *Welt der Arbeit*, 17 November 1950, which referred to the BDI meeting as a "Kungebung der Kulturlosigkeit." Vogel wrote a response to the unions; see "Für und Wider eine 'Kungebung der Kulturlosigkeit,' " *Handels-, Wirtschaft-, und Börsenblatt*, 20 November 1950.

22 "Arbeitnehmner, wehrt Euch gegen den Raub-Vogel!," NL Vogel, box 252, Augsburg.

23 Reusch to Vogel, 11 November 1950, NL Vogel, box 252, Augsburg.

24 Friedrich to Vogel, 17 November 1950, NL Vogel, box 252, Augsburg.

25 The free-spoken Vogel survived the controversy with little effect on his career and reputation. Vogel remained a hard-liner, especially in labor matters, for the rest of his career. In 1958, when Vogel retired from the presidency of the Augsburg IHK, West Germany bestowed on him its highest honor: the Großes Verdienstkreuz, or the Order of the Federal Republic of Germany. Vogel was honored for his service to the economy and to the culture of the Federal Republic. He represented "a synthesis between the kingly *Kaufmann* and the intellectually universal *Kulturmensch.*" Quote excerpted from the *Textil Zeitung*, 20 March 1954, in NL Vogel, box 9, Augsburg.

26 See, e.g., Herr von Bülow of AG der Gerresheimer-Glashüttenwerke to Hermann Reusch, 11 September 1951, NL Hermann Reusch, 40010146/609, RWWA.

27 Wolfgang Dummer to Herrn Froehling of Gesamttextil in Frankfurt, 18 September 1953, NL Vogel, box 204, Augsburg.

28 Ibid. Dummer details a meeting he had with industrialists during a visit to the United States in which they discussed the differences between U.S. and German public relations methods.

29 Nolan, *Visions of Modernity*, 191.

30 Ibid., 192–96.

31 On National Socialism, joyful work, and the "beauty of labor," see Rabinbach, *Human Motor*, 284–88; also Campbell, *Joy in Work*, 312–75.

32 Franz Greiß, "Die Werkszeitung: Was, Wie, Wer, Wem," speech delivered 4 February 1955, B156/170, BAK. See also in file 169, no author, "Gedanken zur Werkszeitung."

33 For a brief introduction, see Berghahn, *Americanisation*, 251.

34 See Maier, "Between Taylor and Technocracy."

35 See, e.g., DIHT Rundschreiben betr. Public and Human Relations, Nr. 22/51, 23 April 1952, NL Vogel, box 146, Augsburg; also Hajek, *Management und Human Relations*, and Diedrich, *"Human relations."*

36 After its mastery by Goebbels and Stalin, the term "propaganda" gradually fell out of use by Germans, who recognized its totalitarian connotations. But in the early 1950s, industrialists were still referring to public relations and publicity unabashedly as "propaganda."

37 For the complete twenty-six-page list of workers' magazines published in 1953, see DIHT Rundschreiben #15, 7 October 1953, B156/169, BAK.

38 DIHT Rundschreiben #4, 7 February 1955, B156/169, BAK.

39 Most prominently, the DGB's *Welt der Arbeit.*

40 Franz Greiß, "Die Werkszeitung: Was, Wie, Wer, Wem," speech delivered 4 February 1955, B156/170, BAK.

41 "Zum Geleit," *Heim und Werk,* 1 September 1950.

42 On the start-up of the *Mitarbeiterbrief des Deutschen Industrieinstituts,* see NL Hermann Reusch, 400101456/310, RWWA. Many industrialists feared that they were spreading themselves too thinly and undermining their own cause with so many competing magazines. The publisher of *Heim und Werk* threatened to stage a boycott of the *Mitarbeiterbrief.*

43 This claim is not born out by the facts. At a DI meeting in 1951, codirector Otto Mejer discussed plans for the launching of *Das Fenster.* See Niederschrift from the DI board meeting, 19 September 1951, NL Hermann Reusch, 40010146/309, RWWA.

44 Promotional letter from Graf Bothmer, publisher of *Das Fenster,* 23 November 1952. Loose copy in *Das Fenster,* November 1952, BfP.

45 On Diesel, see "Erfolgreichen auf der Spur," *Das Fenster,* July 1952; for Friedrich's article, see *Das Fenster,* May 1952, 7, 28.

46 Volkmar Muthesius, "Wir brauchen mehr Millionäre," *Das Fenster,* December 1953/January 1954.

47 *Das Deutsche Wunder* (Munich: Co-Presse Europäische Hefte, 1953). Another book glorifying Germany's industrial history was Krosigk, *Große Zeit des Feuers. Die Waage* also put out an advertisement in 1952 with the motto *Das Deutsche Wunder.* See Greiß, "Erhards soziale Marktwirtschaft," 100.

48 On Hauser, see Regnery, *Memoirs,* 39, and Hauser's autobiography, *Time Was.*

49 The book had the working title "Das Buch der Deutschen Industrie." For industrialists' extensive input into the Hauser project, see IHK Essen Papers, #28-15-7, RWWA. Also, NL Hermann Reusch, 40010145/152, RWWA.

50 "Für die Freie Wirtschaft!" (a one-page appeal from Hauser and his publisher to the attention of all industrialists), NL Hermann Reusch, 40010145/152, RWWA.

51 Ibid.

52 Hauser, *Unser Schicksal.*

53 Schulz, *Das goldene Dach.*

54 Ibid., 63.

55 Ibid., 73.

56 On gender roles, family, and anticommunism in the Adenauer era, see Moeller, *Protecting Motherhood,* 104–5; on households, women, and the division of labor, see Heineman, *What Difference Does a Husband Make?,* 216–17.

57 See NL Hermann Reusch, Kulturkreis files, 40010146/612, RWWA.

58 Reusch to Stein, 28 August 1952, NL Hermann Reusch, 40010146/612, RWWA.

59 See Kuester to Klass, 2 April 1953, NL Wilmowsky, FAH 5 W 37c, KA.

60 On the fear of the deproletarianization of the worker in West Germany, see Mooser, *Arbeiterleben,* 224–36, and Carter, *How German Is She?,* 29–30.

61 Gustav Stein, "Kultur-Fundament der Wirtschaft."

62 Gustav Stein, *Unternehmer als Förderer der Kunst.*

63 Brochure for *Das goldene Dach,* NL Hermann Reusch, 40010146/610, RWWA.

64 On conservatism and family policy in West Germany, see Moeller, *Protecting Motherhood*, esp. chap. 4.

65 Berghahn, "United States and the Shaping of West Germany's Social Compact."

66 An indication of the change in worker and union tactics and culture is the number of strikes and lockouts in the 1950s, which went from 2,529 in 1952, to 1,395 in 1953, to 538 in 1954, to 28 in 1960. From Berghahn, *Modern Germany*, 305.

CHAPTER SEVEN

1 This comment came from IG Farben founder Carl Duisberg's son, who had been a loyal Nazi. See Duisberg, *Nur ein Sohn*, 182.

2 On the high commissioner's release of industrialists and other prisoners, see Buscher, *U.S. War Crimes Trial Program;* 49–64; Bird, *Chairman*, 332–36; and Schwartz, *America's Germany*, 156–84. On the role of the Catholic Church in the release of Alfried Krupp, see Klee, *Persilscheine und Falsche Pässe*, 61–82.

3 In 1950 Günter Henle, Mannesmann director and CDU politician, had prematurely assured his fellow delegates in the Bundestag that "whoever might have been prosecuted as war criminals certainly no longer occupies a leading position in German industry." See the manuscript titled "Schwerindustrie," 10 August 1949, NL Henle 1384/483, BAK.

4 For a scholarly study, see Jörg Friedrich, *Kalte Amnestie*, 266–76. For a more journalistic account, typical of the 1950s and 1960s, see Tetens, *New Germany and the Old Nazis*, 220. For its part, East Germany published a list of Nazis active in West Germany in Nationale Front des Demokratischen Deutschlands, *Brown Book*.

5 See Schwartz, "John J. McCloy and the Landsberg Cases."

6 On the public's view of the clemency decisions, see Merritt, *Democracy Imposed*, 150–78.

7 On the public pressure on McCloy and a good introduction to the amnesty question, see Brochhagen, *Nach Nürnberg*, chap. 2.

8 On the Heidelberger Juristenkreis, see Buscher, *U.S. War Crimes Trial Program*, 91–113, and Frei, *Vergangenheitspolitik*, 163–95. Also active from industry circles was Rudolf Müller, attorney for IG Farben, and Otto Kranzbühler, defender of Krupp, Flick, and Röchling and future legal counsel for the Krupp firm.

9 "Denkschrift über die Notwendigkeit einer Generalamnestie," in Frei, *Vergangenheitspolitik*, 165.

10 See Alfried Krupp to Clay, 21 August 1948, HM 37 (Muench Collection), box 132, folder 2, NARA. Many thanks to Suzanne Brown-Fleming for this and other documents relating to the appeals.

11 On the distribution of care packages to the prisoners, see the files "IG Prozess Pressemeldungen" and "Sonstiges aus Nürnberger Prozess-Curiosa," BAL.

12 Gert Whitman to Henle, 26 February 1951, NL Henle 1384/3, BAK. See the original edition: Houdremont, *Handbuch der Sonderstahlkunde*.

13 Fritz von Bülow to Louis Lochner, 24 November 1954, NL Wilmowsky, FAH 5 37c, KA.

14 HICOG, Frankfurt 251 to State Department re. Board Meeting of Ruhr Steel Industry Leaders, 26 July 1950, RG 59, 862A.33/7-2650, box 5238, NARA. See also Bührer, "Return to Normality."

15 HICOG, Frankfurt 251 to State Department re. Board Meeting of Ruhr Steel Industry Leaders, 26 July 1950, RG 59, 862A.33/7-2650, box 5238, NARA.

16 Reusch's memo was also leaked to the press. On 10 July 1950 the *Rhein Echo* criticized the proposal. See NL Hermann Reusch, 40010148/5, RWWA.

17 Bührer, "Return to Normality."

18 AMCONGEN Düsseldorf to State Department, 18 September 1951, RG 59, 682A.33/9-1851, NARA.

19 See Dr. Klaus Hennig, "Nürnberger Betrachtungen," speech delivered in front of Essen's judges on 24 September 1948, D 6641, IWW; Kranzbühler, *Rückblick auf Nürnberg* (September 1949 speech at the University at Göttingen); and Kranzbühler, "Nürnberg als Rechtsproblem," April 1950 lecture at the Tagung der Deutschen Gesellschaft für Völkerrecht (in author's possession).

20 Friedrich Vorwerk of the Evangelisches Verlagswerk to Dr. Eugen Mündler of Essen, 10 October 1949, NL Wilmowsky, FAH 5 W 41, KA. Note the double meaning of *richten*—to pass judgment upon, or to hang/execute. On Kranzbühler, see Wolmar, *Als Verteidiger in Nürnberg*.

21 See undated, handwritten letter from Wilmowsky to Kranzbühler, ca. fall 1949, in NL Wilmowsky, FAH 5 W 41, KA. Also, Kranzbühler to S. Jonathan Wiesen, 14 September 1995.

22 For more on Wilmowsky, see his autobiography, *Rückblickend möchte ich sagen*, and Manchester, *Arms of Krupp*, 237–50. See also correspondences between Paul Reusch and Wilmowsky in NL Paul Reusch, 40010124/18, RWWA.

23 Wilmowsky to Berthold von Bohlen, 20 November 1949, NL Wilmowsky, FAH 5 W 41, KA.

24 Huber, *Verfassungsrecht des Grossdeutschen Reiches*. On Huber, see Müller, *Hitler's Justice*, 42, 69. The most prominent case of a Nazi whose career was reactivated in the 1950s was Hans Globke, the author of the official legal commentary on the Nuremberg Race Laws of 1935 and later Adenauer's chief aide in the Chancellery. See Brochhagen, *Nach Nürnberg*, 301–4.

25 On Heinrichsbauer's participation, see, e.g., Wilmowsky to Berthold von Bohlen, 15 December 1949; Heinrichsbauer to Wilmowsky, 23 May 1950; and Wilmowsky to Huber, 7 May 1950, all in NL Wilmowsky, FAH 5 W 41, KA.

26 See Wilmowsky, *Warum wurde Krupp verurteilt?*, 217.

27 Ibid., 8, 100.

28 Alfred W. Kames to Wilmowsky, 2 November 1950, NL Wilmowsky, FAH 5 W 37a, KA.

29 Max Ilgner to Wilmowsky, 26 May 1950, NL Wilmowsky, FAH 5 W 41, KA.

30 Wollstädter of Krupp Verbindungsstelle in Bonn to Wilmowsky, 7 December 1951, NL Wilmowsky, FAH 5 W 42, KA.

31 See Vorwerk to Wilmowsky, 27 September 1951, and the succeeding correspondences in NL Wilmowsky, FAH 5 W 42, KA. See NL Wilmowsky, FAH 5 W 37a,

KA, for copies of the form letter that was sent with the book to influential Americans, including the CEO of Sears Roebuck, Robert E. Wood, and Senator James Eastland.

32 See review in the organization's publication *Voice of the Federation,* 16 April 1951.

33 Wilmowsky to the editors of *New Statesmen and Nation,* 16 March 1951, NL Wilmowsky, FAH 5 W 41, KA.

34 Wilmowsky to Vorwerk, 29 November 1949, NL Wilmowsky, FAH 5 W 41, KA.

35 Bird, *Chairman,* 335.

36 On the members of the Peck Panel, see ibid.

37 Wilmowsky to Huber, 5 April 1950, and to Vorwerk, 25 April 1950, NL Wilmowsky, FAH 5 W 41, KA.

38 Huber to Wilmowsky, 7 May 1950, NL Wilmowsky, FAH 5 W 41, KA.

39 In May 1950 Krupp offered the book to West German firms at a special price. It also sent a copy to each of the eleven industrialists in Landsberg, as well as the defense lawyers. Kranzbühler, however, warned Wilmowsky not to thank the attorneys for their input on the original manuscript. "One never knows in whose hands such a letter could end up or in what manner it could be used" (Kranzbühler to Wilmowsky, 2 June 1950, NL Wilmowsky, FAH 5 W 41, KA).

40 On the Schuman Plan, see Gillingham, *Coal, Steel, and the Rebirth of Europe,* 97–177; Berghahn, *Americanisation,* 111–54; and Schwartz, *America's Germany,* chap. 4.

41 On Law No. 27, see Warner, *Steel and Sovereignty,* 11–93.

42 On industrial output during this period, see Kramer, *West German Economy,* 197–200.

43 Text of McCloy's address, delivered 16 June 1950, RG 59, 762A.00/6-1650, box 3845, NARA.

44 See Bird, *Chairman,* 338, and "McCloy Lashes Out at German Critics of Western Policy," *New York Times,* 17 June 1950.

45 See HICOG Reactions Analysis Staff/Office of Public Affairs, "Further Study of Post-Korean Rumors in Germany," RG 59, 762A.00/8-2950, box 3846, NARA.

46 On rearmament in West Germany, see Large, *Germans to the Front,* and Geyer, *Deutsche Rüstungspolitik,* 176–204.

47 On industry and the Korean War, see Berghahn and Friedrich, *Otto A. Friedrich,* chap. 6.

48 On industry's hesitations about rearmament, see Hallgarten and Radkau, *Deutsche Industrie und Politik,* 483–84; speeches in NL Carl Becker, ACDP; scattered reports in *Mitteilungen des BDI,* esp. throughout 1954; and Berghahn, *Americanisation,* 260–82.

49 Kranzbühler to Wilmowsky, 30 June 1950, NL Wilmowsky, FAH 5 W 41, KA.

50 See undated memo on the *Kirchentag,* in NL Wilmowsky, FAH 5 W 41, KA.

51 Schwartz, *America's Germany,* 163.

52 Some war criminals' death sentences were commuted; others were carried out.

53 Quoted from Horne, *Return to Power,* 102.

54 Bird, *Chairman,* 368.

55 Ibid., 369.

56 Gert Whitman to Henle, 26 February 1951, NL Henle 1384/3, BAK. On Krupp's re-

lease and his public relations blunder, see Bird, *Chairman*, 368; Manchester, *Arms of Krupp*, 661; and Friz, *Die Stahlgiganten*, 46.

57 The British government and public also maintained a suspicion of West Germany's industrial elites. See *Who Controls West German Industry? How the Ruhr Magnates Have Made a Come-Back* (London: L.R.D. Publications Ltd., 1954).

58 Daub to Linz, 27 January 1951, VSt/3057, Thyssen.

59 See uncredited notes and cover sheet accompanying a manuscript copy of Martin's book, NL Henle, 1384/190, BAK.

60 Ibid.

61 See Horne, *Return to Power*. Other books included Wheeler-Bennett, *Nemesis of Power*, and Taylor, *Nuremberg Trials* and *Sword and Swastika*.

62 Pounds, *The Ruhr*. On Pounds, see Wilmowsky to Lochner, 7 January 1953, NL Wilmowsky, FAH 5 W 37c, KA. See also Lochner, *Tycoons and Tyrant*, 20.

63 Gollancz, *In Darkest Germany*.

64 Utley, *High Cost of Vengeance*; Belgion, *Victors' Justice*; Hankey, *Politics, Trials, and Errors*. Freda Utley was in regular contact with some of Germany's industrialists, such as Hermann Reusch, who had tremendous words of praise for a writer whom he saw as a savior of Germany. See Reusch to Gustav Stein, 21 November 1952, NL Hermann Reusch, 40010146/614, RWWA.

65 Rothfels, *German Opposition to Hitler*; Ernst Jünger, *The Peace*; Friedrich Georg Jünger, *Failure of Technology*; Röpke, *Economics of the Free Society* and *Humane Economy*.

66 See Buckley, *God and Man at Yale*, and Kirk, *Conservative Mind*.

67 Kranzbühler to Wilmowsky, 2 June 1950, NL Wilmowsky, FAH 5 W 41, KA.

68 Ibid., 25 May 1950.

69 Wilmowsky to Vorwerk, 26 June 1950, NL Wilmowsky, FAH 5 W 41, KA.

70 Kranzbühler to Wilmowsky, 30 June 1950, NL Wilmowsky, FAH 5 W 41, KA; Wilmowsky to Brüning, 4 September 1950, NL Wilmowsky, FAH 5 W 37a, KA. On Brüning's postwar views on the innocence of German industry, see Schuker, "Ambivalent Exile."

71 See Pohle to Wilmowsky, 23 October 1950, NL Wilmowsky, FAH 5 W 37a, KA. See also Franz von Papen, *Memoirs* (London: A. Deutsch, 1952).

72 Wilmowsky to Scheffer, 26 October 1951, NL Wilmowsky, FAH 5 W 37a, KA. On Dirksen's career, see Dirksen, *Moscow, Tokyo, London*.

73 Dirksen to Wilmowsky, 21 July 1950, NL Wilmowsky, FAH 5 W 37a, KA.

74 K. Busse of the Siemens company library to Vorwerk, 7 June 1950, NL Wilmowsky, FAH 5 W 41, KA. Busse continued: "It seems that everywhere people have overestimated the powers of industry.... The idea popular in the 1920s that industry can and should be entrusted with political decisions was a disastrous mistake, both on a historical-political level and on a practical policy level."

75 Dirksen to Belgion, 7 September 1950, NL Wilmowsky, FAH 5 W 37a, KA.

76 Dirksen to Wilmowsky, 21 July 1950, NL Wilmowsky, FAH 5 W 37a, KA.

77 Belgion to Dirksen, 15 September 1950, NL Wilmowsky, FAH 5 W 37a, KA.

78 Wilmowsky to Kuhnke, 8 July 1952, NL Wilmowsky, FAH 5 W 37b, KA.

79 During the war Hesse had served as a propagandist for the Wehrmacht.

80 I have been unable to locate this unpublished document, titled "Die politischen Anklagen gegen die deutschen Industrieführer." However, Louis Lochner cites a copy that Hesse gave to him during an interview. See Lochner, *Tycoons and Tyrant*, 118.

81 Pohle to Wilmowsky, 23 October 1950, NL Wilmowsky, FAH 5 W 37a, KA.

82 Wilmowsky to Pohle, 5 January 1951, NL Wilmowsky, FAH 5 W 37a, KA.

83 On the interesting career of Paul Scheffer and his input in, among others, the Rothfels and Utley books, see Regnery, *Memoirs*, 59–63.

84 Wilmowsky to Dirksen, 21 February 1951, NL Wilmowsky, FAH 5 W 37a, KA.

85 See, e.g., Davidson, *Death and Life of Germany*.

86 Scheffer to Wilmowsky, 20 September 1951, NL Wilmowsky, FAH 5 W 37a, KA.

87 Wilmowsky to Müller, 13 November 1950, NL Wilmowsky, FAH 5 W 37a, KA.

88 Belgion to Dirksen, 4 November 1950, NL Wilmowsky, FAH 5 W 37a, KA.

89 Dulles, *Germany's Underground*.

90 Vorwerk was a Protestant activist whose declared goal was to publish books with a humanitarian purpose. During the 1950s his press published works on the Prussian nobility and royal family, Christian theology, military honor, and hunting.

91 For all these suggestions, see Scheffer to Wilmowsky, 8 September 1951, NL Wilmowsky, FAH 5 W 37a, KA.

92 Chamberlin, *America's Second Crusade*. On the book's origins, see Regnery, *Memoirs*, 84–87.

93 Prince Louis Ferdinand, *Rebel Prince*.

94 Goebbels, *Goebbels Diaries;* Lochner, *Henry Ford* and *Herbert Hoover and Germany.*

95 See Peter Hoffmann, *History of the German Resistance*, 214–15.

96 On Lochner's life and career, see Lochner, *Always the Unexpected.*

97 Lochner to Wilmowsky, 7 November 1951, NL Wilmowsky, FAH 5 W 37a, KA.

98 Belgion to Dirksen, 12 December 1950, NL Wilmowsky, FAH 5 W 37a, KA.

99 Regnery's very first publication was a pamphlet consisting of two speeches by Hutchins. Since 1945 Hutchins had been calling for a sympathetic treatment of occupied Germany. Hutchins wrote the introduction to Victor Gollancz's *In Darkest Germany*. On the relationship between Hutchins and Regnery, see Regnery, *Memoirs*, 31.

100 Kranzbühler to Wilmowsky, 12 October 1951, and Regnery to Wilmowsky, 20 December 1951, NL Wilmowsky, FAH 5 W 37a, KA. For the final contract and more precise financial details, see Regnery to Wilmowsky, 22 January 1951, NL Wilmowsky, FAH 5 W 37a, KA. For a list of the various companies and their contributions, see Kuester (of IHK Essen) to Kranzbühler, 15 December 1952, NL Wilmowsky, FAH 5 W 37b, KA.

101 Kranzbühler to Goldschmidt, 18 March 1952, NL Wilmowsky, FAH 5 W 37b, KA.

102 Wilmowsky to Scheffer, 3 November 1951, NL Wilmowsky, FAH 5 W 37a, KA.

103 Scheffer to Wilmowsky, 15 November 1951, NL Wilmowsky, FAH 5 W 37a, KA.

104 Scheffer to Wilmowsky, 16 February 1952, NL Wilmowsky, FAH 5 W 37b, KA.

105 Scheffer to Wilmowsky, 20 December 1951, NL Wilmowsky, FAH 5 W 37a, KA.

106 Wilmowsky to Fritz Berg, 28 February 1952, NL Wilmowsky, FAH 5 W 37b, KA.

107 Walter Gong to Wilmowsky, 8 May 1952, NL Wilmowsky, FAH 5 W 37b, KA.

108 Scheffer to Wilmowsky, 19 March 1952, NL Wilmowsky, FAH 5 W 37b, KA.

109 After the trials were over, Nagel moved the archive, under Theo Goldschmidt's tutelage, to an office in the IHK Essen. On the fate of the Industry Office after Nuremberg, see IHK Essen, "Nagel Informationdienst," 28-117-3, and NL Hermann Reusch, 40010145/173, RWWA. See also "Aufzeichnung über das Büro Dr. Nagel: Stand, August 1951," NL Wilmowsky, FAH 5 W37b, KA, and file VSt/1422, Thyssen.

110 Pohle to Wilmowsky, 7 February 1952, NL Wilmowsky, FAH 5 W 37b, KA. For a list of the attendees, see Pohle to Wilmowsky, 23 February 1952, in same file.

111 Wilmowsky to Berg, 28 February 1952, FAH 5 W 37b, NL Wilmowsky, KA.

112 The Wilmowsky correspondences contain extensive details about royalties, advances, and profits. See, e.g., Regnery to Wilmowsky, 20 December 1951, NL Wilmowsky, FAH 5 W 37a, and various letters and contracts in file FAH 5 W 37b, KA.

113 The industrialists whom Lochner consulted are too many to list, but they included many prominent names, including the "Brothers von Bohlen" (Alfried Krupp von Bohlen und Halbach and Berthold von Bohlen und Halbach), Friedrich Flick, Hugo Stinnes Jr., Josef Winschuh, Wolf-Dietrich von Witzleben, and Max Ilgner from IG Farben. For a partial list of those consulted, see Lochner, *Tycoons and Tyrant*, vii–viii.

114 See the unpublished study by Ficker (an expert on international and European law) commissioned by Theo Goldschmidt, in Sonstiges aus Nürnberger Prozessen, BAL. On Theo Goldschmidt's sponsorship, see Pohle to Wilmowsky, 23 October 1950, NL Wilmowsky, FAH 5 W 37a, KA.

115 Heinrichsbauer to Hermann Reusch, 9 December 1952, NL Hermann Reusch, 40010145/173, RWWA.

116 On his meeting with Paul Reusch, see P. Reusch to Wilmowsky, 21 November 1952, NL Hermann Reusch, 40010124/18, RWWA. On his meeting with Hermann Reusch, see Reusch to Heinrichsbauer, 10 December 1952, NL Hermann Reusch, 40010145/173, RWWA.

117 Lochner to Wilmowsky, 3 November 1952, NL Wilmowsky, FAH 5 W 37b, KA, and Lochner, *Tycoons and Tyrant*, 197.

118 On Rohland, see his autobiography, *Bewegte Zeiten*.

119 See the Rohland/Lochner exchanges from 1955/1956 in reel 21, Lochner Papers, Wisconsin.

120 Lochner, *Tycoons and Tyrant*, 79.

121 Lochner to Wilmowsky, 2 September 1952, NL Wilmowsky, FAH 5 W 37b, KA.

122 For a series of correspondences about the 1932 speech at the Industry Club, see BC. For the most thorough examination of the speech and party financing in the early 1930s, see Henry A. Turner, *German Big Business*, 204–29.

123 Kranzbühler to Wilmowsky, 5 January 1953, NL Wilmowsky, FAH 5 W 37c, KA. On the financing of the Nazi Party, see Henry A. Turner, *German Big Business*, e.g., 291–304.

124 On the concept of *Resistenz*, see Broszat, "Resistenz und Widerstand."

125 In 1954 John caused an uproar when he traveled to East Berlin to condemn the return to power of Nazi industrialists and militarists in West Germany. See Broch-

hagen, *Nach Nürnberg*, 216–22. On John and the anti-Hitler resistance, see Peter Hoffmann, *History of the German Resistance*, 246–48.

126 Gleason, *Totalitarianism*, 158.

127 Despite his role in the resistance, Löser was tried by a U.S. military tribunal in 1947 and sentenced to seven years in prison the next year. In December 1949 he obtained an early release due to illness. See the British profile of Löser in FO 1029/47, PRO, and Manchester, *Arms of Krupp*, 434–35.

128 On Bosch, see Treue, "Widerstand von Unternehmern und Nationalökonomen."

129 See Erker, *Industrie-Eliten*, 37.

130 Lochner, *Tycoons and Tyrant*, 233.

131 Strolin, *Verräter oder Patrioten?*

132 For one of the most recent studies of the anti-Hitler resistance, see Hamerow, *On the Road to the Wolf's Lair*. On the anti-Semitic ideas within the resistance, see Peter Hoffmann, *History of the German Resistance*, 318.

133 For a short overview of the events following Krupp's release, see Bührer, "Return to Normality."

134 Wollstädter to Wilmowsky, 4 March 1953, NL Wilmowsky, FAH 5 W 37c, KA.

135 "Aktenvermerk über Public Relations," 23 March 1953, NL Wilmowsky, FAH 5 W 37c, KA.

136 Wollstädter to Wilmowsky, 12 June 1953, NL Wilmowsky, FAH 5 W 37b, KA.

137 Hundhausen to Beitz, 21 December 1954, NL Wilmowsky, FAH 5 W 37c, KA.

138 See Knieriem, *Nürnberg*. On the preparation of this book, see Pohle to Kranzbühler, 31 December 1952, NL Wilmowsky, FAH 5 W 37b, KA. Industry tried unsuccessfully to get Knieriem's book translated into English. See Knieriem to Krupp's lawyers, 17 June 1953, NL Wilmowsky, FAH 5 W 37c, KA.

139 Paul Reusch gave his nod after reading the manuscript; see P. Reusch to Wilmowsky, 21 November 1952, NL Wilmowsky, FAH 5 W37b, KA.

140 Lochner to Regnery, 15 February 1953, reel 20, Lochner Papers, Wisconsin.

141 The Chicago general consulate found the book impressive, "especially because it was not a whitewash but an objective study" (Walter Gong to Lochner, 5 February 54, FAH 5 W 42, KA). For correspondence between Lochner and the German Embassy, see reel 8, Lochner Papers, Wisconsin.

142 Hans Kohn, "The Support Was Wide," *New York Times*, 14 November 1954.

143 A collection of Lochner reviews and summaries of reviews can be found in WA 55/3007, KA.

144 Excerpted and undated in ibid.

145 *New Leader*, 29 November 1954, in ibid.

146 Lochner, *Mächtigten und der Tyrann*. The German translation became the cornerstone of a renewed attempt by the DI to bury the myths of the past. See "Entkräftung der Schuldlüge gegen die Industrie," *Schnelldienst des Deutschen Industrieinstituts*, 17 December 1954, 2–4, and "Ein Amerikaner entkräftet die Schuldlüge gegen die deutsche Industrie," *Material zum Zeitgeschehen*, 15 December 1954, 1–8. On Lochner's painstaking attempts to find a German publisher for his book, see, e.g., Wilmowsky to Lochner, 21 September 1954, NL Wilmowsky, FAH 5 37c, KA.

147 Herbert Gross, "Die Magnaten und der Tyrann," *Handelsblatt,* 6 December 1954.

148 Adenauer to Lochner, 27 June 1955, reprinted in Morsey and Schwarz, *Adenauer,* 304–5.

149 "Möhrenwäsche für Krupp, Flick, und Co.," *Die Wirtschaft* (East Berlin), 19 May 1955.

150 On the demise of this relationship, see, e.g., Regnery to Wilmowsky, 16 September 1954, NL Wilmowsky, FAH 5 37c, KA.

151 "In this book I have tried to clear away the rubble of legend and misrepresentation which obstructs one of the paths which lead to the truth about the past. My faith in Germany as a valuable and indeed indispensable member of the Western Community was greatly strengthened by the facts with which my researches brought me face to face" (Lochner, *Tycoons and Tyrant,* 294).

152 Burnham, *Managerial Revolution,* 73.

153 On the concept of totalitarianism in postwar Germany, see Gleason, *Totalitarianism,* 157–66. See the classic study by Arendt, *Origins of Totalitarianism.*

CONCLUSION

1 Hans Merkle has referred to the "social romantic" self-understanding of the industrialist. See Merkle, *Reden bei der Festveranstaltung.*

2 Silberschmidt, *Bedeutung des Unternehmers,* 16.

3 See Heineman, "Hour of the Woman"; Moeller, "War Stories"; Carter, *How German Is She?;* Poiger, *Jazz, Rock, and Rebels;* and Fehrenbach, *Cinema in Democratizing Germany.*

4 In the words of Carl Becker, a prominent clothing manufacturer, "The key to the economy lies in the hands of the woman" (Carl Becker, "Die wirtschaftliche 'Schlüsselgewalt' der Frau in der Volkswirtschaft," speech delivered to the Arbeitsgemeinschaft Hauswirtschaft, e.V., Bonn, 26 January 1954, NL Becker, I-162-110, ACDP).

5 *Die deutschen Industrie und Wirtschaft im Spiegel der Volksmeinung: Eine aufschlußreiche Studie über aktuelle Probleme unserer Zeit,* duchgeführt vom DIVO-Institut für Markt- und Meinungsforschung GmbH im Auftragen *des Spiegels* (Frankfurt, 1955).

6 Carl Hundhausen established the chair in public relations at Erlangen in 1975.

7 Knieriem, *Nuremberg Trials.* See Kannapin's similarly apologetic *Wirtschaft unter Zwang.*

8 Deutsches Industrieinstitut, *Legende von Hitler und der Industrie* (Cologne, 1963), and Deutscher Gewerkschaftsbund, *Hitler und die Industrie* (Anhang zu *Für die Demokratie—Informationen—Kommentare—Presseschau,* [1963]). Both documents can be found in IW. I thank Henry A. Turner for giving me his copy of the latter.

9 This event is richly documented in the Potthoff Collection, 101/5, Böckler.

10 See Schwarz, "Modernisierung oder Restauration?" For polemical accounts of Nazi industrialists' postwar wealth, see Pritzkoleit, *Wem gehört Deutschland,* and Engelmann, *Das Reich zerfiel.*

11 Geyer, *Deutsche Rüstungspolitik*, 176–231.

12 On the pre- and postfascist continuities in the German economy, see Reich, *Fruits of Fascism*, and Tolliday, "Enterprise and State."

13 Michael Wildt sees 1955 as a time when economic "hard times" truly ended. See Wildt, "Privater Konsum," 275.

14 See Ferencz, *Less Than Slaves*.

15 The chief individual representing German industry in the United States was Julius Klein, a retired general and former commander of the Jewish War Veterans of America. See ibid., 49.

16 On such controversial transactions, see Glouchevitch, *Juggernaut*, 165–79.

17 See Pinto-Duschinsky, "Fund-Raising and the Holocaust."

18 Firms such as Krupp, Degussa, the Dresdner Bank, Bertelsmann, and Ford have recently hired respected historians to research their actions during the Third Reich. On the moral and historical responsibility of historians who study industry during the Third Reich, see Feldman, *Unternehmensgeschichte*.

19 Lochner to Regnery, 23 December 1952, Lochner Papers, reel 20, Wisconsin.

20 Some of the terms in German are *Arbeitereinsatz, Zwangsarbeit, Fremdarbeit, Gastarbeit,* etc. See Otto Kranzbühler, "A Short Survey of the Krupp Trial" (n.p., ca. 1949), for an example of the use of the term "manpower."

21 On the social aspects of memory, see Fentress and Wickam, *Social Memory*.

Bibliography

ARCHIVAL SOURCES

Archiv der Thyssen AG, Duisburg
   Company Files in Bestand VSt
   NL Heinrich Dinkelbach
Archiv für Christlich-Demokratische Politik an der Konrad Adenauer Stiftung,
   Sankt Augustin
   NL Siegfried Balke (I-175)
   NL Curt Becker (I-162)
   NL Paul Binder (I-105)
   NL Fritz Hellwig (I-083)
   NL Gustav Stein (I-288)
   Verband Deutscher Maschinen- und Anlagenbauverein (VI-003)
Bayer-Archiv, Leverkusen
   Miscellaneous Company Files
   NL Ulrich Haberland
   Nuremberg Trial Files
Private Papers of Dr. Werner Bührer, Technische-Universität, Munich
   Wilhelm Salewski Papers
Bundesarchiv, Koblenz
   Bestand Deutscher Industrie- und Handelstag (B156)
   Bestand Stahltreuhändervereinigung (B109)
   NL Abraham Frowein (NL 112)
   NL Günter Henle (NL 1384)
   NL Theodor Heuss (NL 221)
   NL Josef Winschuh (NL 1223)
   Südosteuropa Gesellschaft e.V. (R63)
Degussa Archiv, Frankfurt am Main
   Files Relating to the Trial of Gerhard Peters

Miscellaneous Company Reports
F. C. Delius Private Collection, Berlin
  Papers Relating to Siemens AG
DGB-Archiv in der Hans Böckler Stiftung, Düsseldorf (collection has recently
  moved to the Friedrich Ebert Stiftung, Bonn)
  Erich Potthoff Collection
Hessisches Hauptstaatsarchiv, Wiesbaden
  Spruchkammerakte zu Fritz Thyssen
Historisches Archiv Krupp, Essen
  Miscellaneous Company Reports
  NL Tilo Frhr. von Wilmowsky
Industrie- und Handelskammer für Augsburg und Schwaben, Augsburg
  NL Otto A. H. Vogel
Institut für Zeitgeschichte, Munich
  Nuremberg Files
  Ludwig Vaubel Sammlung (ED 321/1–18)
Landesarchiv, Berlin
  Deutsche Industrie-Ausstellung Files
Mannesmann-Archiv, Düsseldorf
  Oskar Altmann Correspondences
  Wolfgang Pohle Correspondences
  Wilhelm Zangen Correspondences
National Archives Records Administration, College Park, Md.
  Papers of the Office of the U.S. Military Government in Germany
  State Department Files
Nordrhein-Westfälisches Hauptstaatsarchiv, Düsseldorf
  NL Wolfgang Pohle (RWN 218)
Office of the Conference on Jewish Material Claims against Germany, Frankfurt am
  Main
  NL Ernst Katzenstein
    Max Stein, "Report on the Employment of Slave Work by the Siemens Concern
    during World War II," in file "Siemens"
Public Record Office, London
  Miscellaneous Foreign Office Files
Paul-Jürgen Reusch Private Collection, Backnang
  Private Correspondences, Hermann Reusch and Paul Reusch
Rheinisch-Westfälisches Wirtschaftsarchiv, Cologne
  Archiv der Gutehoffnungshütte Aktiengesellschaft
    NL Hermann Kellermann
    NL Hermann Reusch
    NL Paul Reusch
    Selected Company Files
    IHK Duisburg
  IHK Düsseldorf

IHK Essen
IHK Köln
Siemens-Archiv, Munich
  Investigative Committee Reports
  NL Hanns Benkert
  NL Fritz Jessen
  Scattered Files on "Wiederaufbau" (Reconstruction)
State Historical Society of Wisconsin, Madison
  Louis Lochner Papers
Stiftung Archiv für Massenparteien- und Organisationen der ehemaligen DDR,
  Bundesarchiv-Berlin
  Miscellaneous Files Relating to West German Industry
  Newspaper Clipping Files on Siemens and Other German Firms
  Vereinigung der Verfolgten des Naziregimes Files
Stiftung Westfälisches Wirtschaftsarchiv, Dortmund
  Akten der Nürnberg Industrieprozess

LIBRARIES AND NEWSPAPER CLIPPING REPOSITORIES

Arbeitsgemeinschaft selbständiger Unternehmer, Bonn/Bad-Godesberg
Bibliothek Institut für Publizistik, Freie Universität, Berlin
Bund Katholischer Unternehmer, Cologne
Institut der Deutschen Wirtschaft, Cologne
Institut der Weltwirtschaft, Kiel
Otto Suhr-Institut, Freie Universität, Berlin

MAGAZINES, NEWSLETTERS, AND JOURNALS

Der Arbeitgeber
Die Aussprache
Das Fenster
Handelsblatt
Industriekurier
Jahresbericht des BnDI
Junge Wirtschaft
Kundgebung und Mitgliederversammung des BDI
Material zum Zeitgeschehen (DI publication)
Mitarbeiterbrief des deutschen Industrieinstituts
Mitteilungen des Bundesverband der Deutschen Industrie
Rundfunkspiegel des deutschen Industrieinstituts
Schnelldienst des deutschen Industrieinstituts
Unternehmerbrief des deutschen Industrieinstituts
Vortragsreihe des deutschen Industrieinstituts
Welt der Arbeit

Abelshauser, Werner. "The First Post-Liberal Nation: Stages in the Development of Modern Corporatism in Germany." *European History Quarterly* 14, no. 3 (July 1984): 285–317.

Adenauer, Konrad. *Memoirs.* Vol. 1. Chicago: Regnery, 1966.

Ahrens, Hanns D. *Demontage: Nachkriegspolitik der Alliierten.* Munich: Universitas, 1982.

Almond, Gabriel A. "The Politics of German Business." In *West German Leadership and Foreign Policy.* Edited by Hans Speier and W. Phillips Davison, 195–241. Evanston, Ill.: Rowe, Peterson, 1957.

Ambrosius, Gerold. *Die Durchsetzung der sozialen Marktwirtschaft in Westdeutschland, 1945–1949.* Düsseldorf: Deutsche Verlags-Anstalt, 1972.

Andreae, Clemens August, and Burghard Freudenfeld. *Sündenbock Unternehmer? Das Risiko der Freiheit im Wandel der Gesellschaft* Cologne: Informedia-Verlags-GmbH, 1973.

Arendt, Hannah. *The Origins of Totalitarianism.* New York: Harcourt Brace, 1951.

Arndt, Ino. "Das Frauenkonzentrationslager Ravensbrück." In *Studien zur Geschichte der Konzentrationslager.* Edited by Hans Rothfels and Theodor Eschenburg, 93–129. Stuttgart: Deutsche Verlags-Anstalt, 1970.

Backer, John H. *The Decision to Divide Germany: American Foreign Policy in Transition.* Durham, N.C.: Duke University Press, 1978.

———. *Priming the German Economy: American Occupational Policies, 1945–1948.* Durham, N.C.: Duke University Press, 1971.

Balabkins, Nicholas. *Germany under Direct Controls: Economic Aspects of Industrial Disarmament, 1945–1948.* New Brunswick, N.J.: Rutgers University Press, 1964.

Barkai, Avraham. *From Boycott to Annihilation: The Economic Struggle of German Jews, 1933–1943.* Hanover, N.H.: University Press of New England, 1989.

———. "German Entrepreneurs and Jewish Policy in the Third Reich." *Yad Vashem Studies* 21 (1991): 122–55.

Belgion, Montgomery. *Victors' Justice.* Hinsdale, Ill.: Regnery, 1949.

Berg, Fritz. *Die Westdeutsche Wirtschaft in der Bewährung.* Hagen: Linnepe, 1966.

Berghahn, Volker R. *The Americanisation of West German Industry, 1945–1973.* Cambridge: Cambridge University Press, 1983.

———. "Ideas into Politics: The Case of Ludwig." In *Ideas into Politics: Aspects of European History, 1880–1950.* Edited by R. J. Bullen, H. Pogge von Strandmann, and A. B. Polonsky, 178–92. London: Croom Helm, 1984.

———. *Modern Germany: Society, Economy, and Politics in the Twentieth Century.* Cambridge: Cambridge University Press, 1987.

———. "The United States and the Shaping of West Germany's Social Compact, 1945–1966." *International Labor and Working-Class History* 50 (fall 1996): 125–32.

———. *Unternehmer und Politik in der Bundesrepublik.* Frankfurt: Suhrkamp, 1985.

———. "West German Reconstruction and American Industrial Culture, 1945–1960." In *The American Impact on Postwar Germany.* Edited by Reiner Pommerin, 65–81. Providence: Berghahn, 1995.

Berghahn, Volker R., and Paul J. Friedrich. *Otto A. Friedrich, Ein Politischer Unternehmer.* Frankfurt am Main and New York: Campus, 1993.

Berghahn, Volker R., and F. L. Karsten. *Industrial Relations in West Germany.* Oxford: Berg, 1987.

Best, Gary Dean. *Herbert Hoover: The Postpresidential Years, 1933-1964.* Vol. 2, *1946-1964.* Stanford: Hoover Institution Press, 1983.

"Big Business Is Still in Trouble." *Fortune,* May 1949, 67-71.

Binder, Elisabeth. *Die Entstehung unternehmerischer Public Relations in der Bundesrepublik Deutschland.* Münster: Lit, 1983.

Bird, Kai. *The Chairman, John J. McCloy: The Making of the American Establishment.* New York: Simon & Schuster, 1992.

Blaich, Fritz. *Wirtschaft und Rüstung im "Dritten Reich."* Düsseldorf: Schwann, 1987.

Boehling, Rebecca. *A Question of Priorities: Democratic Reforms and Economic Recovery in Postwar Germany: Frankfurt, Munich, and Stuttgart under U.S. Occupation, 1945-1949.* Providence: Berghahn, 1996.

Bourdieu, Pierre. *Language and Symbolic Power.* Cambridge: Harvard University Press, 1993.

Bower, Tom. " 'Alle deutschen Industriellen saßen auf der Anklagebank': Die Nürnberger Nachfolgerprozesse gegen Krupp, Flick und die IG Farben." In *Gegen Barbarei: Essays Robert M. W. Kempner zu Ehren.* Edited by Rainer Eisfeld and Ingo Müller, 239-56. Frankfurt am Main: Athenäum, 1989.

———. *The Pledge Betrayed: America and Britain and the Denazification of Postwar Germany.* New York: Doubleday, 1982.

Braunthal, Gerard. *The Federation of German Industry in Politics.* Ithaca: Cornell University Press, 1965.

Bräutigam, Petra, Andrea Schuster, and Astrid Welck. "Drei württembergische Unternehmer während des Nationalsozialismus: Rolf Boehringer, Ernst Stütz, Richard Schweizer." In *Regionale Eliten zwischen Diktatur und Demokratie.* Edited by Cornelia Rauh-Kühne and Michael Ruck, 221-46. Munich: Oldenbourg, 1993.

Briefs, Goetz. *Zwischen Kapitalismus und Syndikalismus: Die Gewerkschaften am Scheideweg.* Munich: L. Lehnen, 1952.

Brochhagen, Ulrich. *Nach Nürnberg: Vergangenheitsbewältigung und Westintegration in der Ära Adenauer.* Hamburg: Junius, 1994.

Broszat, Martin. "Resistenz und Widerstand: Eine Zwischenbilanz des Forschungsprojekts." In *Bayern in der NS-Zeit.* Edited by Martin Broszat, Elke Frölich, and Falk Wiesemann, 691-709. Munich: Oldenbourg, 1977.

Buchheim, Christoph. "Die Währungsreform 1948 in Westdeutschland." *Vierteljahrshefte für Zeitgeschichte* 36 (1988): 189-231.

Buckley, William F., Jr. *God and Man at Yale: The Superstitions of Academic Freedom.* Chicago: Regnery, 1951.

Bührer, Werner. *Die Adenauer-Ära: Die Bundesrepublik Deutschland, 1949-1963.* Munich: Piper, 1993.

———. "Der Kulturkreis im Bundesverband der Deutschen Industrie und die 'kulturelle Modernisierung' der Bundesrepublik in den 50er Jahren. In

Modernisierung im Wiederaufbau: Die westdeutsche Gesellschaft der 50er Jahre.
Edited by Axel Schildt and Arnold Sywottek, 583–95. Bonn: Dietz, 1993.

———. "Return to Normality: The United States and Ruhr Industry, 1949–1955." In *American Policy and the Reconstruction of West Germany, 1945–1955.* Edited by Jeffry M. Diefendorf, Axel Frohn, and Hermann-Josef Rupieper, 135–53. Cambridge: Cambridge University Press, 1993.

———. *Ruhrstahl und Europa: Die Wirtschaftsvereinigung Eisen- und Stahlindustrie und die Anfänge der europäischen Integration, 1945–1952.* Munich: Oldenbourg, 1986.

———. "Die Unternehmerverbände nach den beiden Weltkriegen." In *Lernen aus dem Krieg? Deutsche Nachkriegszeiten, 1918/1945.* Edited by Gottfried Niedhart and Dieter Riesenberger, 140–57. Munich: Beck, 1992.

Bunn, Ronald F. "The Federation of German Employers' Associations: A Political Interest Group." *Western Political Quarterly* 13, no. 4 (July 1959): 652–69.

Burnham, James. *The Managerial Revolution.* New York: John Day, 1941.

Buscher, Frank M. *The U.S. War Crimes Trial Program in Germany, 1946–1955.* Westport, Conn.: Greenwood Press, 1989.

Campbell, Joan. *The German Werkbund: The Politics of Reform in the Applied Arts.* Princeton: Princeton University Press, 1978.

———. *Joy in Work, German Work: The National Debate, 1800–1945.* Princeton: Princeton University Press, 1989.

Carter, Erica. *How German Is She? Postwar West German Reconstruction and the Consuming Woman.* Ann Arbor: University of Michigan Press, 1997.

Chamberlin, William Henry. *America's Second Crusade.* Chicago: Regnery, 1950.

Chandler, Alfred D. *The Visible Hand: The Managerial Revolution in American Business.* Cambridge: Harvard University Press, 1977.

Chrysler, Walter. *Life of an American Workman.* New York: Dodd, Mead, 1950.

Clay, Lucius D. *Decision in Germany.* Garden City, N.Y.: Doubleday, 1950.

Collins, Robert. *The Business Response to Keynes, 1929–1964.* New York: Columbia University Press, 1981.

Confino, Alon. "Collective Memory and Cultural History: Problems of Method." *American Historical Review* 102, no. 5 (December 1997): 1386–1402.

———. *The Nation as a Local Metaphor: Württemberg, Imperial Germany, and National Memory, 1871–1918.* Chapel Hill, University of North Carolina Press, 1997.

Crane, Susan A. "Writing the Individual Back into Collective Memory." *American Historical Review* 102, no. 5 (December 1997): 1371–85.

Cutlip, Scott M. *Public Relations History: From the Seventeenth to the Twentieth Century: The Antecedents.* Hillsdale, N.J. and Hove, U.K.: Erlbaum, 1995.

Czichon, Eberhard. *Wer verhalf Hitler zur Macht? Zum Anteil der deutschen Industrie an der Zerstörung der Weimarer Republik.* Cologne: Rugen, 1967.

Davidson, Eugene. *The Death and Life of Germany.* New York: Knopf, 1961.

Deist, Wilhelm, Manfred Messerschmidt, Haüs-Erich Volkmann, and Wolfram Wette. *Ursachen und Voraussetzungen des Zweiten Weltkrieges.* Frankfurt am Main: Fischer, 1995.

Delius, F. C. *Unsere Siemens-Welt.* Hamburg: Rotbuch, 1972.

Diedrich, Karl Friedrich. *"Human relations" als soziales und wirtschaftliches Potential im Betrieb.* Munich: Steinebach, 1951.

Diegmann, Dietrich. "American Deconcentration Policy in the Ruhr Coal Industry." In *American Policy and the Reconstruction of West Germany, 1945–1955.* Edited by Jeffry M. Diefendorf, Axel Frohn, and Hermann-Josef Rupieper, 197–215. Cambridge: Cambridge University Press, 1993.

Diggins, John P. *Up from Communism: Conservative Odysseys in American Intellectual History.* New York: Harper & Row, 1977.

Dirksen, Herbert von. *Moscow, Tokyo, London: Twenty Years of German Foreign Policy.* Norman: University of Oklahoma Press, 1952.

Doering-Manteuffel, Anselm. "Die Kultur der 50er Jahre im Spannungsfeld von 'Wiederaufbau' und 'Modernisierung.'" In *Modernisierung im Wiederaufbau: Die westdeutsche Gesellschaft der 50er Jahre.* Edited by Axel Schildt and Arnold Sywottek, 533–40. Bonn: Dietz, 1993.

Domaniewski, Zbigniew. *Intellectual Capitalism: A Study of Changing Ownership and Control in Modern Industrial Society.* New York: World University Press, 1950.

DuBois, Josiah E., Jr. *Generals in Grey Suits.* London: Bodley Head, 1953.

Duisberg, Curt. *Nur ein Sohn: Ein Leben mit der Großchemie.* Stuttgart: Seewald, 1981.

Dulles, Allen. *Germany's Underground.* New York: Macmillan, 1947.

Eells, Richard. *The Corporation and the Arts.* New York: Macmillan, 1967.

Emmet, Christopher. *Zerstörung auf unsere Kosten: Wie die Demontage von Fabriken in Deutschland der Inflation in den Vereinigten Staaten hilft und den Marshallplan sabotiert.* Hamburg: Hamburger Buchdruckerei, 1948.

Engelmann, Bernd. *Das Reich zerfiel, die Reichen blieben.* Berlin: Verlag der Nation, 1974.

Erker, Paul. *Industrie-Eliten in der NS-Zeit: Anpassungsbereitschaft und Eigeninteresse von Unternehmern in der rüstung-und Kriegswirtschaft, 1936–1945.* Passau: Wissenschaftsverlag, 1994.

Erker, Paul, and Toni Pierenkemper. *Deutsche Unternehmer zwischen Kriegswirtschaft und Wiederaufbau: Studien zur Erfahrungsbildung von Industrie-Eliten.* Munich: Oldenbourg, 1999.

Eschenburg, Theodor. *Herrschaft der Verbände?* Stuttgart: Deutsche Verlags-Anstalt, 1955.

Fabian, Franz. *Der Rat der Götter: Nacherzählt nach dem gleichnamigen DEFA-Film.* Berlin: Deutscher Filmverlag, 1950.

Fehrenbach, Heide. *Cinema in Democratizing Germany: Reconstructing National Identity after Hitler.* Chapel Hill: University of North Carolina Press, 1995.

Feldenkirchen, Wilfried. *Siemens, 1918–1945.* Munich: Piper, 1995.

———. *Siemens, 1918–1945.* Translated by Tom Rattray and John Taylor. Columbus: Ohio State University Press, 1999.

Feldman, Gerald D. *Hugo Stinnes: Biographie eines Industriellen, 1870–1924.* Munich: Beck, 1998.

———. "Jakob Goldschmidt, the History of the Banking Crisis of 1931, and the Problem of Freedom of Manoeuvre in the Weimar Economy." In *Zerrissene*

Zwischenkriegszeit, Wirtschaftshistorische Beiträge: Knut Borchardt zum 65. Geburtstag. Edited by Christoph Buchheim, Knut Borchardt, Michael Hutter, and Harold James, 307–37. Baden Baden: Nomos, 1994.

———. "Politische Kultur und Wirtschaft in der Weimarer Zeit: Unternehmer auf dem Weg in die Katastrophe," *Zeitschrift für Unternehmensgeschichte* 43, no. 1 (1998): 1–18.

———. "The Social and Economic Policies of German Big Business, 1918–1929." *American Historical Review* 75, no. 1 (October 1969): 47–55.

———. *Unternehmensgeschichte des Dritten Reichs und Verantwortung des Historiker: Raubgold und Versicherung, Arisierung und Zwangsarbeit.* No. 23 of series Gesprächskreis Geschichte. Bonn: Friedrich-Ebert Stiftung, 1999.

Fentress, James, and Chris Wickham. *Social Memory.* Oxford: Blackwell, 1992.

Ferencz, Benjamin. *Less Than Slaves: Jewish Forced Labor and the Quest for Compensation.* Cambridge: Cambridge University Press, 1979.

Flender, Alfred. *Die Stunde des Unternehmers.* Bonn, 1954.

Flieger, Heinz, and Franz Ronnenberger, eds. *Public Relations Anfänge in Deutschland: Festschrift zum 100. Geburtstag von Carl Hundhausen.* Wiesbaden: Verlag für Deutsche Wirtschaftsbiographien, 1993.

Fones-Wolf, Elisabeth. *Selling Free Enterprise: The Business Assault on Labor and Liberalism, 1945–1960.* Urbana: University of Illinois Press, 1994.

Foschepoth, Josef. "German Reaction to Defeat and Occupation." In *West Germany under Construction: Politics, Society, and Culture in the Adenauer Era.* Edited by Robert Moeller, 73–89. Ann Arbor: University of Michigan Press, 1997.

Frankenburg, Richard Alexander von. *Porsche: Der Weg eines Zeitalters.* Stuttgart: Steingruben-Verlag, 1951.

Frei, Norbert. *Vergangenheitspolitik: Die Anfänge der Bundesrepublik und die NS-Vergangenheit.* Munich: Beck, 1996.

Friedman, Milton. *Capitalism and Freedom.* 2d ed. Chicago: University of Chicago Press, 1982.

Friedrich, Jörg. *Die Kalte Amnestie: NS-Täter in der Bundesrepublik.* Munich: Piper, 1984.

Friedrich, Otto. *Das Leitbild des Unternehmers wandelt sich.* Stuttgart: Seewald, 1959.

Friz, Maria. *Die Stahlgiganten Alfried Krupp and Berthold Beitz.* Frankfurt am Main: Ullstein, 1990.

Fürstenau, Justus. *Entnazifizierung: Ein Kapitel deutscher Nachkriegspolitik.* Neuwied: Luchterhand, 1969.

Gall, Lothar, and Manfred Pohl, eds. *Unternehmen im Nationalsozialismus.* Munich: Beck, 1998.

Geary, Dick. "The Industrial Elite and the Nazis in the Weimar Republic." In *The Nazi Machtergreifung.* Edited by Peter D. Stachura, 49–67. London: Allen & Unwin, 1983.

Gehrig, Astrid. *Nationalsozialistische Rüstungspolitik und unternehmerischer Entscheidungsspielraum: Vergleichende Fallstudien zur württembergischen Maschinenbauindustrie.* Munich: Oldenbourg, 1996.

Gehrig, Herbert. *Die Persönlichkeit des Unternehmers.* Düsseldorf: Triltsch, 1954.

Geyer, Michael. *Deutsche Rüstungspolitik, 1860-1980.* Frankfurt am Main: Suhrkamp, 1984.

Gillingham, John. *Coal, Steel, and the Rebirth of Europe, 1945-1955: The Germans and French from Ruhr Conflict to Economic Community.* Cambridge: Cambridge University Press, 1991.

———. *Industry and Politics in the Third Reich: Ruhr Coal, Hitler, and Europe.* London: Methuen, 1985.

Gillis, John R. "Memory and Identity: The History of a Relationship." In *Commemorations: The Politics of National Identity.* Edited by John R. Gillis, 3-24. Princeton: Princeton University Press, 1994.

Glaser, Hermann. *The Rubble Years: The Cultural Roots of Postwar Germany.* New York: Paragon House, 1986.

Gleason, Abbott. *Totalitarianism: The Inner History of the Cold War.* Oxford: Oxford University Press, 1995.

Glouchevitch, Philip. *Juggernaut: The Keys to German Business Success.* New York: Touchstone, 1993.

Goebbels, Joseph. *The Goebbels Diaries.* Edited by Louis P. Lochner. Garden City, N.Y.: Doubleday, 1948.

Gollancz, Victor. *In Darkest Germany.* Hinsdale, Ill.: Regnery, 1947.

Grebing, Helga. "Demokratie ohne Demokraten? Politische Denken, einstellungen und Mentalitäten in der Nachkriegszeit." In *Wie neu war der Neubeginn?: Zum deutschen Kontinuitätsproblem nach 1945.* Edited by Helga Grebing, 6-19. Erlangen: Universität Erlangen-Nürnberg, 1989.

———. *Konservative gegen die Demokratie: Konservative Kritik an der Demokratie in der Bundesrepublik Deutschland nach 1945.* Frankfurt am Main: Europäische Verlagsanstalt, 1971.

Gregor, Neil. *Daimler-Benz in the Third Reich.* New Haven: Yale University Press, 1998.

Greiner, Bernd. *Die Morgenthau Legende: Zur Geschichte eines umstrittenden Planes.* Hamburg: Hamburger Edition, 1995.

Greiß, Franz. "Erhards soziale Marktwirtschaft und DIE WAAGE." In *Ludwig Erhard: Beiträge zu seiner politischen Biographie, Festschrift zum 75. Geburtstag.* Edited by Gerhard Schröder and Ludwig Erhard, 94-109. Frankfurt am Main: Propyläen, 1972.

Greiß, Franz, and Martin Lohmann. *Die Gründung des Bundes Katholischer Unternehmer 1949.* Bonn: BKU, 1985.

Gross, Herbert. *Sozialismus in der Krise.* Frankfurt am Main: Lutzeyer, 1952.

Grube, Frank, and Gerhard Richter. *Das Wirtschaftswunder: Unser Weg in den Wohlstand.* Hamburg: Hoffmann und Campe, 1983.

Habermas. Jürgen. *Legitimation Crisis.* Boston: Beacon Press, 1973.

Hajek, Karlfranz A. *Management und Human Relations.* Vienna: F. Brabec, 1955.

Halbwachs, Maurice. *On Collective Memory.* Chicago: University of Chicago Press, 1992.

Hallgarten, George W. F., and Jürgen Radkau, *Deutsche Industrie und Politik von Bismarck bis heute.* Frankfurt am Main: Athenäum, 1974.

Hamerow, Theodore. *On the Road to the Wolf's Lair: German Resistance to Hitler.* Cambridge: Harvard University Press, 1997.

Hankey, Maurice Pascal Alers. *Politics, Trials, and Errors.* Chicago: Regnery, 1950.

Hartewig, Karen. "Die 'allierte Besatzungsmacht' in den Lebensgeschichten westdeutscher Unternehmer." *BIOS Zeitschrift für Biographieforschung Oral History* 6 (special issue) (1993): 95–121.

Hartman, Geoffrey, ed. *Bitburg in Moral and Political Perspective.* Bloomington: Indiana University Press, 1986.

Hartmann, Heinz. *Authority and Organization in German Management.* Princeton: Princeton University Press, 1959.

Hauser, Heinrich. *Time Was: Death of a Junker.* New York: Reynal & Hitchcock, 1942.

———. *Unser Schicksal: Die Deutsche Industrie.* Munich: Steinebach, 1952.

Hayek, Friedrich A. *The Road to Serfdom.* Chicago: University of Chicago Press, 1944.

Hayes, Peter. "Big Business and 'Aryanization' in Germany." *Jahrbuch für Antisemitismusforschung* 3 (1994): 254–81.

———. "Fritz Roessler and Nazism: The Observations of a German Industrialist, 1930–1937." *Central European History* 20 (1987): 58–79.

———. "Industrial Factionalism in Modern German History." *Central European History* 24 (1991): 122–31.

———. *Industry and Ideology: IG Farben in the Nazi Era.* Cambridge: Cambridge University Press, 1987.

———. "Profits and Persecution: Corporate Involvement in the Holocaust." In *Perpetrators, Victims, and Bystanders: Essays in Honor of Raul Hilberg.* Edited by James S. Pacy and Alan P. Wertheimer, 51–73. Boulder, Colo.: Westview Press, 1993.

Hayse, Michael R. "Recasting West German Elites: Higher Civil Servants, Business Leaders, and Physicians in Hessen, 1945–1955." Ph.D. diss., University of North Carolina, 1995.

Head, David. *"Made in Germany": The Corporate Identity of a Nation.* London: Hodder & Stoughton, 1992.

Heineman, Elizabeth. "The Hour of the Woman: Memories of Germany's 'Crisis Years' and West German National Identity." *American Historical Review* 101, no. 2 (April 1996): 354–95.

———. *What Difference Does a Husband Make? Women and Marital Status in Nazi and Postwar Germany.* Berkeley and Los Angeles: University of California Press, 1999.

Heinrichsbauer, August. *Schwerindustrie und Politik.* Essen-Kettwig: West-Verlag, 1948.

Hellwig, Fritz. *Carl Ferdinand Freiherr von Stumm-Halberg, 1836–1901.* Heidelberg: Westmark, 1936.

———. "Die Echte Unternehmer in der Marktwirtschaft." In *Unternehmer, Marktwirtschaft und Sozialpolitik. 4 Vorträge gehalten auf der Jahreshauptversammlung der Arbeitsgemeinschaft selbständiger Unternehmer (ASU) am 30 March 1951 in Wiesbaden.* Edited by the ASU, 3–25. Frankfurt am Main: ASU, 1951.

Helt, Richard C., and Marie E. Helt. *West German Cinema since 1945: A Reference Handbook.* Metuchen, N.J.: Scarecrow Press, 1987.

Henke, Klaus-Dietmar. *Die Amerikanische Besetzung Deutschlands.* Munich: Oldenbourg, 1995.

Henle, Günter. *Three Spheres: A Life in Politics, Business, and Music.* Chicago: Regnery, 1971.

Hentschel, Volker. *Ludwig Erhard: Ein Politikerleben.* Munich: Olzog, 1996.

Herbert, Ulrich. *Hitler's Foreign Workers: Enforced Foreign Labor in Germany under the Third Reich.* Cambridge: Cambridge University Press, 1997.

Herbst, Ludolf. *Der Totale Krieg und die Ordnung der Wirtschaft.* Stuttgart: Deutsche Verlags-Anstalt, 1982.

Herf, Jeffrey. "Belated Pessimism: Technology and Twentieth-Century German Conservative Intellectuals." In *Technology, Pessimism, and Postmodernism.* Edited by Yaron Ezrahi, Everett Mendelsohn, and Howard Segal, 115–36. Amherst: University of Massachusetts Press, 1994.

———. *Divided Memory: The Nazi Past in the Two Germanys.* Cambridge: Harvard University Press, 1997.

Herman, Arthur. *The Idea of Decline in Western History.* New York: Free Press, 1997.

Hermand, Jost. *Kultur im Wiederaufbau: Die Bundesrepublik Deutschland, 1945–1965.* Munich: Nymphenburger, 1986.

Herzog, Bodo. *Paul Reusch und das Deutsche Museum in München: Zum 100. Geburtstag von Paul Reusch.* Munich: Oldenbourg, 1967.

Hetzer, Gerhard. "Unternehmer und leitende Angestellte zwischen Rüstungseinsatz und politischer Säuberung." In *Von Stalingrad zur Währungsreform: Zur Sozialgeschichte des Umbruchs in Deutschland.* Edited by Martin Broszat, Klaus-Dietmar Henke, and Hans Woller, 551–91. Munich: Oldenbourg, 1989.

Hoffmann, Hilmar. *The Triumph of Propaganda: Film and National Socialism, 1933–1945.* Providence: Berghahn, 1996.

Hoffmann, Peter. *The History of the German Resistance, 1933–1945.* London: Macdonald and Jane's, 1970.

Holdermann, Karl. *Im Banne der Chemie: Carl Bosch, Leben, und Werk.* Düsseldorf: Econ, 1953.

Homburg, Heidrun, *Rationalisierung und Industriearbeit: Arbeitsmarkt-Management-Arbeiterschaft in Siemens-Konzern Berlin, 1900–1939.* Berlin: Haude and Spener, 1991.

Horkheimer, Max, and Theodor Adorno. *Dialectic of Enlightenment.* New York: Continuum, 1999.

Horne, Alistair. *Return to Power: A Report on the New Germany.* New York: Praeger, 1956.

Houdremont, Eduard. *Handbuch der Sonderstahlkunde.* Berlin: Springer, 1943.

Huber, Ernst Rudolf. *Verfassungsrecht des Grossdeutschen Reiches.* Hamburg: Hanseatische Verlagsanstalt, 1939.

Hundhausen, Carl. *Werbung um öffentliches Vertrauen: "Public Relations."* Essen: W. Girardet, 1951.

Hunold, A., ed. *Wirtschaft ohne Wunder*. Erlenbach-Zurich: E. Rentsch, 1953.

Hutton, Patrick H. *History As an Art of Memory*. Hanover, N.H.: University Press of New England, 1993.

Huyssen, Andreas. *Twilight Memories: Marking Time in a Culture of Amnesia*. London: Routledge, 1995.

Irwin-Zarecka, Iwona. *Frames of Remembrance: The Dynamics of Collective Memory*. New Brunswick, N.J.: Transaction, 1994.

James, Harold. "The Deutsche Bank and the Dictatorship, 1933–1945." In *The Deutsche Bank, 1870–1995*. Edited by Lothar Gall, Gerald D. Feldman, Harold James, Carl-Ludwig Holtfrerich, and Hans E. Büschgen, 277–357. London: Weidenfeld & Nicholson, 1995.

——. *The German Slump: Politics and Economics, 1924–1936*. Oxford: Clarendon Press, 1986.

Jefferies, Matthew. *Politics and Culture in Wilhelmine Germany: The Case of Industrial Architecture*. Oxford: Berg, 1995.

Jones, Larry Eugene. "Carl Friedrich von Siemens and the Industrial Financing of Political Parties in the Weimar Republic." In *Von der Aufgabe der Freiheit: Politische Verantwortung und bürgerliche Gesellschaft im 19. und 20. Jahrhundert— Festschrift für Hans Mommsen zum 5. November 1995*. Edited by Christian Jansen, Hans Mommsen, Lutz Niethammer, and Bernd Weisbrod, 231–46. Berlin: Akademie, 1995.

Jung, Susanne. *Rechtsprobleme der Nürnberg Prozesse, dargestellt am Verfahren gegen Friedrich Flick*. Tübingen: J. C. B. Mohr, 1992.

Jünger, Ernst. *The Peace*. Hinsdale, Ill.: Regnery, 1948.

Jünger, Friedrich Georg. *The Failure of Technology: Perfection without Purpose*. Hinsdale, Ill.: Regnery, 1949.

Kannapin, Hans Eckhardt. *Wirtschaft unter Zwang*. Cologne: Deutsche Industrieverlagsgesellschaft, 1966.

Karrenbrock, Paul. *Die Lösung der Judenfrage in Deutschland zugleich eine wissenschaftliche Auseinandersetzung mit der Gedankenwelt des "Mythos."* Düsseldorf: privately printed, 1935.

Kater, Michael. "Heinrich Himmler's Circle of Friends, 1931–1945." *MARAB: A Review* 2 (winter 1965–66): 74–93.

Kershaw, Ian. *The Nazi Dictatorship: Problems and Perspectives of Interpretation*. 3d ed. London: Edward Arnold, 1993.

Kindleberger, Charles. "Toward the Marshall Plan." In *The Marshall Plan and Germany: West German Development within the Framework of the European Recovery Program*. Edited by Charles S. Maier, 71–114. New York: Berg, 1991.

Kirk, Russel. *The Conservative Mind: From Burke to Eliot*. Chicago: Regnery, 1953.

Kittel, Manfred. *Die Legende von der "Zweiten Schuld": Vergangenheitsbewältigung in der Ära Adenauer*. Berlin: Ullstein, 1993.

Klass, Gert von. *Albert Vögler*. Tübingen: Wunderlich, 1957.

——. *Die drei Ringe: Lebensgeschichte eines Industrieunternehmens*. Tübingen: Wunderlich, 1954.

———. *Die Wollspindel: Ein Schwäbisches Familienporträt*. Tübingen: Wunderlich, 1955.

Klee, Ernst. *Persilscheine und Falsche Pässe: Wie die Kirchen den Nazis halfen*. Frankfurt am Main: Fischer, 1991.

Knieriem, August von. *Nürnberg: Rechtliche und menschliche Probleme*. Stuttgart: Klett, 1953.

———. *The Nuremberg Trials*. Chicago: Regnery, 1959.

Kocka, Jürgen. *Unternehmensverwaltung und Angestelltenschaft am Beispiel Siemens, 1847-1914*. Stuttgart: Klett, 1969.

Koehne, Rainer. *Das Selbstbild deutscher Unternehmer, Legitimation und Leitbild einer Institution*. Berlin: Duncker and Homblot, 1976.

———. *Unternehmertum im Wandel: Wie sehen sich die Unternehmer, wie werden sie gesehen?: Herausforderungen an eine Institution*. Cologne: Walter-Raymond Stiftung, 1975.

Koshar, Rudy. *Germany's Transient Pasts: Preservation and National Memory in the Twentieth Century*. Chapel Hill: University of North Carolina Press, 1998.

Kramer, Alan. *The West German Economy: 1945-1955*. New York: St. Martin's Press, 1991.

Kranzbühler, Otto. *Rückblick auf Nürnberg*. Hamburg: Zeit-Verlag E. Schmidt, 1949.

Kreimeier, Klaus. *The Ufa Story: A History of Germany's Greatest Film Company, 1918-1945*. New York: Hill and Wang, 1996.

Krosigk, Graf Lutz Schwerin von. *Die Große Zeit des Feuers: Der Weg der deutschen Industrie*. Tübingen: Wunderlich, 1957.

Krumm, Heinrich. *Tagebuch eines deutschen Unternehmers, 1937-1947*. Frankfurt am Main: private printing, 1956.

Kuby, Erich. *Das Mädchen Rosemarie*. Hamburg: Konkret Literatur, 1985.

Kugler, Anita. "Vor der Werkstatt zum Fließband: Etappen der frühen Automobilproduktion in Deutschland." *Geschichte und Gesellschaft* 13, no. 3 (1987): 304-39.

Lademacher, Horst. "Zur Bedeutung des Petersberger Abkommens vom 22. November 1949." In *Die Britische Deutschland- und Besatzungspolitik, 1945-1949*. Edited by Josef Foschepoth and Rolf Steininger, 240-65. Paderborn: Schöningh, 1985.

La Mure, Pierre. *König der Nacht: Das Leben des John D. Rockefeller*. Hamburg: C. Wegner, 1954.

Langbein, Hermann. "Arbeit im KZ-System." In *Sklavenarbeit im KZ* (Dachauer Hefte 2), 3-12. Munich: DTV, 1993.

Large, David Clay. *Germans to the Front: West German Rearmament in the Adenauer Era*. Chapel Hill: University of North Carolina Press, 1995.

Le Goff, Jacques. *History and Memory*. New York: Columbia University Press, 1992.

Lehming, Eva-Maria. *Carl Hundhausen: Sein Leben, sein Werk, sein Lebenswerk; Public Relations in Deutschland*. Wiesbaden: Deutscher Universitäts-Verlag, 1997.

Lenk, Kurt, "Zum westdeutschen Konservatismus." In *Modernisierung im Wiederaufbau: Die westdeutsche Gesellschaft der 50er Jahre*. Edited by Axel Schildt and Arnold Sywottek, 636-45. Bonn: Dietz, 1993.

Lepsius, M. Rainer. *Interessen, Ideen, und Institutionen.* Opladen: Westdeutscher Verlag, 1990.

Link, Werner. *The Contribution of Trade Unions and Businessmen to German-American Relations, 1945-1975.* Bloomington, Ind.: Institute of German Studies, 1978.

Lochner, Louis P. *Always the Unexpected: A Book of Reminiscences.* New York: Macmillan, 1956.

———. *Henry Ford: America's Don Quixote.* New York: International Publishers, 1925.

———. *Herbert Hoover and Germany.* New York: Macmillan, 1960.

———. *Die Mächtigen und der Tyrann.* Darmstadt: Schneekluth, 1955. Translation of *Tycoons and Tyrant.*

———. *Tycoons and Tyrant: German Industry from Hitler to Adenauer.* Chicago: Regnery, 1954.

Ludwig, Johannes. *Boykott, Enteignung, Mord: Die "Enjudung" der deutschen Wirtschaft.* Munich: Piper, 1992.

Maier, Charles S. "Between Taylor and Technocracy: European Ideologies and the Vision of Industrial Productivity in the 1920s." *Journal of Contemporary History* 5, no. 2 (1970): 27-61.

———, ed. *The Marshall Plan and Germany: West German Development within the Framework of the European Recovery Program.* New York: Berg, 1991.

———. *The Unmasterable Past: History, Holocaust, and German National Identity.* Cambridge: Harvard University Press, 1988.

Manchester, William. *The Arms of Krupp.* Boston: Little Brown, 1968.

Marchand, Roland. *Creating the Corporate Soul: The Rise of Public Relations and Corporate Imagery in American Big Business.* Berkeley and Los Angeles: University of California Press, 1998.

Markovits, Andrei S. *The Politics of the West German Trade Unions: Strategies of Class and Interest Representation in Growth and Crisis.* Cambridge: Cambridge University Press, 1986.

Marshall, Barbara. "German Attitudes to British Military Government 1945-47." *Journal of Contemporary History* 15, no. 4 (1980): 655-81.

———. *The Origins of Post-War German Politics.* London: Croom Helm, 1988.

Martin, James Stuart. *All Honorable Men.* Boston: Little Brown, 1950.

Mason, Tim. "The Primacy of Politics: Politics and Economics in National Socialist Germany." In *Nazism and the Third Reich.* Edited by Henry A. Turner, 175-200. New York: Quadrangle, 1972.

Mathias, Peter. "Entrepreneurs, Managers, and Business Men in Eighteenth-Century Britain," In *Enterprise and Labor.* Edited by Peter Mathias and John A. Davis, 12-32. Oxford: Blackwell, 1996.

Matsuda, Matt K. *The Memory of the Modern.* Oxford: Oxford University Press, 1996.

Meinecke, Friedrich. *The German Catastrophe: Reflections and Recollections.* Cambridge: Harvard University Press, 1950.

Menne, Alexander. *Das Nürnberger Urteil gegen die IG Farbenindustrie: Eine Stellungnahme.* Frankfurt am Main: Arbeitsgemeinschaft Chemische Industrie des Vereinigten Wirtschaftsgebietes, 1948.

Merkle, Hans. *Reden bei der Festveranstaltung aus Anlass der Ernennung von Prof. Dr. h. c. Hans L. Merkle zum Ehrenburger der Universität Stuttgart, 4. Februar 1994.* Stuttgart: Universitätsbibliothek Stuttgart, 1994.

Merritt, Richard. *Democracy Imposed: U.S. Occupation Policy and the German Public, 1945-1949.* New Haven: Yale University Press, 1995.

Mitchell, Maria. "Materialism and Secularism: CDU Politicians and National Socialism, 1945-1955." *Journal of Modern History* 67 (June 1995): 278-308.

Mitscherlich, Alexander, and Margarete Mitscherlich. *Die Unfähigkeit zu trauern: Grundlagen kollektiven Verhaltens.* Munich: Piper, 1977.

Moeller, Robert G. *Protecting Motherhood: Women and the Family in the Politics of Postwar West Germany.* Berkeley and Los Angeles: University of California Press, 1992.

————. "War Stories: The Search for a Usable Past in the Federal Republic of Germany." *American Historical Review* 101, no. 4 (October 1996): 1008-48.

Mollin, Gerhard. *Monatkonzerne und "Drittes Reich": Der Gegensatz zwischen Monopolindustrie und Befehlswirtschaft in der deutschen Rüstung und Expansion, 1939-1944.* Göttingen: Vandenhoeck & Ruprecht, 1988.

Mommsen, Hans. *Das Volkswagenwerk und seine Arbeiter im Dritten Reich.* Düsseldorf: Econ, 1996.

Mooser, Josef. "Arbeiter, Angestellte, und Frauen in der 'nivellierte Mittelstandsgesellschaft.' Thesen." In *Modernisierung im Wiederaufbau: Die westdeutsche Gesellschaft der 50er Jahre.* Edited by Axel Schildt and Arnold Sywottek, 362-76. Bonn: Dietz, 1993.

————. *Arbeiterleben in Deutschland, 1900-1970: Klassenlagen, Kultur, und Politik.* Frankfurt am Main: Suhrkamp, 1984.

Morsey, Rudolf, and Hans-Peter Schwarz. *Adenauer: Briefe 1953-55.* Berlin: Siedler, 1995.

Mörtzsch, Friedrich. *Offenheit macht sich bezahlt: Die Kunst der Meinungspflege in der amerikanischen Industrie.* Düsseldorf: Econ, 1956.

Müller, Ingo. *Hitler's Justice: The Courts of the Third Reich.* Cambridge: Harvard University Press, 1991.

Muthesius, Volkmar. *Geld und Geist: Kulturhistorische und Wirtschaftspolitische Aufsätze.* Frankfurt am Main: F. Knapp, 1961.

————. *Moral des Geldes.* Frankfurt am Main: F. Knapp, 1956.

————. *Was wir der Marktwirtschaft verdanken.* Frankfurt am Main: F. Knapp, 1951.

Naasner, Walter. *Neue Machtzentren in der deutschen Kriegswirtschaft, 1942-1945: Die Wirtschaftsorganisation der SS, das Amt des generalbevollmächtigten für den Arbeitseinsatz und das Kreigsproduktion im nationalsozialistischen Herrschaftssystem.* Schriften des Bundesarchivs 45. Boppard am Rhein: Harald Boldt, 1994.

Naimark, Norman. *The Russians in Germany: A History of the Soviet Zone of Occupation, 1945-1949.* Cambridge: Harvard University Press, 1995.

Nationale Front des Demokratischen Deutschlands. *Brown Book: War and Nazi Criminals in West Germany.* East Berlin: Verlag Zeit im Bild, 1965.

Neebe, Reinhard. *Grossindustrie, Staat, und NSDAP, 1930-1933: Paul Silverberg und der Reichsverband der Deutschen Industrie.* Göttingen: Vandenhoeck & Ruprecht, 1981.

Negt, Oskar. "In Erwartung der autoritären Leistungsgesellschaft: Zum gesellschaftlichen Bewußtsein der wirtschaftlichen und militärischen Führungsschichten." In *Der CDU-Staat: Studien zur Verfassungswirklichkeit der Bundesrepublik*. Edited by Gert Schäfer and Carl Nedelmann, 200–37. Munich: Szczensy, 1967.

Neumann, Franz. *Behemoth: The Structure and Practice of National Socialism*. London: Gollancz, 1942.

Nicholls, A. J. *Freedom with Responsibility: The Social Market Economy in Germany, 1918-1963*. Oxford: Clarendon Press, 1994.

Nolan, Mary. *Visions of Modernity: American Business and the Modernization of Germany*. Oxford: Oxford University Press, 1994.

Nora, Pierre, ed. *Realms of Memory: The Construction of the French Past*. Vol. 1. New York: Columbia University Press, 1996.

Ogger, Günter. *Friedrich Flick der Grosse*. Berlin: Scherz, 1971.

Orlow, Dietrich. *The Nazis in the Balkans: A Case Study in Totalitarian Politics*. Pittsburgh: University of Pittsburgh Press, 1968.

Ortega y Gasset, José. *The Revolt of the Masses*. New York: Norton, 1930.

Overy, Richard. "State and Industry in Germany in the Twentieth Century." *German History* 12, no. 2 (1994): 180–89.

Pätzold, Kurt, and Manfred Weissbecker. *Geschichte der NSDAP, 1920-1945*. Cologne: Pahl-Rugenstein, 1981.

Pence, Katherine. "Labours of Consumption: Gendered Consumers in Post-War East and West German Reconstruction." In *Gender Relations in German History: Power, Agency, and Experience from the Sixteenth to the Twentieth Century*. Edited by Lynn Abrams and Elizabeth Harvey, 211–39. London: UCL Press, 1996.

Petzina, Dieter. *Autarkiepolitik im Dritten Reich: Der nationalsozialistische Vierjahresplan*. Stuttgart: Deutsche Verlags-Anstalt, 1968.

Pinto-Duschinsky, Michael. "Fund-Raising and the Holocaust: The Case of Dr. Gert-Rudolf Flick's Contribution to Oxford University." In *Integrity in the Public and Private Domains*. Edited by Alan Montefiore and David Vines, 211–49. London: Routledge, 1999.

Plato, Alexander von. "Lebenswelten und politische Orientierung im Revier: Zur Struktur politischen Bewußtseins bei Arbeitern und Unternehmern im Ruhrgebiet." In *Die Eisen- und Stahlindustrie im Dortmunder Raum: Wirtschaftliche Entwicklung, soziale Strukturen und technischer Wandel im 19. und 20. Jahrhundert*. Edited by Ottfried Dascher and Christian Kleinschmidt, 283–304. Dortmund: Stadtarchiv, 1992.

Plettner, Bernhard. *Abenteuer Elektro-Technik: Siemens und die Entwicklung der Elektrotechnik seit 1945*. Munich: Piper, 1994.

Plumpe, Werner. "Unternehmerverbände und industrielle Interessenpolitik." In *Das Ruhrgebiet im Industriezeitalter*, vol. 1. Edited by Wolfgang Köllmann et al., 655–727. Düsseldorf: Schwann im Patmos, 1990.

Poiger, Uta G. *Jazz, Rock, and Rebels: Cold War Politics and American Culture in a Divided Germany*. Berkeley and Los Angeles: University of California Press, 2000.

Pommerin, Reiner, ed. *Culture in the Federal Republic of Germany, 1945-1995*. Oxford: Berg, 1996.

Pool, James, and Suzanne Pool. *Who Financed Hitler?* New York: Dial Press, 1978.

Pounds, Norman. *The Ruhr: A Study in Historical and Economic Geography*. London: Faber and Faber, 1952.

Prince Louis Ferdinand of Prussia. *The Rebel Prince*. Chicago: Regnery, 1952.

Pritzkoleit, Kurt. *Wem gehört Deutschland? Ein Chronik von Besitz und Macht*. Vienna: Kurt Desch, 1957.

Prowe, Diethelm. "Economic Democracy in Post–World War II Germany: Corporatist Crisis Response, 1945-1948." *Journal of Modern History* 57 (September 1985): 463-70.

———. "Foundations of West German Democracy; Corporatist Patterns." In *Coping with the Past: Germany and Austria after 1945*. Edited by Kathy Harms, Lutz-Reiner Reuter, and Volker Duerr, 105-30. Madison: University of Wisconsin Press, 1990.

Rabinbach, Anson. *The Human Motor: Energy, Fatigue, and the Origins of Modernity*. New York: Basic Books, 1990.

Rahner, Karl. "Der Unternehmer und die Religion." In *Vorträge anläßlich der Internationalen Herbsttagung des Wirtschaftsring e.V. Bonn* (Munich, 26-27 October 1962), 26-42. Aachen: Heinrich Kutsch, 1962.

Redlich, Fritz. *Der Unternehmer: Wirtschafts- und sozialgeschichtliche Studien*. Göttingen: Vandenhoeck & Ruprecht, 1964.

Regnery, Henry. *Memoirs of a Dissident Publisher*. Chicago: Regnery, 1985.

Reich, Simon. *The Fruits of Fascism: Postwar Prosperity in Historical Perspective*. Ithaca: Cornell University Press, 1990.

Reiner, Ludwig. *Wir alle können besser leben*. Munich: Verlag Wilhelm Steinberg, 1953.

Ritter, Gerhard. *The Corrupting Influence of Power*. Oxford: Cowley, 1952.

Robin, Ron. *The Barbed-Wire College: Reeducating German POWs in the United States during World War II*. Princeton: Princeton University Press, 1995.

Rohland, Walter. *Bewegte Zeiten: Erinnerungen eines Eisenhüttenmannes*. Stuttgart: Seewald, 1978.

Roper, Elmo. "The Public Looks at Big Business." *Harvard Business Review* 27, no. 2 (March 1949): 165-74.

Röpke, Wilhelm. *Economics of the Free Society*. Chicago: Regnery, 1963.

———. *Die Gesellschaftskrise der Gegenwart*. Erlenbach-Zurich: E. Rentsch, 1942.

———. *A Humane Economy: The Social Framework of the Free Market*. Chicago: Regnery, 1960.

Roseman, Mark. *Recasting the Ruhr, 1945-1958: Manpower, Economic Recovery, and Labour Relations*. Providence: Berg, 1992.

Rosenfeld, Gavriel. *Munich and Memory: Architecture, Monuments, and the Legacy of the Third Reich*. Berkeley and Los Angeles: University of California Press, 2000.

Rossiter, Clinton. *Conservatism in America: The Thankless Persuasion*. New York: Vintage, 1962.

Roth, Michael. *The Ironist's Cage: Memory, Trauma, and the Construction of History*. New York: Columbia University Press, 1995.

Rothfels, Hans. *The German Opposition to Hitler*. Hinsdale, Ill.: Regnery, 1948.

Rühl, Manfred. *Public Relations der Gewerkschaften und Wirtschaftsverbände.* Düsseldorf: Verlag für deutsche Wirtschaftsbiographie, 1981.

Sachse, Carola. *Siemens, der Nationalsozialismus und die moderne Familie: Eine Untersuchung zur sozialen Rationalisierung in Deutschland im 20. Jahrhundert.* Hamburg: Rasch & Röhring, 1990.

———. "Zwangsarbeit jüdischer und nichtjüdischer Frauen und Männer bei der Firma Siemens 1940 bis 1945." *Internationale wissenschaftliche Korrespondenz zur Geschichte der deutschen Arbeiterbewegung* 27 (1991): 1–12.

Saint-Simon, Claude-Henri de. "Letter to the Industrialists." In *The Political Thought of Saint-Simon.* Edited by Ghita Ionescu, 162–63. Oxford: Oxford University Press, 1976.

Schäfer, Hans-Dieter. *Das gespaltene Bewusstsein: Über deutsche Kultur und Lebenswirklichkeit, 1933–1945.* Munich: Carl Hanser, 1982.

Scharf, Claus, and Hans-Jürgen Schröder, eds. *Die Deutschlandpolitik Grossbritanniens und die Britische Zone, 1945–1949.* Wiesbaden: Steiner, 1979.

Schelsky, Helmut. "Die 'nivellierte Mittelstandsgesellschaft.'" 1953. Excerpted in *50 Jahre Bundesrepublik Deutschland: Daten und Diskussionen.* Edited by Eckart Conze and Gabriele Metzler, 190–93. Stuttgart: Deutsche Verlags-Anstalt, 1999.

Schildt, Axel. "Ende der Ideologien? Politisch-ideologische Strömungen in den 50er Jahren." In *Modernisierung im Wiederaufbau: Die westdeutsche Gesellschaft der 50er Jahre.* Edited by Axel Schildt and Arnold Sywottek, 627–35. Bonn: Dietz, 1993.

———. *Konservatismus in Deutschland: Von den Anfängen im 18. Jahrhundert bis zur Gegenwart.* Munich: Beck, 1998.

———. *Moderne Zeiten: Freizeit, Massenmedien, und "Zeitgeist" in der Bundesrepublik der 50er Jahre.* Hamburg: Christians, 1995.

———. *Zwischen Abendland und Amerika: Studien zur Westdeutschen Ideenlandschaft der 50er Jahre.* Munich: Oldenbourg, 1999.

Schindelbeck, Dirk, and Volker Ilgen. *"Haste Was, Biste Was!": Werbung für die Soziale Marktwirtschaft.* Darmstadt: Primus, 1999.

Schlabrendorff, Fabian von. *Eugen Gerstenmaier im Dritten Reich: Eine Dokumentation.* Stuttgart: Evangelisches Verlagswerk, 1965.

Schlenzka, Peter A. *Unternehmer, Direktoren, Manager: Krise der Betriebsführung?* Düsseldorf: Econ, 1954.

Schleussner, C. A., ed. *Fibel der sozialen Marktwirtschaft: Zur Orientierung für Unternehmer und Unternehmensleiter.* Düsseldorf: Econ, 1953.

Schmidt, Klaus-Dieter. *Soziale Gerechtigkeit durch unternehmerische Initiative: Der Bund Katholischer Unternehmer, 1949–1990.* Paderborn: Schöningh, 1994.

Schuker, Stephen A. "Ambivalent Exile: Heinrich Brüning and America's Good War." In *Zerrissene Zwischenkriegszeit, Wirtschaftshistorische Beiträge: Knut Borchardt zum 65. Geburtstag.* Edited by Christoph Buchheim, Knut Borchardt, Michael Hutter, and Harold James, 329–56. Baden Baden: Nomos, 1994.

Schulte, Jan Erik. "Rüstungsunternehmen oder Handwerksbetrieb? Das KZ-Häftlinge ausbeutende SS-Unternehmen 'Deutsche Ausrüstungswerke GmbH.'" In *Die nationalsozialistischen Konzentrationslager.* Edited by Ulrich Herbert, Karin

Orth, and Christoph Dieckmann. Vol. 2, *Entwicklung und Struktur*, 558–83. Göttingen: Wallstein, 1998.

Schulz, Eberhard. *Das goldene Dach*. Munich: Steinebach, 1952.

Schulze, Rainer. "Representation of Interests and Recruitment of Elites: The Role of the *Industrie- und Handelskammern* in German Politics after the End of the Second World War." *German History* 7, no. 1 (1989): 71–91.

———. "Unternehmerische Interessenvertretung in Westdeutschland nach dem Ende des zweiten Weltkrieges." *Tel Aviver Jahrbuch für deutsche Geschichte* 19 (1990): 283–311.

Schulze, Winfried. *Der Stifterverband fur die deutsche Wissenschaft, 1920-1995*. Berlin: Akademie, 1995.

Schumpeter, Joseph A. *Essays: On Entrepreneurs, Innovations, Business Cycles, and the Evolution of Capitalism*. New Brunswick, N.J: Transaction, 1951.

———. *Kapitalismus, Sozialismus, und Demokratie*. Munich: Francke, 1980.

Schwartz, Thomas. *America's Germany: John McCloy and the Federal Republic of Germany*. Cambridge: Harvard University Press, 1991.

———. "John J. McCloy and the Landsberg Cases." In *American Policy and the Reconstruction of West Germany, 1945-1955*. Edited by Jeffry M. Diefendorf, Axel Frohn, and Hermann-Josef Rupieper, 433–54. Cambridge: Cambridge University Press, 1993.

Schwarz, Hans-Peter. *Konrad Adenauer: A German Politician and Statesman in a Period of War, Revolution, and Reconstruction*. Vol 1. Providence: Berghahn, 1995.

———. "Modernisierung oder Restauration? Einige Vorfragen zur künftigen Sozialgeschichtsforschung über die Ära Adenauer." In *Rheinland-Westfalen im Industriezeitalter*. Edited by Kurt Düwell and Wolfgang Köllmann, 278–93. Wuppertal: Peter Hammer, 1982.

Schweitzer, Arthur. *Big Business in the Third Reich*. Bloomington: Indiana University Press, 1964.

Seherr-Thoss, Hans Christoph. ed. *Zwei Männer—Ein Stein: Gottlieb Daimler und Karl Benz in Bildern, Daten, und Dokumenten*. Düsseldorf: VDI Verlag, 1950.

Selle, Gerd. "Das Produktdesign der 50er Jahre: Rückgriff in die Entwurfsgeschichte, vollendete Modernisierung des Alltagsinventars oder Vorbote der Postmoderne?" In *Modernisierung im Wiederaufbau: Die westdeutsche Gesellschaft der 50er Jahre*. Edited by Axel Schildt and Arnold Sywottek, 612–24. Bonn: Dietz, 1993.

Siegel, Tilla. "Die Doppelte Rationalisierung des 'Ausländereinsatzes' bei Siemens." *Internationale wissenschaftliche Korrespondenz zur Geschichte der deutschen Arbeiterbewegung* 27 (1991): 12–24.

Siegel, Tilla, and Thomas von Freyberg. *Industrielle Rationalisierung unter dem Nationalsozialismus*. Frankfurt am Main and New York: Campus, 1991.

Siegrist, Hannes. "Ende der Bürgerlichkeit? Die Kategorien 'Bürgertum' und 'Bürgerlichkeit' in der westdeutschen Gesellschaft und Geschichtswissenschaft der Nachkriegsperiode." *Geschichte und Gesellschaft* 20 (1994): 548–83.

Siemens, Georg. *History of the House of Siemens*. Vol. 2, *The Era of World Wars*. Freiburg: Karl Alber, 1957.

Siemens, Werner von. *Lebenserinnerungen*. Munich: Prestel, 1966.

Silberschmidt, Max. *Die Bedeutung des Unternehmers in weltgeschichtlicher Sicht*. Zürich: Arbeitgeberverband schweizerischer Maschinen- und Metall-Industrielle, 1956.

Simpson, Christopher. *The Splendid Blond Beast: Money, Law, and Genocide in the Twentieth Century*. New York: Grove Press, 1993.

Sklavenarbeit im KZ (Dachauer Hefte 2). Munich: DTV, 1993.

Smith, Arthur L. *The War for the German Mind: Re-educating Hitler's Soldiers*. Providence: Berghahn, 1996.

Sohl, Hans-Günther. *Notizen:* private printing, 1983.

Solomon, Ernst von. *The Questionaire*. Garden City, N.J.: Doubleday, 1955.

Speer, Albert. *Infiltration*. New York: Macmillan, 1981.

———. *Inside the Third Reich*. New York: Macmillan, 1970.

Stachura, Peter D. *Gregor Strasser and the Rise of Hitler*. London: Allen & Unwin, 1983.

Stallbaumer, Lisa M. "Strictly Business? The Flick Concern and 'Aryanizations': Corporate Expansion in the Nazi Era." Ph.D. diss., University of Wisconsin, 1995.

Stein, Gustav. "Kultur-Fundament der Wirtschaft." *Der Volkswirt* 8 (1954): 70–73.

———. "Unternehmer nach 1945: Verpflichtung und Aufgabe." In *5 Jahre BDI: Aufbau und Arbeitsziele des industriellen Spitzenverbandes*. Edited by BDI. Bergisch Gladbach: Hieder-Verlag, 1954.

———. *Unternehmer als Förderer der Kunst*. Bonn: Lutzeyer, 1952.

Stein, Gustav, and Herbert Gross, eds. *Unternehmer in der Politik*. Düsseldorf: Econ, 1954.

Stern, Fritz. *The Politics of Cultural Despair: A Study in the Rise of the Germanic Ideology*. Berkeley and Los Angeles: University of California Press, 1961.

Stokes, Raymond. *Divide and Prosper: The Heirs of I. G. Farben under Allied Authority, 1945–1951*. Berkeley and Los Angeles: University of California Press, 1988.

Strolin, Karl. *Verräter oder Patrioten? Der 20. Juli 1944 und das Recht auf Widerstand* Stuttgart: Vorwerk, 1952.

Struve, Walter. *Elites against Democracy: Leadership Ideals in Bourgeois Political thought in Germany, 1890–1933*. Princeton: Princeton University Press, 1973.

Taylor, Telford. *The Anatomy of the Nuremberg Trials: A Personal Memoir*. New York: Knopf, 1992.

———. "The Krupp Trial: Fact vs. Fiction." *Columbia Law Review* 53 (February 1953): 197–210.

———. *Nuremberg Trials: War Crimes and International Law*. International Conciliation, no. 450. New York, Carnegie Endowment for International Peace, 1949. Pp. 241–371.

———. *Sword and Swastika: Generals and Nazis in the Third Reich*. New York: Simon & Schuster, 1952.

Tetens, T. H. *The New Germany and the Old Nazis*. New York: Random House, 1961.

Thum, Horst. *Wirtschaftsdemokratie und Mitbestimmung von den Anfängen 1916 bis zum Mitbestimmungsgesetz 1976*. Cologne: Bund Verlag, 1991.

Tolliday, Steven. "Enterprise and State in the West German Wirtschaftswunder: Volkswagen and the Automobile Industry, 1939–62." *Business History Review* 69 (autumn 1995): 273–350.

Tornow, Ingo. "Die deutschen Unternehmerverbände, 1945–50: Kontinuität oder Diskontinuität." In *Vorgeschichte der Bundesrepublik Deutschland.* Edited by Josef Becker, Theo Stammen, and Peter Waldmann, 241–67. Munich: Fink, 1987.

Treue, Wilhelm. "Widerstand von Unternehmern und Nationalökonomen." In *Der Widerstand Gegen den National-Sozialismus.* Edited by Jürgen Schmädke and Peter Steinbach, 917–38. Munich: Piper, 1986.

Treue, Wilhelm, and Helmut Uebbing. *Die Feuer verlöschen nie: August Thyssen-Hütte, 1926–1966.* Düsseldorf: Econ, 1969.

Trials of War Criminals before the Nürnberg Military Tribunals. Vol. 6, *The U.S. versus Flick;* vols. 7 and 8, *The U.S. versus Krauch* (the I. G. Farben case); and vol. 9, *The U.S. versus Krupp.* Washington, D.C.: U.S. Government Printing Office, 1950–53.

Turner, Henry A. "Fritz Thyssen und 'I Paid Hitler.' " *Vierteljahrshefte für Zeitgeschichte* 19, no. 3 (July 1971): 225–44.

———. *German Big Business and the Rise of Hitler.* Oxford: Oxford University Press, 1985.

Turner, Ian. "British Policy toward German Industry, 1945–9: Reconstruction, Restriction, or Exploitation?" In *British Occupation Policy and the Western Zones, 1945–1955.* Edited by Ian Turner, 67–92. Oxford: Berg, 1989.

———, ed. *British Occupation Policy and the Western Zones, 1945–1955.* Oxford: Berg, 1989.

Ullmann, Hans-Peter. *Interessenverbände in Deutschland.* Frankfurt am Main: Suhrkamp, 1988.

Der Unternehmer im Wandel der Zeiten: Teilnehmertreffen der Baden-Bädener Unternehmergespräche am 29 September 1984 in Baden-Baden (Symposium zum Dreissigjährigen Bestehen der Bad-Bädener Unternehmergespräche). Frankfurt am Main: F. Knapp, 1985.

Utley, Freda. *The High Cost of Vengeance.* Chicago: Regnery, 1949.

Vaubel, Ludwig. *Unternehmer gehen zur Schule: Ein Erfahrungsbericht aus USA.* Düsseldorf: Droste, 1952.

———. *Zusammenbruch und Wiederaufbau: Ein Tagebuch aus der Wirtschaft, 1945–1949.* Munich: Oldenbourg, 1985.

Vogelsang, Reinhard. *Der Freundeskreis Himmler.* Göttingen: Musterschmidt, 1972.

Vollrath, Ernst. "Perspectives of Political Thought in Germany after 1945." In *Culture in the Federal Republic of Germany, 1945–1995.* Edited by Reiner Pommerin, 37–58. Oxford: Berg, 1996.

Wagenfuhr, Horst. *Schöpferische Wirtschaft: Pionier-Leistungen deutscher Erfinder und Unternehmer.* Heidelberg: Werkschriften Verlag, 1954.

Warner, Isabel. *Steel and Sovereignty: The Deconcentration of the West German Steel Industry, 1949–54.* Mainz: P. von Zabern, 1996.

Wege der Wirtschaftspublizistik: Festgabe für Dr. Fritz Pudor zur Vollendung seines 60. Lebensjahres. Essen: West-Verlag, 1959.

Weisbrod, Bernd. *Schwerindustrie in der Weimarer Republik: Interessenpolitik zwischen Stabilisierung und Krise.* Wuppertal: P. Hammer, 1978.

Wember, Heiner. *Umerziehung im Lager: Internierung und Bestrafung von Nationalsozialisten in der britischen Besatzungszone Deutschlands.* Essen: Klartext, 1992.

Wessel, Horst A. *Kontinuität im Wandel: 100 Jahre Mannesmann, 1890-1990.* Düsseldorf: Mannesmann, 1990.

———. "Die Überlieferung von Filmquellen in Archiven von Unternehmen, Kammern, und Verbänden der Wirtschaft." In *Film schätzen auf der Spur: Verzeichnis historischer Filmbestände in Nordrhein-Westfalen.* Edited by Paul Hofmann, 143-47. Düsseldorf: Nordrhein-Westfälisches Hauptstaatsarchiv, 1994.

Wheeler-Bennett, John. *The Nemesis of Power: The German Army in Politics, 1918-1945.* London: Macmillan, 1953.

Wiesen, S. Jonathan. "Coming to Terms with the Worker: West German Industry, Labour Relations, and the Idea of America, 1949-1960." *Journal of Contemporary History* 13, no. 4 (2001).

———. "Overcoming Nazism: Big Business, Public Relations, and the Politics of Memory, 1945-50." *Central European History* 29 (1996): 201-26.

Wildt, Michael. "Privater Konsum in Westdeutschland in den 50er Jahren." In *Modernisierung im Wiederaufbau: Die westdeutsche Gesellschaft der 50er Jahre.* Edited by Axel Schildt and Arnold Sywottek, 275-89. Bonn: Dietz, 1993.

Williams, Ernest. *Made in Germany.* London: W. Heineman, 1896.

Willis, F. Roy. *The French in Germany, 1945-1949.* Stanford: Stanford University Press, 1962.

Wilmowsky, Tilo Frhr von. *Rückblickend möchte ich sagen.* Oldenbourg: G. Stalling, 1961.

———. *Warum wurde Krupp verurteilt? Legende und Justizirrtum.* Frankfurt am Main: Vorwerk, 1950.

Winschuh, Josef. *Männer, Traditionen, Signale.* Berlin: F. Osmer, 1940.

———. *Das neue Unternehmerbild: Grundzüge einer Unternehmerpolitik.* Baden-Baden: Lutzeyer, 1954.

———. *Der Unternehmer im neuen Europa.* Berlin: Buchholz & Weisswange, 1941.

———. "Young Businessmen and Germany's Future." *Harvard Business Review* 29, no. 3 (May 1951): 35-42.

Wirtschaftspolitische Gesellschaft von 1947. *Deutsche Initiative: Wortlaut der Referate gehalten auf der Kundgebung der Wirtschaftspolitischen Gesellschaft von 1947 am 19. und 20. Oktober 1950 in Frankfurt a.M.* Heidelberg-Ziegelhausen: Vita-Verlag, 1951.

Wojak, Irmtrud, and Peter Hayes, *"Arisierung" im Nationalsozialismus: Volksgemeinschaft, Raub, und Gedächtnis.* Jahrbuch 2000 zur Geschichte und Wirkung des Holocaust. Frankfurt am Main and New York: Campus, 2000.

Wolmar, W. von. *Als Verteidiger in Nürnberg: Otto Kranzbühler und die Nürnberger Prozesse.* Hamburg: Staats- und Wirtschaftspolitische Gesellschaft, e.V., 1982.

Zangen, Wilhelm. *Aus Meinem Leben.* Düsseldorf: private printing, 1968.

Zippe, Herbert. *Große Unternehmer: Lebensbilder aus fünf Jahrhunderten.* Thansau-Rosenheim: H. Riedler, 1954.

Zur Frage der Demontagen in der Eisenindustrie. Duisburg: "Überreicht durch VSt," 1948.

Index

Socialism, 120; and West German mentalities, 126–27, 157, 171–72, 233–34; and workers' family life, 163, 197; and resistance to Hitler, 229, 233. *See also* Industrialists: self-understanding as elites; Masses; Totalitarianism; *Unternehmer*

Burnham, James, 137, 233. *See also* Managers

Buscher, Frank, 82

Business. *See* Industry

Businessmen. *See* Independent businessmen; Industrialists; Industry; *Unternehmer*

Capitalism: reputation of, 3, 7, 95, 128, 156, 157, 173, 176, 237; publicity on behalf of, 10, 101, 198–99; Marxist/East German view of, 11–12, 48, 102, 173; relationship to fascism and Nazism, 11–12, 49, 118; survival of during Nazi years, 13; ideological debates over, 26, 27, 41–44; American critiques of, 101; folklore of, 134, 156, 194, 236. *See also* Anticommunism; Economic Miracle; Industry; Public relations; United States; *Unternehmer*

Carnegie, Andrew, 134

Carnegie Foundation, 158

Carp, Werner, 53

Catholic Church: economic and social views, 26, 123–24, 164; and support of industry during Nuremberg trials, 82; and support of Fritz Thyssen, 83; and support of industrial organizations, 123. *See also* Bund Katholischer Unternehmer; Christian Democratic Union

Central Federation of German Handcrafts, 274 (n. 76)

Chamberlin, William Henry, 220

Chambers of Industry and Commerce. *See* Industrie- und Handelskammer (IHK)

Christian Democratic Union (CDU), 26, 45, 101, 109, 121, 181, 238; and Allied industrial policies, 61, 67, 87, 91, 149. *See also* Adenauer, Konrad

Christian socialism, 123, 129. *See also* Catholic Church

Chrysler, Walter, 134

Churchill, Winston, 41, 62, 258 (n. 46)

Claims Conference, 25, 29, 241

Clay, Lucius, 89, 91, 97, 203–4

Codetermination: introduction of in British zone (1947), 58, 65, 67, 91, 180; workers' and Left's support of, 88, 180–88, 240; introduction of in West Germany (1950–51), 110, 111, 116, 200; industry's hostility toward, 164, 180–88, 213, 240; definition of, 180. *See also* Labor unions; Reusch, Hermann; Vogel, Otto

Codetermination Act (1951), 180, 186

Cold War, 2, 48, 64, 242; and legacy of industrial guilt, 11, 12, 52, 187, 232–33; and Allied industrial policies, 65, 69, 214; industry's views of, 92; and free enterprise, 144, 237; and consumer culture, 145; and culture, 160; rhetoric of, 184; and amnesty of industrialists, 203, 214. *See also* Anticommunism; *Bürgertum;* Masses; Totalitarianism

Collectivism. *See* Anticommunism; Totalitarianism

Committee for the Support of Steel Production, 86

Communism: ideological critique of industry in, 87; and art, 160; and industry's relationship to National Socialism, 181, 185. *See also* Anticommunism; Communist Party of Germany

Communist Party of Germany (KPD), 25, 27, 45, 238

Comte, Auguste, 174

Conference on Jewish Material Claims against Germany. *See* Claims Conference

Conservatism/conservatives: industrialists as, 8, 133, 168, 169, 173, 175, 201–2, 238; in the FRG, 26, 121, 123, 160, 173, 175, 177, 195; and pro-German public relations in United States, 65, 123, 137, 215–29 passim; in Weimar and Nazi Germany, 84–85, 112, 151; and fears of mass consumption and mass culture, 126, 130, 141; and relationship to capitalism, 156, 173–74, 194; and culture,

Eastland, Robert, 284 (n. 31)
Economic Miracle (*Wirtschaftswunder*), 25, 94, 124, 161; as national myth, 4, 176, 194–95, 238
Edison, Thomas, 134
Einaudi, Luigi, 132
Entrepreneurs. *See* Independent businessmen; Industrialists; Industry; *Unternehmer*
Erdmann, Gerhard, 111
Erhard, Ludwig, 94, 123, 147, 148, 150, 182, 225, 274 (n. 76); and social market economy, 131, 133
Ernst Poensgen Stiftung, 158
Europe: ideal of, 60, 109, 170–71. *See also* West, the
European Coal and Steel Community (Schuman Plan), 42, 202, 209, 210, 212, 218, 229
European Recovery Plan. *See* Marshall Plan
Expressionism, 159

Factories: bomb damage to, 17; hierarchies in, 138, 183, 191, 192, 197–98, 238; artistic depictions of, 140, 159, 165–66, 277 (n. 28); ideas about during Weimar and Nazi years, 190–91; industry's celebration of, 191, 193, 195–97; and family life, 197. *See also* DINTA; Hauser, Heinrich; Human relations
Factory community (*Betriebsgemeinschaft*), 25, 190
Family: and anticommunism, 121, 123; as embodiment of conservative and Western values, 123, 197–99, 230, 238. See also *Bürgertum;* Home; Industry: and German youth; Winschuh, Josef; Workers
Family business, 111; as romanticized image, 118, 122, 126, 134, 236. *See also* Arbeitsgemeinschaft selbständiger Unternehmer; Independent businessmen; *Unternehmer*
Federal Republic of Germany (FRG), 4; economic recovery of, 3, 94, 125, 160, 237–38; former Nazis active in, 11, 106, 107, 152, 206, 283 (n. 24), 287 (n. 125); founding of, 94, 101; ideological divisions in, 129, 160; competition with GDR, 145
Federation of American Citizens of German Descent, 207
Federation of German Industry. *See* Bundesverband der Deutschen Industrie
Fehrenbach, Heide, 163
Feininger, Lyonel, 148
Feldenkirchen, Wilfried, 23
Fenster, Das (magazine), 193–94
Ficker, Hans, 224
Films: about companies, 10, 138–42, 265 (n. 18). *See also* Industrialists: movies about
Fischer-Tropsch Works, 66
Flick, Friedrich, 137, 150, 155, 242, 260 (n. 84), 272 (n. 37); Nuremberg trial of, 69, 71, 72, 74, 80, 96, 97; industrial holdings and wealth of, 152, 202, 241; interviewed for biography of Vögler, 152–53; imprisonment and release of, 202, 215, 219; and *Tycoons and Tyrant*, 219, 287 (n. 113); verdict against, 261 (n. 97)
Flick (company): Nuremberg trial of, 68, 69, 74, 82; rebuilding of in 1950s, 202, 241; imprisonment and release of directors of, 213
Flossenbürg, 25
Forberg, Kurt, 172
Forced labor: compensation for survivors of, 1–2, 241, 242; and industry's self-conception, 8; industry's use of during World War II, 14–15, 22–51 passim; automobile firms' use of, 16, 224; industry's justifications regarding, 22–51 passim, 207, 208, 214; as criminal charge in Nuremberg trials, 69, 97, 205; euphemisms for, 244; definition of, 246 (n. 2). *See also* Claims Conference; Siemens: and forced labor; Siemens: and Jews
Ford, Henry, 117–18, 134, 194, 221, 271 (n. 27)
Fordism, 159, 190, 271 (n. 27). *See also* Ford, Henry; Mass production
Fort Reno (POW camp), 109
Fortune, 102, 108

194; movies about, 139–42; conservative views of, 169, 201–2; portrayed as Nazis, 185–86, 240, 256 (n. 8); as ethical figures, 233–34, 237; self-perceptions of, 236–38; and Nazi espionage, 255 (n. 120)

Industrial organizations, 55, 99, 101–13 passim, 132, 147. *See also* Arbeitsgemeinschaft selbständiger *Unternehmer;* Bundesverband der Deutschen Industrie; Bundesvereinigung deutscher Arbeitgeberverbände; Bund Katholischer Unternehmer

Industrie- und Handelskammer Essen (IHK), 55, 62, 97, 113, 131, 134, 167, 196, 198, 211, 223

Industry: reputation of, 3, 7, 94, 206; definitions of, 7, 247 (n. 18); as milieu, 8, 202; and German youth, 10, 121–22, 140, 151–52, 194, 196; during National Socialism, 11–16, 215, 227; ethical responsibilities of, 35, 81, 111, 115, 116, 123–28, 227, 237; *Geist* (spirit) of, 37, 50; Allied policies toward, 41–44, 53, 54, 55, 60, 64, 86–92, 209, 212; leadership changes in, 54, 107–10, 122, 241, 272 (n. 37); Allied suspicions of former Nazis in, 54, 215, 285 (n. 57); commissioned books about, 73–81, 150–56, 288 (n. 146); and ideas about politics, 77–79, 84–85, 86, 103, 116, 127, 226; and religion, 81, 121–25, 262 (n. 114); political power of, 104–6, 180, 241; social responsibilities of, 111–13; and ideas about profit, 116, 123–24, 127, 137, 138–39, 160, 178, 189, 194, 198, 237; generational changes in, 135–38, 240; and nostalgia, 137–38, 187, 236; boycotts of, 142; and philanthropy, 157–59, 166–70, 176–78, 241–42; cultural ideas and activities of, 157–78 passim; and Germany's spiritual condition, 160–62, 169; and freedom, 164, and modernization, 172, 175, 187; and workers, 193–97; and ideas about wealth, 194, 237; and portrayal of behavior during Nazi years, 207, 224; pragmatism of, 227; after 1955, 241–44; war criminals active in, 282 (n. 3). *See also* Capital-ism; Hitler, Adolf; Industry; National Socialism; *Unternehmer*

Industry Office, 70, 71, 72, 223, 260 (n. 77). *See also* Nuremberg trials: and public relations

Institute for Juridical Studies (Heidelberg University), 70

Institut für Demoskopie (Allensbach Institut), 109–10, 130, 131, 132, 177

Institut für Weltwirtschaft und Seeverkehr, 108

Iron and Steel Exhibition, 165–66, 169. *See also* Culture; Factories

Iron Industry Group, 224

Jaenecke, Walter, 177

Jannings, Emil, 138

Jarres, Karl, 261 (n. 94)

Jessen, Fritz, 21, 28, 29, 30, 33, 47, 48, 255 (n. 120)

Jews: industry's treatment of during Third Reich, 11–15, 22–23; industrialists' help with emigration of, 14, 206, 228; legacy of persecution of, 22–51 passim, 243; postwar testimonies by, 38, 85; portrayed as capitalists, 173. *See also* Anti-Semitism; Aryanization; Claims Conference; Forced labor; National Socialism; Siemens: and Jews

John, Otto, 228, 287 (n. 125)

Joint Chiefs of Staff Policy Directive (JCS 1067), 43, 44, 55, 60

Jünger, Ernst, 112, 217

Jünger, Friedrich Georg, 217

Junkers, 174

Kant, Immanuel, 178

Karrenbrock, Paul, 262 (n. 123)

Kastl, Ludwig, 224, 261 (n. 94)

Kellermann, Hermann, 54

Khrushchev, Nikita, 176

Kirdorf, Emil, 87; support of Hitler, 12, 82, 83, 158, 225; and cultural patronage, 158

Kirk, Russell, 217

Klass, Gert von, 134, 152, 154–55. *See also* Vögler, Albert

Klee, Ernst, 82

Klee, Paul, 148

Klein, Julius, 296 (n. 15)

threat to bourgeois, Western values, 115, 187; as threat to the *Unternehmer*, 120; in United States, 142–43; and Germany's spiritual renewal, 160–64; and ideas of decline, 170–72. *See also* Culture; Industry
Mass production, 159, 161–62; industry's ambivalence about, 142–44, 162–63. *See also* Advertising; Marketing
Meinecke, Friedrich, 165
Mejer, Otto, 267 (n. 50)
Memory: theories of, 2, 4, 5, 6, 244; collective, 2, 234, 242, 244; selective, 118–19, 165, 179, 234, 243–44. *See also* Industry; National Socialism
Menne, Alexander, 182
Messerschmitt, Willy, 28
Metal Workers' Union, 89
Milch, Erhard, 33
Mitscherlich, Alexander, 5
Mitscherlich, Margarete, 5
Mitscherlich Thesis, 5
Mohler, Armin, 220
Moral Rearmament Movement, 123, 229
Mörder sind unter uns, Die (The Murderers Are among Us) (film), 139
Morgenthau, Henry, 43, 61, 207
Morgenthau Plan, 207, 229
Müller-Armack, Alfred, 123, 177
Museum of Science and Industry (New York), 144
Muthesius, Volkmar, 135–36, 150, 177, 194, 274–75 (n. 89), 267 (n. 54)

Nachrichten für Außenhandel (publication), 108
Nagel, Heinz, 70, 71, 74, 75, 223, 224
National Association of Manufacturers, 102
National Council for Prevention of War, 65
National Socialism: legacy of in West Germany, 6, 9, 52, 175, 186, 187, 201, 233–34, 237; industrial behavior under, 11–14; and persistence of Nazi terminology in postwar Germany, 57, 90, 92, 175–76, 183–86, 191, 193, 200, 243; German resistance against, 76, 77, 227–29, 233;

and workers, 190–91, 200. *See also* Hitler, Adolf; Industrialists; Industry
Nazi Party. *See* National Socialism; NSDAP
Nazis: "return to power" of, 216, 287 (n. 125)
Neoliberalism. *See* Liberalism
Neue Deutsche Biographie (book), 134–35
Neues Deutschland (newspaper), 27
Neumann, Carl, 111, 177
New School for Social Research, 220
Nicholls, A. J., 131
Niemöller, Martin, 82, 83
Night of the Long Knives (Röhm Putsch), 74
Nölting, Erik, 62
North German Iron and Steel Control Commission, 56, 57
Northwest German Radio (NWDR), 185
NSDAP (National Socialist German Workers' Party/Nazi Party), 14, 89, 215, 216, 228. *See also* Hitler, Adolf; National Socialism
Nuremberg trials, 9, 53, 68–72, 213; and Britain, 69; and Soviet Union, 69, 259 (n. 68); and public relations, 70–80, 203–14 passim; and Churches, 82–83; industry's reaction to verdicts of, 87–98, 203–9, 264 (n. 9); and amnesty of industrialists, 202–5; legal argument against verdicts of, 205–9. *See also* Flick, Friedrich; Krupp; Krupp von Bohlen und Halbach, Alfried; Public relations; United States

Office of the United States High Commissioner for Germany (HICOG), 204, 215, 225. *See also* McCloy, John J.
Office of the United States Military Government in Germany (OMGUS), 97, 144, 203, 216
Orff, Carl, 168
Ortega y Gasset, José, 170–71
O'Sheah, Benjamin, 40, 48
Oxford University, 242

Papen, Franz von, 218, 225
Peck, David W., 208